Concise Encyclopedia of
NATURE

Left: The giraffe's long neck enables it to browse on the juicy upper leaves of trees.

Right: Pangolins are able to roll themselves up into a ball when danger threatens. The horny plates then provide them with an effective suit of armour.

Editor-in-Chief Michael W. Dempsey
Executive Editor Angela Sheehan
Production Manager Peter Sackett
Picture Researcher Marion Gain
Picture Editor Sarah Tyzack

Consultant Editors
Robert W. Burton
Robin Kerrod

ISBN 0 361 01739 1

Published 1971 by Purnell Books,
Paulton, Bristol BS18 5LQ,
a member of the BPCC Group
Printed in Hong Kong
Reprinted 1972, 1976, 1981
New edition 1984

Concise Encyclopedia of NATURE

Michael Chinery M.A.

Purnell

Contents

Living Things

Nature or natural history is sometimes taken to mean the study of all natural things—things that have not been made by man. More commonly, however, it means the study of living things. The word organism is used for anything that is alive or that has been alive at some time. Trees and flowers, butterflies and tortoises, fishes and elephants are all living things or organisms. Rocks, metals and water are not organisms.

The first thing we must do if we are going to study living things is to find out what it is that makes living things different from non-living objects. We do not know the vital ingredient necessary to make something alive, although some scientists think they are near to discovering it, but we can list six features possessed by living things. These features are not shown by any non-living object, so we can call them the characteristics of living things.

Characteristics of Life

One of the most obvious features of living things is that they can *move* in search of food or to escape from enemies. *Feeding* (including drinking) is another feature of living things. They have to take in food to provide themselves with energy and with body-building materials. Energy is released when food is 'burnt' or combined with oxygen, and so living things have to take in oxygen from the air, although this is not true of some bacteria. The process of taking in oxygen is called *breathing* or respiration. Body-building materials in the food are added to the organism's body, so that it grows. Stalactites and stalagmites in a cave get longer and thicker with time, but only because extra material is added to the outside. There is no production of new material inside them so their growth is not like that of a living organism. Breathing and the other processes that go on inside the living organism result in the production of waste materials. These must be removed, and all organisms have some way of *excreting*, or getting rid of these waste materials.

Another characteristic of living things is that they are *sensitive* to changes in their surroundings. A fly will soon be off if it senses the approaching fly swatter, and a potted plant will soon turn upwards again if the pot is laid on its side. Finally, living things *reproduce* themselves. Organisms do not live for ever, but why they grow old is still a mystery. They ensure that more of the same kind will take their place by reproducing by means of seeds, eggs or babies.

Plants are as much alive as animals. They feed by taking in energy from the sun and minerals from the soil. They reproduce by seeds and even move by turning to face the sun.

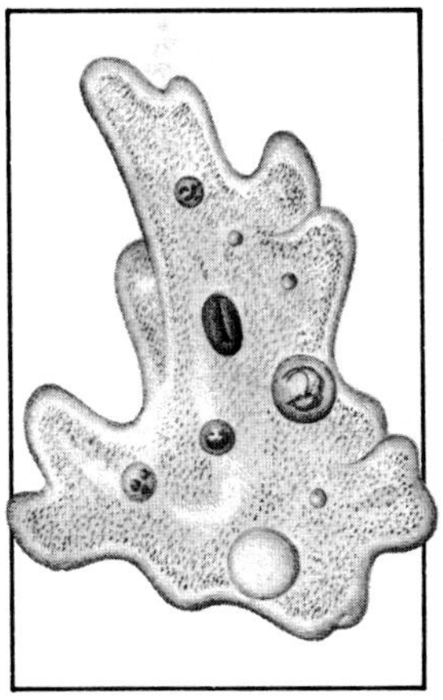

Amoeba, smaller than a pinhead, is a complete animal with all the characteristics of living things.

Even when taking a rest, this serval cat is alert and sensitive to what is going on–an important feature of living things.

The Living Cell

Just as a house is built of bricks, so animals and plants are made of units called cells. Cells are extremely small and they cannot usually be seen without a microscope. Some animals and plants—known as the Protozoa or Protista—consist of only one tiny cell, but larger organisms consist of millions of cells. There are many different kinds of cells and each kind has a particular job to do in the body. There are skin cells covering the outside and lining the various internal organs; nerve cells carrying messages; bone cells forming skeletons; and muscle cells for movement. Plants have a variety of cells, too. There are food-making cells in the leaves, tube-like water-carrying cells in the roots and stems, and food-storing cells.

Animals and plants are built up of cells just as a house is built up of bricks. The cells are not all of the same shape. Different shaped cells have different jobs to do. The picture shows a selection of human body cells.

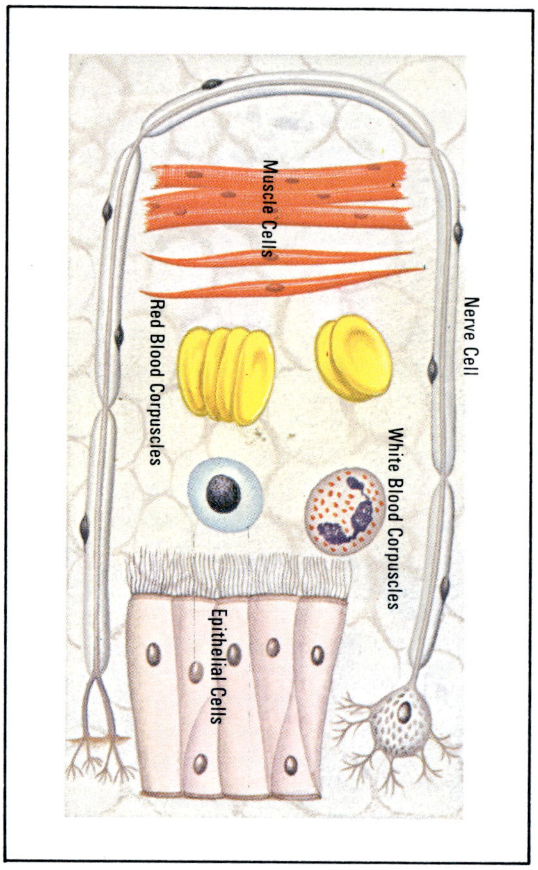

Below: Although cells are so tiny, they have complicated structures. Fine channels carry chemical materials from the nucleus to all parts of the cell.

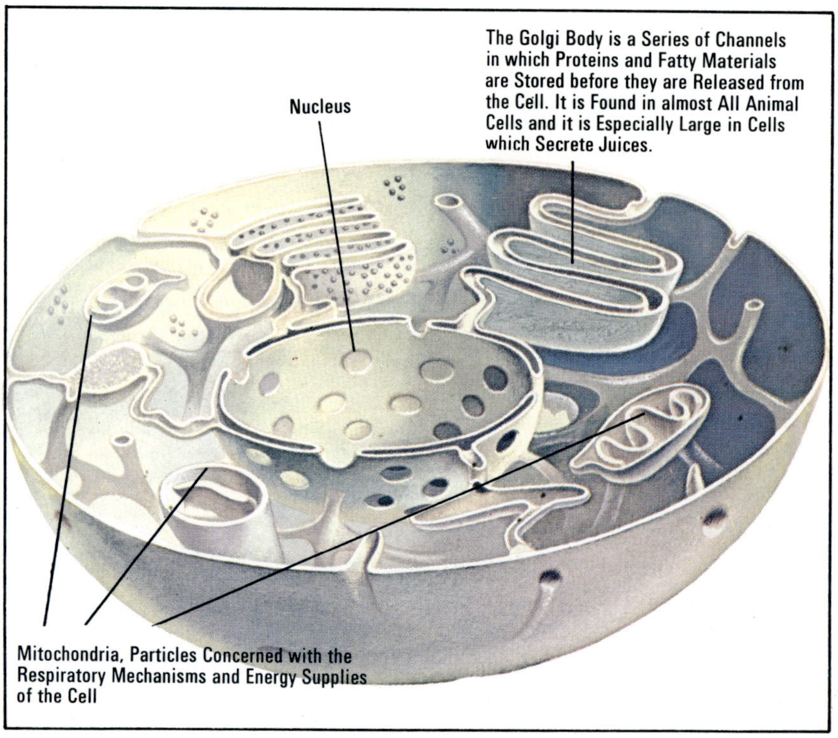

Plants and Animals

Plant cells differ from animal cells mainly in having a stiff cellulose wall around them. This gives them a fixed, regular shape. Plant cells in leaves contain small green chloroplasts which make food (p. 17). Animal cells never contain chloroplasts.

Inside the Cell

All cells are bounded by a very thin cell membrane. In plants it is just inside the cellulose wall. The cell is filled with protoplasm. This is a watery material in which there are very complicated mixtures of proteins and other materials. It is here that all the processes of life take place.

In the centre of the cell there is a nucleus, made of a special type of protoplasm. This is the 'brain' of the cell. Inside the nucleus are the chromosomes. These are minute threads which carry the genes. Genes are very complicated chemicals which carry the 'plans' for the body. The nucleus instructs its cell to manufacture substances according to these plans.

Cell Division

Living things start out as single cells. The single cell divides into two. The two cells then divide into four, and so on. Cell division of this sort takes place even in the fully grown plant or animal because new cells have to replace those that have worn out. The chromosomes play a very important part in cell division because it is essential that the new cells have the same 'instructions' as the old cells. Each chromosome produces an exact copy of itself and, when the cell divides into two, one set goes to each new cell.

The Origins of Life

When the Earth first came into existence some 4,500 million years ago there was no life on the planet. Starting probably as a dense ball of dust, the Earth passed through a very hot and partly liquid stage. The atmosphere contained carbon dioxide and large amounts of methane (marsh gas) and ammonia. The whole of the Earth was surrounded by a thick blanket of steam. It gradually cooled down and much of the steam blanket turned into water and formed the ocean. The Earth was ready to support its first life.

The Primeval Soup

We shall never know exactly how life started on Earth, but we can make some intelligent guesses. The atmosphere of our planet in its younger days consisted largely of methane, carbon dioxide, ammonia and water. These are simple substances but they contain all the major elements of life—carbon, oxygen, hydrogen and nitrogen. The Sun's ultra-violet light was able to get through this atmosphere and, under the influence of this radiation, some of the simple materials probably linked up to form sugars and amino-acids. These substances are the building bricks of living material.

Experimentally, bombardment of methane/ammonia mixtures with ultra-violet rays and artificial lighting in the laboratory has produced sugar and amino-acids. If these reactions went on for a long time on the young Earth, they would have formed what is known as the 'primeval soup'—a rich mixture of life's building bricks.

Presumably some of the sugars and amino-acids linked up and produced proteins and other complicated materials that could duplicate themselves. If these materials then formed a membrane around themselves they would have produced the first cell.

Viruses

Viruses can be seen only with the powerful electron microscope. Some are not much more than one millionth of a millimetre across. They appear to be on the border-line between living and non-living matter. They can be crystallised, dried, and then can 'come to life' again. Viruses can grow and reproduce only inside living cells. The virus particles contain plans rather like those of the ordinary cell nucleus, and the virus then 'instructs' the cell to make more virus material instead of normal cell materials. This interferes with the normal working of the cell and produces illness or disease in the animal or plant. Fowl pest and myxomatosis are animal diseases caused by viruses. Plant diseases include tobacco mosaic.

Virus particles are of many shapes and sizes when they are crystallised, as shown by two types of 'flu virus (top) and the smallpox virus (bottom).

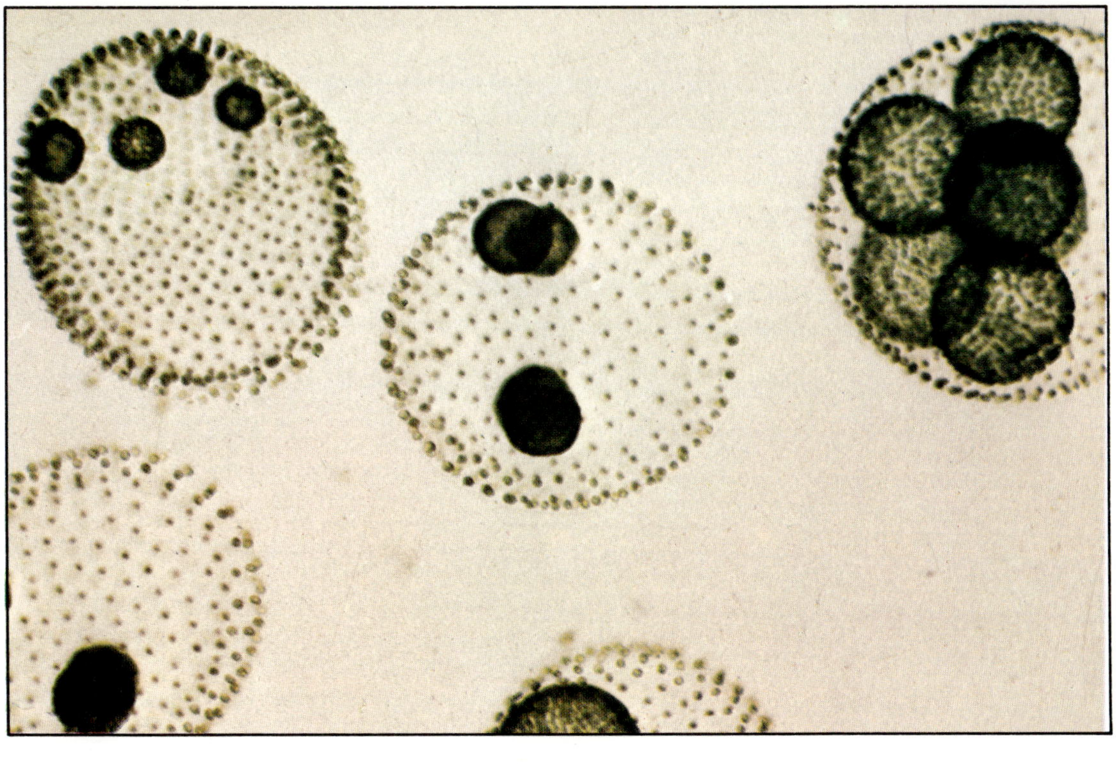

Microscopic algae may have been an early form of life. These consist of balls of cells which reproduce by forming new balls inside.

Plants and Animals

We do not know what the earliest living things were like, and we probably never will. They might have been something like today's bacteria, little more than specks of protoplasm obtaining energy by carrying out chemical processes. Whatever they were like, we can be fairly certain that they have given rise to all of today's living things with the possible exception of the viruses.

Apart from the viruses, all of today's living things fall into one of two large groups—plants and animals. Examples of plants include mosses, seaweeds, trees, grasses and cabbages. Examples of animals include jellyfishes, spiders, snakes, birds and dogs. Man is also an animal.

It is easy to tell the difference between a cabbage and a dog, but it is not so easy to tell the difference between all plants and animals. You might think that animals move about and plants stay still, but this is not always so. There are many animals, such as the sea anemone, that stay in one place and there are many tiny plants that swim about in the water. Then there is the insect-eating sundew—a plant whose sticky 'fingers' can move to trap a small fly. You might say that animals have eyes and ears, while plants do not.

Plants certainly do not have such sense organs, but there are also many animals, for instance the earthworm and the jellyfish, with only simple senses, but they are still much more obvious than the senses which control the plant's movements.

Most animals grow to a definite size and shape and then stop growing, whereas plants generally go on growing indefinitely, but the most important distinction between the two groups concerns the way in which they get their food. Plants are nearly all able to make their own food, nearly always with the help of energy from the Sun. Those plants that cannot do this are obviously plants from their other features. Animals cannot make food and they have to feed on plants or upon other animals, that have themselves eaten plants.

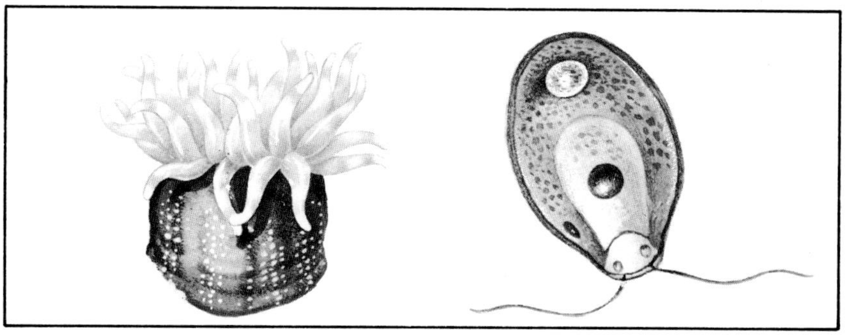

It is easy to distinguish between a typical plant, such as the buttercup (top) and a typical animal, such as this antelope. It is less easy to say which of the above organisms is a plant and which is an animal. The sea anemone (left) is actually an animal, while the other is a plant that swims in the water.

Plant and Animal Species

There are probably well over a million different animal species, and something like half a million plant species. All the individuals in a species look and behave alike. All polar bears, for example, look like polar bears and act like polar bears.

We know today that the appearance and behaviour of an organism are controlled by the genes present in its cells. All members of the species have the same arrangement of genes and chromosomes in their cells. When the animals mate or the plants are fertilised this same pattern is passed on to the next generation, and so they will also conform to the general appearance and behaviour of the species. The structure and behaviour of different animals normally prevents them from mating other than with members of the same species. Even if animals of two species could mate together, the chances are that the arrangement of the genes in the two animals would be so different that they could not join up to give a new animal. Each species is thus maintained as a separate kind of organism. We can define a species, therefore, as a group of plants or animals which all have the same appearance and behaviour and which can breed among themselves.

Species and Genera

Linnaeus, the eighteenth-century Swedish naturalist, recognised that some species were very alike (these were the ones that had most recently separated from each other) and he concluded that they were related to each other. He grouped similar species into larger units called genera (singular genus). He then gave a scientific name to every plant and animal that he knew. The scientific name was made up of the name of the genus and the name of the individual species. We still use Linnaeus' method today. The scientific name of the large white butterfly is *Pieris brassicae*, while that of the small white butterfly is *Pieris rapae*.

The Species and Evolution

Although all the members of a species look basically alike, there are always some minor variations. You have only to look at people to see this variation: they all belong to the same species, but none of them looks exactly alike. When all the members of the species are free to breed among themselves these small differences are evened out and the species stays more or less the same. But suppose that the members of a species become separated into two regions—by a chain of mountains for example. Very small changes may occur in one population and not in the other. Over a very long time these changes might spread throughout this population and it would be slightly different from the other population. Perhaps the difference might simply be that one population had a slightly different colour. At this stage, the members of the two populations would probably be able to interbreed. They would still belong to the same species, and would probably be known as geographical races or varieties of that species. If the two populations continued to be separated, the differences between them might well increase until there came a time when they were no longer able to interbreed. The two populations would then be separate species. This sort of process has obviously taken place many times during the history of animals and plants and has given rise to all the many species we know today. Species which are very similar have been separated most recently.

Closely related species have many features in common because they have evolved fairly recently from a common ancestor. The picture shows a great tit (left), a varied tit (top right) and a blue tit (bottom right) which have rather different habits from each other.

Although one species does not normally mate with another, closely related species do sometimes mate and produce offspring. These offspring are called hybrids. One of the best known examples is the mule, the offspring of a male donkey and a female horse. The mule is a strong animal, but, like most hybrids, it is sterile and unable to reproduce. The offspring of a female donkey and a male horse is a smaller animal called a hinny.

The Soil

Soil is a very complex material that is formed mainly from the underlying rocks. You can see the soil-forming processes at work in old quarries and in road or railway cuttings. Wind and rain attack the bare surfaces and small pieces begin to crumble away. If the slope is very steep the particles may roll to the bottom, but they are often trapped by the mosses and lichens. These little rock particles form what is known as the soil skeleton. Small grasses and other plants can take root among them and the roots find their way into tiny cracks in the rock, thus helping to break it up further. When the plants die their remains decay and add organic matter called humus to the soil skeleton. A true soil is now beginning to form and larger plants can take root in it. The underlying rock is broken down further and the soil gets deeper. In time it becomes a mature soil, with plenty of humus. As well as rock particles and humus, a soil contains air spaces, water and hordes of tiny organisms which help to break down dead plants and animals into the nutrient-rich humus.

Different types of rocks produce different kinds of soils. Soft clay has very tiny mineral particles which hold a lot of water and stick together to produce wet sticky soils. Sandy rocks, on the other hand, produce large particles and light, well-drained soils.

These types of soil support very different types of vegetation. Sticky clays, for example, support oak woods. Sandy soils are acidic and support pine woods or heathland. Chalk and limestone rocks are alkaline and only lime-loving plants will be able to grow on such soils. The chalk lands of Europe originally carried forests but, through the activity of man and his grazing animals, the forests have now been converted into grasslands.

Chalk and limestone rocks do not provide much material for the soil skeleton. The soils are therefore rather thin, but they carry a wealth of attractive lime-loving plants.

Climate and Soil

Although the nature of the underlying rock has a very great effect on the nature of the soil, the climate is also very important. In the cold temperate regions, the rainfall exceeds the evaporation of water from the soil. Humus and minerals such as iron and calcium are therefore continually washed down from the surface layers. This action, known as leaching, is especially obvious in sandy soils and the surface layers become quite pale. Leached soils are called podsols.

In the warm temperate regions the evaporation of water more or less equals the rainfall and so there is not much downward movement of humus and minerals. The surface layers are brown and the soils are called brown earths. Black earths are found under the grass of the steppes and prairies. These regions are fairly dry and water is nearly always moving up to the surface. Minerals and humus remain at the surface and the surface layers are black.

The chalk downs of England are famous for their orchids, although there are not nearly so many now as there were 100 years ago. The fragrant and pyramidal orchids, seen here with yellow bird's foot trefoil, are among the commonest species.

Roots and Stems

If you have ever tried to pull up a tree seedling, or even a dandelion plant, you will know that it is hard work. The root holds the plant very firmly in the ground. This is one of the main jobs of the root. It anchors the plant so that the wind cannot pull it out of the ground. The other job of the root is to absorb water for the plant.

Dandelions, thistles and many other plants have tap roots. Each plant has just one main root which grows more or less straight down into the ground. There may be a few branches, but they are never as large as the main root. Not all plants have tap roots. If you pull up a grass or a daisy plant you will see that it has lots of roots, all more or less the same size. Roots of this type are called fibrous roots.

The root anchors the plant by growing down between the soil particles and filling the spaces very tightly. The finer regions of the roots, a little way behind the root tip, bear thousands of root hairs. These are very tiny and they are usually broken off when a plant is uprooted, but you can see them very well on cress seedlings if you grow them on blotting paper. The root hairs grow between the soil particles and, because they have such thin walls, water can seep into them from the soil. This water, containing dissolved minerals, passes to the centre of the root and enters the long conducting tubes. It then begins its journey up to the leaves. The conducting tubes have very tough walls and they give the root its strength. You can see them in the centre of the root if you slice through a carrot or a parsnip.

The Stem

The stem of a plant has to carry the water from the roots to the leaves. It also has to hold up the leaves (and the flowers if there are any) so that they get plenty of light. Stems are usually upright and they may or may not have branches. Some stems are quite soft and juicy. Other stems are woody.

The water is carried in conducting tubes which are continuous with those in the roots, although the arrangement is different in the stem. The tubes of a young stem are arranged in little clusters called vascular bundles. They form a ring in the outer half of the stem. The tough walls of the tubes, together with the sclerenchyma fibres that surround them, give great strength to the

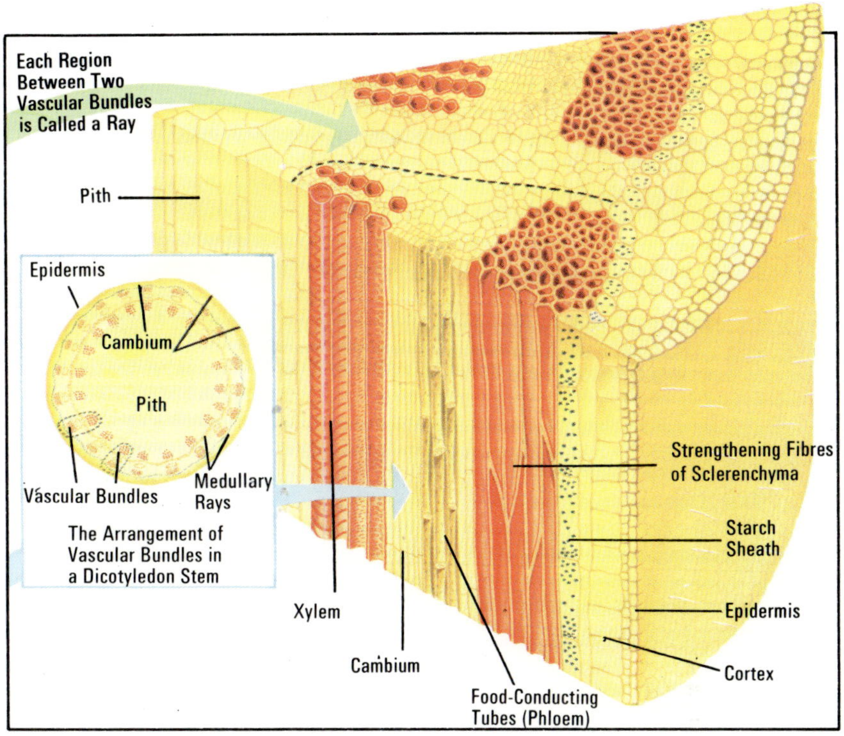

The conducting tubes in a young stem are collected into bundles and arranged in a ring.

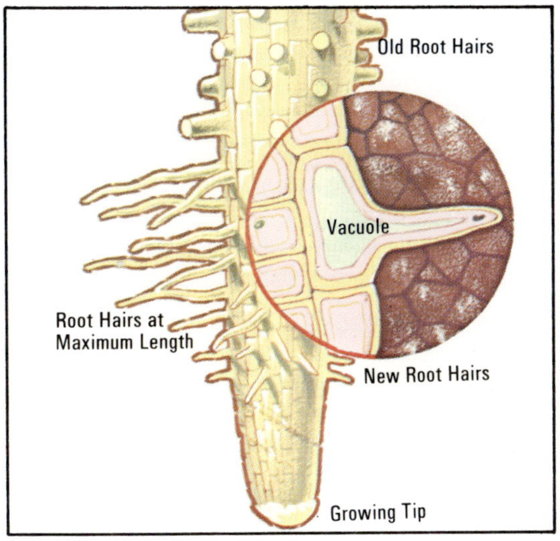

Root hairs grow out from the outer cells of the root and greatly increase its surface area.

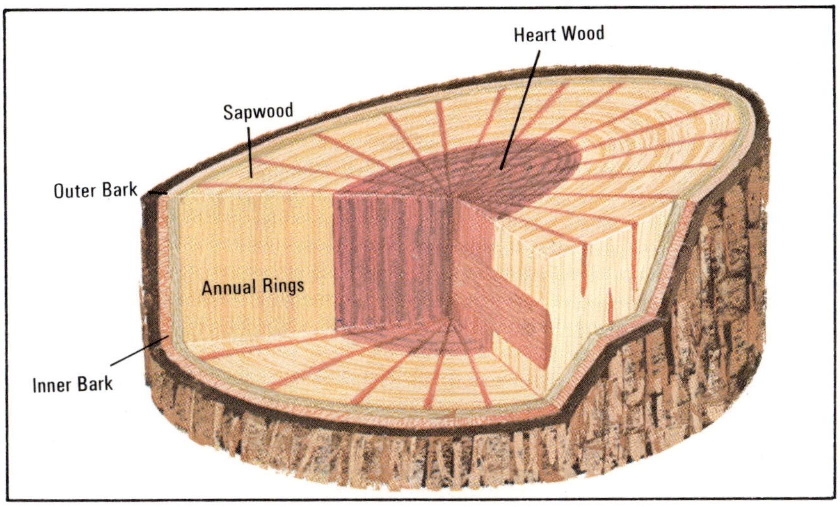

A tree trunk consists almost entirely of tough fibres and water-carrying tubes. Food is carried only by tubes in the inner bark. The dark region in the centre of this section is heartwood, which no longer carries water.

A tap root system, shown by the thistle, has one main root with several smaller branches. A fibrous root system consists of many similar sized roots, none of which can be called a main root. Grasses all have fibrous roots.

Deciduous trees, which lose their leaves for the winter, bear the scars of the leaves on their twigs. The large terminal bud at the tip of the twig contains the new leaves. Overlapping scales, sticky in this horse chestnut twig, protect the young leaves from the winter winds.

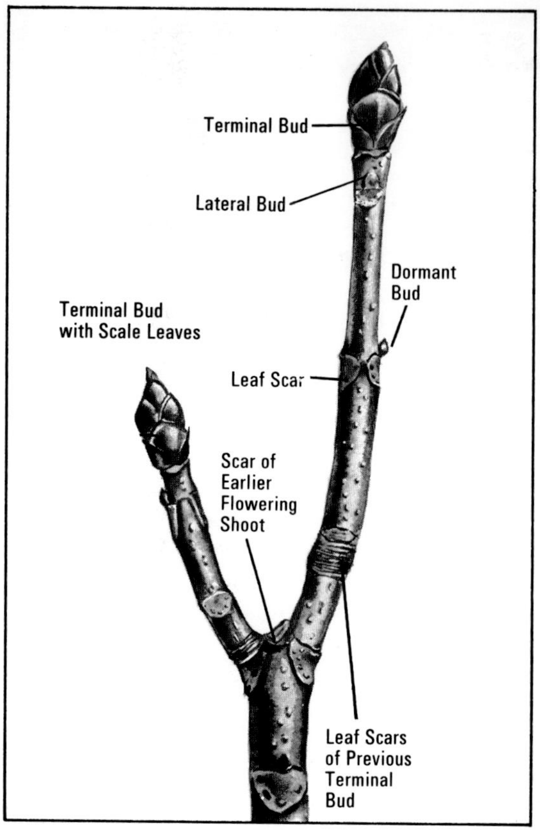

stem yet they still allow it to bend in the wind. As well as the water-carrying xylem tubes, the vascular bundles contain food-carrying phloem tubes. These carry food from the leaves to other parts of the plant.

Woody plants form more tubes and fibres each year and the trunk gets thicker and thicker. It consists almost entirely of tubes and fibres. The older ones get squashed in the middle of the trunk as heartwood. They no longer carry water. The outer regions, which do carry water, form the sapwood.

Annual Rings

In parts of the world where there are definite seasons, trees form only narrow conducting tubes in autumn and none are formed in winter, then large ones are formed in spring. There is a distinct boundary between the autumn wood and the spring wood and so, when a tree is cut down, we can see the annual rings.

Why a Plant Needs Water

Food materials are absorbed from the soil and carried about in the plant in solution. Water is one of the basic raw materials from which plants make sugar and starch (see page 17). Plants also use water for support. The water makes the cells firm, or turgid. This is very important in herbaceous plants which do not have many woody fibres to support them. If water is lost, the plant droops.

Right: The tallest stem is the trunk of the redwood which rises over 90 metres above the ground. These massive trees grow in a narrow strip near the Pacific Coast of the U.S.

How Plants Make Food

The sun provides almost all of the energy on the earth, including all the energy that we use in our bodies to move about and to keep warm. But our bodies cannot harness the sun's energy directly—nor can any other animal's. This can be done only by green plants. They are the primary converters of energy. They make use of the sun's light energy and they convert some of it into chemical energy which they store in their tissues. Animals obtain some of this energy by eating the plants. If it were not for the plants, animals would be unable to survive, because only plants can make energy-containing foods from simple materials in the air and the soil. The prophet Isaiah did not know much about energy conversion, but he was quite right when he said 'all flesh is grass': all animal flesh does come from plant material. This holds true in the sea as well as on the land. The fishes and the whales all depend upon the millions of tiny floating plants for their food.

Photosynthesis

The basic source of all food is the remarkable process called photosynthesis, which takes place in all green plants. Photosynthesis means 'building with light' and it is the process by which green plants make sugars from carbon dioxide and water. It takes place only in the presence of sunlight and in the presence of the green colouring matter called chlorophyll.

The chlorophyll absorbs some of the light energy falling on it and it uses it to power a complicated chain of reactions involving water and carbon dioxide. Energy is passed from stage to stage of the process and finally ends up in the sugar that is made. Oxygen is given off in the process, but the chlorophyll is unchanged and it is able to go on absorbing more light.

Leaves

Most photosynthesis takes place in the leaves. The leaves are the 'food factories' of the plant and they are specially constructed for this work. Most leaves sit horizontally on the plant and the stems ensure that the leaves are arranged so as to catch the greatest possible amount of light. You rarely see one leaf sitting directly on top of another.

The leaf is covered with a thin, transparent skin or cuticle and the inner region consists of numerous rather loosely packed cells. Most of the chlorophyll is concentrated in the upper layers where there is the most light. It is not spread throughout the cells, but packed into little 'envelopes' called chloroplasts. The water needed for photosynthesis comes from the roots and enters the leaves through the veins. The carbon dioxide comes from the air and enters the leaves through tiny breathing pores called stomata. Most of these are on the lower surface of the leaves. As well as letting carbon dioxide into the leaf, they let the unwanted oxygen out. They also let the excess water vapour out, but if water is in short supply they will close up and prevent the plant from losing water.

The cells inside the leaf are always surrounded by a film of water and the carbon dioxide dissolves in this film. It can then pass

Carbon dioxide enters the plant through the leaves. Water enters through the roots. They combine in the leaves to form sugar, which is then carried away to all other parts of the plant. Oxygen is given out during the process and it escapes through the leaves. The whole process is powered by sunlight and therefore takes place only during the daytime.

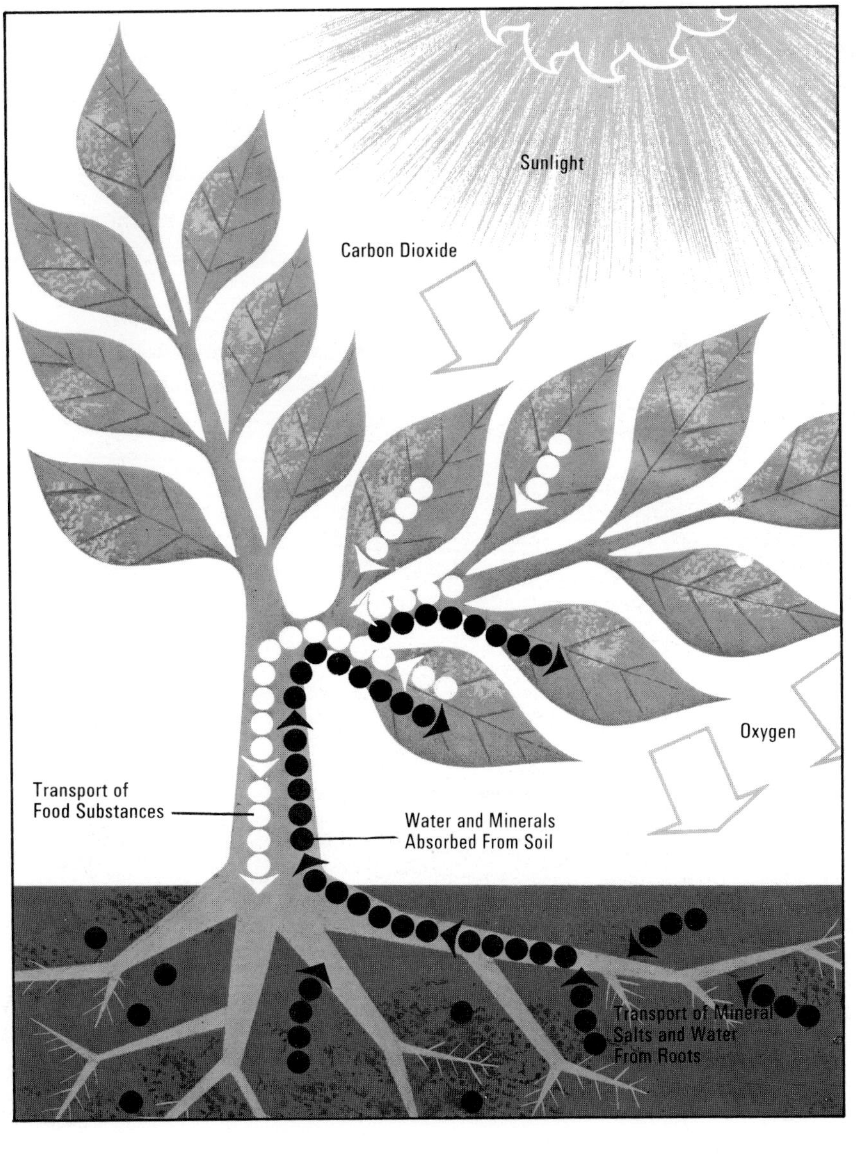

Right: Spraying trace elements on pastureland in New Zealand. Large areas have been made more fertile by the addition of small, but vital amounts of 'trace' elements such as manganese, molybdenum, zinc and copper.

through the cell walls and into the protoplasm. The speed at which photosynthesis takes place depends upon several things, including the amount of carbon dioxide entering the plant, the temperature, the brightness of the light, and the amount of chlorophyll in the leaves. Plants which grow in shady places often make up for the low light intensity by having more chlorophyll in

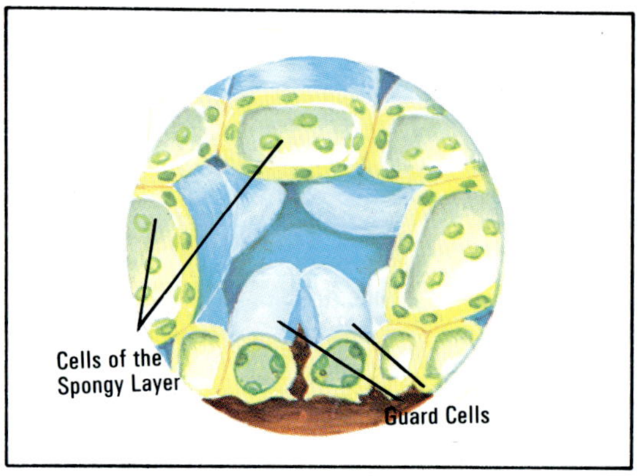

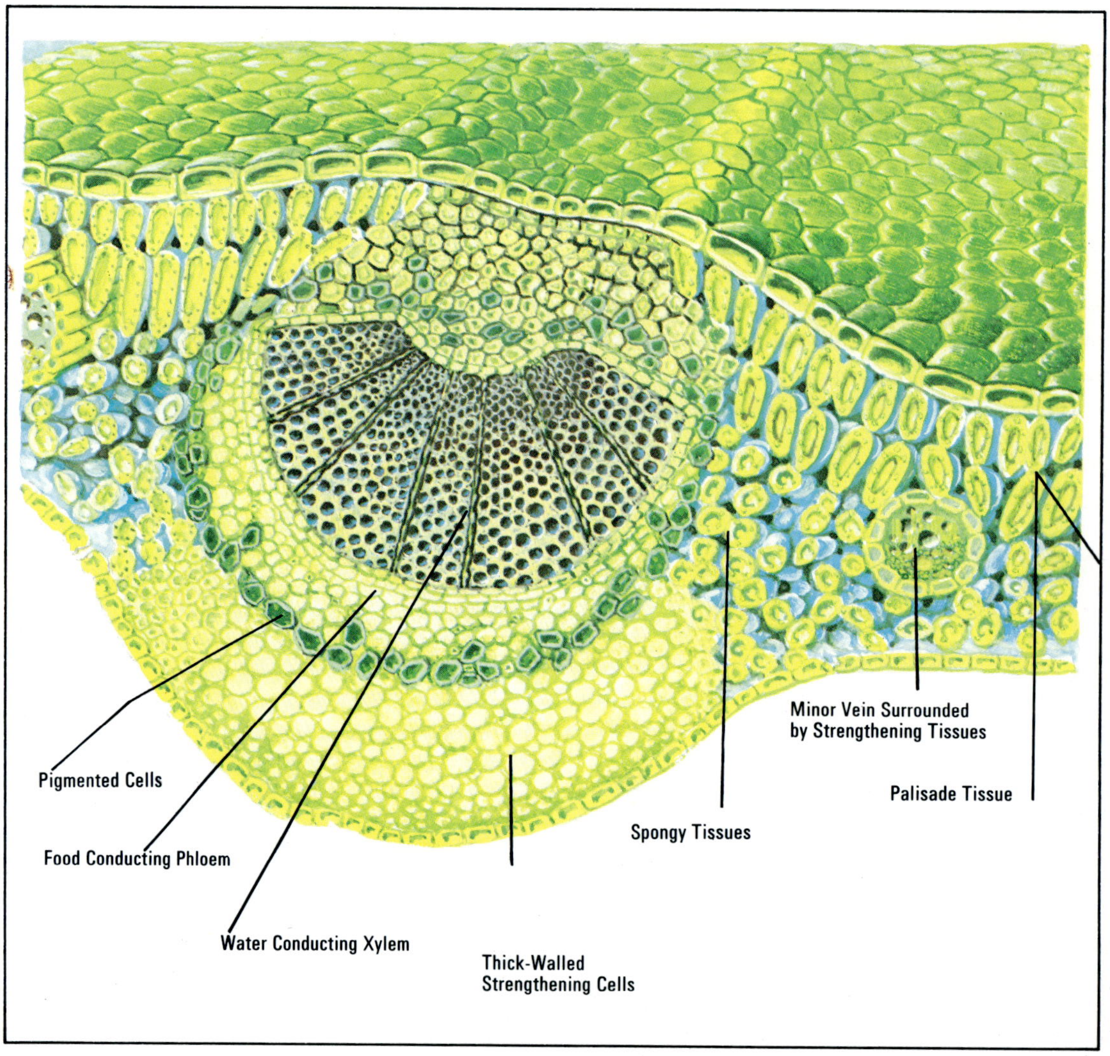

The leaf is well constructed for its work. It presents a large surface area to the light and its chlorophyll is found mainly in the upper region, where it can trap the most light. The main vein or midrib sends branches to all parts of the leaf and these pass water out to the cells and spaces. Excess water escapes through the tiny breathing pores on the lower surface. One of these breathing pores, with its sausage-shaped guard cells, is shown above. The guard cells control the size of the pore.

their leaves. This makes them somewhat darker than plants growing in full light.

After Photosynthesis

The sugars produced by photosynthesis are carried to other parts of the plant and used to provide energy. They can also be converted into starch and stored until they are needed. Some of the sugars are converted into cellulose and used to build up more plant material. But the plant cannot exist just on the sugars and starches. Protoplasm contains proteins, which contain various materials which must be obtained from the soil and combined with the sugars to form proteins.

Mineral Nutrition

The plant body consists mainly of the four elements hydrogen, carbon, oxygen, and nitrogen. The first three elements are obtained from water and carbon dioxide and they are always freely available. There is plenty of nitrogen in the air as well, but plants cannot use this atmospheric nitrogen. They have to absorb nitrates or other nitrogen-containing compounds from the soil. Nitrogen is essential for the growth of plants because it is a constituent of all proteins, and proteins are the basis of all living matter. If a plant is not able to get enough nitrogen it will become stunted.

Left: The effect of nitrogen on plant growth. A. Nitrogen encourages rapid leaf growth. B. Insufficient nitrogen means poor. weak growth. C. Excessive nitrogen can cause soft rank growth.

If a plant is analysed chemically it will be found to contain much more than the four elements mentioned above. Among the other elements will be iron, magnesium, calcium, potassium, sodium, silicon, phosphorus, sulphur, and chlorine. Scientists have found out which elements are essential and which are not by carrying out water culture experiments. In these experiments plants are grown in bottles containing solutions of various elements. One bottle has all the elements in it, and the plant in this bottle grows well. The other bottles each have one element missing. If a plant does not grow well in any of these bottles it is because it needs the missing element. Apart from hydrogen, carbon, oxygen, and nitrogen, the main substances or minerals needed by plants are magnesium, iron, calcium, potassium, phosphorus, and sulphur. A lack of any of these in the soil will interfere with the proper growth of the plant.

When plants die, their remains decay. The minerals are then returned to the soil for a new generation of plants. The farmer and the gardener, however, do not leave their crops to rot on the land. They take them away to sell or to eat. Minerals are not returned to the soil and they must be added in the form of manure or fertilizer. Most soils contain plenty of calcium, iron, and sulphur but nitrogen, phosphorus, and potassium have to be added.

Food Storage in Plants

Much of the food that a plant makes is stored for later use. It may be stored up to tide the plant over the winter and to get it going again in the spring, or it may be stored up in readiness for flowering and the production of fruits and seeds.

Relatively few plants actually store the sugar made by photosynthesis. Most of them convert it to starch. Proteins and fats or oils are stored by some plants, usually in seeds.

It is very lucky for mankind that plants do accumulate stores of food materials because we can take the food for ourselves. Our vegetable crops have all come from wild plants and most of them have been cultivated for a very long time. During that time, the size of the various food-storing regions has been greatly increased.

The tulip bulb stores food in fleshy scale leaves. Food from the green leaves goes back to the scale leaves of the new bud which makes the next year's bulb. The old scale leaves remain as thin brown coating scales.

A corm stores food in the swollen stem. Buds develop on the corm which forms each year at the base of the flower shoot.

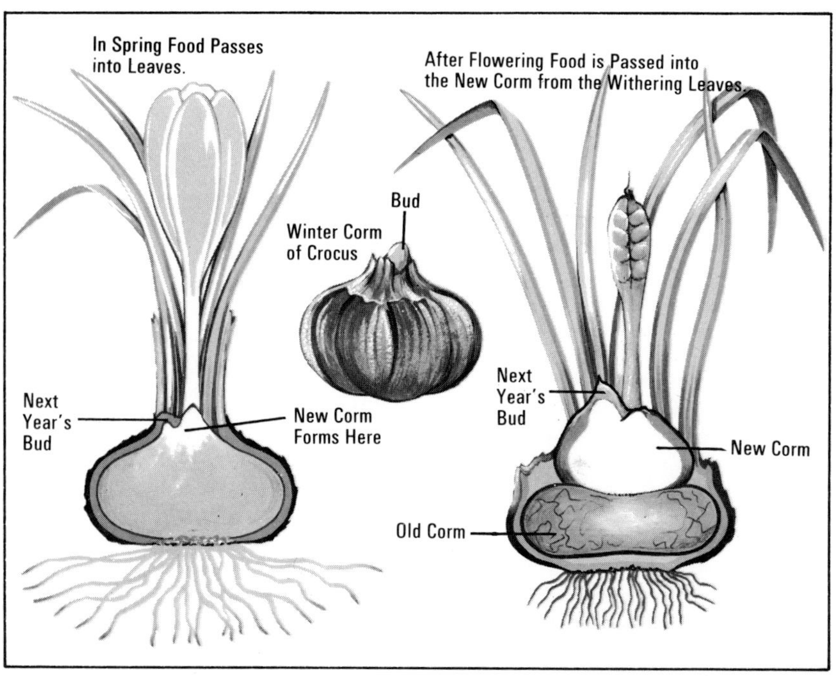

Storage in Roots

Many plants store their food in swollen roots. Two well known examples are the carrot and the sugar beet. These plants, and most of the others like them, are biennials. This means that they live for two seasons. During the spring and summer of the first year the plants make food and store it in their swollen tap roots. The plants die down in the autumn and the food reserve in the roots is used to produce new leaves in the spring.

Other plants storing food in their roots include the dahlia and the lesser celandine, but these do not have tap roots. The food is stored in a number of swollen roots called root tubers. It is used when the plant shoots up in the spring.

Storage in Stems

Many plants store food in their stems without any special modifications. Others, however, develop specially swollen stems. The kohl rabi, a member of the cabbage family, stores food in a tennis ball sized swelling just above the ground. Irises and several other plants possess horizontal underground stems called rhizomes. These are usually full of food. Potato tubers are also underground stems used for storing food. They develop at the tips of finer stems growing horizontally through the soil.

Corms are underground stems as well. Although often called bulbs, they are really quite different. The crocus corm is a short, rounded stem with one or more buds on the top. After flowering a new corm develops at the base of the leaves.

Leaves and Flowers

The ordinary cabbage consists of a tightly packed bunch of leaves, all full of food. This food is passed to the flowers when they develop and the leaves become thinner. Bulbs also store food in leaves, although these are rather special leaves. A bulb consists almost entirely of swollen, juicy leaves called scales. These surround one or more buds. When the bulb starts to grow the food is passed from the scales to the buds. The scales then wither, but a new set of scales is formed inside them. This new set will be next year's bulb. The papery coverings are the shrivelled old scales.

Some plants even store food in their flowers. The large creamy heads of the cauliflower are the young flowers.

Fruit and Seeds

All seeds must have some sort of food reserve which will enable the young seedlings to grow to the stage at which they can start making their own food. Many of the larger seeds—peas, beans, cereal grains, nuts, and so on—are used for human food. Many fruits also contain food materials. Sweet, juicy fruits attract animals, which then scatter the seeds.

Above: Collecting roots of sugar beet for processing. The swollen tap roots contain the plants' food reserves, designed to produce new leaves, flowers and seeds in the spring.

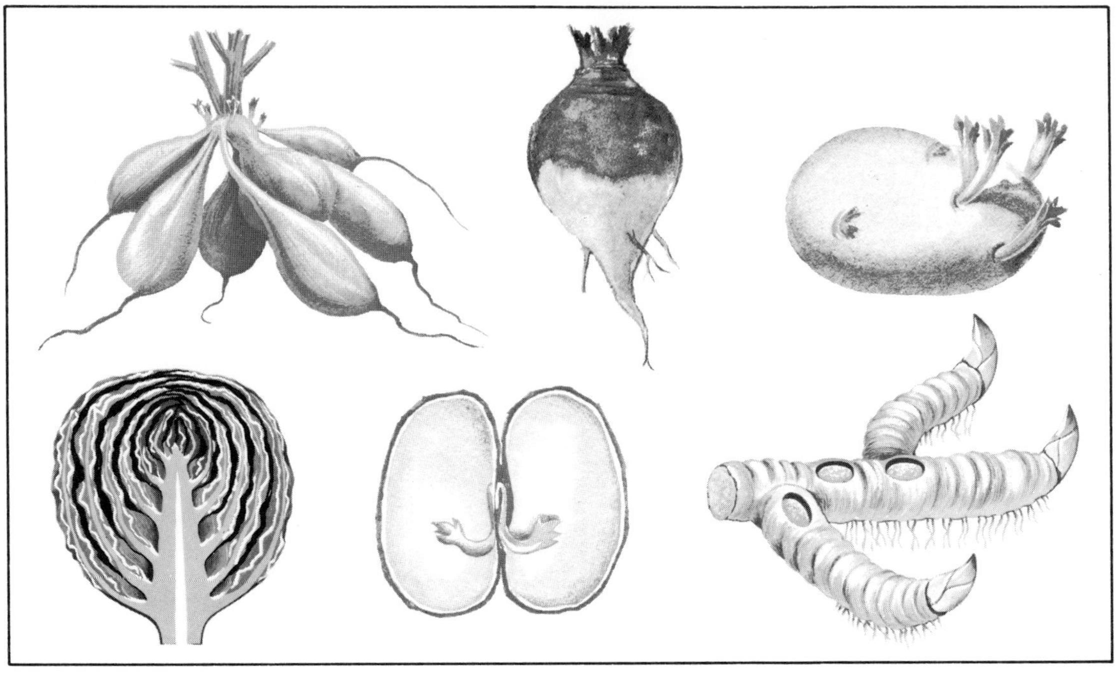

Left: A selection of plant food stores including roots (dahlia tubers and sugar beet), stems (potato tuber and rhizome), seeds (bean seed) and leaves (cabbage).

Plant Growth and Movement

One of the main differences between the higher plants and the higher animals is that the plants do not have such a fixed shape or size. A lion always has four legs, two eyes, one tail, and so on. But we cannot say how many branches an oak tree will have because the growth pattern of a plant is flexible. A tree growing in the middle of a wood has a very different shape from the same kind of tree growing by itself in the middle of a field, as the growth of the woodland tree is influenced by the trees around it.

By marking a root or a shoot with equally spaced lines you can find out the region in which most of the growth takes place.

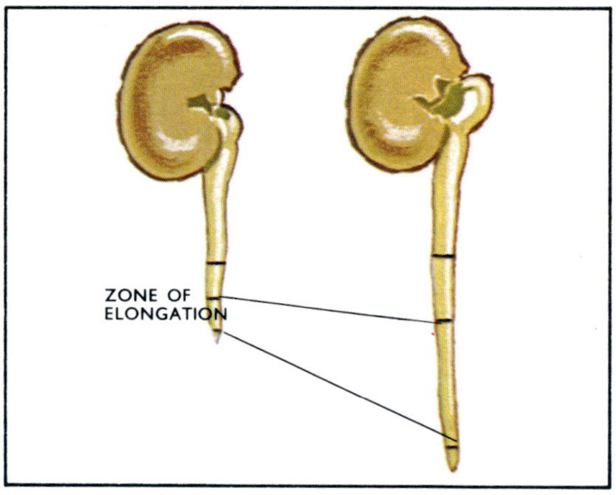

Many climbing plants have tendrils which grow rapidly when touched and coil tightly around a support.

Stems and Roots

You can learn quite a lot about plant growth if you watch buds, such as those of the horse chestnut, opening in the spring. The buds are actually very short stems surrounded by young leaves. The leaves on the outside, called scale leaves, protect the bud during the winter. The bases of all the leaves are very close together. In other words, the internodes of the stem—the regions between the leaf bases—are very short. When spring comes the leaf scales fall from the outside of the bud and the internodes begin to lengthen. The new leaves become separated and they begin to unfold. If the bud contains a flower, as most of the terminal buds do, its growth soon stops. The growth of the stem continues through one or more of the subsidiary buds. The stem tips of these buds continue to grow and produce more cells. The cells get longer and so the stem itself grows. The actual tip of the stem is never seen because it is always sheathed by developing leaves. Later in the summer more scale leaves are produced around the stem tip and growth slows down.

Many of the subsidiary buds on a stem never open. They are reserve buds, which develop only if the main stem is damaged. Some trees produce a great many new shoots when the branches are cut. The lime is a good example. It is often grown along drives and pathways and it is regularly cut back to the main branches. The cut ends produce dense clusters of twigs. Treating trees in this way is called pollarding.

Roots grow in a similar way to stems, although they are simpler because there are no leaves. The tip of the root produces new cells continuously. As the top of the root is

Many flowers close up at night or when the weather is cold. The daisy closes its flowers when the light begins to fade in the evening. These movements are called nastic movements.

fixed, the tip is driven down into the soil. The tip is protected by a special layer of cells called the root cap. These cells are always being worn away, but new ones are being produced all the time to replace them.

The Mechanism of Growth

A plant grows basically by producing new cells at the tips of its stems and roots. Most of the actual growth, however, takes place a little way behind the tip. It is possible to show this by marking a young root with dye as shown in the diagram. The marks are equally spaced to start with, but after a while those that were just behind the tip become widely separated. Although growth actually takes place just behind the tip, it is controlled by the tip. The tip of the root or shoot produces a material called auxin. The auxin causes the cells to grow longer. If the shoot tip is removed, the auxin supply is lost and the cells do not grow.

Growth Movements

If you grow a plant in a room with only one window, you will soon notice that the plant bends towards the window. This bending movement is very useful for the plant because it ensures that it gets as much light as possible. It is produced by auxin. When a plant receives light from one side only, the cells on the other side grow longer than those on the lighter side. So the plant bends over towards the light. Bending movements of this kind, in which the movement depends on the direction of the stimulus, are called tropisms. Bending movements caused by light are called phototropisms.

If you grow some cress seedlings and then lay some of them down flat in the dark, you will find that the stems start to grow up again and the roots try to grow down again. These are some more bending movements, but this time the plants are responding to gravity and the movements are called geotropisms. Like phototropisms, they are controlled by auxin. Recent experiments have shown that auxin collects on the lower side of the stem and causes the cells to grow on that side. This produces an upward curve in the stem. Auxin collecting on the lower side of a root, however, slows down growth on that side. The upper side grows more quickly and the root bends downwards.

Above: A number of plants bend round during the day and thus remain facing the sun. This is particularly noticeable in a field of sunflowers where nearly every flower faces in the same direction.

Other bending movements include the bending of roots towards water, and the curling of tendrils around sticks and other supports when they are touched. All of these movements take place in the growing region, just behind the tip of the root or shoot. They are therefore called growth movements.

Another kind of bending movement is shown by the leaves of several plants. The garden nasturtium, for example, bends its leaves round during the day and keeps them facing the sun. They get the maximum amount of light this way. The movements are controlled by changes in the pressure of water in the cells of the leaf stalks.

Vegetative Reproduction

Bracken is a serious weed when it gets on to farm land because its underground rhizomes creep through the soil and soon cover a very large area. One original plant can become several plants if part of the connecting rhizome dies away.

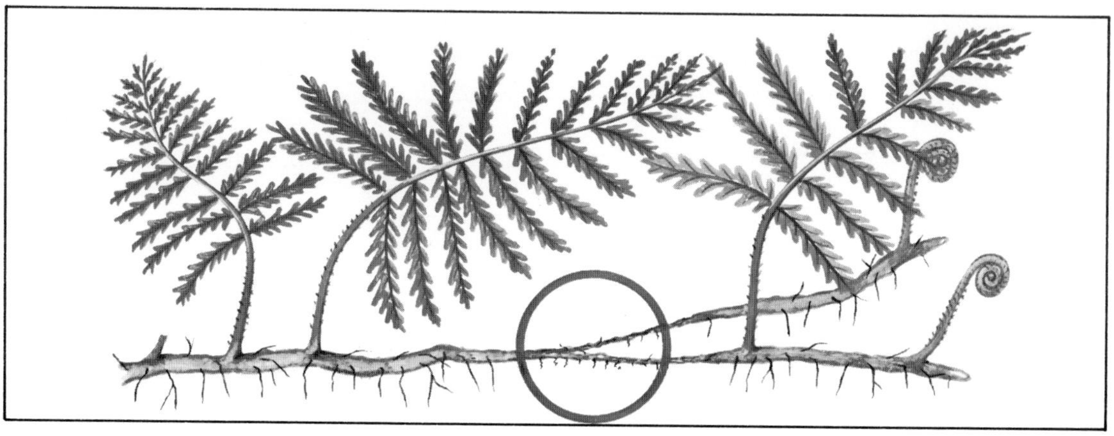

Many of the simplest plants reproduce by splitting into two similar halves. This is very similar to the reproductive methods of some of the simplest animals—the Protozoa. The more advanced plants, however, generally have special organs for sexual reproduction. In addition, many plants have a second method of reproduction, known as vegetative reproduction. Parts of the plant become separated and grow into new plants.

The strawberry plant sends out slender stems, called runners, that grow over the surface of the ground and then develop roots at their tips. Leaves grow and the runners decay, leaving a number of new plants. Some plants spread with underground stems called rhizomes—mint spreads in this way, for example. Many rhizomes store food as well.

Vegetative reproduction is an efficient way of spreading a plant over a small area, as we can see by the way in which couch grass or mint soon forms a large clump. But it does not carry the plants into new regions. A more important point is that the new plants are all the same, because they are just pieces of the parent plants. There is no variation of the sort that we get when cells join together in sexual reproduction. And without variation there can be no change or evolution.

Several plants, such as bryophyllum (near right) and coral root (far right), produce detachable buds or plantlets which grow into new plants.

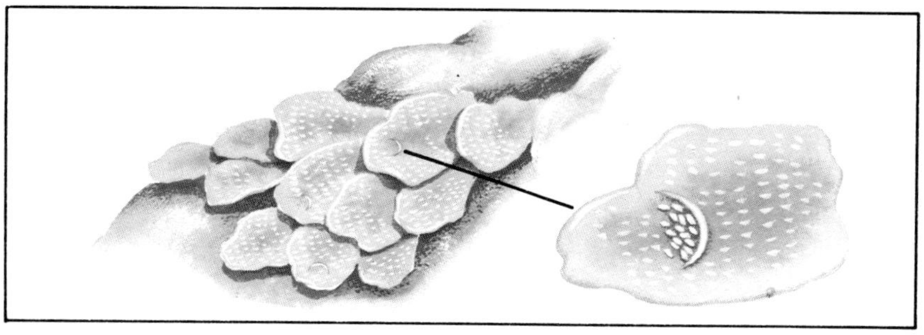

Some liverworts (page 33) produce detachable buds called gemmae. They are formed in little cups and they are washed away by the rain.

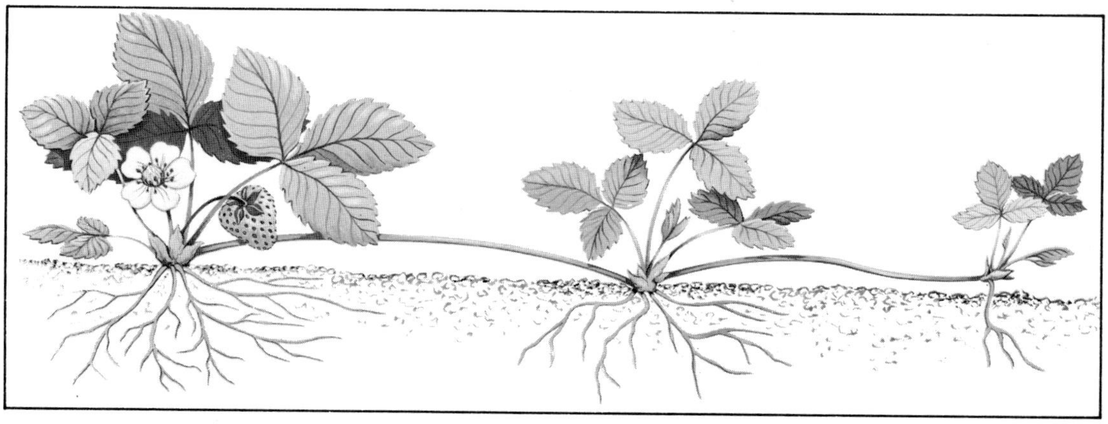

Strawberry runners grow very rapidly and soon cover the ground with young plants.

Plant Classification

There are more than 350,000 different species of plants in the world. The members of one species are all quite similar. Two bluebell plants have more in common than a bluebell and a daffodil. There is a closer connection between a bluebell and a daffodil, however, than between a bluebell and a primrose. And there is a closer connection between a bluebell and a primrose than between a bluebell and a fern. These similarities and differences are used to classify plants, or to divide them into groups.

Most people who study plants divide the plant kingdom into four major groups. They are called thallophytes, bryophytes, pteridophytes and spermatophytes. Each group is further divided into orders and families as shown on the chart or 'family tree' on the next page.

Thallophytes

The thallophytes are the simplest of the plants alive today and the earliest plants must have been of this type. There are no flowers and the plant body is not even divided into root, stem and leaf. There are two main groups: the algae and the fungi. The algae nearly all live in water. They all have green chlorophyll, although this may be masked by other colours. Seaweeds are algae and so are the slimy green threads that choke fish ponds in the summer and make the water green. Many algae are microscopic organisms that swim freely in the water. The fungi and bacteria have no chlorophyll and they cannot carry out photosynthesis to make their own food (see page 17). Some scientists do not think they are plants at all. Fungi include moulds and toadstools. Bacteria are also sometimes classed as thallophytes as well.

Bryophytes

The bryophytes are green plants which usually have distinct stems and leaves. There are no true roots, however, and no flowers. Bryophytes are divided into two main sections: the mosses and the liverworts.

Pteridophytes

This group includes the ferns, horsetails and club mosses. They are green plants and they are generally much larger than the mosses and liverworts. They have stems and leaves as a rule, and they also have proper roots. Associated with their larger size, they also have special tubes which carry water and food around the plant. There are no flowers.

Spermatophytes

These are the seed-bearing plants. Roots, stems and leaves are normally well developed. Apart from a few parasites (see page 47), they all contain chlorophyll and make their own food.

The two major sections of the seed-bearing plants are the gymnosperms and the angiosperms. Most of the gymnosperms carry their seeds in cones and are therefore called conifers. Other gymnosperms include the cycads, the yews and the ginkgo or maidenhair tree.

The angiosperms are the flowering plants. They account for something like 250,000 of the known plant species. There are two main sections: the monocotyledons and the dicotyledons. The basic difference between the two sections is found in the seed. The seed of a monocotyledon has only one seed leaf (cotyledon) whereas the seed of a dicotyledon has two seed leaves. Monocotyledons include plants such as grasses, irises, daffodils, tulips and orchids. Their leaves are normally narrow and the veins run parallel to each other. The flowers frequently have either three or six petals. The dicotyledons normally have broader leaves, with a network of veins. Their flowers usually have either four or five petals. Almost all flowering trees are dicotyledons and so are most of the flowers and vegetables that we grow in our gardens.

Plants are arranged in many families, the arrangement depending very much on the structure of the flower. The leaves and stems are not of much use in classifying plants because they vary so much according to the conditions under which the plants live. Unrelated plants growing in the same habitat often look alike because they are adapted to the same conditions. Conversely, related plants growing in different habitats may look very different. A dandelion living in a damp meadow may have large upright leaves and long flowering stems. If transplanted to a wind-swept mountainside, this same plant would start to produce much shorter leaves and they would lie flat and form a rosette on the ground. The flowering stems would also

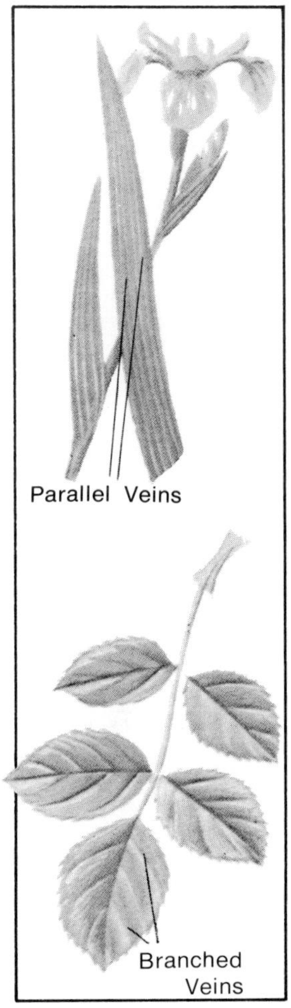

The leaves of a monocotyledon such as an iris normally have narrow leaves with parallel veins. The leaves of a dicotyledon such as a rose are normally broader and have a network of veins.

CYCADS
CONIFERS
FERNS
GINKGOS
CLUBMOSSES
DICOTYLEDONS
MONOCO
GYMNOSPERMS
HORSETAILS
ANGIOSPERMS
MOSSES
FUNGI
LIVERWORTS
BACTERIA
ALGAE
THALLOPHYTA
BRYOPHYTA
PTERIDOPHYTA
SPERMATOPHYTA

be shorter, although the flowers themselves would remain the same.

Bacteria

Bacteria are minute organisms. The largest bacteria are only about 0.01 millimetre across, and they can be seen only with a good microscope. There are three main groups of bacteria: bacilli are rod-shaped, cocci are spherical, and spirilli are like minute curved or twisted sausages. Many bacilli and most of the spirilli possess flagella, which enable them to swim.

Many bacteria cause diseases, such as tuberculosis and tetanus, but the majority are very useful. Whereas green plants get their energy from sunlight, bacteria get their energy from various chemical reactions. The soil teems with bacteria which break down dead plants and animals. They release minerals which growing plants can use. Bacteria therefore play a vital role in the workings of nature.

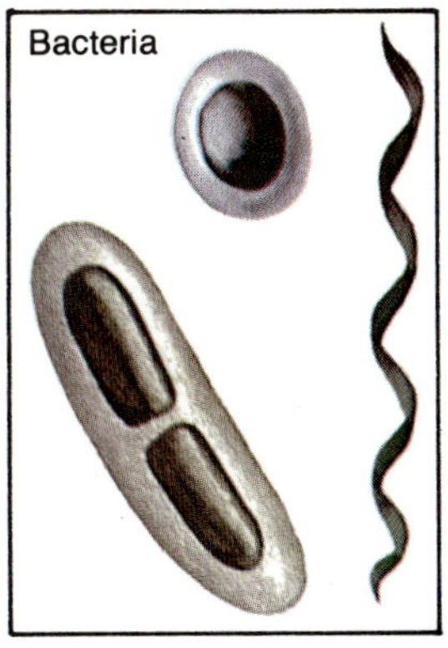

The Algae

Right: Pandorina is a colonial alga consisting of 16 individual cells embedded in a sphere of jelly. A diatom, one of the algae with glassy shells.

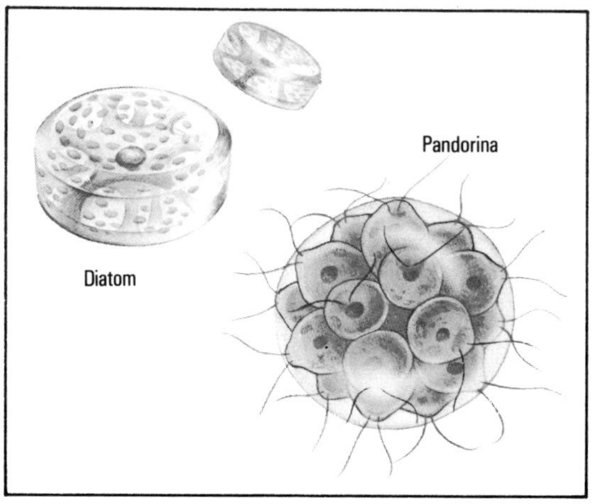

Right: Spirogyra, showing the spiral chloroplast which gives the plant its name.

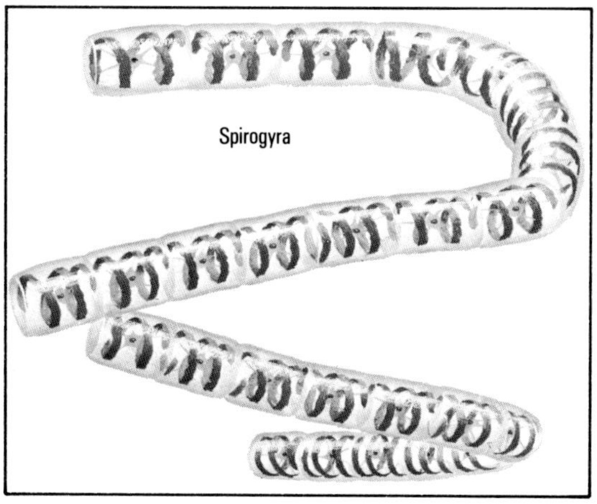

Chlamydomonas, greatly magnified, showing the cup-shaped chloroplast and the two flagella. The dark sphere in the centre is the nucleus.

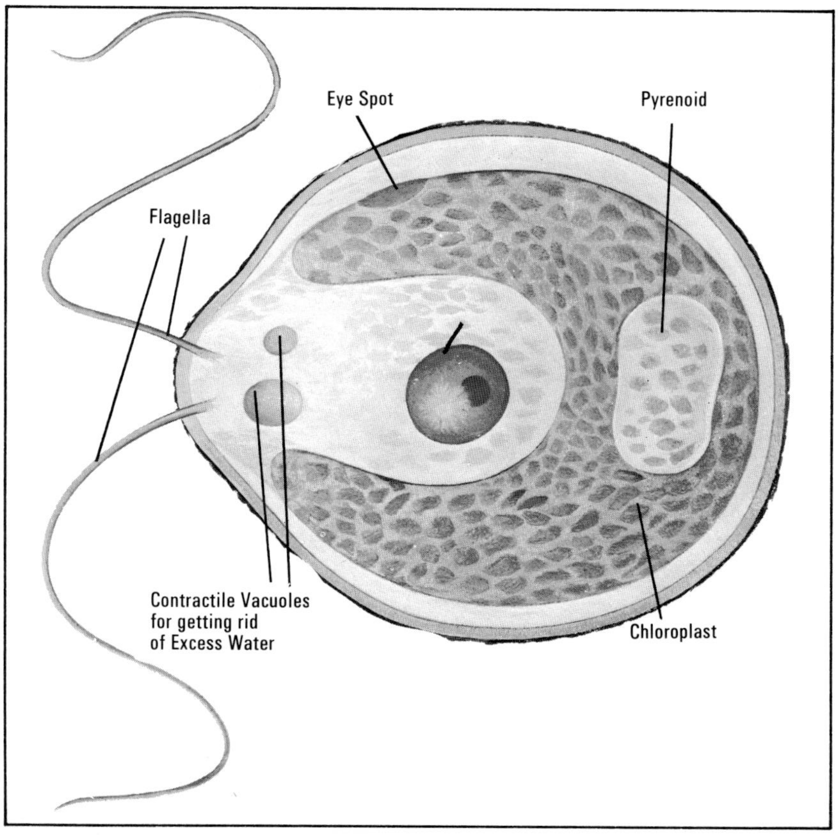

The algae are simple plants belonging to the large group known as the thallophytes. The plant body is called a thallus. It is not divided into roots, stems and leaves, although some of the seaweeds have root-like holdfasts which fix them to the rocks. There are no special cells for carrying water or food around the plants. And there are, of course, no flowers. All algae possess chlorophyll, although it is often masked by brown or red pigments, so they make their own food like any other green plants.

Plants That Move About

The simplest algae are single-celled organisms and most of them are extremely small. Some live in damp soil and some clothe tree trunks in damp places, but most of them live in water. They possess little whip-like hairs called flagella and they swim by lashing these hairs.

One of the commonest algae in fresh water is called chlamydomonas. Its single oval cell is so tiny that fifty of them would only just about stretch across a pin's head. But it is a complete plant with a cellulose cell wall, a nucleus to control its activity and a chloroplast in which it makes food. The little plant also has a red 'eye spot' which is sensitive to light. This eye spot controls the movement of the plant, directing it towards areas of moderately bright light. This ensures that the plant remains in a position where it can carry out photosynthesis efficiently. When the water is warm chlamydomonas grows rapidly and it splits into two every day or so.

Chlamydomonas is a solitary plant, with each individual leading a separate existence. There are, however, several common pond-dwelling algae which live in clusters or colonies. The colonies consist of eight or more cells, all more or less like chlamydomonas and acting as separate individuals.

Spirogyra

During the summer many ponds become choked with tangled green strands known as blanketweed. Each strand is an alga and one of the commonest kinds is called spirogyra. The strands are unbranched and each is composed of a number of cylindrical cells. These cells are all more or less alike and each acts independently. When the cells divide into two, the two new cells do not separate:

they remain in the strand and continue to grow. The strand therefore increases in length. Spirogyra can also reproduce in another way. Neighbouring strands send side branches into each other, forming a sort of 'ladder'. The contents of one cell moves across into the neighbouring cell and forms a tough walled 'egg'. The parent strands then decay and the eggs develop into new strands.

Above: The algae are prominent on rocky sea-shores where seaweeds grow in profusion. They provide a retreat for many small animals when the tide goes out.

Seaweeds

Seaweeds include the largest and the most complicated algae. Some are red, some are brown and some are green, but they all contain chlorophyll and they all make their own food with the aid of sunlight. The need for sunlight means that the seaweeds can grow only in shallow water, where light reaches the bottom.

Green seaweeds, such as the common sea lettuce, normally grow on the upper parts of the sea-shore and they make the rocks very slippery. A little lower down on the shore there is usually a zone of brown seaweeds. These include the largest of the algae, some of the oarweeds or kelps being many metres long. One of the commonest of the brown seaweeds is the bladder wrack, so called because its fronds bear numerous air bladders which pop if squeezed. The bladders help to buoy the plants up when the tide comes in. The fronds of the brown seaweeds are covered here and there, especially at the tips, with pale spots. These are tiny pits in which the reproductive bodies develop. Tiny free-swimming spores are released from the pits. Some of them have to pair up before growing into new seaweeds, but others can grow directly into new plants.

Red seaweeds are generally much smaller than the brown ones and many of them are constructed in a different way. Instead of having broad blades, many of them have slender branching filaments made up of chains of cells. Some secrete chalky skeletons around themselves and these seaweeds play an important part in building coral reefs in the warmer seas. Red seaweeds normally grow further down the shore than the brown ones and, unless there are rock pools, they do not very often reach above low tide level. They extend into deeper and darker water, because the red pigment helps the chlorophyll to absorb light more efficiently.

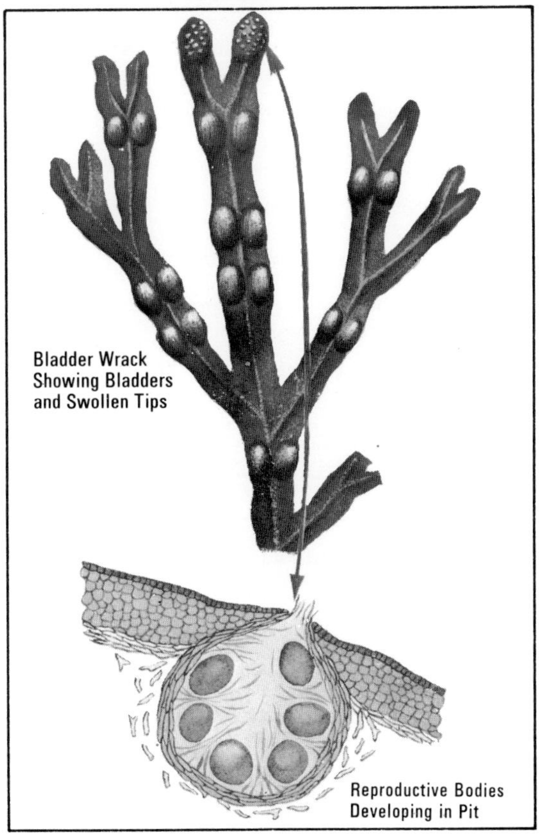

The bladder wrack is one of the commonest brown seaweeds and covers many of the rocks of the middle shore. The bladders contain air which helps to buoy up the plant. The tips of the thallus bear pimply swellings. Each pimple is the opening of a reproductive organ.

Below: A few of the many varieties of seaweed.

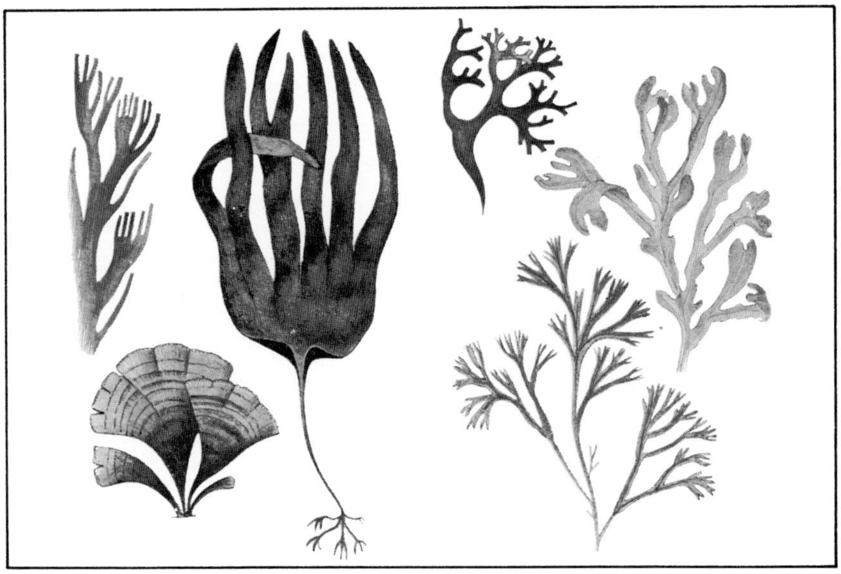

Fungi

Right: The beautiful but poisonous fly agaric.

Moulds and toadstools belong to the large group of plants called fungi. None of them ever has any chlorophyll. Fungi cannot, therefore, make their own food. They have to get 'ready-made' food just like animals. Most of them get it from dead and decaying matter, such as dead leaves and rotting wood. Fungi getting food in this way are called saprophytes. Some fungi, however, are parasites and they obtain food from living plants or animals. Many serious crop diseases are caused by parasitic fungi. Potato blight is a well known one and the rust disease of wheat is another. Fungi also produce various skin diseases, such as ringworm, in animals.

Because the fungi do not make their own food they do not need sunlight. This is why we can grow mushrooms in dark damp cellars. Like the algae, the fungi belong to the division of plants called the thallophytes. They have no roots, stems, or leaves. Their bodies are composed of slender threads called hyphae. These creep over or through the food materials and secrete digestive juices which dissolve the food. The resulting solution is then absorbed. Fungi are a nuisance when they start to grow on our jam or our floorboards, but they are of great importance in nature. They play a major part in breaking down dead leaves and returning the goodness to the soil.

Below: The mushroom begins as a small, round cap and grows into the familiar parasol shape, showing the spore-bearing 'gills' underneath.

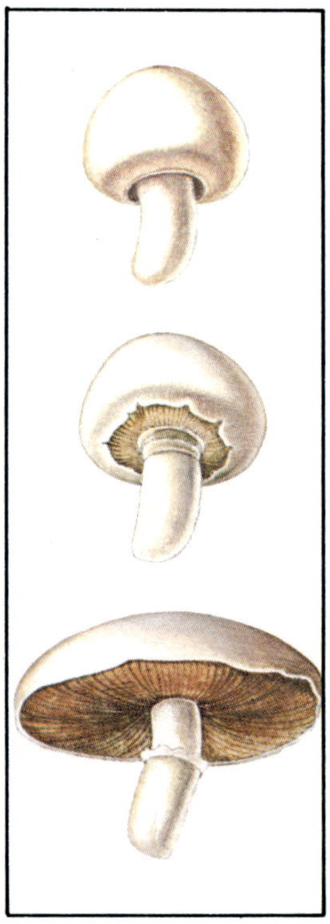

Moulds

Moulds consist of a mass of fluffy threads that cover the material they are growing on. One of the common moulds is the pin mould or mucor. Like nearly all fungus threads, the hyphae are white, but upright branches form after a while and they bear little black capsules at their tips. These look like tiny pin-heads and give the mould its common name. Each capsule contains hundreds of tiny spores and, when the capsule splits, the spores are scattered like dust into the wind. If they land in a suitable place they will grow into new threads. This is a form of vegetative or asexual reproduction. Sexual reproduction takes place when side branches join together and form tough-walled 'eggs'. These can survive cold and drought and, when good conditions return, they start to grow. A spore capsule develops and scatters lots of spores which can then grow into new threads.

Toadstools

Toadstools are more complicated fungi than the moulds and the familiar umbrella-shaped toadstool is only a part of the fungus. For most of the year the fungi exist as slender threads just like those of the moulds. They grow and branch and then, usually in the

Few organic materials are safe from the attacks of fungi. Mucor, the pin mould, grows on stale bread, cheese, leather, animal dung and many other substances. The left-hand pictures show the little black capsules which contain the spores, greatly enlarged.

autumn, they become tightly packed together and they start to form the toadstool. At first it is a little button-shaped object in the ground, but it grows rapidly and breaks through the surface. The cap then opens out to reveal either the familiar gills radiating out from the stalk or a mass of tiny pores. Spores are formed on the gills or in the pores.

The mushroom is simply one particular kind of toadstool that happens to be very good to eat. There are many other toadstools that are good to eat, but some of them are very poisonous. You should never eat fungi unless you are absolutely sure that they are edible. Two of the most deadly kinds are the death cap and the red and white fly agaric. Both have little 'cups' at the base of the stalk and both have rings higher up on the stalk.

Two other groups of fungi that are commonly found are the bracket fungi and the puffballs. Bracket fungi grow on living and dead trees and, instead of forming umbrella-shaped spore-bearing bodies, they form shelf-like structures on the trunks. Puff-balls are ball-shaped or club-shaped fungi that grow on the ground. When they are ripe they split open and when they are touched, or even blown by the breeze, huge clouds of spores shoot out.

Penicillin

One of the biggest advances in medical science was the discovery of penicillin. It was discovered quite by accident in 1928, when Alexander Fleming found that a little green mould was growing among some bacteria he was studying. Fleming then noticed that the germs near the mould were dying. In fact, the mould was producing a germ-killing substance. It was a long time before scientists managed to isolate this substance, but they succeeded in the end and found that it could be used to fight a wide variety of diseases. The mould was called *Penicillium notatum* and the substance was therefore called penicillin. Large amounts are now produced in huge tanks.

Yeasts

Yeasts are rather special kinds of fungi which consist of tiny egg-shaped cells instead of threads. They produce digestive juices which turn sugar into alcohol. Yeasts are therefore used in making wine and beer.

Lichens

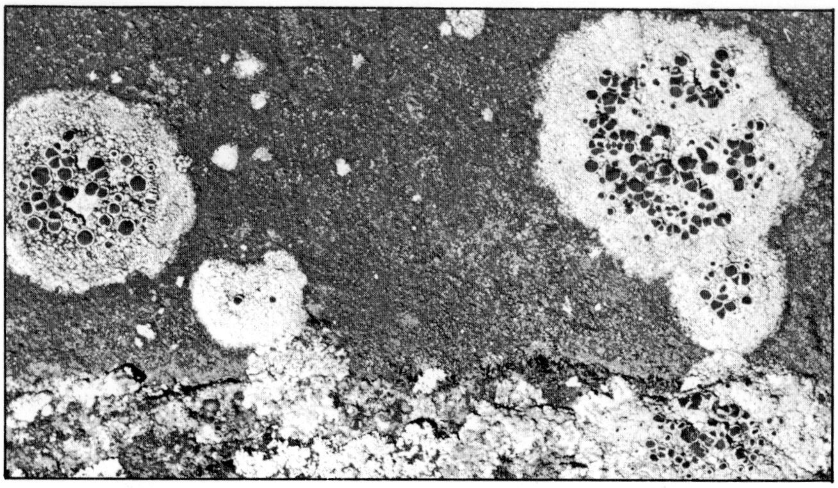

Above: Patches of crustose lichens growing on an old wall.

Old walls, especially in country areas, are often encrusted with grey or yellow patches more or less circular in outline. These patches, despite their rather lifeless appearance, are growing plants and they are called lichens (pronounced like-ens). They are extremely hardy plants—hardy enough to grow on exposed rocks—and their hardiness results mainly from their curious construction. A lichen is, in fact, two plants rolled into one. The two plants are a fungus and an alga, each kind of lichen having its own combination of fungus and alga species.

The bulk of the lichen plant is made up of fungus threads, but there is a great difference between the tough, hardy lichen and the soft body of a normal fungus. This is one of the many mysteries still surrounding the lichens. The tiny algae are bound up among the fungus threads and are normally concentrated near the upper surface where they can receive the maximum amount of sunlight. Botanists now believe that lichens are special kinds of fungi.

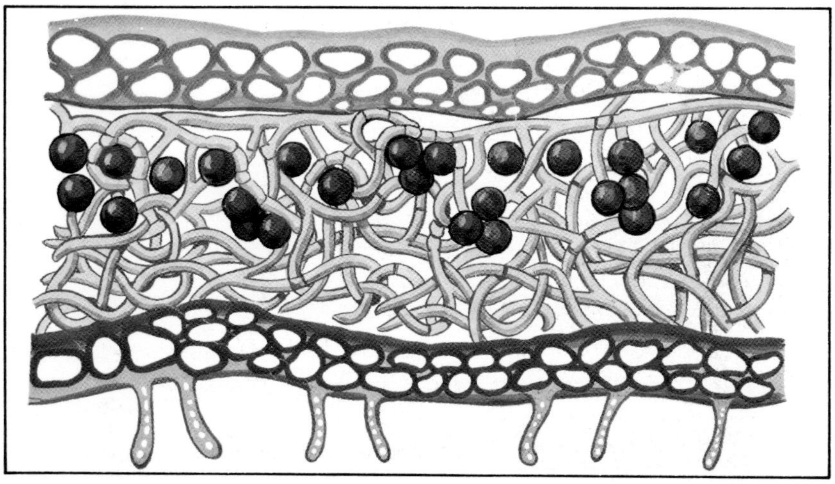

The bulk of the lichen body is formed by the tangled fungus threads. The algal cells are found mainly in the upper layers, where they get enough light to make food. Botanists now consider that lichens are just special kinds of fungi which use algae to help them to feed.

The fungus threads of the lichen absorb and store water when it is available. They then pass it on to the algae. The algae contain chlorophyll and they can carry out photosynthesis. Mineral salts are obtained partly from the dust that falls on the plants and partly from the rock or soil: the fungus threads produce acids that dissolve the rock and release the minerals. The minerals and sugars are combined by the algae to make food for themselves and for the fungus. The lichen is therefore very much a partnership, with each partner having certain jobs. It is a good example of a symbiotic association (see page 134).

There are three main groups of lichens, according to the shape of the thallus or body. Fruticose lichens are often branched and they look like miniature trees or bushes. Foliose lichens consist of spreading 'fingers', often rather leaf-like. Crustose lichens cover surfaces with a delicate crust lacking any distinct lobes or 'fingers'.

Reproduction takes place in two ways in the lichens. The fungus produces spores in brightly coloured patches. These tiny spores are scattered in the wind but they contain no algae and will not develop into lichens unless they meet the right kind of alga. The lichen fungi cannot live alone. The other method of reproduction involves the production of sporedia. These are little granules that break off from the lichen surface. They contain fungus threads and algae and they can grow directly into new lichens.

Lichens are so hardy that they can grow almost everywhere, from the hottest deserts to the coldest polar regions. Desert lichens grow mostly underground, getting their light through a small hole in the ground. The wandering lichen, which is spread by the wind, may have been the manna which was eaten by the Israelites in the desert. An unusual lichen lives in Antarctic seas. Large areas of the Arctic Circle are covered with lichens known as reindeer moss because they are the main summer food of the reindeer. Lichens have been widely used for making dyes, including litmus for detecting acids. They are sometimes eaten or used in medicines and perfumes. As well as growing on the ground, especially where the soil is poor, lichens grow on rocks, walls and tree trunks. The one thing that they cannot survive, however, is air pollution and they are rarely found in large cities.

Mosses and Liverworts

Most people can recognise mosses when they see them. Their slender stems are rarely more than a few centimetres long and they carry thin, almost transparent leaves. There are no proper roots, although short hair-like outgrowths anchor the plants to the ground. Mosses usually grow in dense clusters, forming bright green mats or cushions.

Mosses are not flowering plants, but dense clusters of leaves develop at the tops of the stems. Among these leaves there are the reproductive organs. The male organs are club-shaped and the female organs, which are usually on separate branches, are like tiny flasks. In damp weather, when the plants are covered with a film of moisture, the male cells are released. They possess minute hairs called flagella and these enable them to swim to the female 'flasks' where they pair up with the egg cells in the flasks. The new cell formed by this union begins to grow and eventually forms a little oval box or capsule. This has its own stalk and it grows up above the rest of the moss plant. It contains the spores—minute dust-like particles that can grow into new moss plants. The spore capsule usually has a pointed cap to start with, but this comes off when the spores are ripe and reveals a complicated system of 'teeth'. When the air is dry these teeth curl back and allow the breeze to scatter the spores. The capsule closes up again in damp weather, for the spores would not drift away if they were wet.

When the moss spore germinates it sends out a thin green thread. This is called the protonema and it soon grows several branches. Buds develop on the branches and each bud grows into a new moss plant. As a result, the young mosses are clumped together right from the start. By clumping together, mosses retain a good deal of moisture around themselves.

Liverworts

The liverworts are less well known than the mosses. There are two main groups: flat and leafy. The flat liverworts grow in very damp places. They are especially common by waterfalls, where the water is always splashing them. They look rather like tough green seaweeds, creeping over the surface, and it is possible that the earliest land plants were of this type. The leafy liverworts are very much like the mosses, and are readily distinguished only when they are carrying spore capsules.

The life histories of liverworts are very similar to those of the mosses, but the spore capsules are very much simpler. They are round and black to start with, but when the spores are ripe they split open and become star-shaped. The spores are scattered by the wind and, when they reach suitable places, they grow into new liverworts. There is no protonema. Many liverworts can also reproduce vegetatively by producing gemmae. These are tiny detachable buds, produced in little cups. They are scattered by raindrops and grow into new liverworts.

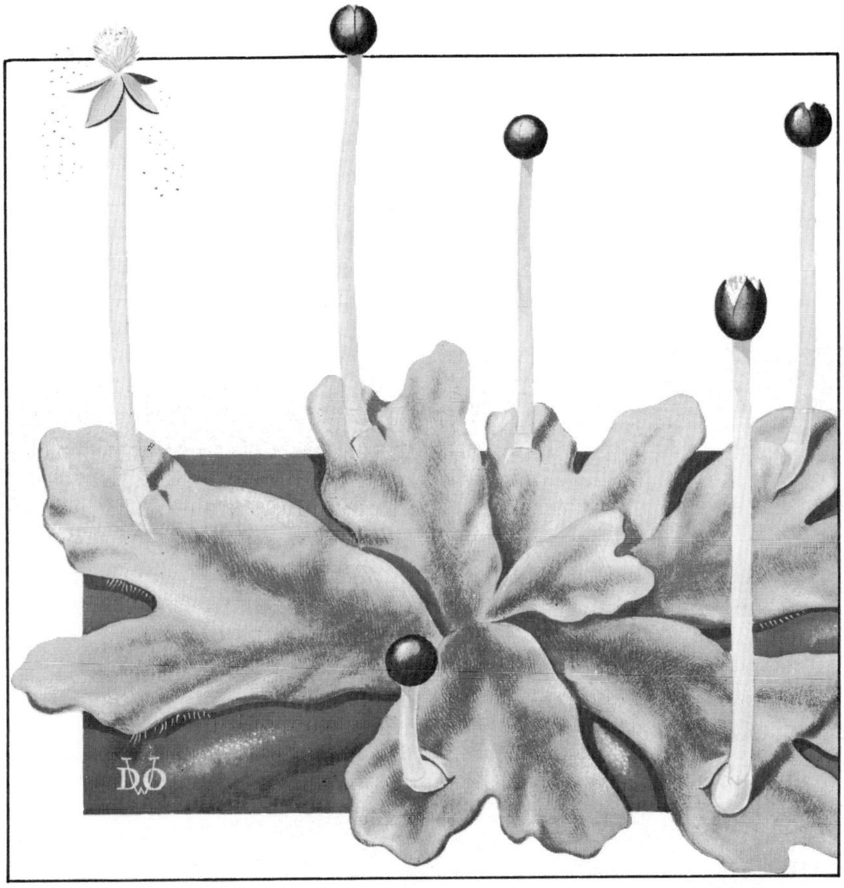

Pellia, one of the flat liverworts, showing the tough thallus and the simple spore capsules.

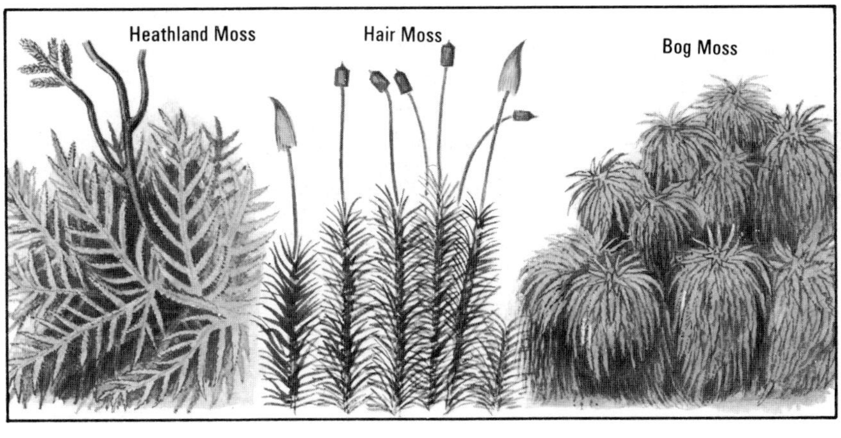

Some common mosses of damp heathland.

Ferns and Horsetails

The ferns and their relatives belong to a very ancient group of plants known as the Pteridophyta. This group was in existence at least 400 million years ago and its members included some of the earliest of all land plants. The pteridophytes reached their peak about 250 million years ago, when they formed great forests. Most of our coal consists of the remains of these plants and so we know quite a lot about them. Some of them reached heights of more than 30 metres. These huge plants have long since died out and today's pteridophytes rarely exceed a few metres in height. Although there are several other types of pteridophyte still in existence only the ferns make a significant contribution to today's plant life.

Ferns and the other pteridophytes normally have roots and stems. Most of them also have leaves but none of them ever has any flowers. They reproduce by scattering tiny spores, rather like those of the mosses and liverworts. The possession of proper roots is an advance over the lowly mosses, but even more important is the development of a system of tubes carrying water and food from one part of the plant to another. Once the plants had evolved such a system they could begin to increase in size.

Ferns

Most of the ferns possess roots, stems and leaves. Except in the tropical and subtropical tree ferns, which may reach a height of 20 metres, the stems are small and usually remain under the ground. Fern stems are normally unbranched, but the bracken and some other ferns have branching underground stems called rhizomes. These spread through the soil and throw up leaves. The rhizomes enable bracken to spread rapidly and make it very difficult to get rid of. Fern leaves, often called fronds, may be quite large and they are frequently divided into many small leaflets. There are some exceptions, such as the hart's tongue fern. Fern stems are normally under the ground and unbranched, but the bracken is one of a few species with creeping rhizomes. A field of bracken may, in fact, consist of a single bracken plant which has sent up thousands of fronds from its rhizomes.

The spores are normally produced on the undersides of the leaves and if you look at fern fronds in late summer you will see hundreds of little brown patches. These are patches of spore capsules. In some species they are covered by protective flaps. Each capsule has a little stalk and looks like a tiny club. When it is ripe it bursts open and the spores are scattered in the wind.

When a spore falls on suitable ground it begins to grow, but it does not grow into a new fern plant. It forms a little heart-shaped plate up to 10 mm across. This plate is called the prothallus. It is green and it has little root-like hairs on its underside. After a while the prothallus produces reproductive cells. These are of two kinds: egg cells and male cells. The male cells are released in wet weather and they swim about by means of tufts of flagella (movable hairs). They are attracted to the egg cells and they join up in pairs. The combined cell then starts to grow into a new fern plant. It is supported by the prothallus at first, but it soon starts to make its own food. The first fronds are quite small and simple, but later ones take on a more mature appearance. It may be several years before the young fern plant begins to produce its own spores.

Many fern plants can grow in dry places but, because the life cycle depends on damp

The fern's spore capsules are normally carried on the underside of the fronds and they are often hidden by a protective shield, as here.

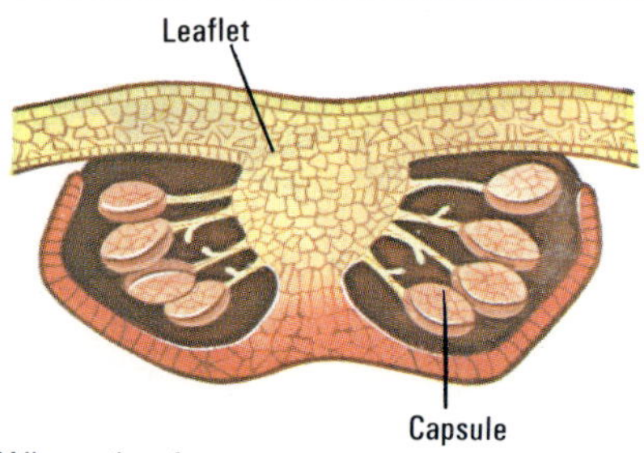

When the fern spore germinates it grows into a little heart-shaped structure called the prothallus.

Ferns thrive in a warm, damp climate in considerable variety.

conditions during the prothallus stage, the ferns are found mainly in damp places. Shady woods and spray-soaked places around waterfalls are probably the best places in which to look for them.

Horsetails

About 250 million years ago the horsetails played a very prominent part in the world's plant life. There were many different species and some of them were more than 30 metres tall. Today there are only about 25 species alive and they are rarely more than about 90 cm tall. Many of them live in marshy places and ponds, although some live in much drier places.

Horsetails are rather spiky plants without proper leaves. Some species have whorls of thin branches, but others have no branches at all and the stems look rather like long pencils sticking up out of the ground or the water. The stems are always somewhat ridged and they bear a number of little 'collars'. These collars are made up of tiny scale leaves and they occur at intervals all the way up the stem. They mark the position of the nodes or joints and the stems snap very easily at these points.

Under the ground, the horsetails have creeping rhizomes, like those of the bracken fern, and they are difficult plants to get rid of in a garden. The stems usually die down every year, but the rhizome lives on to produce the next year's stems.

The spores are produced in little 'cones' at the tips of the stems. Some horsetail species produce special spore-bearing stems which are brown and which come up before the green stems, but other species carry their cones at the tips of ordinary stems. The spores are green and they grow very quickly when they have been scattered. They grow into prothalli rather like those of the ferns, although they usually have upright 'fingers' on the upper surface. Egg cells and male cells are produced and, after pairing up, they grow into new horsetail plants.

Club Mosses

Living club mosses are all quite small plants and, as their name suggests, they look rather like mosses. They generally grow more or less flat on the ground and their leaves are very small. The stag's-horn moss grows to 3 metres. They are, however, more closely related to the ferns and they have the same sort of life history. The spores are borne in 'cones' at the tips of upright shoots, and the cones are rather club-shaped — hence the common name of these plants. The prothallus of the club moss is something like a small sausage. It normally lives under the ground and gets its food by forming a partnership with a fungus.

Bracken is one of the few species of ferns that has creeping rhizomes.

Conifers

Silver Fir

Giant Fir

Seeds are produced only by the two most advanced groups of plants—the cone-bearers and the flowering plants. The ferns and the other more primitive groups of plants scatter tiny spores. Apart from the palm-like cycads, the cone-bearers are generally large trees, often called conifers. Examples include the pines, spruces (Christmas trees), cedars, larches and monkey puzzle trees. The conifers nearly all have small narrow leaves called needles and most of them are evergreens. The needles are very tough and coated with thick cuticles. The breathing pores are sunk well below the surface and water loss is therefore kept to a minimum. This is very important, for the conifers often live in regions where water is scarce.

Conifers stretch in an unbroken belt from Norway to eastern Siberia and also right across Canada. The soil in these regions is frozen during the winter and water is not readily available to the trees. Also, the winds are strong and tend to remove water by evaporation from the leaves. Without some means of cutting down water loss, the trees would soon die. Conifers also flourish in the Mediterranean area and in other regions with moist winters and hot, dry summers.

Coniferous trees grow more quickly than the broad-leaved or flowering trees and this is why the conifers are planted so widely for timber. Their wood is softer than that of most broad-leaved trees and coniferous timbers are generally known as softwoods. Most of them are less durable than the hardwoods and they rot more quickly, although the western red cedar (not a true cedar) contains natural preservatives that make it resistant to nearly all wood-rotting organisms.

The Conifer's Life History

Reproduction in the conifers centres on the cones. There are two types of cones—male cones and female cones—and they start to grow in the spring. Both types are normally found on one tree. The male cones are small and yellowish. They are usually rather inconspicuous, but they are easily seen in the pine because they are grouped into large clusters at the bases of the new shoots. The female cones develop near the tips of the new shoots.

Each cone consists of a series of overlapping scales which are no more than special leaves. The scales of the male cone carry pollen sacs and the female cone-scales each carry a pair of ovules which will eventually become the seeds. In dry weather the scales of the cones separate a little and pollen escapes from the male cones. Blown by the wind, the pollen grains enter the female cones. The cones then close up again. The female cones then begin to grow brown and woody. The pollen grains send out fine tubes which grow into the ovules. Inside each ovule there is an egg cell and a tiny cell from the pollen grain joins with this egg cell to form an embryo plant. Food material is deposited around it and it gradually forms a root and a little shoot with several leaves. While this is going on the ovule wall becomes hard. The whole thing—embryo plant plus food reserve plus coat—is now a seed. The seed coat has a thin 'wing' growing out from one side and, when the cone opens, the seed can float away on the wind. If it lands in suitable soil it will grow into a new conifer. The whole process, from cone formation to the release of the seeds, takes just over a year in most conifers. In pines, however, it takes two years.

Spores and Seeds

There is a big difference in the reproductive process of the ferns and the conifers. The ferns produce spores, while the conifers produce seeds with baby plants in them.

Spanish Fir

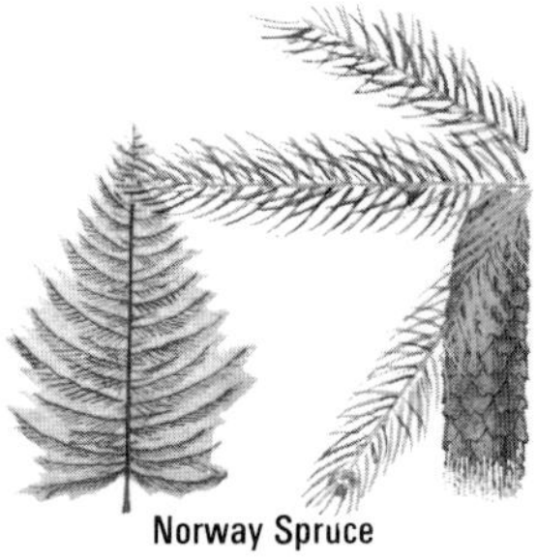

Norway Spruce

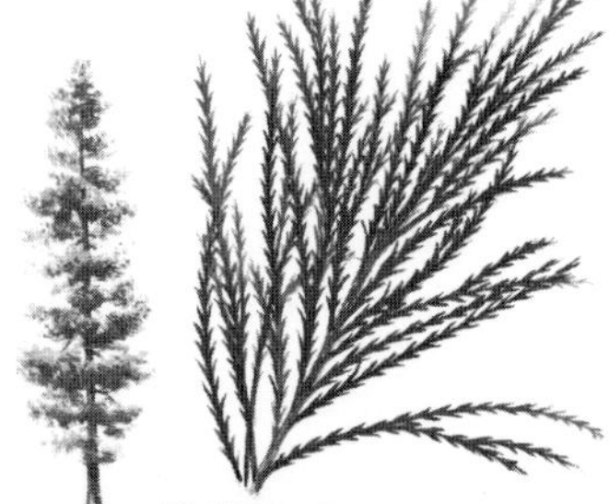

Wellingtonia

Deodar

Most ferns produce only one kind of spore and all the prothalli (see page 34) are alike. Some ferns, however, produce separate male and female spores, which develop into male and female prothalli. This is what happens in the conifers, but the prothalli are very much reduced and do not lead a separate existence.

The pollen grains are male spores. The male prothalli are simply the pollen tubes and the few cells inside them. The ovules are the female spore capsules and the female spores are represented by cells inside the ovules. These spores are never released from their capsules. Only one spore grows in each ovule, and it grows into a bunch of cells representing the prothallus. One cell becomes the egg cell—as it does on the fern prothallus—and is fertilised by a male cell.

In ferns, the male cell has to swim towards the egg cell. By retaining the female spore and prothallus inside the ovule, the conifers avoid the need for free water and reproduction becomes a much less chancy affair. Pollen is blown to the female cones by the wind. The early growth of the young plant takes place inside the parent, where it is protected.

Cycads

The cycads are strange plants with many features part way between ferns and conifers. They have seeds, however, and clearly belong with the conifers. They grow in the warmer parts of the world. Most of them have short, stout trunks crowned with tufts of large fern-like leaves. The pollen and seeds are carried in large cones, although the female cones of one species are little more than bunches of ordinary leaves. When the pollen grain reaches the ovule it puts out a pollen tube but it does not grow towards the egg cell. It bursts and releases the male cell which swims to the egg cell.

Coniferous forests cover vast areas in northern lands. They are our main source of timber.

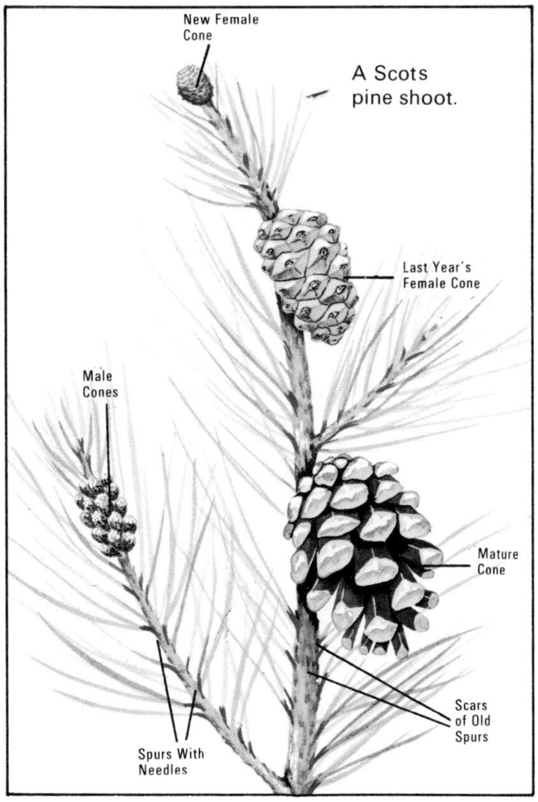

Left: The development of pine cones.

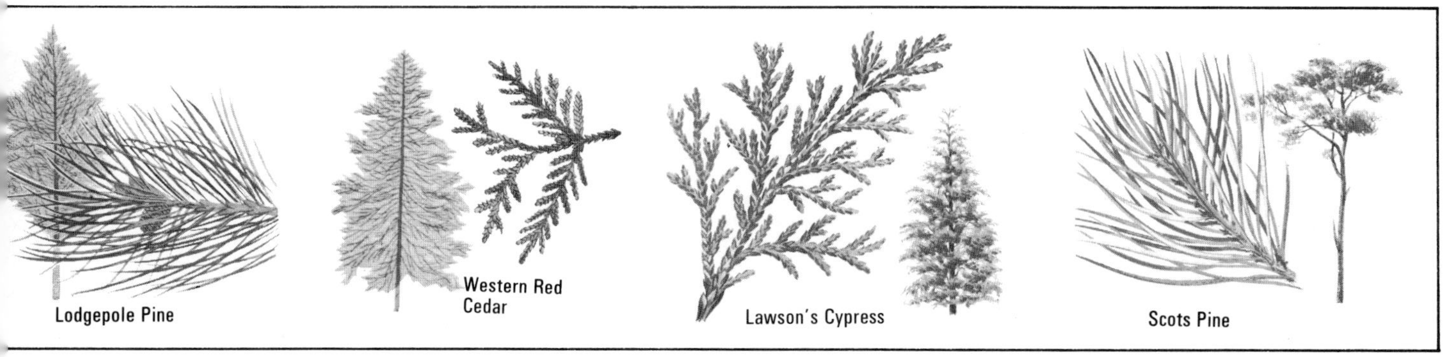

Flowering Plants

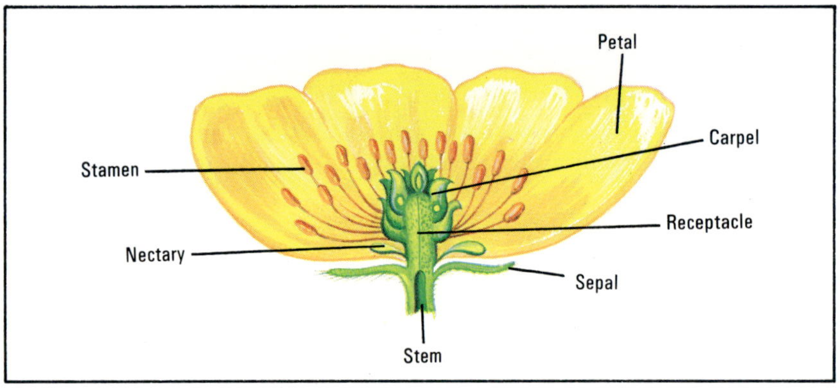

The flowering plants are the most advanced of all plants. Nearly every plant you see around you is a flowering plant. There are about 250,000 different kinds and they include all the most useful plants as well as the most attractive ones.

Flowering plants range in size from the tiny floating duckweeds to huge forest trees. Their structure varies a great deal but, with the exception of a few parasitic and saprophytic species (see page 47), they all contain chlorophyll and they all make food by photosynthesis. Flowering plants also grow in much the same way as the non-flowering plants. It is their methods of reproduction that make the flowering plants so different from the mosses, ferns and conifers.

The previous chapter describes how the conifers have overcome the need for free water during reproduction. This advance has been maintained in the flowering plants and other improvements have led to better and less wasteful methods of reproduction.

The Structure of the Flower

Conifers produce 'naked' seeds on the scales of their cones. Flowering plants, however, enclose their seeds in containers

Top: The buttercup is known as a perfect flower because it has all four kinds of floral organs in it. Above: After pollination, the petals fall off and the carpels swell to become fruits. The flowers on the right are arranged in different types of heads, called inflorescences.

called fruits. Flowers are composed of very special leaves of which there are four main kinds. Around the outside of a flower there are usually a number of greenish leaves called sepals. When the flower is still in bud the sepals surround the other parts and protect them. When the flower opens the sepals bend back, or they may even fall off in some flowers. Just inside the sepals we find the petals. These vary a great deal in colour, shape and arrangement. They are often joined together. The petals are normally large and brightly coloured and their job is to attract insects to the flowers. Inside the petals there are normally a number of pin-like objects. These are the stamens—the male parts of the flower—and their job is to produce pollen. Right in the centre of the flower we find one or more carpels. These are the female parts of the flower. Each carpel contains one or more ovules which will eventually become seeds. Each carpel has a sticky tip called a stigma, which may be raised up on a slender stalk.

Most flowers contain stamens and carpels, but there are some which contain only one or the other. Marrow flowers, for example, are either male or female—they have stamens or carpels, but not both. There are even some species which have male and female flowers on different plants. Examples include willows and holly trees. Only the female trees will bear fruit and seeds.

Pollination

Before a flower can form seeds it must be pollinated. This means that pollen of the right kind must fall on to the stigmas of the carpels and begin to grow. Some flowers are self-pollinated, that is pollen falls from the stamens to the stigmas of the same flower. Most flowers, however, have some way of preventing or discouraging self-pollination. The stamens may ripen and scatter their pollen before the stigmas are ready, or the stigmas may ripen before the stamens are ready. The flowers may also be self-sterile, which means that the pollen will not grow on the stigmas of the same flower. These flowers must be cross-pollinated with pollen from another flower of the same kind.

Some plants, including grasses and many trees, rely on the wind to carry their pollen from flower to flower. Such wind-pollinated plants generally have small and inconspicuous flowers, often without any petals. The stamens and carpels are often in separate flowers and the male flowers often hang in long clusters called catkins. These scatter clouds of pollen when blown by the wind. The stigmas of the wind-pollinated plants are usually branched and feathery and they have a better chance of trapping pollen.

Most flowering plants rely on insects to carry their pollen from flower to flower. The insects are attracted to the flowers by the brightly coloured petals and also by the scent and the sugary nectar that many flowers produce. The insects thus get dusted with pollen which they then carry to the stigmas of another flower. Because the pollen is carried directly from flower to flower, the plants do not have to make so much.

Above: Most flowers are pollinated by insects. The insects are attracted by nectar, scent and brightly coloured petals, as in this cactus flower.

Above left: The sweet pea can be pollinated only by insects heavy enough to weigh down the keel petal and get into the flower.

Wind pollinated flowers, such as these plantains, are generally drably coloured and they usually have long hanging stamens which scatter pollen in the breeze.

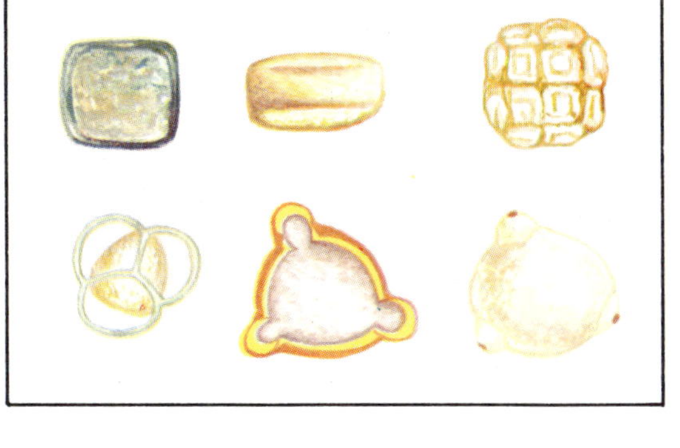

Each kind of flower has its characteristically shaped pollen grain. Scientists use the pollen grains preserved in peat bogs to tell them about the plants that lived long ago.

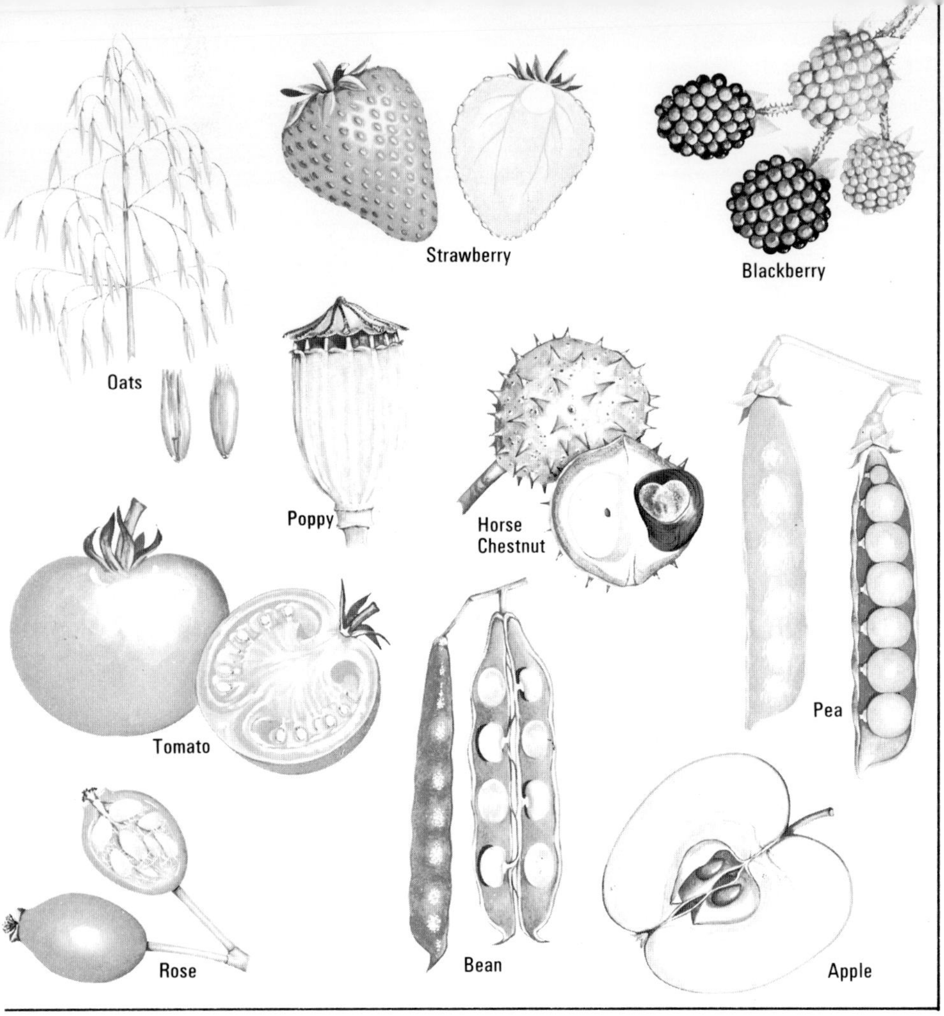

A selection of fruits. The apple, strawberry and rose hip are false fruits because they are not formed from the carpels alone.

Many juicy fruits are eaten by birds. The seeds are then scattered far and wide.

The seeds of the poppy and snapdragon are scattered as the capsules are rocked by the wind. The seeds of the stock and violet are shot out as the fruits dry out and shrink.

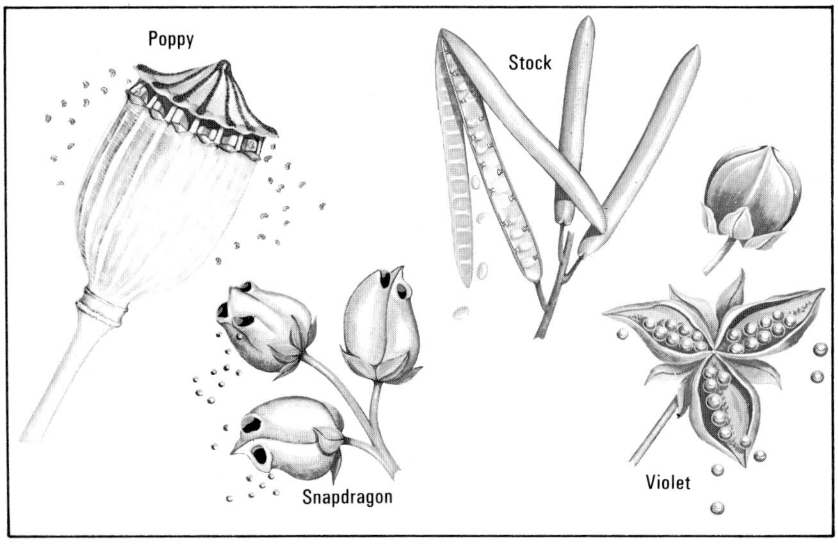

The Formation of Fruits and Seeds

When a pollen grain falls on to a ripe stigma of the right kind it begins to grow. It sends out a thin tube which forces its way down through the stigma and into the carpel. Two minute cells from the pollen grain move down the tube and enter an ovule. One of them pairs up with the egg cell in the ovule. The egg cell is now said to be fertilised and it rapidly grows into an embryo. This is a tiny plant, with root, shoot and either one or two leaves. Food materials are deposited in or around these leaves and the wall of the ovule becomes tough. The whole thing is now a seed.

While the seed or seeds have been growing, the carpel around them has been growing and changing too. It has become the fruit. Fruits come in many shapes and sizes. Some are hard and woody, some are soft and juicy, some are tough and leathery. They all contain one or more seeds. Most fruits are formed from the carpel or carpels alone, but some are formed from other parts of the flower. Apples and pears, for example, are formed mainly from the flower stalk. The carpels of the apple flower are concealed inside the flower stalk, below the petals. After fertilisation the flower stalk swells up to form the fruit. The original carpels become the core of the fruit, with the seeds inside them.

Scattering Fruits and Seeds

When the seeds are ripe the parent plant must release them so that they can grow. Most plants have some method of ensuring that the seeds are carried some way away. The fruits play a large part in this scattering or dispersal of the seeds.

Some fruits, including the pods of peas and beans, dry out as they ripen. When completely ripe, the pods burst open and throw out their seeds. They make quite a noise in doing so and the seeds may travel several metres.

Larger numbers of plants rely on the wind to scatter their seeds. Very small seeds are blown about by the wind quite easily. Larger fruits and seeds may have feathery outgrowths, such as the parachutes of dandelions and thistles. Many trees carry fruits which have wing-like flaps. When the fruits fall they are borne away on the wind and come to earth some way away from the parent tree.

Juicy fruits are attractive to birds and other animals, which eat the fleshy parts and spit out the seeds. The smaller seeds may pass right through the birds' food canal and come out unharmed with the droppings. In both examples, the seeds are scattered far away from the parent plant. Many fruits have small hooks on them and the hooks catch into the fur of animals. By the time the animal shakes off the fruit it might be several kilometres away.

Germination

When the seed has fallen on suitable ground, and when the temperature is high enough, it will begin to grow, or germinate. It will absorb water and swell up, the seed coat will burst and out will come the little root. No matter which way up the seed was lying in the ground, the root will always grow downwards and anchor the young plant in the ground. The young shoot soon follows the root out of the seed and it grows upwards to the light. The seed leaves may grow up as well, although they often stay inside the seed. While the seed is germinating it relies on the food stored up in it by the parent plant. Then, when its own shoot and leaves have grown up into the light, it starts to make food for itself and becomes an independent plant. In time it will produce flowers and seeds of its own and start the whole cycle again.

Annuals, Biennials and Perennials

Many plants live for only one season. They germinate as seeds in the spring, flower in the summer and then die. The seeds then lie in the ground until the next spring. These plants are called annual plants. Some of them actually have several generations in one year, taking only a few weeks to grow and produce their own seeds. Most of the annual plants are rather small. Biennial plants take two seasons to complete their life histories. They grow from seed in the first season and store up supplies of food. These food stores keep them going through the winter and enable them to produce flowers and seeds in the following spring or summer. After flowering the plants die. Perennial plants go on living for several years—hundreds of years for some species of trees. Most of them flower many times during their lives. All trees are perennials.

Composite flowers, such as thistles and dandelions, produce fruits with little 'parachutes' of hairs. These carry the fruits away very efficiently.

The fruit of maize and other grasses consists of nothing more than a thin case around the starch-filled seed and it is called a grain. When it reaches a warm and moist place it will start to germinate. Like all seeds, it contains enough food to last the seedling until it can make food for itself. The root is the first to grow out from the seed. It begins to absorb water and then the shoot grows up above the ground. When the leaves open out the young plant can make its own food.

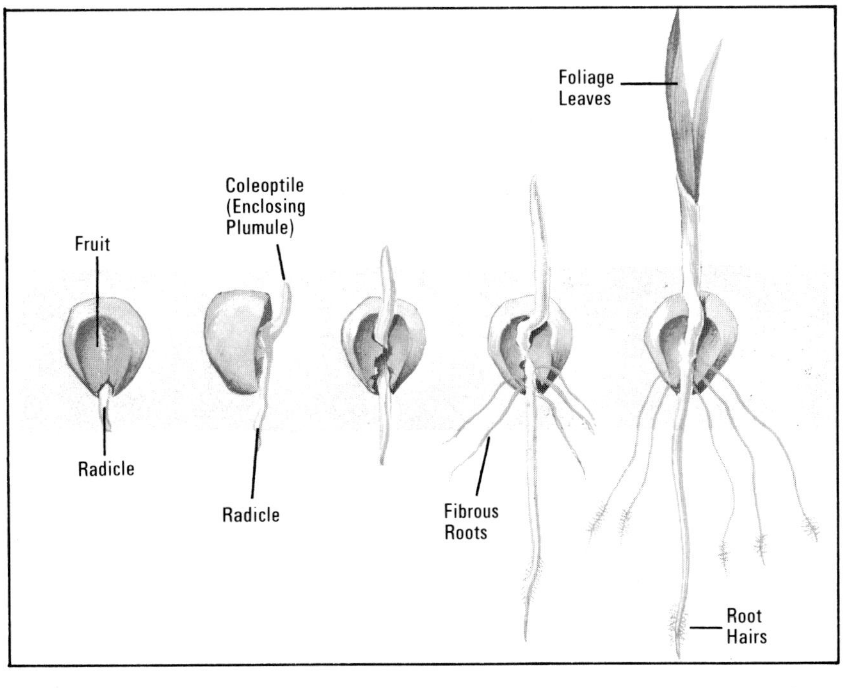

Flowering Trees

Japanese Maple

Lombardy Poplar

Silver Birch

Beech

Common Ash

Oak

White Poplar

Goat Willow

Trees are plants, just as much as daisies, daffodils and cabbages are plants. The main difference is that trees are much taller than other plants and have strong woody trunks to support them. The trunk takes a long time to grow, however, and young trees are much like any other young plants when they first leave their seeds.

All modern trees produce seeds, but there are two main kinds of trees—the conifers and the flowering trees. The conifers are described on page 36. All the other trees are flowering trees, although their flowers may not always be conspicuous.

Flowering trees belong to a wide range of families. Some trees, such as the elms, have families to themselves. Others share their families with small herbaceous plants. The violet family, for example, contains many large tropical trees as well as the familiar violets. The pea family contains the herbaceous peas and clovers, the shrubby gorse and broom and the attractive but poisonous laburnum tree. These plants all look very different, but you can see the connection if you look at the flowers.

Some flowering trees have very attractive flowers. Examples include apple, almond, lilac, horse chestnut, magnolia and pussy willow. Some of these are cultivated in parks and gardens. Many other trees, however, have small and rather dull flowers which are easily overlooked. Examples of these trees include oak, ash, elm, maple, holly and poplar. It might be a surprise that these trees have flowers.

Reproduction

Most of the inconspicuous flowers are pollinated by the wind, although the lime or linden tree is a notable exception. Its hanging bunches of yellowish flowers produce abundant scent and nectar and the trees literally buzz with bees in June and July. The wind-pollinated flowers usually open early in the year, often before the leaves have started to open. The hazel is an early flowering tree.

All flowering trees carry their seeds in fruits of some kind or other. Many trees bear juicy fruits which are brightly coloured. These are eaten by birds, which then scatter the seeds over a wide area. Other trees may bear woody fruits. These may have 'wings' which help them to drift away, or they may simply fall to the ground to be carried away by squirrels and other rodents. Poplars and willows have hairy seeds which drift away on the wind.

Trees and Shrubs

The gorse, the gooseberry and the rhododendron are clearly not herbaceous plants because they have woody stems. But we can hardly call them trees either. Trees are woody plants which normally have one main stem or trunk carrying branches some way above the ground. The gorse and the other plants mentioned above have several stems of more or less the same size, all arising at about ground level. Plants which normally grow in this way are called shrubs.

A bush is any woody plant with several stems arising at about ground level. It may be a true shrub, or it may be a tree which has been cut down and allowed to send up side shoots from the base.

Below: The rhododendron is one of the most beautiful of the flowering shrubs.

London Plane

Tulip Tree

Small-leaved Lime

Spanish Chestnut

Walnut

Maple

Purple Beech

Sycamore

Grasses

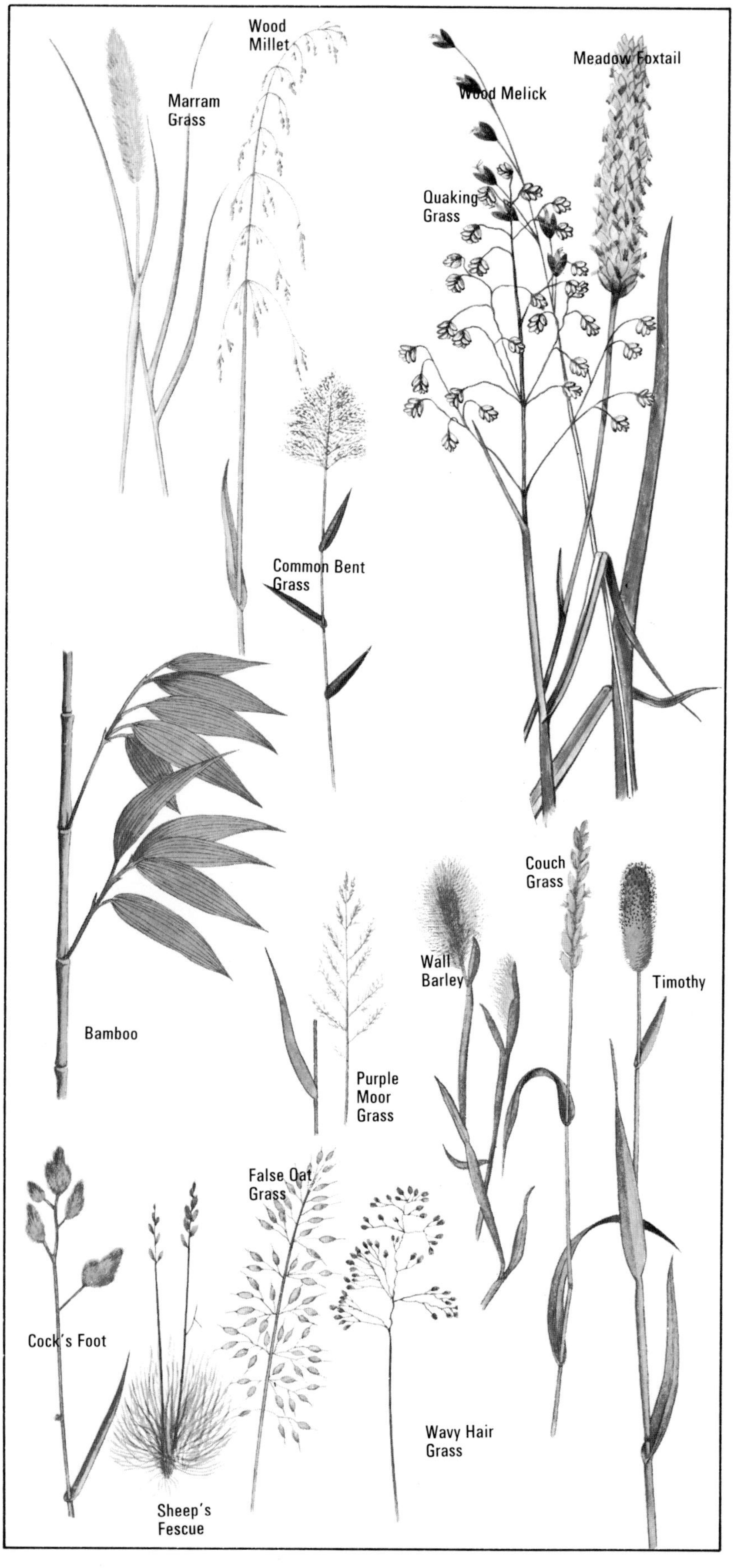

The grass family, known as the Gramineae, is the most important of all plant families as far as man is concerned. From this one family come all our cereal crops. Maize, wheat, oats, barley, rice and many other cereals have been developed from various wild grasses. These cereals provide flour and they are the staple foods in most parts of the world. About two-thirds of the world's sugar comes from the tall grass that we call sugar cane. As well as feeding us, the grasses also feed our important meat-producing animals such as cattle and sheep and rabbits.

If all the world's grasses were to disappear we would lose a very large proportion of our food and we would also lose our lawns, parks and playing fields. Much of the land surface would become a barren waste because the grasses play a very important part in binding the soil together.

The grasses belong to the group of flowering plants called monocotyledons (see page 25) and, like the other members of the group, they have narrow leaves with parallel veins. They are nearly all small herbaceous (non-woody) plants, although some of the bamboos are very woody and reach heights of 30 metres.

The stems of most grasses are normally very short and close to the ground. Only the leaves grow upwards at first, and if you look at a lawn or a meadow in the spring you will see that it is nearly all leaf. This is what enables the grasses to stand up to repeated mowing or grazing. The stems are not normally removed and they can easily send up a new crop of leaves. The stems also send out a number of side shoots at ground level. These are called tillers and they enable the grass to cover the ground and form a turf quite quickly. If the main stem is damaged or removed the plant will produce even more tillers and so mowing, trampling and grazing actually help the grass to form a thick turf. Many grasses also produce runners or rhizomes (see page 24) and spread even more quickly over the ground.

The Grass Flower

It might surprise many people to know that grasses have flowers. This is partly because lawns and playing fields are mown before they get a chance to flower and partly because the grass flowers are rather dull and inconspicuous. Stems that are to bear flowers turn upwards and end in a head of flowers. The head consists of a number of small oval structures called spikelets, each of which contains one or more flowers.

The flowers have no petals, no bright colours and no scent. They consist simply of the stamens and carpels. When they are ripe the stamens hang out of the spikelets and scatter their pollen to the wind. Some of the pollen reaches the feathery stigmas of the grasses but, as with all wind-pollinated flowers, much of it is wasted. Grass pollen is the main cause of hay fever. Many people are sensitive to the pollen blowing about in the air and it affects their noses, giving them the symptoms of a nasty cold.

After a grass flower has been pollinated its ovary develops into the grain. The grain contains a food reserve composed mainly of starch and this is what makes the grasses so important as human food. Several wild species have been cultivated to produce bigger and better yields of starch (flour). The plant breeders are also interested in the type of flour produced as well as the quantity, because flour that is good for making bread is not good for making biscuits or macaroni.

Cultivated grasses are far and away the world's most important crops. In temperate countries wheat is the chief cereal crop. The great wheat-fields of the North American and Russian plains often stretch unbroken to the horizon. Harvesting the crop is a highly mechanized affair carried out by teams of combine harvesters (bottom). Rice is the chief cereal crop in much of Asia. Often it is planted, gathered and threshed by hand and the farmers can produce hardly enough grain for their own families on their own small fields (left). Both wheat and rice have been grown for many centuries and through selective breeding the grain yields are now far greater than the original wild strains.

Insect-Eating Plants

Pitcher plants trap insects in various kinds of jars which are formed from the leaves. The jars contain fluids which attract the insects and then digest them when they fall in. The digested materials are absorbed by the plant. Some pitcher plants have lids on their pitchers. The lids prevent rain from getting in and diluting the juices.

Although most plants are able to make their own food from simple substances in the air and the soil, a number of plants supplement their food supplies by catching and digesting insects. The insects provide additional nitrates and other minerals and so plants with insect-catching habits are often able to survive on poor soils. Most of the insect-eating plants live in peat bogs and similar wet places. There are relatively few soil bacteria in such places and plants do not decay very rapidly. Their partially decomposed remains accumulate to form peat and very little mineral matter becomes available for growing plants.

Insects are caught by specially modified leaves and the plants then digest them with juices not very different from those in our own intestines. All of the insect-eating plants can survive without catching insects. They possess chlorophyll and they can make their own food. If they are grown in good soil they will grow and flower quite normally even if they cannot catch insects. When grown on their normal soil, however, they need the extra minerals and they do not flower well if they are unable to catch insects.

The sundew attracts insects with the shiny droplets on its leaf tentacles. The insects are trapped by the sticky fluid and the leaf closes up while the insect is digested.

Parasitic Plants

The mistletoe is best known as a Christmas decoration, although in some parts of Europe it is also believed to protect homes from fire and lightning. But apart from its various legendary properties, the mistletoe is interesting because of its strange way of life. It has no roots of its own and it grows on the branches of other trees, especially apples and poplars. It sends suckers into the branches and these suckers take in water and mineral salts. The mistletoe is therefore a parasite. Yet it is actually only a partial parasite, because it does contain its own chlorophyll and it can make its own food when once it has 'stolen' water and minerals from its host plant.

Another very common partial parasite is the eyebright, a little plant with nettle-like leaves and pink and white flowers. The eyebright has roots of its own, but they are not very efficient and they obtain most of their water and minerals by sending suckers into neighbouring grass roots. The eyebright can grow without the help of the grasses, but it then makes only a small plant and it does not flower well.

A number of flowering plants have taken the parasitic habit a stage further and have become complete parasites. They have no chlorophyll and they can make no food for themselves: they take everything they need from other plants. The only thing these parasites have to do for themselves is produce flowers and seeds.

The dodder is a well-known parasite whose tangled red stems often smother low growing gorse and heather in the summer. The thread-like stems twine around the host stems and send suckers into them. The upper parts of affected host plants often become discoloured and they may die off. The dodder's leaves are reduced to tiny scales on the stem, and it does not even have a root. Bunches of pale pink flowers cluster around the stems and each flower produces a vast number of tiny seeds. When conditions are suitable the seed germinates and the thread-like stem emerges together with a temporary root. The stem lengthens rapidly and if it finds a suitable host it will coil around it and send in suckers. The root then dies, leaving the dodder completely dependent upon its host. If the seedling does not find a host within a few days it will die.

Looking like pink strands of cotton, the dodder twines around a heather plant and sends suckers into it to obtain food. The dodder's flower clusters are clearly seen.

The World's Biggest Flower

One of the most amazing plants of all is rafflesia, which grows in Malaysia and neighbouring countries. It has no roots, stems, or leaves but it produces the world's biggest flower. Rafflesia is a parasite of various vines. A seed becomes wedged in the bark and it sends a number of hair-like threads into the wood. These threads take food from the host and they later produce a little flower bud at the surface. The bud takes about nine months to develop and then opens to produce a huge flower, sometimes more than 60 centimetres across and weighing about 9 kilogrammes. It has a nasty smell which attracts pollinating flies.

Parasites and Saprophytes

A parasite is a plant or an animal that lives in or on another living creature, taking food from it without giving anything in return. The creature attacked is called the host and it may be a plant or an animal. The parasite sometimes kills its host, but they often live together for a long time.

A saprophyte is a plant that takes food from dead and decaying organisms. As a result they cannot make their own food by photosynthesis like other plants do. Most fungi are saprophytes, taking their food from decaying leaves and so on.

Right: The mistletoe is only a partial parasite because it does make some of its own food. But it sends suckers into its host plant for its water supply. Far right: The toothwort gets all its food by sending suckers into the roots of trees such as the elm and hazel. The dodder sends out suckers (haustoria) which penetrate the host plant's tissues and suck up food materials.

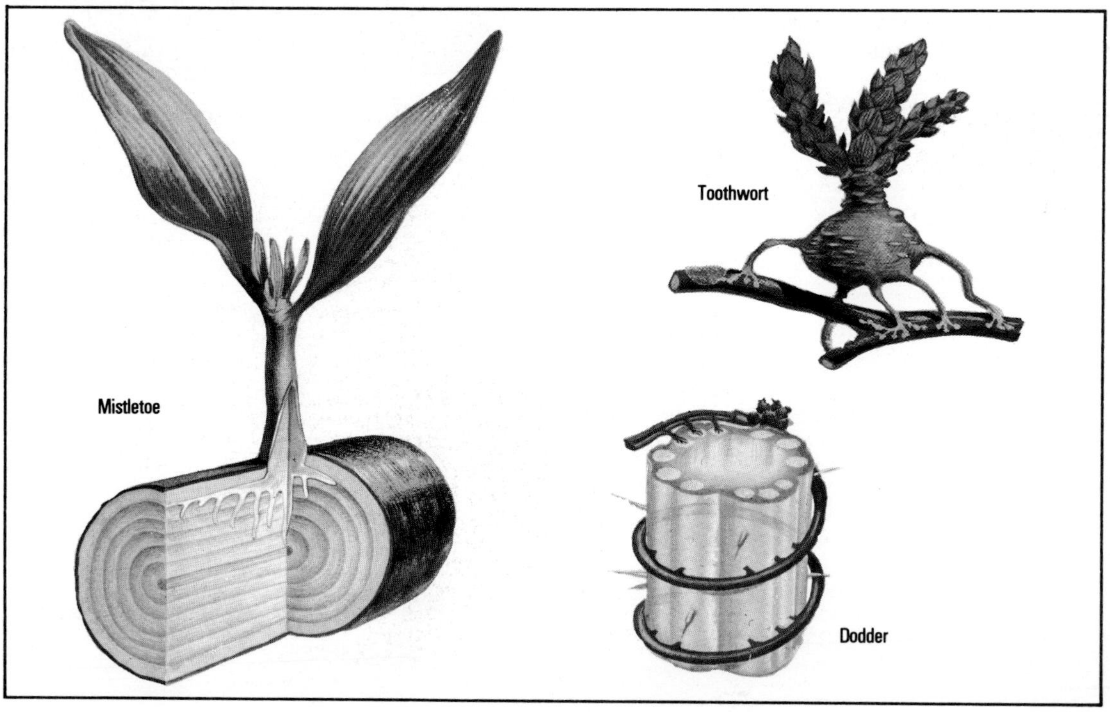

Climbing Plants

The taller a plant grows, the more chance it has of getting up above its neighbours and getting the full benefit of the sunlight. Tall plants, however, need sturdy stems to support them and this means that they grow rather slowly as a rule. But some plants have overcome this problem by climbing over their neighbours. These climbing plants do not need strong stems of their own and they can put all their efforts into upward growth. They grow very quickly.

The ivy is one of the best known climbing plants. The young stems creep over the ground and when they find a wall or a tree trunk they turn upwards. Small roots grow out from the stems and take a hold in little cracks and pores. They hold the slender ivy stems tightly against the support and allow them to continue their upward growth. The ivy does not take food from the tree on which it grows, but a lot of ivy can weaken a tree.

Many plants climb by simply twisting or twining themselves around their neighbours. Honeysuckle and bindweed are common examples, and so are the runner beans or stick beans. Some species twine clockwise and others twine anticlockwise.

Peas and several other plants possess tendrils. They are often specially modified leaves. They coil tightly around any twig they touch. The curved prickles of roses or blackberries are not basically for protection. They serve as climbing aids.

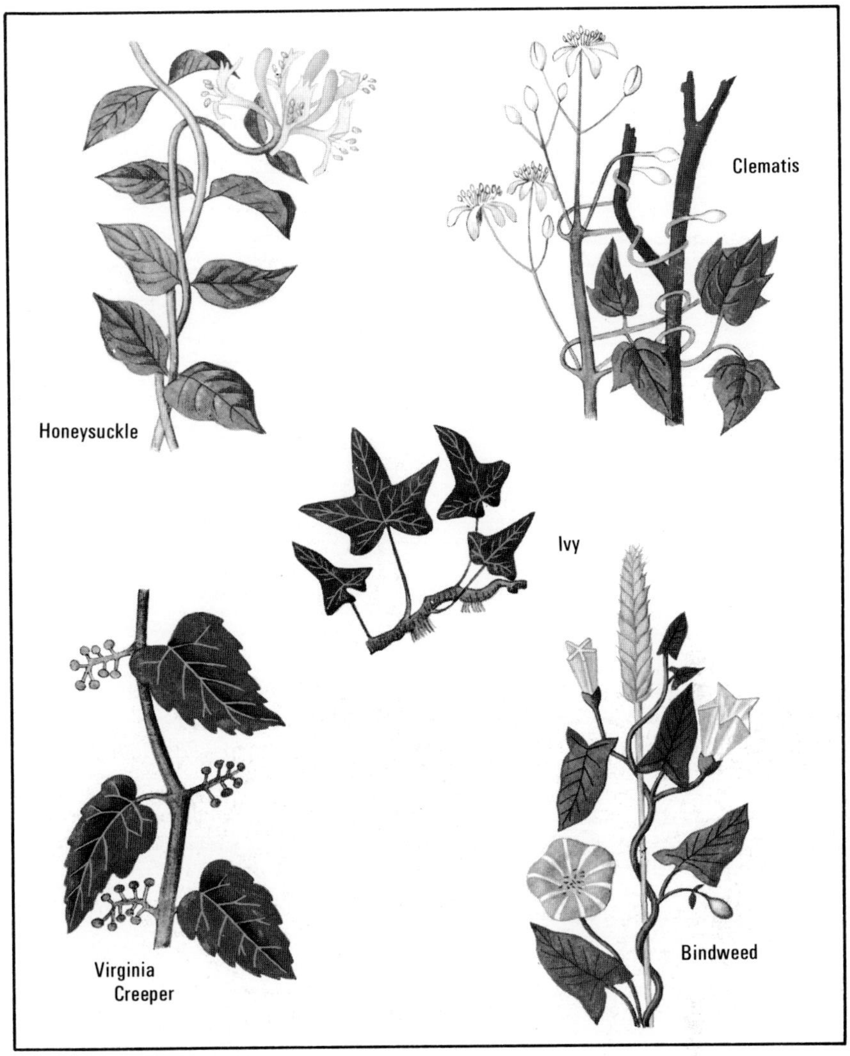

Above: A selection of climbing plants. Clematis climbs by twining its tendrils about supports. Honeysuckle is the best known of the 'clockwise' twiners and convolvulus or bindweed one of the most common 'anticlockwise' climbers. Ivy climbs by means of aerial roots developed on the lower part of the stems. The tendrils of the Virginia creeper may develop into adhesive discs which enable the plant to climb.

Left: Ivy is a common climber of both trees and walls. Its aerial roots secrete a sticky fluid which glues them to the support.

Protection in Plants

Some plants are carefully avoided by man and other animals because they are unpleasant to touch. Many of them have sharp thorns or prickles capable of inflicting painful wounds. Others possess poisonous hairs that produce irritating rashes.

Thorns and Spines

When picking blackberries or gooseberries we always try to avoid the prickles and we do not pay any particular attention to them. A careful look at them, however, will show that they are not all alike and that there are in fact several different types of prickles.

Hawthorn and the blackthorn or sloe prickles are actually dwarf branches and they often carry leaves. Prickles of this kind should really be called thorns.

In some other plants the leaves themselves form the prickles. They are called spines. Gooseberry and acacia spines are outgrowths from the leaf bases. Gorse bushes have both thorns and spines: the leaves are needle-like, and short, pointed stems grow in their axils. Another form of spine is formed by the edges of leaves drawn out into sharp points, as in holly and thistles, for example. The spines of cacti are greatly modified leaves. They always arise on little 'cushions' called aeroles and these will always distinguish a cactus from any similar prickly plant.

The curved prickles of roses and blackberries are neither stems nor leaves. They are outgrowths from the skin and they are often called emergences. Although they certainly do protect the plants, their main job is to help the plants climb (see page 49).

The Function of Prickles

Most prickly plants live in dry or semi-dry regions, or else in places where water drains readily from the soil. The plants must not lose too much water by evaporation, and one of the commonest ways of cutting down water loss is by reducing the size of the leaves. The leaves tend to become spiny and, the drier it is, the more woody they become. Prickles therefore seem to be mainly concerned with reduction of water loss, but they certainly protect the plants from animals as well. Some spines, however, are probably basically for protection. The holly, for example, has very spiny leaves on its lower branches—where animals can browse—but

The ocotillo is a desert plant of America. Its spines are modified leaf midribs.

The spines of the thistle are formed from the stiffened margins of the leaves.

The prickles of the blackberry are climbing aids. The spines of cacti are rather a puzzle. They probably have several functions, including the trapping of a layer of still air around the plants. This helps to cut down evaporation. The spines of the gooseberry and acacia are outgrowths from the leaf bases. Those of the barberry are modified leaves, while the gorse has both thorns and leaf spines.

The thorns of the hawthorn are dwarf branches, shown by the fact that they often carry leaves.

the leaves on its upper branches are frequently quite smooth.

Stinging Hairs

Most plants have some sort of hair on their stems and leaves. Long coats of hair may keep a plant warm in a cold climate, or they may keep the sun off it in a hot climate. The hairs also help to cut down the loss of water. The goosegrass or cleavers has tiny hooked hairs which help it to climb.

Many hairs secrete oils and other fluids, and the stinging hairs come under this heading. The stinging hairs of the stinging nettle grow on the stem and leaves. They are strengthened with a glassy material called silica and they end in little spherical swellings. These break off when something brushes against the nettle and the sharp needle-like point sticks into the animal. Poison then flows into the wound from the cavity of the hair and it sets up an irritating rash. The poison has no real antidote.

Several other plants have stinging hairs. The fever nettle of West Africa has a very strong poison that can make a man quite ill. Even elephants are said to avoid this plant.

Left: Blackberry fruit, with the curved prickles also visible on the stem.

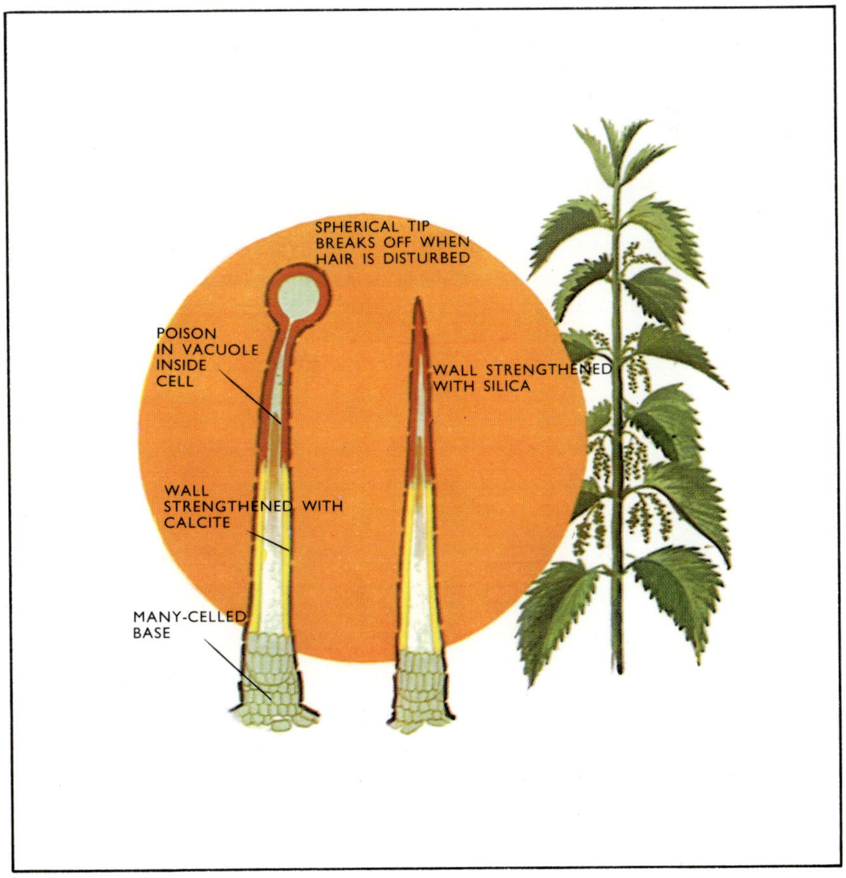

The stinging hairs of the nettle end in a little round swelling. This breaks off when the plant is touched, leaving a sharp needle which injects poison into the skin.

Dictionary of Flower Families

Arrowhead family (Alismataceae) A family of monocotyledons living in water or wet places. The plants have erect and/or floating leaves and some have submerged leaves as well. The flowers, usually carried on whorls of slender branches, have three rounded petals and three sepals. The petals are usually pink or white, often with a darker patch at the base. There are about 80 species, mainly in the Northern Hemisphere. They include the arrowhead, named for its leaves, and the water plantains.

Arum family (Araceae) A family of monocotyledons containing about 2,000 species. The flowers are normally small and they are crowded together on a fleshy stalk called a spadix. This is very often surrounded by a leaf-like sheath called the spathe. There are often separate male and female flowers. The family has its headquarters in the forests of South America, but it is widely distributed. One of the commonest European species is the cuckoo pint, also known as lords and ladies. It grows in shady woods and hedgerows and is most obvious in the autumn when its bright red fruits are ripe. The flowers have an unpleasant smell which attracts flies. The insects crawl down to the base of the spathe and become trapped there by a ring of hairs. The female flowers open first and they are pollinated by the flies. The male flowers then open and dust the flies with fresh pollen. The hairs wither and the flies escape, only to be lured into another arum where they pollinate another batch of female flowers.

Balsa family (Bombacaceae) A family of trees found in many parts of the Southern Hemisphere. The balsa itself is an evergreen tree growing in the forests of Ecuador and Peru. It is best known for its very light wood. Another famous member of the family is the baobab, found in Africa and Australia. The trunk is quite short but it may be 10 metres across. It bears a crown of branches at the top and looks as if it has been uprooted and thrust into the ground again upside down. The large white flowers are usually hidden among the leaves, but the trees are deciduous and when the leaves fall they reveal the large gourd-like fruits. These contain a pleasant-tasting pulp. The durian tree of South East Asia is another member of the family.

Balsam family (Balsaminaceae) A family of dicotyledonous herbs with succulent stems. There are over 500 different kinds, most of them living in tropical Africa and Asia. Most of the species belong to the genus *impatiens*, so named because of the 'impatient' way in. which the fruits burst when touched and throw their seeds out. The flowers are frequently pink or orange and they are very irregular. There are usually five petals and three sepals, although some of the sepals look like petals. Many of the species live along river banks and in other damp places.

Banana family (Musaceae) A family of monocotyledons found mainly in the tropics. There are about 200 species, including the striking bird-of-paradise flowers of South Africa. Cultivated banana plants may reach a height of 12 metres and they may be 30 cm across, but the 'trunk' is composed entirely of leaf stalks wrapped around a very slender stem. The leaf blades may be 4 metres long and they form a large crown at the top of the plant. The real stem emerges from the crown and carries the flowers. The flowers start out in a bunch of purple bracts about the size of a rugby ball. The bracts turn back one by one to reveal clusters of tubular flowers, each with six yellow petals. Each cluster of flowers produces a hand of bananas, and there are dozens of hands on a stem. There is only one flowering stem and the whole shoot is finished when it has produced its fruit. New shoots are always being produced, however, from an underground rhizome.

Bedstraw family (Rubiaceae) A large family of dicotyledons including both herbs and woody plants. The flowers are small, often white or yellow, and have four or five petals. Most of the 5,000 species live in the Tropics, but some of the bedstraws are common in cooler regions. One of the best known of these is the goosegrass. The coffee plant also belongs to this family.

Beech family (Fagaceae) A family of trees and shrubs including oaks and sweet chestnuts as well as beeches. There are over 800 species, more than 500 being oaks. They are found mainly in the Northern Hemisphere, although the southern beeches are found in South America, Australia and New Zealand. There are separate male and female flowers. The male flowers are usually in catkins or in tassel-like clusters. Their pollen is scattered by the wind. The female flowers give rise to nuts.

Beet family (Chenopodiaceae) A family of dicotyledons consisting mainly of herbs and shrubs. The leaves often appear downy. Several species have succulent leaves. Most of the species live in open situations, often in quite dry places. Many live on sand dunes by the sea, and several are common weeds in cultivated land. Fat hen and goosefoot are typical examples. Beetroot and sugar beet are both cultivated varieties of the wild beet that grows on coastal dunes and cliffs.

Begonia family (Begoniaceae) A family of succulent dicotyledons found mainly in the forests of South America and the Pacific islands. Their large and colourful flowers have made them popular for growing indoors. The male and female organs are carried in separate flowers. The female flowers have between two and five petal-like parts, formed from both sepals and petals. The male flowers have two petals and two larger sepals. The many stamens also add to the appearance of the flower.

Bellflower family (Campanulaceae) A large family of dicotyledons whose members nearly all have bell-shaped flowers. The five petals are all joined together to form the bell, but their outer ends are separated to form five lobes. Nearly all the 2,000 species are herbaceous plants and they are found in most parts of the world. Examples include the harebell, the clustered bellflower and Canterbury bells.

Right: The baobab tree.

Below: Arum lily cutaway to show the clusters of male and female flowers.

Arrowhead, showing the characteristic shape of the leaf.

Sweet chestnuts, showing the spiny cups surrounding the fruits.

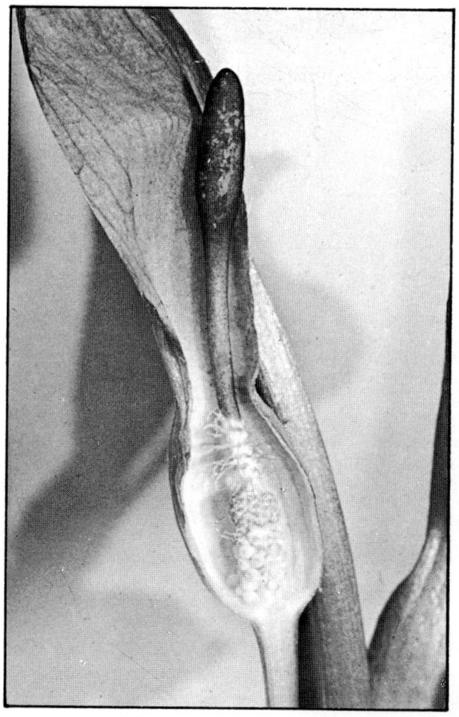

Bindweed family (Convolvulaceae) A family of dicotyledons including herbs, shrubs and some trees. Many are climbers and the plants often contain a white, milky juice. The flowers are regular, with the five petals joined to form a funnel or a bell. There are five separate sepals. There are about 1,500 different species in the family. Most of them live in the Tropics, but there are some common ones in cooler regions. As well as the familiar bindweeds, the family contains the parasitic dodders, the morning glory and the sweet potato. The latter comes from South America, where its sweet, starch-filled roots are an important food.

Birch family (Betulaceae) A family of deciduous trees and shrubs containing the birches and alders. They are found mainly in the temperate regions of the Northern Hemisphere. Some of the species, such as the dwarf birch, reach far into the tundra. The alder grows in damp places. The male flowers are carried in hanging catkins and their pollen is scattered in the wind. The female flowers are carried in little upright catkins. These are quite slender in the birch, but they are cone-like in the alder. The fruits have little wings and they are carried away by the wind. The female cones of the alder remain on the trees long after the fruits have gone.

Black bryony family (Dioscoreaceae) A family of monocotyledons, although its members have broad leaves more like those of the dicotyledons. Most of the 750 species are climbing plants. Some are woody and some are herbaceous. Most of them have tuberous underground stems. The flowers are small and pale, with male and female flowers usually on separate plants. Each flower has six petal-like parts, united at the base to form a short tube. Most of the species live in the tropics, but the black bryony is very common in Europe. It climbs over hedges and its bright berries make a pleasant sight in the autumn. Several species are cultivated in tropical lands. Their starch-filled root tubers and rhizomes are called yams. They are an important food and look like sweet potatoes, but they are in fact sweeter.

Box family (Buxaceae) A small family of dicotyledons, with about 100 species scattered throughout the world. Most of the species belong to the genus called *buxus* and they are nearly all evergreen shrubs. The flowers are small and green, consisting of four sepals without any petals. Male and female flowers are separate, but both kinds grow on one plant. The box is quite common on the limestone and chalk of southern England.

Broomrape family (Orobanchaceae) A family of dicotyledons whose members are all root parasites. They have no chlorophyll and they obtain their food by sending suckers into the roots of other plants. The aerial shoots are scaly and they are cream, pink, or brown in colour. They carry dense clusters of flowers in which the petals are joined to form a twisted tube. Like all parasites, these plants produce huge numbers of seeds. Many of the species are pollinated by bumble bees. There are about 130 species, mainly in the Old World. Common species include the toothwort, which attaches itself to the roots of hazel and other trees, and the various kinds of broomrapes. The broomrapes parasitise clovers, gorse, thistles and many other herbaceous and shrubby plants.

Buckbean family (Menyanthaceae) A small family of dicotyledons whose members are all marsh-loving plants. There are less than 40 species. The buckbean is widespread in the Northern Hemisphere. It grows in bogs and marshes and also around the edges of lakes and ponds. Its large shiny leaves each have three leaflets and they look like huge clover leaves sticking up out of the water. The flowers are pink or white, densely packed on tall stalks. The edges of the petals are divided up to form dense fringes. The family also contains the fringed waterlily, which has small yellow flowers.

Buckthorn family (Rhamnaceae) A family of dicotyledonous trees and shrubs with about 900 members. The flowers are generally small and inconspicuous, often being greenish in colour. The sepals form a little tube, with four or five lobes at the top. The petals, if there are any, are attached to the rim of this tube. The fruits are often fleshy and brightly coloured. The buckthorn and the alder buckthorn are common in Europe. The buckthorn is a thorny shrub, found mainly on limestone soils. Its fruits are black. The alder buckthorn is not thorny.

Buddleia family (Buddlejaceae) A family of dicotyledons found mainly in the tropical regions. The 150 or so species are all trees and shrubs whose flowers are generally rather small but grouped into dense clusters. Each flower has four sepals united into a tube. The four petals also form a tube, although their outer parts fold back to form a star-shaped flower. The best known member of the family is the cultivated buddleia, which is a native of China. It is sometimes called the butterfly bush, because it is very attractive to butterflies and other insects.

Two members of the buttercup family: the lesser celandine (top) and traveller's joy, or wild clematis (bottom).

Top: Birch catkins, female erect, male hanging.
Bottom: Lady's smock, or cuckoo flower (cabbage family).

Right: Exquisite blooms from two species of cacti.
Below: Aubretia, a ground cover plant of the cabbage family.

Buttercup family (Ranunculaceae) A large family of dicotyledons containing herbs, shrubs and woody climbers. There are about 1,900 species, most of them found in the cooler regions of the Northern Hemisphere. Most of the plants in this family have a bitter taste, and many of them are very poisonous. The flowers are usually regularly arranged, although there are some irregular flowers in the family. All the parts of the flower are separate. Distinct sepals and petals are normally present, although some flowers have sepals that look just like petals. There are many stamens in the flowers. Among the many members of the family, there are buttercups, lesser celandines, anemones, marsh marigolds, delphiniums, columbines (granny's bonnets) and clematis.

Butterwort family (Lentibulariaceae) A small family of dicotyledons whose members increase their food supplies by catching insects. There are about 250 species. Many live in marshes or in water, and some live as epiphytes on trees. The petals are united to form a hood-shaped tube. The flowers are often carried singly on slender stalks. The butterworts grow in bogs and wet grassland. They have rosettes of leaves which are covered with sticky secretions. Insects get stuck on the leaves and are digested. The bladderwort also belongs to this family. It grows in water and catches small water creatures in little balloon-shaped traps, or bladders, up to 2 cm long.

Cabbage family (Cruciferae) A large family of dicotyledons with about 3,000 species. Most of them live in the Northern Hemisphere. The majority are herbs, but there are some woody plants in the family. There are four petals, arranged in the form of a cross. This gives the family its name because crucifer means 'to carry a cross'. There are four sepals as well, and usually six stamens. Two of the stamens have short stalks and the other four have long stalks. There are two carpels joined together, but all the other parts of the flower are separate. Most of the flowers are white, yellow, or pink. Among the members of the family are wild cabbage (and its many cultivated varieties), turnip, candytuft, honesty, lady's smock, water cress, wallflower and aubretia. All of them contain strongly flavoured juices, particularly noticeable in the mustard plant.

Cactus family (Cactaceae) A family of dicotyledons with about 1,700 members. With one possible exception, they all come from the New World. The stems are all thick and fleshy and modified for water storage. Leaves are generally absent, but the stems bear a number of large or small spines. These spines arise on little 'cushions' called areoles. Cactus flowers are very showy, with numerous petals and sepals all grading into one another. Most of the cacti live in dry places, but the Christmas cactus grows in the rain forests of South America. Some species are now rare because too many have been collected.

Carrot family (Umbelliferae) A large family of dicotyledons in which the flowers are carried in large heads called umbels. The individual flower stalks all leave the main stem at one point and, although the individual flowers are small, they form large circular patches. There are nearly 3,000 species, most of them in the cooler parts of the Northern Hemisphere. Nearly all of them are herbaceous plants, with ridged, hollow stems. The leaves are usually greatly divided and fern like, and most of them are pleasantly scented. Among the members of the family are: carrot, hogweed, parsnip, celery and ground elder. Many herbs used in cooking also come from this family. They include parsley, dill, fennel, chervil and coriander. However, some members of the family are very poisonous.

Cocoa family (Sterculiaceae) A small family of trees growing in the warmer parts of the world. The cocoa tree itself, often called the chocolate tree, is a native of South and Central America, although most of today's cocoa is grown in West Africa. The tree reaches a height of about 10 m and carries large leathery leaves. The flowers are carried not on the branches, but on little 'cushions' on the main trunk. The flowers are pink, with pink sepals as well. The petals are united at the base. The flowers are followed by large fruits rather like rugby balls. Each fruit contains numerous seeds which are the cocoa beans. Cocoa is obtained from the roasted beans. Another member of the family is the kola tree of West Africa. The fruits, borne among the foliage in the normal way, yield seeds which are used to make refreshing drinks.

Cucumber family (Cucurbitaceae) A family of dicotyledons with about 700 species, mainly found in tropical regions. Most of the species are herbaceous, although some are shrubs. Many of the species are climbers. The leaves are broad and their veins spread out like the fingers of a hand. The leaves and stems are often covered with coarse hairs. Male and female flowers are normally separate, but they often grow on one plant. The flower is trumpet-shaped, although the petals are not completely joined. The fruit is a berry or a rather large and thick-skinned object called a pepo. The cucumber is a pepo. As well as the cucumber, the family contains melons, marrows, pumpkins, gourds and the white bryony. The latter is a common wild plant in the hedgerows of Britain and Europe. The flowers are small and greenish. Male and female flowers are carried on separate plants.

Currant family (Grossulariaceae) A family of shrubs with about 150 species, all in the genus ribes. The leaves are broad and often palmately lobed—like the fingers of a hand. The flowers are often small and inconspicuous, but they are

Top left: A prickly pear cactus covered with juicy fruits.

Left: A showy cactus flower, with numerous petals, greenish and sepal-like on the outside, but brilliantly white in the centre.

Top right: The deadnettle can be recognised by its rather square stems and the whorls of irregular flowers.

Bottom left: The dandelion is composite. Each floret produces its own fruit, which is borne away by a 'parachute' of hairs.

Left: The sunflower is another composite, made up of many florets. Only the outer florets have the broad yellow rays.

Bottom right: Section through a snowdrop, a member of the daffodil family. This family differs from the lily family because the seed box, or ovary, is located outside the petals.

followed by prominent berries. Several species are cultivated. They include red, white and black currants as well as the gooseberry.

Daffodil family (Amaryllidaceae) A family of monocotyledons with about 1,000 species, nearly all of which have bulbs. Most of them come from temperate regions. The flowers, which are often solitary, are enclosed in a leafy or papery sheath before they open. There are six petals, joined to form a bell in the snowflakes but separate in daffodils and snowdrops. The cup or trumpet of the daffodil is just an outgrowth from the petals. The members of this family are very similar to the lilies, but the ovary (seed box) lies outside the petals. In the lilies the ovary is inside the petals. Many members of the family are cultivated for their attractive flowers.

Daisy family (Compositae) With about 15,000 species of dicotyledons, this is the largest of all flowering plant families. There are trees, shrubs, herbs and climbers in the family. They inhabit all possible places from ponds and streams to the coldest mountains and the driest deserts. But the flowers are remarkably alike. What we normally call the flower is a collection of many tiny flowers packed tightly into a single head. Each tiny flower is called a floret and it is made up of five little petals joined up to form a tube. It has five stamens and a carpel at the base. The sepals are never leaf-like and they are usually represented by a ring of little hairs. After flowering they grow up to form the 'parachute' that carries away the fruit. The florets are of two main types, called ligulate and tubular. The petals of a ligulate floret grow out on one side to form a flat blade or ligule. Dandelion florets are all of this kind. Tubular florets do not have a ligule. Thistle florets are all tubular. Sunflowers, daisies and many other composite flowers have both types of floret. The ligulate florets are on the outside, helping to make the flower heads conspicuous, and the tubular ones are in the centre. As well as the flowers already mentioned, the family includes knapweed, ragwort, hawkweed, coltsfoot and chicory. Many species are cultivated for their flowers. They include asters, dahlias, zinnias, cornflowers and marigolds. Lettuce, endive and globe artichoke are among the species cultivated as vegetables.

SOME COMPOSITES

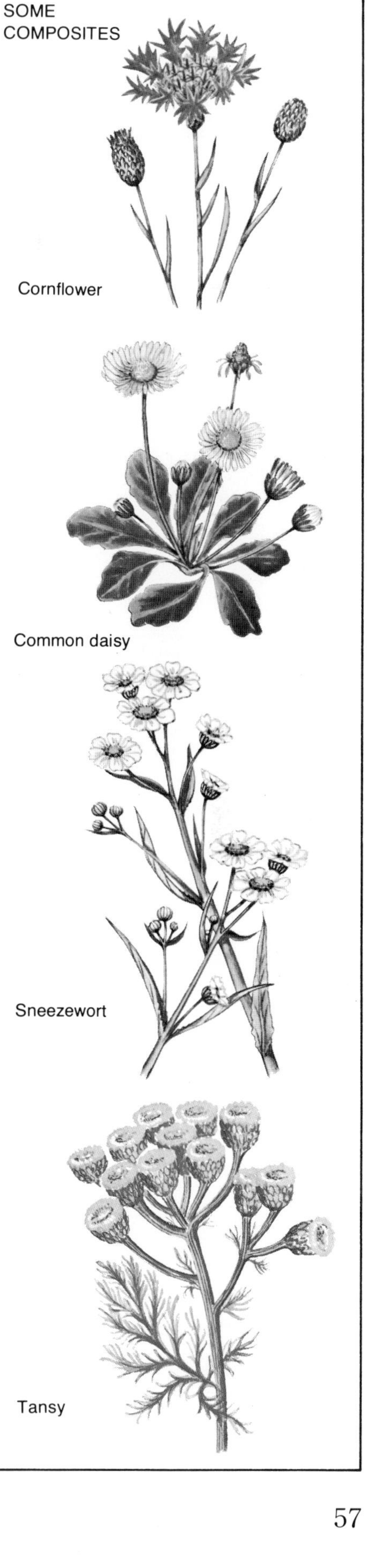

Deadnettle family (Labiatae) A family of dicotyledons with about 3,000 species, nearly all of them herbaceous. The stems are rather square and they carry the leaves in opposite pairs. The flowers usually form whorls around the stem. The five sepals from a toothed tube and the five petals are joined to form a helmet-shaped flower. The four stamens are concealed in the upper part of the helmet. There are two carpels, but each is divided into two so that there appear to be four little 'nutlets' at the base of the sepals when the petals fall. Many members of the family contain fragrant oils. As well as the deadnettles, the family contains lavender, rosemary, mint, thyme and others which are used as herbs in cooking or for making scents.

Dock family (Polygonaceae). A family of dicotyledons with about 800 species, mainly in the temperate parts of the world. There are herbs, shrubs and climbers, together with a few trees. The flowers are often small and dull, but they are grouped into dense clusters in many species. Many of the plants, including the docks and knotgrasses, are troublesome weeds. Among the few useful plants in the family are rhubarb and buckwheat. Himalayan knotweed has escaped from gardens in many places.

Dogwood family (Cornaceae) A family of about 100 dicotyledons, mainly trees and shrubs. The small flowers usually hang in clusters and they are normally followed by small stone fruits (drupes). The European dogwood is a deciduous shrub found especially on chalky soils. It can be recognised easily by its purplish stems and the deep red colour of its leaves in late summer. It bears small white flowers with four petals. The flowers are followed by black fruits. The wood of the dogwood is extremely hard and was once used for making skewers and wooden spikes known as 'dogs'.

Duckweed family (Lemnaceae) This family of monocotyledons contains the smallest of all flowering plants. They are all tiny floating plants, consisting of a little green disc only a few millimetres across. There may or may not be a root hanging down into the water. The minute flowers are borne in 'pockets' on the disc. There are separate male and female flowers and they consist simply of stamens or a carpel. Some species rarely flower but reproduce by budding—small pieces become detached and then grow into new plants. They often form continuous green carpets over ponds in the summer. There are about 30 species of duckweeds, found in fresh waters throughout the world.

Ebony family (Ebenaceae) The hard black wood known as ebony can be obtained from the heartwood of several tropical trees, but most of it comes from the true ebony trees of India and Africa. The 500 or so members of this family are all trees and shrubs. The flowers are of two types: solitary female ones and male flowers hanging in large clusters towards the tips of the branches. Some of the stamens may be modified into bright petal-like structures. The flowers produce abundant nectar and they are very attractive to bees. The persimmon is another member of the family. This is a small tree that produces a pleasant tomato-like fruit.

Eelgrass family (Zosteraceae) A small family of monocotyledons containing some of the few flowering plants that live in the sea. The plants have creeping rhizomes, slender stems and grass-like leaves. There are separate male and female flowers, borne on the sides of the stem and more or less enclosed by a sheath. They are pollinated by water and have no petals. The plants more often reproduce vegetatively by breakage of the rhizome. There are about a dozen species, found around the coasts and estuaries of most of the temperate seas. Most of them grow round about low tide level. They are important food for geese and turtles.

Elm family (Ulmaceae) A family of trees with about 150 species, mostly in the Northern Hemisphere. The elms themselves are the most

Left: Flax has been cultivated for its fibres and oil for centuries.

Below left: The dandelion flower head is a collection of tiny florets at the top of a leafless stem. The green objects surrounding the florets are bracts, not sepals.

Below: The blue funnel-shaped flowers of the stemless gentian are typical of the gentian family.

important members of the family. They are large deciduous trees and their clusters of tiny reddish flowers are produced very early in the year, long before the leaves appear. The leaves are often unevenly developed at the base. The fruits have little circular wings around them and they are scattered by the wind. Elms have very tough wood, suitable for furniture, but they are attacked by bark beetles and by the fungus causing Dutch elm disease. They are not planted as often as they were in the past. Another member of the family is the hackberry. This small tree grows in the warmer regions and produces small plum-like fruits.

Flax family (Linaceae) A family of dicotyledons containing herbs, shrubs and trees. There are nearly 300 species. The flowers are regularly arranged, with four or five petals, and they contain both stamens and carpels. The flax itself is probably a native of the Mediterranean region and it has been cultivated for a very long time. The fibres from its stems are used to make linen, while the seeds yield linseed oil. The plant is also grown in gardens for its attractive blue flowers.

Flowering rush family (Butomaceae) The only member of this family, closely related to the arrowhead family, is the flowering rush, a tall plant with broad strap-like leaves and pink flowers arising in a cluster from the top of the stem. There are six petals, three large and three small. The plant is found in ditches and along the edges of ponds and streams in Europe and Asia.

Forget-me-knot family (Boraginaceae) A large family of dicotyledons with about 2,000 species. Most of them live in Europe and Asia. Most of them are herbs, but there are some woody plants in the family. The five sepals are joined to form a tube and the five petals are also joined. They sometimes form a bell-shaped flower, sometimes a funnel-shaped flower and sometimes they open out to form a saucer-shaped flower. The throat of the flower may be partly closed by scales or hairs. Many of the flowers are blue. The leaves and stems are often very hairy. The family also includes lungwort, borage, comfrey and viper's bugloss.

Frogbit family (Hydrocharitaceae) A family of monocotyledons whose members are all aquatic herbs. They live in fresh water or in the sea. Some species float freely at the surface, others are rooted and completely submerged. The frogbit is a floating plant with palette-shaped leaves and conspicuous white flowers. There are separate male and female flowers, but each has three large petals and three smaller sepals. Several flowers normally arise from a cluster of bracts on the stem. In the autumn, buds called turions drop off and lie on the bottom until spring. The water soldier is a similar kind of plant, but it has large spiky leaves. Both float in ponds and ditches, especially in chalky districts. Other members of the family include vallisneria and Canadian pondweed. Both are commonly grown in aquarium tanks. They are rooted plants.

Gentian family (Gentianaceae) A family of dicotyledons famous for the brilliant blue colours of many of its members. They are all herbs, usually with hairless, shiny leaves. There are about 800 species, mainly found in the temperate regions. The petals are joined together and are generally funnel-shaped, although the outer regions may turn back to form a four or five armed star. The petals do not fall when they wither, but remain around the developing fruit. Many of the most famous gentians are alpine plants and they are widely grown in rock gardens. Other members of the family include the pink centaury and the yellow-wort. Gentians are used in medicines.

Geranium family (Geraniaceae) A family of dicotyledons with about 700 species, most of them herbaceous. The leaves are broad and lobed or deeply divided. The flowers, which are usually some shade of pink or purple, are more or less regular. They have five free petals, 10 stamens, and several joined carpels which are prolonged into a long 'beak', hence the names of cranesbill and storksbill. This is especially prominent when the fruits swell up after flowering. As well as the cultivated geraniums, the family includes the cranesbills, storksbills and the very common herb robert. Cultivated geraniums belong to the genus pelargonium and come from South Africa. They are distinguished from other members of the family by having two types of petals and one sepal.

Below: A more useful grass, the invaluable cereal crop, wheat.
Bottom left: The common forget-me-not.
Bottom right: Flower head of annual meadow grass.

Grass family (Gramineae) A very large family of monocotyledons of great importance to man and other animals. There are about 10,000 species, nearly all of them herbaceous. Grasses dominate large parts of the world where they form steppes, prairies and savannahs. They survive fires and being cropped by mammals. The leaves are strap-shaped and they sheath the stems at their lower ends. The flowers have no petals and they are borne in little spikelets. Each spikelet consists of two leaf-like scales which enclose one or more flowers. Each flower normally has three stamens and a carpel. The spikelets are arranged in various ways in tight or loose heads. The stamens hang from the spikelets when they are ripe and they scatter their pollen to the wind. It is picked up by the feathery stigmas of other flowers. Grasses grow in all possible places. As well as the wild grasses that grow in our open spaces, the family includes all the cereals, rice, sugar cane and bamboos. Bamboos are woody and one species grows to 40 metres. They are important food for gorillas and pandas.

Hazel family (Corylaceae) A small family of deciduous trees and shrubs found mainly in the northern temperate regions. The male flowers are carried in hanging catkins, while the female flowers are carried in little bud-like catkins. The fruits are nuts. The best-known member of the family is the hazel.

Heather family (Ericaceae) A family of dicotyledonous shrubs with about 1,600 species. Most of them live in the cooler parts of the world, including mountain slopes. The flowers are more or less regular, with the petals attached to the edge of a fleshy disc. As a rule the petals are partly or completely joined to each other, forming bell-shaped or lantern-shaped flowers. About half of the members of the family belong to the rhododendron genus. The heathers and heaths are well known plants on sandy soils. Another well known member of the family is the bilberry whose juicy black fruits make delicious pie fillings.

Holly family (Aquifoliaceae) A family of about 300 kinds of trees and shrubs. Some species are deciduous, while others are evergreen. The small white flowers appear in the summer months. There are separate male and female flowers, and they normally grow on different trees. This is why some trees never bear the familiar red fruits.

Honeysuckle family (Caprifoliaceae) A family of dicotyledons nearly all of which are shrubs. There are about 400 species, most of

Top left: Rye grass, showing the large hanging stamens which scatter the pollen. This is one of the most nutritious grasses and is widely sown.

Left: The honeysuckle gives off an almost overpowering scent.

Below: The hazel produces its pollen in catkins, which appear early in the year before the leaves come out.

Top: Garden irises.
Bottom: Yellow forsythia flowers.

them living in the northern temperate regions. The five petals are joined together to form a long or short tube. The tube may have two distinct lips. The stamens are usually five in number and they are attached to the petals. Many species produce attractive berries and stone fruits. As well as the honeysuckles, the family contains the elder, the guelder rose and the wayfaring tree.

Hop family (Cannabidaceae) A small family containing only three species of dicotyledonous herbs. The two species of hops are climbing herbs, with male and female flowers on separate plants. The male flowers are small and brownish and they are carried on branching stalks. The female flowers develop in cone-like clusters. These clusters are used in making beer. They give the beer its bitter taste. The other member of the family is the hemp, from which we get valuable rope-making fibres and the drug known as marijuana.

Horse chestnut family (Hippocastanaceae) A small family with about 25 species of trees and shrubs in the Northern Hemisphere. The flowers are grouped into large pyramidal bunches at the ends of the twigs. The large nut-like seeds (conkers) are carried in leathery capsules which are often prickly. The common horse chestnut comes from Turkey and Eastern Europe. The seeds were once thought to be useful in treating sick horses but, like most other parts of the plant, they are poisonous.

Hydrangea family (Hydrangeaceae) A family of trees and shrubs with about 200 species. Most of them live in the northern temperate regions. The flowers are regularly arranged and they usually contain both stamens and carpels. Some flowers, however, especially around the outside of a cluster, are sterile. They have large and showy petals which attract insects to the smaller fertile flowers in the centre. As well as the cultivated hydrangeas, which come from China and Japan, the family includes the syringa or mock orange.

Iris family (Iridaceae) A family of monocotyledons with about 1,000 species. They are all herbs with corms, bulbs, or rhizomes. The leaves are slender and grass-like. The flowers are usually regular and they contain both male and female parts. There are six petals, not always alike, and they are usually joined together near the base to form a tube. There are three stamens. The family includes the irises, crocuses and gladioli. It also includes the little sisyrinchium or blue-eyed grass, a common garden plant which also grows wild in Ireland and in North America.

Ivy family (Araliaceae) A family consisting mainly of trees, shrubs and woody climbers. Most of the 700 species live in the tropics. The flowers are small but they often grow in large bunches. They are followed by berries or by stone fruits (drupes). The common ivy grows throughout most of Europe and climbs on trees and rocks. Its greenish flowers open late in the year, usually in October, and they are very attractive to flies, wasps and other insects.

Lilac family (Oleaceae) A family of trees and shrubs with about 600 species, most of them growing in Asia. The flowers are carried in large bunches. Each flower is quite small and usually consists of four petals joined to form a tube. There are rarely more than two stamens. Many of the flowers are sweetly scented, and several of the shrubs are cultivated. As well as lilacs, the family includes the ash, privet, winter jasmine, forsythia and olive. The ash and the olive have no petals and the ash produces its flower clusters long before the leaves are out.

Lily family (Liliaceae) A family of monocotyledons with about 3,700 species. Most of them are herbs, but there are a few shrubby plants in the family. Woody plants are very rare among the monocotyledons. The flowers are regular and usually have six petals. The petals may be free or they may be joined together. There are six stamens. The three carpels are joined together and they are inside the petals. This last feature separates the lily family from the daffodil family. Many of the plants grow in desert climates and survive the dry season as bulbs. Many are cultivated for their pretty flowers. The family includes the lilies, bluebells, hyacinths, colchicums, tulips and onions. The woody plants in the family include the spiky aloes of South Africa. The stems are usually short and they bear rosettes of thick leaves. Slender spikes of bell-shaped flowers rise up from the rosettes. Several species are cultivated as house plants, and some provide useful medicinal drugs.

Lime family (Tiliaceae) A family of trees, shrubs and occasional herbs. There are about 300 species. The lime trees, best called lindens or basswoods to avoid confusing them with the citrus limes, are deciduous trees growing in the Northern Hemisphere. The small greenish or yellowish flowers hang in bunches, each bunch bearing a leaf-like 'wing'. Each flower has five sepals, five petals, and many stamens. The flowers are very fragrant and they attract plenty of insects. The fruits are later carried away by the 'wing'. The inner bark of the trees is very fibrous and it was once used as a source of raffia or bast. The jute plant is grown in India and Pakistan and provides fibres for most of the world's sacks.

Lobelia family (Lobeliaceae) A family of dicotyledons including both herbs and small trees. There are about 400 species, found mainly in the warmer parts of the world. Several species are cultivated for their flowers. The petals are joined to form an irregular tube. The anthers (pollen sacs) of the stamens are also joined together to form a tube around the stigma. Most of the lobelias are some shade of blue, although there are red and white ones as well. Many lobelias, including those grown in gardens, are quite poisonous plants. The family is often regarded as part of the bell-flower family.

Loosestrife family (Lythraceae) A family of dicotyledons with about 500 species. It contains herbs, shrubs and trees. The flowers are usually regular and they contain both male and female

The snake's head fritillary has nodding flowers.

Solomon's seal is a perennial plant of the woodlands.

Butcher's broom has no proper leaves.

Below: Colchicums, like all the other plants on this page, belong to the lily family.

Right: Large flowers of the magnolia, the most magnificent of the early flowering trees.

parts. The sepals, petals and stamens are joined together at the base to make a tube surrounding the ovary. The purple loosestrife, one of the best known members of the family, is a slender plant growing in marshy places. It has long spikes of purple flowers. The yellow loosestrife is quite different and belongs to the primrose family.

Magnolia family (Magnoliaceae) A small family containing about 200 species of trees and shrubs. The magnolias are among the most beautiful of the flowering shrubs. Many of them produce their large star-shaped or cup-shaped flowers before the leaves open in the spring. There are between six and twelve petals and many stamens. The carpels are clustered on a sausage-shaped receptacle in the centre of the flower. Most of the magnolias come from the Far East. Some are evergreen and some are deciduous. Another member of the family is the tulip tree, which comes from North America. There are three sepals which form a 'saucer' for the petals. The latter are six in number and they form a deep cup.

Mahogany family (Meliaceae) A family of trees famous for their hard red wood which is excellent for cabinet making. Several species live in Central America and the West Indies and related species live in Africa. They all have compound leaves, the leaflets of which are arranged in unequal pairs. The small greenish flowers have their stamens joined together. Much of the timber sold today as mahogany actually comes from other types of trees, although the wood is just as good. Many cigar boxes, especially those made in the West Indies, are made of wood from another tree in this family. It is often known as the Spanish cedar. Its strong scent appears to discourage insect pests.

Mallow family (Malvaceae) A family of dicotyledons containing trees, shrubs and herbs. There are nearly 1,000 species. The leaves are usually palmately veined (like the fingers of a hand) and may be sub-divided. The leaves and stems are often covered with star-shaped hairs. The flowers are usually regular and they normally contain both stamens and carpels. There are normally five sepals and five petals. The latter are free but they usually form a trumpet-like tube. Besides the mallows themselves, the family contains the hollyhock, the hibiscus and the cotton.

Mangrove family (Rhizophoraceae) A family of trees that grow in coastal swamps in the warmer parts of the world. They produce great tangles of roots that trap mud and debris and gradually build up dry land. The trees have small flowers, followed by leathery fruits. The seeds germinate in the fruits while they are still on the trees. They each produce a dagger-like root, and when they fall from the trees the roots dig into the mud and get a firm hold. The name mangrove is also given to trees of various other families which live in similar situations and which have developed the same kind of root system.

Maple family (Aceraceae) A family of trees and shrubs with about 200 species, mainly in the northern temperate region. All but ten belong to the genus acer. The leaves are often palmately veined and some are compound (made up of several leaflets). The flowers are small and greenish and they hang down in bunches. They are followed by the familiar double winged fruits which children call 'aeroplanes'. Many oriental species are grown for their attractive foliage. This is especially colourful in the autumn when the leaves turn many shades of red, orange and yellow. The sycamore is one of the largest of the maples, reaching a height of about 30 m. It comes from southern and Central Europe and it seeds so freely that it is becoming a weed in many woodlands.

Milkwort family (Polygalaceae) A family of herbs, shrubs and trees with about 700 species. About 500 of these belong to the genus polygala and are called milkworts. These are herbs or small shrubby plants with irregular flowers. There are five sepals but the inner ones look like petals. There are three petals, joined together and also joined to the eight stamens. The common milkworts of Europe are small plants usually found growing in grassland. The flowers are blue, pink or white.

Mistletoe family (Loranthaceae) A family of shrubby plants, most of which are partial parasites of trees. There are about 1,300 species. The flowers are regular, with sepals and bright petals in many species. In other species the sepals are missing and the petals are then small and green. This is the case with the mistletoe itself. The mistletoe has separate male and female flowers, and these normally develop on different plants. The female flowers are followed by sticky white berries that are eaten by birds, which distribute the seeds.

Nasturtium family (Tropaeolaceae) A family of 90 dicotyledons all belonging to one genus and all coming from America. They are herbaceous plants and many of them climb. The leaves are more or less circular and they have a spicy flavour. They make a pleasant addition to salads. The bright orange and yellow flowers are favourites in many gardens. Some of the wild species possess underground tubers which are a good source of starch.

Orange family (Rutaceae) A family of trees and shrubs with about 1,000 species in the warmer parts of the world. Several species are used for making furniture, but the most important members of the family are the citrus trees that provide us with oranges, lemons, limes, grapefruits and similar fruits. These trees all came originally from South East Asia, although they are now grown in nearly all warm regions of the world. They have shiny, evergreen leaves and most species have white flowers with five petals and many stamens. The fruits are berries in which the outer skin becomes thick and leathery.

Orchid family (Orchidaceae) A family of monocotyledons containing some of the world's most fascinating flowers. The flowers have six petal-like segments, but one of these is always very different from the others. There is often a long spur on one of the petals and the nectar is produced there. Most of the orchids are found in the tropics, but many attractive species grow in cooler regions. Some orchids grow as epiphytes, perched high up on the branches of tropical trees. They rely on humus accumulating on the trees or on nutrients blowing in the air. Others are saprophytes, lacking chlorophyll and getting food from decaying leaves in the soil. Some rely on fungi called mycorrhiza. Many European orchids are named after animals because the petals often take on the shapes of animals. The lower petal of the bee orchid, for example, looks very much like a bumble bee. This attracts male bees to the flower as they mistake it for a female bee and so pollination is effected. Some of the other resemblances are pure chance. The man orchid has its lower lip drawn out to look like the body of a man, complete with arms and legs. The lower lip of the monkey orchid is drawn out in similar fashion, but the 'limbs' are relatively longer and more bent. The pollen is produced in masses called pollinia. They are sticky and adhere to visiting insects. Twayblade has a mechanism which stamps the pollinia onto the insects' backs. There are about 15,000 species of orchids.

Palm family (Palmae) A large family of monocotyledons whose members are all woody plants, either slender trees or climbers. The leaves are large and greatly divided. They usually spring from near the top of the plant. The flowers arise in large bunches and hang down from the tops of the plants. There are about 2,500 species of palms and they provide a great many useful materials. Among the most important are the date palm, the coconut palm, the oil palm (which yields valuable oil used in making margarine and soap), and the raffia palm from which we get raffia. Only the grass family is more important to man than the palm family. Some palms can grow outside the tropics provided that there is no frost. Coconuts have been carried around the world by people, or by the nuts floating in ocean currents. The palms have over 1,000 recorded uses. The nuts take more than one year to ripen.

Pea family (Leguminosae) A large family of dicotyledons with very characteristic flowers and fruits. There are more than 12,000 species, ranging from tiny herbs to large trees. The leaves are usually compound (made up of several leaflets). The flowers have five petals, one of which stands up at the back of the flower and is called the standard. There is a wing petal at each side, and the other two are partly joined to form the keel. The five sepals normally form a tube, and the 10 stamens are also normally joined together. There is a single carpel which develops into the pod. The pod, which is characteristic of the family, contains several seeds and it normally bursts open as it dries. It throws the seeds out. Another characteristic of the family is the possession of root nodules. These are little swellings on the roots and they contain special bacteria which are able to make nitrates (plant foods) from the nitrogen in the air.

Members of the pea family, often called legumes, enrich the soil by means of these nodules. Members of the family include: peas, beans, clovers, lupins, gorse, vetches, laburnum and acacias. Many species are cultivated for their flowers or their fruits and seeds. Most of the 600 species of acacias live in Australia but they are also common in the drier parts of Africa.

Pepper family (Piperaceae) A family of dicotyledons with over 1,500 species in the warmer parts of the world. Many are woody climbers. One of the most important species is *Piper nigrum*, from which we get the pepper in our pepper pots. It is a woody climber that clings to supports by means of special roots. It has broad, shiny leaves and little clusters of flowers without petals. The flowers are followed by little orange berries which are harvested when almost ripe. They are then dried and ground up to make pepper. The plant came originally from South East Asia. Black and white pepper come from the same plant. White pepper has had the outer part removed before drying and is milder. Another species, the cubeb, is used in medicine and others are grown as indoor plants. The red and green peppers that we eat as vegetables are quite different and they belong to the potato family.

Periwinkle family (Apocynaceae) A family of dicotyledons containing about 1,500 species. Most of them are woody plants and many of them are climbers. The majority live in the warmer parts of the world. The petals are joined to form a tubular, funnel-shaped flower. The stems normally contain a milky juice and several species yield useful forms of rubber. Others provide medicinal drugs for treating heart diseases and other ailments. Originally they were used as poisons for putting on arrow heads. The periwinkles are creeping evergreen plants with blue or white flowers. They grow in shady places and are commonly planted in gardens. The oleander is another member of the family. Although it is grown as an ornamental tree, in city streets, it is very poisonous. Only a few seeds will kill if eaten.

Pineapple family (Bromeliaceae) A family of monocotyledons with about 1,500 species, all hailing from the New World. They produce clusters of spiky leaves around fairly short stems. The flowers are more or less regular and densely packed on thick spikes. Some of these flower heads are several metres long. Many members of the family, commonly called bromeliads, live in the rain forests. Some have saw-edged leaves which can make walking through the forest very unpleasant. Some live as epiphytes, perched on the branches of trees (see page 196). The leaf bases hold a great deal of water and many animals make their homes in these 'ponds'. Spanish moss of the southern United States is not a real moss but a plant that hangs from trees and telephone wires in festoons. It does not have roots but collects its water and nutrients from dust particles through fine hairs on its leaves and stems. The pineapple itself is a small plant which is cultivated in fields. It has purple flowers. The fruit is formed by the fusion of the flowers and the leaves and stalks of the spike. Pineapples came originally from southern America but they are now grown in tropical and subtropical regions throughout the world. Commercially pineapples are raised from cuttings, not seeds.

Pink family (Caryophyllaceae) A family of dicotyledons containing about 1,500 species. Most of them are herbs and they live mainly in the northern temperate regions. The leaves are generally narrow. The flowers are regular as a rule and normally contain both male and female parts. There are four or five sepals, sometimes joined at the base. There are four or five petals, but they are often deeply notched so that there appear to be twice as many. All the petals are free. There are commonly twice as many stamens as petals, surrounding between two and five stigmas. The family includes the pinks (and the cultivated carnations), stitchworts, chickweeds, campions, ragged robins, sweet williams and gypsophila. Colobanthus is one of the most southerly of flowering plants. It grows among mosses around the coasts of Antarctica.

Left: Tropical orchids growing high in the treetops, sending sprays of flowers arching down from the branches.

Far left: The fragrant orchid, found in chalk grassland.

Below: The bee orchid looks as if it has a bee sitting on it.

Right: The wild carnation, which grows in southern parts of Asia and Europe.

Below: Dyer's greenwood, broom and vetch belong to the pea family. They have a typical flower shape, with a standard petal forming a kind of hood.

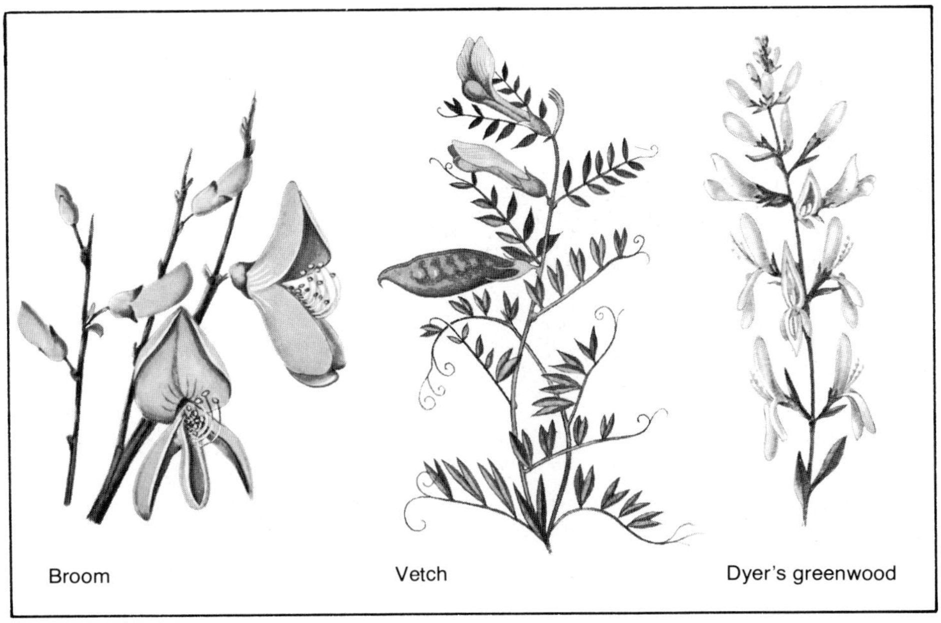

Pitcher plant family (Sarraceniaeceae) A family of dicotyledons in which the leaves are modified for catching insects. There are about a dozen species, found mainly in the eastern parts of North America. They live in peat bogs and in other poorly drained places where normal food materials are in short supply. The leaves of the pitcher plants are like slender beakers or ice cream cornets and they contain water. Insects and other small creatures that fall in gradually decay and the plant absorbs the resulting material. The rim of the pitcher is often brightly coloured and slippery. Insects are attracted to it and then they cannot get out. However, some mosquitoes lay their eggs in pitcher plants and the larvae live in the little pools. Some of the species have little 'lids' on the pitchers. These prevent too much rain from entering. Another family of pitcher plants lives in South East Asia. It is called the *Nepenthaceae*. There are about 60 species. The pitchers are formed by the tips of the leaves and they are provided with 'lids'. Some of these pitchers hold as much as half a litre of water.

Plantain family (Plantaginaceae) A family of dicotyledons, although their leaves are often narrow and have parallel veins like those of monocotyledons. They are herbs and their leaves normally form a rosette on the ground. The small flowers are carried in dense spikes at the top of leafless stalks. Each flower has four pale, scale-like petals, all joined to form a tube. There are both stamens and carpels in each flower, the stamens having very long stalks. The flowers at the bottom of the spike open first and the stigmas ripen before the stamens in each flower. A flowering spike will therefore have several regions: unopened flowers at the top, a ring of spiky stigmas further down, a ring of hanging stamens below that, and a region of developing fruits at the bottom. The flowers are pollinated by the wind. There are about 200 species. They are very common in grassland.

Pondweed family (Potamogetonaceae) A family of monocotyledons. There are about 90 species, all in the genus potamogeton. They are all aquatic herbs living mainly in fresh water. They nearly all have rhizomes buried in the mud. The leaves are generally strap-shaped and all submerged, although some species have oval floating leaves. The flowers are clustered on loose or dense spikes. Each has four pale segments, with four stamens and usually four carpels. Many of the flowers never rise above the surface and their pollen is transferred by the water. Other flowers emerge from the water and are pollinated by the wind.

Poppy family (Papaveraceae) A family of dicotyledons with about 200 species, mainly in the Northern Hemisphere. Most of them are herbs and they all contain a thick milky juice. The flowers are regular, usually with four

Top: Polyanthus, a cultivated primrose.

Above: The oxlip belongs to the primrose family and thrives on chalky boulder clay.

Right: Two hover-flies visiting one of the hundreds of varieties of cultivated roses.

Below: Plantain heads, showing the long hanging stamens.

petals. There are normally two sepals, which fall off as the flower opens. The petals are often crumpled when they first open. There are numerous stamens and the joined carpels are top-shaped. They scatter their tiny seeds through small pores as they sway in the wind. As well as the poppies themselves, the family includes the greater celandine. Many species are cultivated as garden plants. Opium and the pain-killer, morphine, are obtained from poppies.

Potato family (Solanaceae) A family of dicotyledons with about 2,000 species. The flowers are usually regular, with five joined petals. These sometimes form a bell-shaped flower, but they are more often spread out to form a star. The stamens are often joined together and they form a little cone sticking out of the centre of the flower. The fruits are usually berries, although some species produce tough capsules. The family includes herbs, shrubs and small trees. Many of them are poisonous. The members include henbane, deadly nightshade, woody nightshade (bitter-sweet), potato and tomato.

Deadly nightshade

Primrose family (Primulaceae) A family of dicotyledons with about 1,000 species, mainly in the Northern Hemisphere. Most of them are herbs. The flowers are regular, usually with five sepals and five petals. Both the sepals and the petals are joined and they often form tubes. Many of the species are cultivated for their flowers. The family includes primroses, cowslips, oxlips, creeping jenny and yellow loosestrife. It also includes the cyclamen and the many cultivated forms of primula and polyanthus.

Reedmace family (Typhaceae) A small family of monocotyledons with only ten species. They are stout herbs which grow in shallow water. They are often incorrectly called bulrushes. The leaves are broad and sword-like. The flowers are carried in dense cylindrical spikes. The male flowers are in narrow spikes at the tops of the stems, while the female flowers are below them in thicker spikes which become a rich brown when mature. Each flower is surrounded by a few hairs, but there are no petals. The hairs carry the fruits away when they are ripe.

Rockrose family (Cistaceae) A family of dicotyledons with about 200 species, most of them found in the Mediterranean region. They include both herbs and shrubs. The flowers are regular, with three or five sepals and usually with three or five petals as well. The parts are all separate and the petals are easily detached. There are many stamens. The rockroses and their relatives favour warm, dry soils. Several species are common on chalk slopes and grassland, and one lives in the Arctic.

Top: One variety of cultivated primrose.

Above: Ragged robin, a common wildflower of the English grasslands.

Left: Blackthorn, a member of the rose family, has flowers with six petals. Most species have only five.

Below: The white rock rose, a rather rare plant native to limestone regions.

Above: A wood rush, quite a common plant in grasslands.

Below right: Speedwell, a member of the snapdragon family.

Below: A sedge in flower, showing the male flowers in the upper spike and the female flowers in the lower ones.

Rose family (Roseaceae) A very large family of dicotyledons including herbs, shrubs, trees and climbers. There are about 2,000 species, many of which provide us with valuable fruit. Many more are cultivated for their flowers. The leaves, which may be simple or compound, almost always bear little outgrowths called stipules at the base. The flowers are regular. There are usually five sepals, partly joined together, and five free petals. There are many stamens and a variable number of carpels which may or may not be joined. Although the flowers fit a general and easily recognised pattern, the rose family produces a very wide variety of fruits. We only have to think of the many kinds of edible fruits. Among the many members of the family are: roses, blackthorn, blackberry, hawthorn, mountain ash, meadowsweet, cinquefoil and geum. Important fruits provided by the family include apples, pears, plums, cherries, peaches, apricots, raspberries and strawberries, to name only the most important ones. Roses are also used for perfume. Their petals yield a fragrant oil.

Rush family (Juncaceae) A family of herbaceous monocotyledons with grass-like leaves or with leaves reduced to little brown scales. There are about 350 species, most of them growing in damp places. Many species form thick tufts. The stems are long and slender, often round in section and filled with soft pith. They are pointed at the top and many stems bear clusters of flowers emerging from one side near the top. The flowers are small but perfectly formed, with six brownish or greenish petal-like segments arranged in a star shape. They contain both stamens and carpels and they are pollinated by the wind. Members of the genus luzula are more like grasses than the other rushes. Their leaves are more blade-like and they are fringed with soft hairs. The plants are often known as wood rushes and they grow in drier places than the other rushes. The stems of rushes have long been used for making mats and the seats of chairs, but the rushes which used to be strewn on floors belong to another family. 'Rush lights' were made by peeling stems to reveal a pith which acted as a wick.

St John's wort family (Hypericaceae) A family of dicotyledons with about 1,000 species, mainly found in the temperate regions. The family includes herbs, shrubs and trees. More than 400 of the species belong to the genus hypericum and are known as St John's worts. They have yellow flowers, with five sepals and five petals. There are many stamens, often joined together in bunches. The flowers produce abundant pollen, but no nectar. One of the unusual features of the plants is the possession of translucent dots on the leaves of many species. These are easily seen if the leaves are held up to the light: it looks as if the leaves have been pierced all over with a pin. The pale regions are glands and they secrete a poison which is harmful to animals. Several species are weeds in farmland, but others are cultivated for their attractive heads of flowers. One of the best known is a low-growing shrub called the rose of sharon.

Saxifrage family (Saxifragaceae) A family of dicotyledonous herbs with about 500 species, mostly found in the cooler regions. The flowers are usually regular, with four or five petals. They are very similar to the flowers of the rose family, but they have fewer stamens as a rule and their fruits are rather different. Many species grow in cold regions, especially alpine areas, and they form cushions of small, tough leaves. Plants of this type are widely grown in rock gardens. The garden plant called London pride is a member of this family.

Sedge family (Cyperaceae) A family of monocotyledons which are often confused with grasses and rushes. Many of them actually have common names including the words grass or rush. Many sedges can be identified at once by

their triangular stems and the triangular arrangement of the leaves. There are about 4,000 species of sedges and most of them grow in damp places, although many can be found in dry grassland. The flowers have no sepals or petals but each is surrounded by a little scale. Male and female flowers are separate in many species and are carried on separate spikes of the flower head. The male spikes are usually nearer the top and they can be recognised by the long anthers hanging from them. The family includes the cotton grass, the bulrush and a wide variety of true sedges belonging to the genus carex. Many of them grow in large tufts and several are used for thatching. Over 4,000 years ago papyrus was used by the Egyptians to make a form of paper from the 5 metre stems. The rhizomes were used for fuel and the pith was eaten.

Snapdragon family (Scrophulariaceae) A large family of dicotyledons with more than 2,500 species. Most of them are herbs, although there are some trees and shrubs such as the imperial tree which is planted in parks in China and Japan. The petals are joined together and the flowers are usually highly irregular. In many species they are tubular, and they often have two distinct 'lips' which are held closed around the stamens and stigmas. Such flowers can be pollinated only by insects heavy enough to weigh down the lower lip and enter the flower. The four or five stamens are usually in the upper part of the flower and so is the stigma. They are in the right position to touch the head and back of an insect as it enters the flower. As well as the snapdragons, the family includes mulleins, speedwells and many garden plants such as nemesias and calceolarias. There are also many partial parasites in the family. These include the eyebrights and the yellow rattle, all plants which take water and dissolved salts from the roots of other plants (see page 47). Foxgloves, as well as being garden plants, are the source of digitalis for treating heart disease.

Spindle family (Celastraceae) A family of about 850 species of trees, shrubs and woody climbers. Many of the lianas that drape the trees in the tropical rain forests belong to this family. Better known is the European spindle tree. Its pale greenish flowers are inconspicuous, but its gay fruits make it very attractive in the autumn. The fruits are pink and they hang from the branches like little lobed cherries. When ripe, they split open and reveal the bright orange seeds. The leaves turn purple in the autumn, and a related American tree is often called the burning bush because of its autumn colours. The spindle is a deciduous shrub, but many of its relatives are evergreens. It gets its name because it was used for making spindles in textile machinery. It was also destroyed because it harboured the bean aphid, a serious pest.

Spurge family (Euphorbiaceae) A family of dicotyledons with more than 5,000 species. Most of these live in the tropical regions and they inhabit a wide variety of habitats. The plants are therefore very varied in their appearance. There are herbs, shrubs, trees, climbers and aquatic plants in the family. Many of the species contain a milky juice. Most of the plants have no petals, their place being taken by modified leaves which often assume bright colours. These leaves may be taken for a single flower, but they actually surround a cluster of several flowers. The actual flowers are very tiny. Male and female flowers are separate and the male flowers each consist of just a single stamen. The petty spurge is a very common bright green weed in gardens. It pours out its latex when the stem is broken. Other members of the family include the crown-of-thorns and the poinsettia, both popular house-plants. Two useful members of the family are the rubber tree and the castor oil plant. The family also includes the dogs' mercury, a very common plant in European woodlands. It differs from the spurges themselves in having no milky juice.

Right: Crown of thorns, a very prickly red-flowered spurge from Madagascar, where they use the swollen leaves to store water.

Below right: Dog's mercury, a very common member of the spurge family, which grows in shady woods and hedgerows.

Below: Orpine, a large member of the stonecrop family, is a favourite feeding place for autumn butterflies.

Stinging nettle family (Urticaceae) A family of dicotyledons, most of which are herbs or small shrubs. Many, but not all of the 500 species have stinging hairs (see page 51). The flowers are small and greenish, with stamens and carpels usually in separate flowers. The common stinging nettle carries its flowers in drooping spikes. The plant is a common weed throughout the temperate parts of the world. The leaves can be eaten when they are young. They are cooked like spinach.

Stonecrop family (Crassulaceae) A family of dicotyledons which usually have succulent (juicy) leaves. They are all herbs or small shrubs with small star-shaped flowers which are borne in large flat heads. There are over 1,200 species, mostly found in the warm and dry regions of the world. They are especially prominent in rocky places, including sea cliffs, and they are popular rockery plants. Many are particularly attractive to butterflies. The family includes the houseleeks as well as the stonecrops and the orpine. Bryophyllum and kalanchoe will regenerate from a cut piece of leaf which has buds growing on its margins.

Sundew family (Droseraceae) A family of dicotyledons whose members are all adapted for trapping insects. There are about 100 species, all more or less herbaceous. The sundews themselves have glandular hairs all over their leaves and these hairs secrete a sticky fluid which attracts insects and then traps them. The leaves then fold over and pour juices on to the insect which digest its body. The leaves absorb the resulting liquid. Sundews live in peat bogs and other places with poor soil. Their flowers are often small and insignificant. The family also includes the Venus fly trap, which traps insects with a gin-trap arrangement. The end portion of the leaf is hinged and it snaps shut when an insect alights on it.

Tea family (Theaceae) A family of small evergreen shrubs with its headquarters in South East Asia. The flowers are often fragrant, with five white petals and many stamens. As well as the tea plant, the family contains the beautiful camellias which are grown in gardens all over the world. Many varieties of these plants have been produced in a profusion of colours. They have huge flowers with thick waxy petals.

Above: A sundew leaf, showing the glistening, sticky hairs which attract and trap small insects.

Left: The spiky heads of the teasel were once widely used for combing out wool and other fibres.

Right: Thrift growing on a cliff top near the coast, seen in company with dwarf gorse.

Above right: Thrift growing in a rock crevice.

Far right: The large floating leaves of the waterlily provide shelter for many small water creatures and are favourite resting places for insects.

Teasel family (Dipsaceae) A family of dicotyledonous herbs with about 150 species, mainly in the Mediterranean region. The flowers are small and are grouped into dense heads surrounded by sepal-like bracts. The petals are joined to form a small and irregular tube. The teasel head bears numerous stiff bristles between the bluish flowers. These bristly heads were once used for combing out wool. The leaves and stems of the plant are also very spiky. The family also includes the various species of scabious.

Thrift family (Plumbaginaceae) A family of dicotyledonous herbs and shrubs with about 750 species. Many of them live on sea-shores, cliffs and mountains. The flowers are regular. There are five sepals, united into a tube at the base and five petals. The petals may be free or joined to form a tube. There are also five stamens and five stigmas. The flowers are often tightly bunched into heads. The sea lavender and the thrift or sea pink are well known members of the family.

Vine family (Vitidaceae) A family of about 700 species of climbing shrubs found throughout the tropical and temperate regions. The plants climb by means of tendrils. The leaves are palmately veined and often broken up into several leaflets. The flowers are small and greenish and they are followed in many species by the familiar berries which we know as grapes. Several species are grown for their attractive leaves, especially colourful in the autumn. One of the best known of these decorative plants is the Virginia creeper. Its tendrils are branched and each branch ends in a little sticky disc. These attach the plant to trees and walls and allow it to climb up.

Violet family (Violaceae) A family of dicotyledons containing about 800 species of trees, shrubs and herbs. About half of these belong to the genus viola, which includes the familiar violets and the pansies. The flowers of this genus are irregular, with one of the five petals forming a spur. The flowers are followed by rounded capsules which split into three parts when ripe and force the seeds out as they shrink. The family originates in South America.

Walnut family (Juglandaceae) A family of about 50 trees, mainly in the Northern Hemisphere. The leaves are large and compound. Male and female flowers are separate, the male ones being in hanging catkins and the female ones solitary or in small spikes. The petals are very small or missing altogether. The walnuts that we buy in the shops for Christmas are not the complete fruits. The complete fruit is a stone fruit, rather like the plum except that the outer layer is green and leathery. This outer layer is removed as a rule before the 'nuts' go to the shops. The woody part is the equivalent of the plum stone and the seed is inside it. The family also contains the hickory trees of North America. These provide valuable timber and one species also provides pecan nuts.

Waterlily family (Nymphaeaceae) A family of water-dwelling or marsh-dwelling dicotyledons with about 60 species. They usually have sturdy rhizomes buried in the mud and these throw up long-stalked leaves which are usually heart-shaped and which float at the surface. There may also be some thin submerged leaves. The flowers arise singly and usually float, although the flowers of the yellow waterlily or brandy-bottle stand up above the surface. The flowers are regular and they often have numerous petals. There are usually many stamens as well. It is called brandy-bottle because of the shape of its fruits.

Willow family (Salicaceae) A family of deciduous trees and shrubs with about 500 species. About 40 are poplars, and the rest are willows or sallows. Most live in northern regions and some extend right into the Arctic. The flowers have no petals and they are carried in upright or hanging catkins. Male and female catkins are borne on separate trees. The willows and sallows generally have rather narrow leaves and their catkins are erect. They are pollinated by insects and many have sweetly scented flowers. The male catkins are laden with golden pollen in the spring. Poplars are all fairly large trees. Their leaves tend to be triangular and their flowers are carried in hanging, wind-pollinated catkins.

Willowherb family (Onagraceae) A family of dicotyledons with about 500 species. Most of them are herbs, but the fuchsias and a few other members of the family are shrubs. The flowers are usually regular, with two or four free sepals and two or four free petals. Most of the fuchsias come from Latin America, but two are native to New Zealand. The willowherbs themselves have four petals. Willowherbs bear long pod-like fruits which split into four parts and release the hairy seeds. They become weeds because the windblown seeds soon spread to invade bare ground. The rosebay willowherb is a very common plant of waste land. It is also called fireweed because it springs up so readily on burnt ground. Other members of the family include the evening primrose, the enchanter's nightshade and the clarkia. Evening primrose opens its flowers at dusk and closes them at dawn. It often grows as a weed.

Wood sorrel family (Oxalidaceae) A family of dicotyledons with nearly 1,000 species. Most of them are herbs, but there are some shrubs and trees. About 800 species belong to the wood sorrel genus oxalis, in which the leaves are divided into several leaflets rather like clover leaves. It has an acid flavour from the oxalic acid in its leaves. The flowers are regular, with five petals and usually with 10 stamens. The wood sorrel itself is a delicate plant with little white flowers whose petals are streaked with pink or mauve. It is common in the woodlands of Europe and North America. Many related species are cultivated in gardens and oca is cultivated in the Andes for its edible roots. Wood sorrel and others fold their leaves down at night.

Skeletons and Muscles

Most animals have a skeleton. Our own skeletons, like those of all other backboned animals, are inside our bodies and are called endoskeletons. But some animals have skeletons on the outside of their bodies instead. These animals include insects, crabs and snails. Their skeletons are called exoskeletons. They are hard and chalky shells in snails, but insect exoskeletons are made of a horny material called chitin.

Are Skeletons Necessary?

The skeleton takes the weight of the body and all the other parts of the body are normally suspended from it. The skeleton also gives shape to the body.

The skeleton also enables animals to move. The muscles shorten and pull various parts of the body. Such a system works best if the muscles are attached to something firm. The skeleton provides this firm support. The other main job of the skeleton is to protect the animal. Our skulls protect our brains, and our ribs protect our hearts and lungs.

Right: The crab does not have a backbone: its skeleton consists of hard plates on the outside of its body.

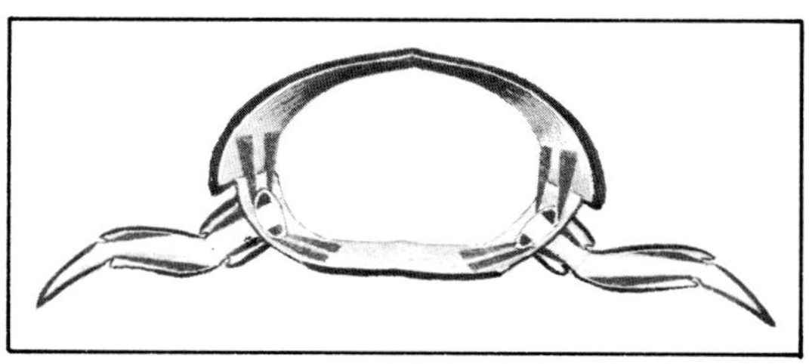

Vertebrate skeletons (below) all have the same basic pattern, but they are adapted for different ways of life.

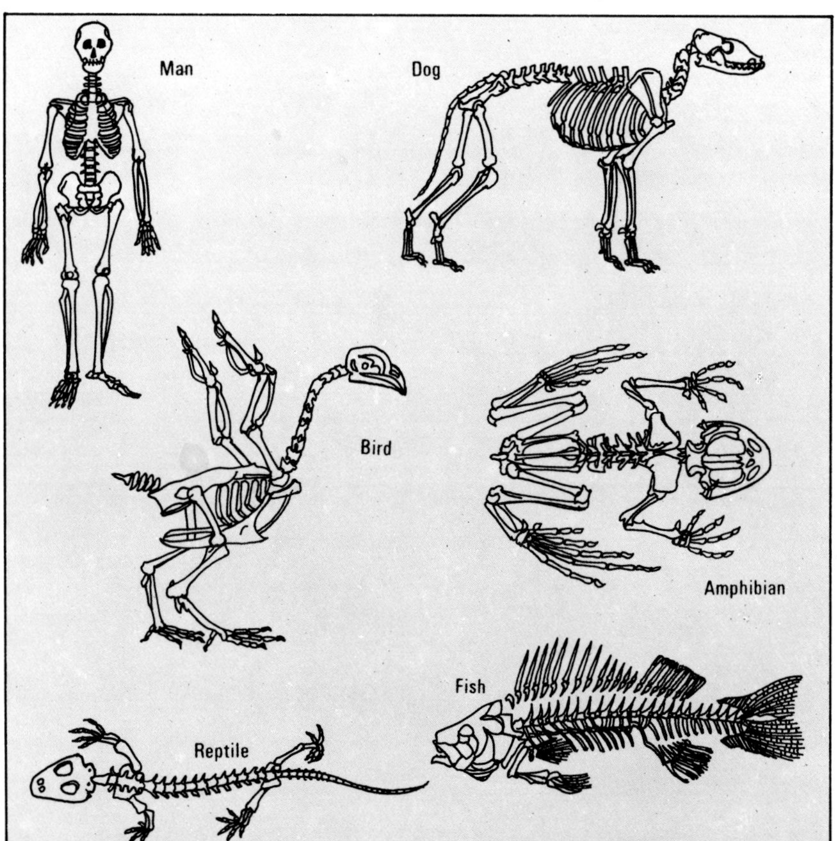

Joints

The skeleton is made up of sections which meet at joints. The joints of an exoskeleton are quite simple, usually little more than thin and flexible regions. The joints of endoskeletons are more complicated. When two bones meet at a joint they are held together by very tough straps called ligaments. The ends of the bones are covered with smooth cartilage and they are often enclosed in a little bag of liquid.

There are several kinds of joints in the vertebrate body. One important type of joint is called a hinge joint. The two bones meet to form a hinge and they can move only in one plane. The best examples are found in our elbows and knees. Another important type of joint in our own bodies is the ball and socket joint. This is found in our hips and shoulders. The upper ends of the leg and arm bones are ball-shaped and they fit into cup-shaped hollows in the hip and the shoulder. The balls can move around in any direction, and so we have a very wide range of movement at the hip and the shoulder. Other joints in the vertebrate body, such as the head joint, allow rather less movement.

Muscles for Movement

Muscles form the flesh of an animal and they generally make up a large proportion of its bulk. They consist of thousands of little tapering cells collected into bundles. A muscle, such as the biceps of the arm, contains several bundles of fibres. Vertebrate muscles are attached to bones by strong cords called tendons.

When a nerve stimulates a muscle the muscle fibres contract. The whole muscle gets shorter and fatter and, because it is attached to a bone at each end, one of the bones must move. A muscle can relax and it can then be stretched out again, but it cannot push a bone. Muscles therefore have to work in pairs. For instance, one muscle contracts to bend the knee and a second straightens it.

The muscles are not always very close to the bones which they pull. The bones of a bird's leg and foot are worked by muscles high up in the leg. These muscles are joined to the foot bones by long tendons—the sinews that you have to remove when you prepare a chicken for the oven.

The muscles that help us to move—the skeletal muscles as they are called—can contract very strongly but they get tired quickly. We can lift heavy weights for a short time, but we soon have to drop them because our muscles get tired.

Involuntary Muscles

The skeletal muscles are also called voluntary muscles, because we can move them when we want to. There are other muscles, however, which go on working without our knowing about them. They include the muscles that push food along the digestive canal and the muscles that control the size of the pupil in the eye. Unlike the skeletal muscles, these involuntary muscles do not get tired.

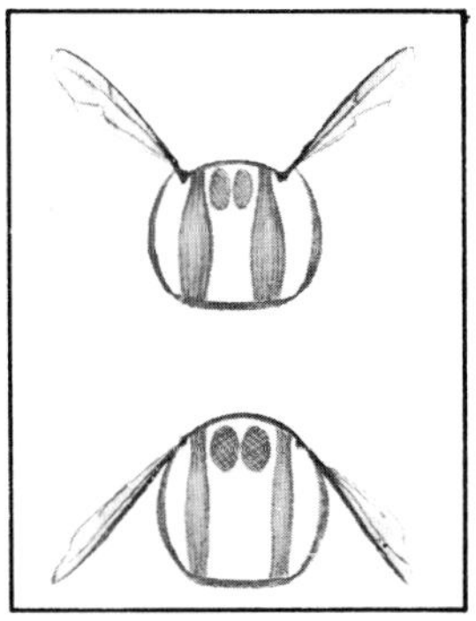

Both the frog and the cheetah have very strong muscles in the upper parts of their legs. Contraction of these muscles straightens the legs and sends the animal hurtling forward. The cheetah is the fastest of all land animals over short distances and can run at 100 kph.

Top: Insect wings are made to vibrate very rapidly by the contraction of two sets of muscles in the thorax.

The Senses of Animals

Animals use their eyes, ears and other sense organs to find out what is going on in their surroundings. Signals are sent from the sense organs to the brain and the brain then instructs the body to react accordingly. Most of the reactions concern the finding and catching of food or escape from danger, so the senses are very important for an animal. An animal that does not detect changes in its surroundings, or an animal that does not react correctly to these changes, will soon perish.

The simplest animals, such as amoeba, have no special sense organs. The whole body surface is sensitive and the animals react to unpleasant sensations by moving away. The more advanced animals have special sense organs, each constructed for picking up different kinds of signals from their surroundings. They also have nerves, which carry signals from one part of the body to another, and a brain which is the control centre. Signals are received in the brain and the brain then sends signals to the body telling it to take the correct action.

We have five main senses: sight, hearing, taste, smell and touch. These are the most obvious senses but there are several more. The senses of balance and temperature, for example, are important, and there are senses that tell us about the conditions inside our bodies. The sense of pain tells us when something is wrong, and other senses in our bodies tell us when we are hungry or thirsty. Similar kinds of sense organs are found in other animals, although they are not always made up in the same way and they are not always on the same part of the body. Some sense organs may be absent: many animals living in the dark, for example, have no eyes.

Right: Hunting animals need to be able to judge distances well. Two eyes at the front (instead of on the sides) help them to do this.

Below right: Man's eyes are his most important sense organs and they tell him a great deal about his surroundings. Light is gathered in by the lens and focused on to the retina at the back. Nerve cells there are stimulated and they send the picture to the brain.

Below: Sounds reaching the human ear drum set up vibrations in three tiny bones. These carry the vibrations to the inner ear, where they are picked up by nerves.

The Eyes

The eyes are the organs of sight. They are normally found on the head and they are sensitive to light rays. The eyes of vertebrate

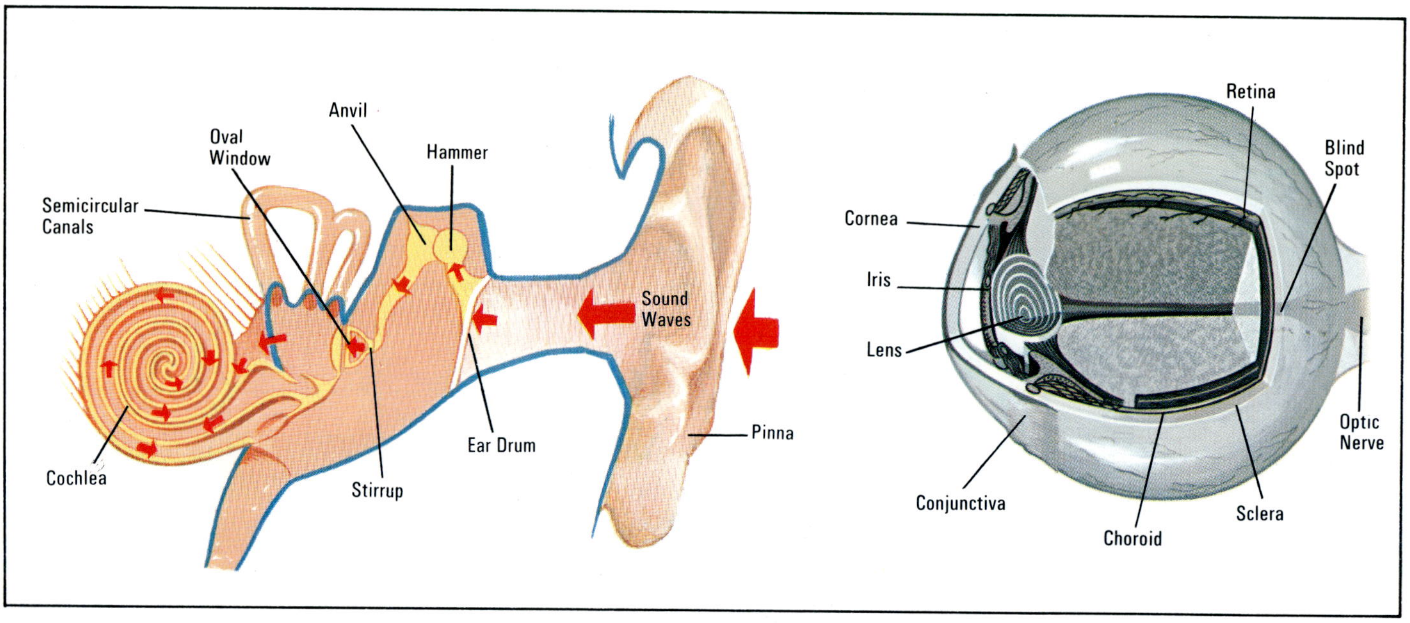

animals are all more or less alike. The basic parts are the lens and the retina. The lens gathers the light rays and focuses them on to the retina. The latter consists of millions of light-sensitivc cells which send signals to the brain. The brain then interprets the signals as a picture.

Insect eyes are constructed on a very different pattern. They are known as compound eyes because they are made up of numerous tiny units. Each unit is cone-shaped and they all fit together so that their lenses form a patchwork pattern on the surface of the eye. Each lens sends its own signals to the brain. Although the image is not very clear, the insect easily spots movements. Dragonflies catch smaller insects in mid air. They rely on sight and their eyes have up to 30,000 units. Insects which rely less on sight have smaller eyes.

The Ears

Sounds play a large part in the lives of many animals. They are used as warnings and as signals to attract mates. The sound-receiving organs, or ears, are normally membranes stretched like drumskins across openings. They vibrate when sound waves hit them and send signals to the brain. Some insects pick up sounds with sensitive hairs. The organs are normally on the head, but may be located elsewhere. For example, crickets have their ears on the front legs.

Chemical Senses

The senses of taste and smell are chemical senses. The sense of smell tells us about chemicals in the air. Most substances give off some sort of vapour or scent and this consists of minute particles called molecules which affect our smelling organs, or olfactory organs to give them their proper name. Our own sense of smell, centred in our noses, is not very good but some other animals have extremely good senses of smell. Insects smell with their antennae, and some male moths have such sensitive smell receptors that they can smell female moths more than a kilometre away.

We taste things only with our tongues, but other creatures use other parts of their bodies. Flies, for example, have taste organs on their feet and they taste things by landing on them.

The Sense of Touch

Most of the body surface is sensitive to touch, although some parts are more sensitive than others. Hairs have tiny nerves wrapped around their bases, and the nerves tell the brain when the hairs are touched. Mice and cats have very sensitive whiskers which help them to find their way in the dark. If the whiskers touch anything the animal draws back.

Below: Insect's eyes have many lenses. The surface of the eye is often brilliantly coloured, as in the horse-fly.

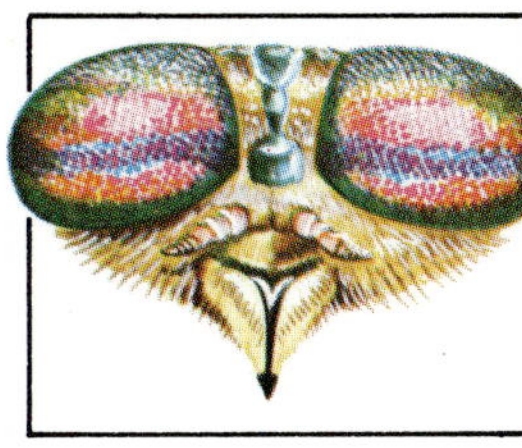

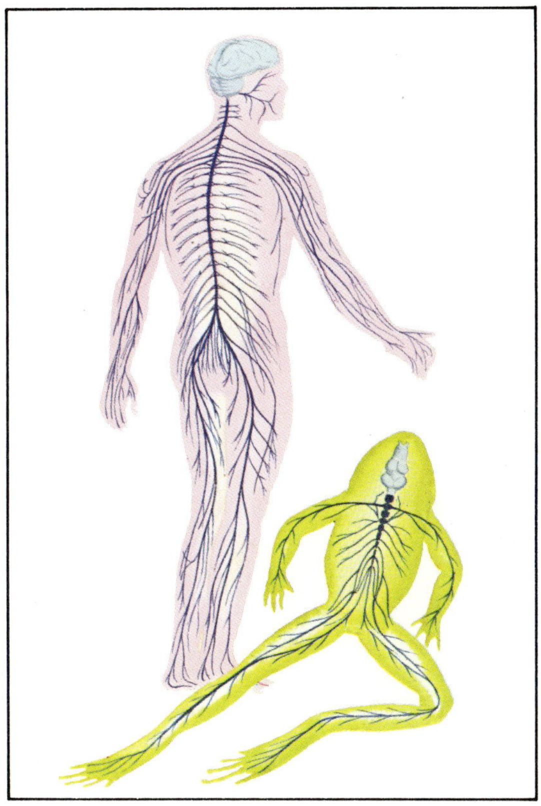

Left: The arrangement of the nervous system is very similar in man and the frog, although man's brain is very much larger and more efficient.

Below: The impala must always be alert to danger. Even while drinking, its eyes are scanning the area and its ears are pricked up waiting for the faintest sound of danger.

Feeding and Digestion

The toad is a carnivore, feeding on slugs and insects which it catches with its long sticky tongue.

The waterbuck eats grass and other leaves and is a typical herbivore.

The food of animals provides energy and the materials they need for building up their own bodies. Green plants get their energy from the sun. Animals cannot do this and they rely on green plants to provide their energy. They either eat plants or other animals, which have eaten plants, but the energy always comes from a plant to start with.

Some animals feed on plants. They are called herbivores. Some species feed on other animals. They are called carnivores or flesh-eaters. Other species feed on both plants and animals. They are called omnivores.

Herbivores

Herbivores or plant-eating animals include voles, rabbits, deer, sheep, horses, snails and caterpillars. Most feed on the leaves and other juicy parts of the plants, but a few feed on wood. Examples include the termites and many beetles. One large group of insects sucks the sap from plants through mouths equipped with 'hypodermic needles'.

Carnivores

Carnivorous or flesh-eating animals include cats, dogs, weasels, owls, snakes, frogs, sharks, ladybirds, starfishes and sea anemones. Some chase their prey, others lie in wait until something comes along. Some spiders and caddis fly larvae set traps for their prey by spinning silken webs or snares. Some snakes and other animals use poison to kill or paralyse their food before they eat it.

Most carnivores catch their food while it is alive, but some feed on dead animals, or carrion. Carrion feeders include vultures and hyenas. Many insects also feed on dead animals, including the burying beetles or sexton beetles. They bury dead animals by dragging soil out from under them. They then lay their eggs on them, as do flies, and their larvae eat the rotting flesh.

Various blood-sucking creatures such as fleas and bed bugs can also be classed as carnivores.

Omnivores

Many herbivorous animals will eat flesh sometimes. For example, voles and other rodents will often eat insects. Carnivores may also eat vegetable food from time to time. But there are some animals which regularly eat a mixture of plant and animal materials. These are the omnivorous animals. They include most bears, the badger, the rat and the cockroaches. Man is also an omnivorous animal.

Filter Feeders

Many animals living in water feed on tiny particles which they filter out from the water. These particles are tiny plants and animals, or decaying matter falling to the bottom of the sea or the pond. The filter feeders are therefore omnivorous animals. Bivalve molluscs have two tubes or siphons, one to suck in water and the other to squirt it out. While the water is flowing through the animal it is strained or filtered (see p. 109). Freshwater mussels are useful in fish tanks because they filter out a lot of the microscopic algae which would otherwise make the water green.

Some marine worms are also filter feeders. They have crowns of feathery arms or tentacles around their heads and these strain out particles falling from above. Some whales, the basking shark and the herring filter small animals from sea water by straining them through sieves in their mouths.

Animal Teeth

Only the backboned animals have proper teeth and jaws. The teeth of fishes, amphibians and reptiles are normally simple spikes, although the snake's fangs are very special teeth. Birds have no teeth, although some extinct birds had them. The most complex teeth are found in mammals. Their job is to catch, cut and chew the food. The number and arrangement of a mammal's teeth depend to some extent upon its food. Flesh-eaters, such as dogs, have large stabbing teeth called fangs, near the front. These stab the prey and rip the flesh. The back teeth of flesh-eaters have sharp edges and they slice the meat into pieces. Grazing animals do not need stabbing teeth, and they have gaps where the eye teeth would normally be. Their back teeth have broad flat surfaces suitable for grinding plants.

Digestion

When an animal has eaten its food it must be broken down into simple substances which can be carried around the body and used to provide energy or to build new cells. This is carried out in the digestive system. The detailed structure of the digestive system varies a great deal, but it is basically a tube which begins at the mouth and ends at the anus. Food is taken in through the mouth, and the front part of the system is concerned mainly with breaking down the food into smaller pieces and simpler substances. The next part of the system is concerned with absorbing the digested food into the blood, and the last part is concerned with getting rid of the undigested material or waste. Sea anemones, jellyfishes and some other simple creatures have only a mouth and this must serve for taking food in and for passing out waste.

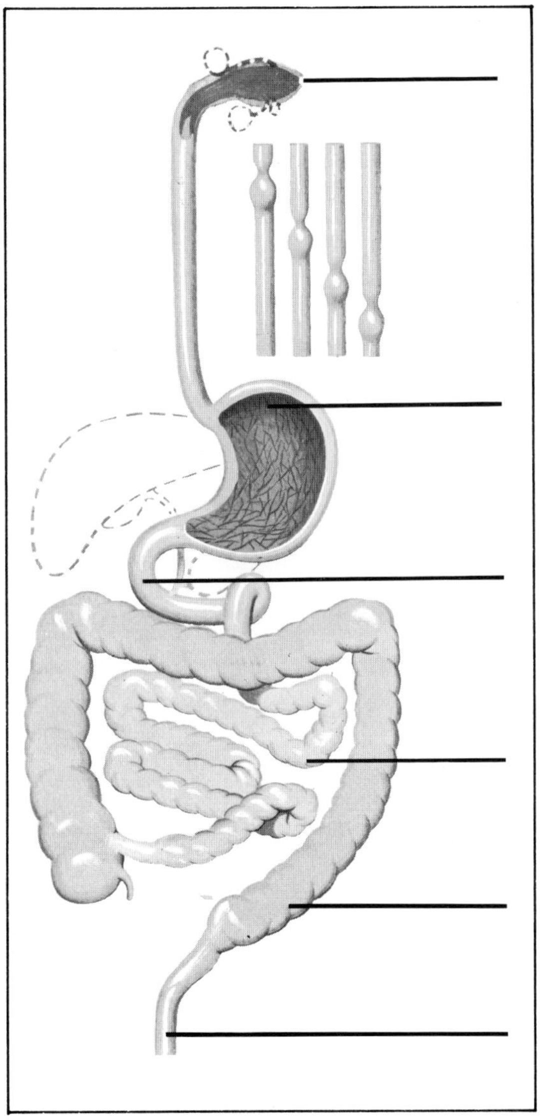

Digestion begins in the mouth, where the salivary glands pour saliva on to the food. The chewed and moistened food then passes down the gullet and into the stomach.

In the stomach the food is churned up with dilute acid and certain digestive juices. Food particles are reduced in size and the chemical breakdown of protein begins. After a few hours the food is reduced to a liquid 'soup' and it is ready to pass on.

In the duodenum the food meets other digestive juices, including some from the liver and pancreas. Chemical breakdown is accelerated.

Chemical breakdown is completed in the small intestine and the food materials are taken into the bloodstream.

Undigested material passes into the large intestine or colon and water is absorbed.

The remaining material passes into the rectum and is then periodically passed out of the body.

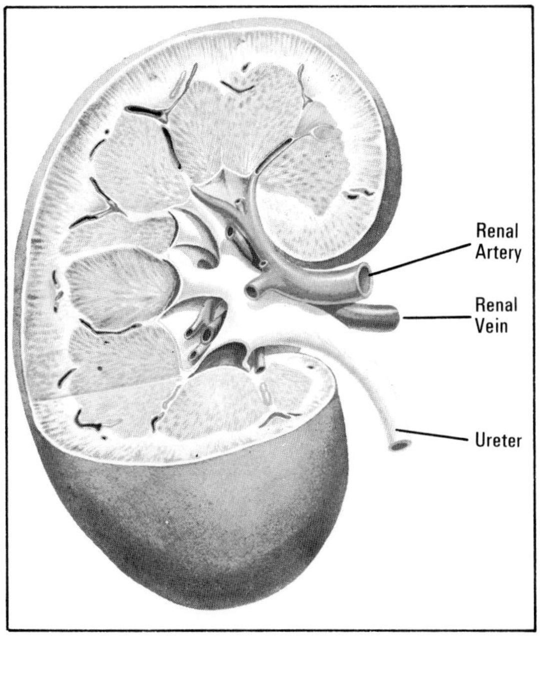

Waste products produced by the body must be removed from the blood. This is called excretion and is done in the kidneys. A kidney consists of about a million tubes. Blood is filtered through them and unwanted materials, including excess water, are retained and flow into a large duct called a ureter. This carries the waste materials (now called urine) to the bladder, and from there to the outside.

How Animals Breathe

Breathing, like feeding, is one of the characteristics of all living things. Breathing involves taking in oxygen, which is then used to 'burn' the food in the cells of the body and to release energy. The whole process of obtaining oxygen and using it in the body is called respiration. One of the waste products of respiration is carbon dioxide. The breathing organs get rid of carbon dioxide as well as obtaining oxygen for the animals.

The simplest animals, such as the protozoans and the jellyfishes, have no special breathing organs. They are quite small creatures and they are not very active. They do not need very much oxygen. Enough oxygen seeps into their bodies without the need for special breathing organs.

Larger and more active animals need special breathing organs and they also need a bloodstream to carry the oxygen from the breathing organs to the rest of the body.

Breathing Under Water

Many aquatic animals come to the surface to breathe air. Examples include whales, seals and some water snails. Many others, however, can remain permanently under the surface and rely on oxygen dissolved in the water. They have breathing organs called gills. In common with all breathing organs, gills have a large surface area for absorbing oxygen.

Fishes' gills consist of columns of little finger-like organs situated in cavities connected to the throat. The cavities also open on to the sides of the body. The fish takes in a mouthful of water and forces the water over the gills.

The gills of the crabs and lobsters are feathery outgrowths covered by the shell. One of the limbs wafts a current of water through the gill chamber. This brings a continuous supply of oxygen to the gills. The gills of bivalves (cockles and mussels) are very large and they serve to trap food particles as well as to absorb oxygen. Many water snails breathe by means of gills. Water is pumped in and out of the gill cavity and the gills absorb oxygen. Land snails have lost their gills, but they still have the gill cavity. It is lined with blood vessels and acts as a lung. Some snails returned to the water after a period of life on land. Most of them still breathe air and they come to the surface now and then to renew the air.

Air-breathing Vertebrates

The reptiles, birds and mammals all breathe by means of lungs. These are thin-walled sacs in the chest cavity. Most amphibians also have lungs, although these are rather inefficient organs. The amphibians are moist-skinned animals and they can absorb a good deal of oxygen through the skin. The lining of the frog's mouth and throat is also very thin and well supplied with blood vessels and a frog can often be seen pumping air into its throat.

The reptiles cannot breathe through their skin. The lungs are elaborately folded to give

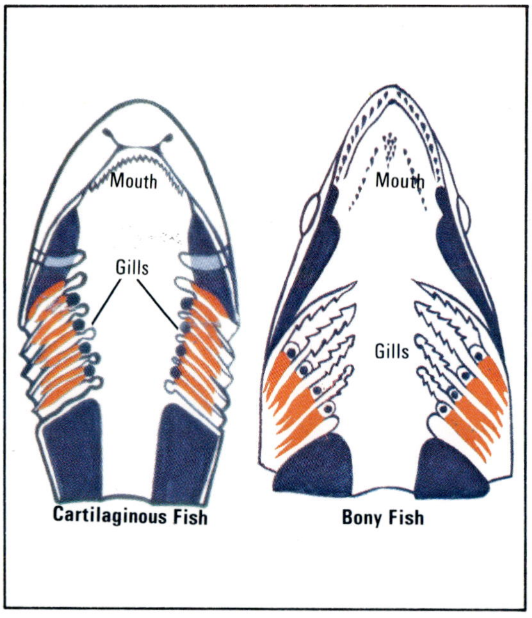

The fish's gills lie in pouches at the back of the throat. In the shark-like fishes (left) each gill has its own separate opening on the side of the body. The gills of the bony fishes (right) are covered by the operculum and there is only one opening to be seen.

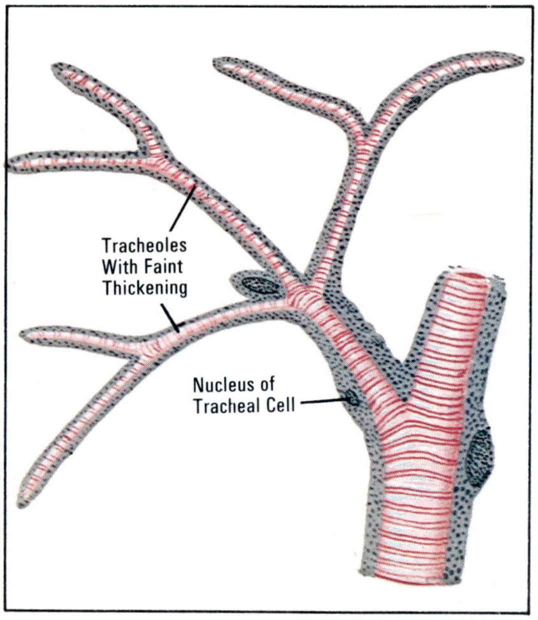

Far right: Part of an insect's breathing system. The fine tubes reach all parts of the body and carry oxygen to all the tissues. The rings prevent the tubes from collapsing.

them a large surface area. This folding is taken even further in the lungs of mammals. Each lung is made up of thousands of tiny air pockets called alveoli, each of which is surrounded by blood vessels. This arrangement provides a very large surface area for the absorption of oxygen, but it does mean that not all the air can be exchanged at each breath.

Birds are extremely active animals and they need large amounts of oxygen. Instead of being closed at the end, the lungs lead on to thin-walled air-sacs. When the bird breathes in the air rushes in through the lungs to the air-sacs. At each breath, the air in the lungs is completely changed.

Insect Breathing Systems

The insects, together with the centipedes and a few other arthropods, have a breathing system quite different from that of other animals. The body is penetrated by masses of tiny tubes called tracheae, which open on to the body surface at holes called spiracles. Air flows along the tracheae and carries oxygen to all parts of the body.

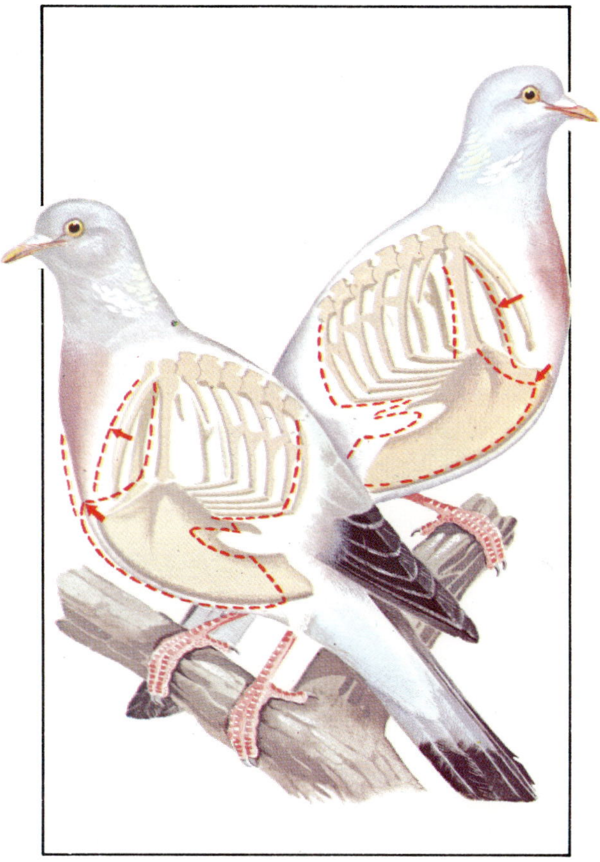

Birds are very active animals and they need a good supply of oxygen. Their ribs and keel move backwards and forwards, forcing air in and out of the lungs and air-sacs.

Below left: The oxygen concentration in the lungs is higher than that in the blood. Consequently oxygen spreads, or diffuses, through the wall of the alveoli into the blood capillaries. At the same time carbon dioxide passes from the blood into the lungs. At the tissues the situation is reversed. The blood is now richer in oxygen and poorer in carbon dioxide. So oxygen passes from the blood to the tissues and carbon dioxide from the tissues to the blood.

Human lungs. The small diagram shows how the tubes end in clusters of thin-walled pouches or alveoli where oxygen is absorbed.

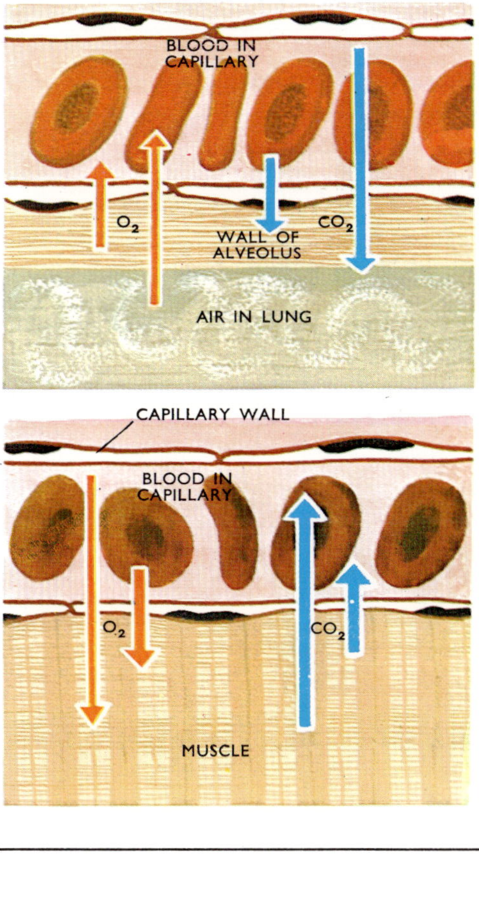

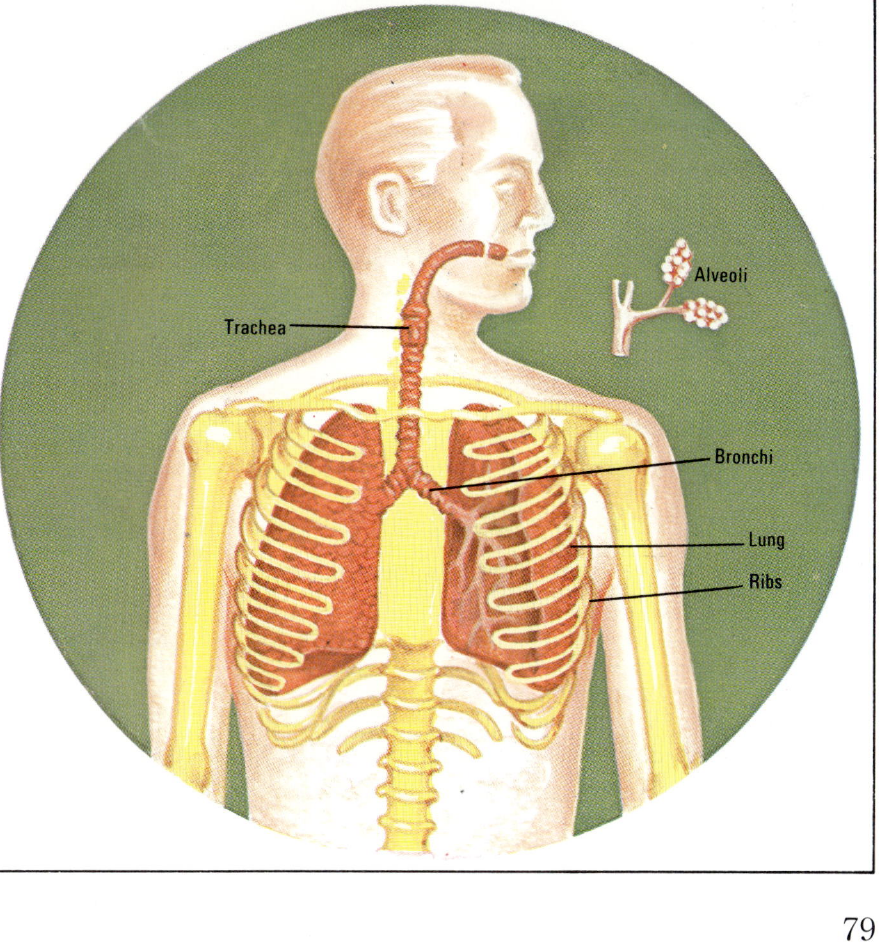

The Blood System

All but the simplest animals have some sort of blood system. It is the transport system, carrying materials from one part of the body to another. Food is carried from the digestive organs to all parts of the body, and waste products are carried from the tissues to the excretory organs. In most animals the blood carries oxygen from the breathing organs to the tissues. Hormones—chemical 'messengers'—are also distributed by the blood. A less obvious function, but still a very important one, is the distribution of heat around the body. The blood plays a very important part in keeping the bodies of birds and mammals at constant temperatures. Yet another function of the blood is fighting infections and destroying germs.

Mammalian Blood

Mammalian blood, like that of the other vertebrates, consists mainly of a liquid called plasma. Plasma is mainly water, but it contains a very complicated mixture of proteins, sugars and dissolved minerals. Floating in the plasma there are millions of tiny cells called corpuscles. The corpuscles

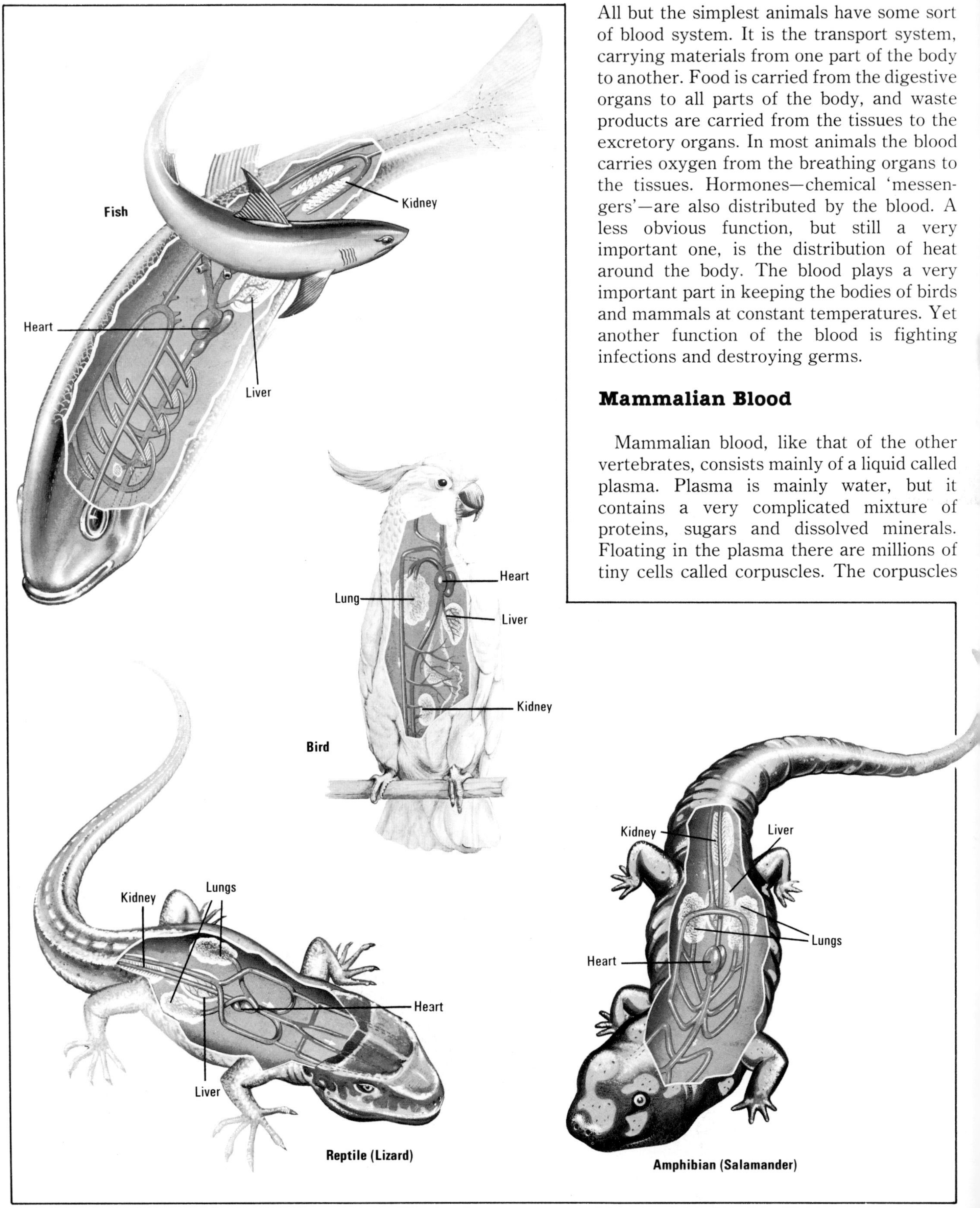

are of two main types: red and white. Red corpuscles, which give the blood its red colour, are minute disc-shaped cells. Their job is to carry the oxygen around the body. The red colouring matter, haemoglobin, takes up the oxygen in the lungs and releases it again as the blood flows around the body (see page 79).

White blood corpuscles are concerned with the control of infection, by fighting germs that get into the blood. In addition to the red and white corpuscles, the blood contains some smaller bodies called platelets. These break down when they come in contact with the air and they cause the blood to clot.

The Heart and the Blood Vessels

The insects and other arthropods have an open blood system. The blood lies in large cavities and surrounds all the internal organs. Most animals, however, have a closed blood system with the blood running in narrow vessels.

The heart is a pump for pushing the blood around the body. It is a muscular bag and it is divided into two or more chambers. The blood vessels that carry blood away from the heart are called arteries. The main arteries have thick, muscular walls. When these blood vessels reach their destination they divide up into tiny vessels called capillaries. These have very thin walls and materials can pass very easily between the blood and the tissues. The capillaries then join up again to form the veins which carry the blood back to the heart.

Warm-blooded or Cold-blooded?

The birds and mammals can keep their bodies at constant high temperatures. For this reason, we call them warm-blooded animals. Fishes, frogs, snakes and all the invertebrate animals are unable to keep a high temperature and we call them cold-blooded animals. But this does not mean that they are always cold. Their bodies are always more or less at the temperature of their surroundings. A snake basking in the sunshine will actually be quite warm—warmer than a warm-blooded animal sometimes. Birds and mammals use up energy to keep them warm, and they thus need regular food.

Far left: The diagrams show the arrangement of the major blood vessels in various vertebrate animals.

Below left: Red and white corpuscles. The red ones have no nuclei.

Below: A drawing of the human heart showing the various chambers and the valves which ensure that the blood flows in the right direction.

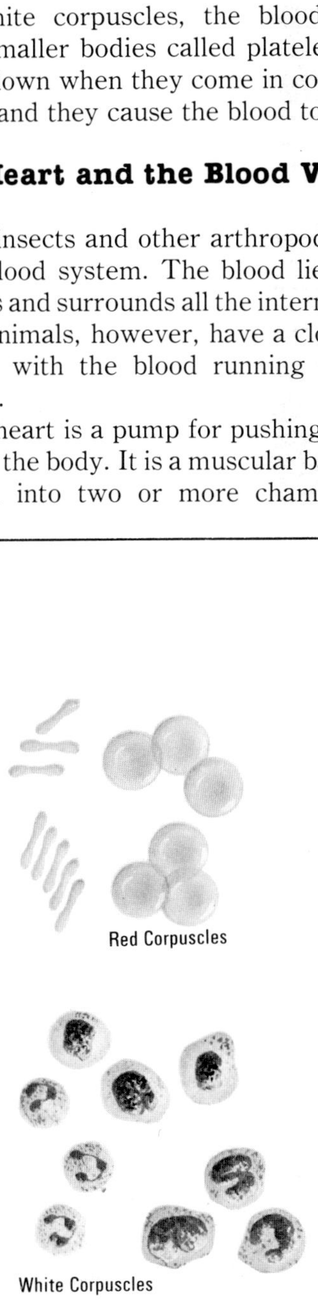

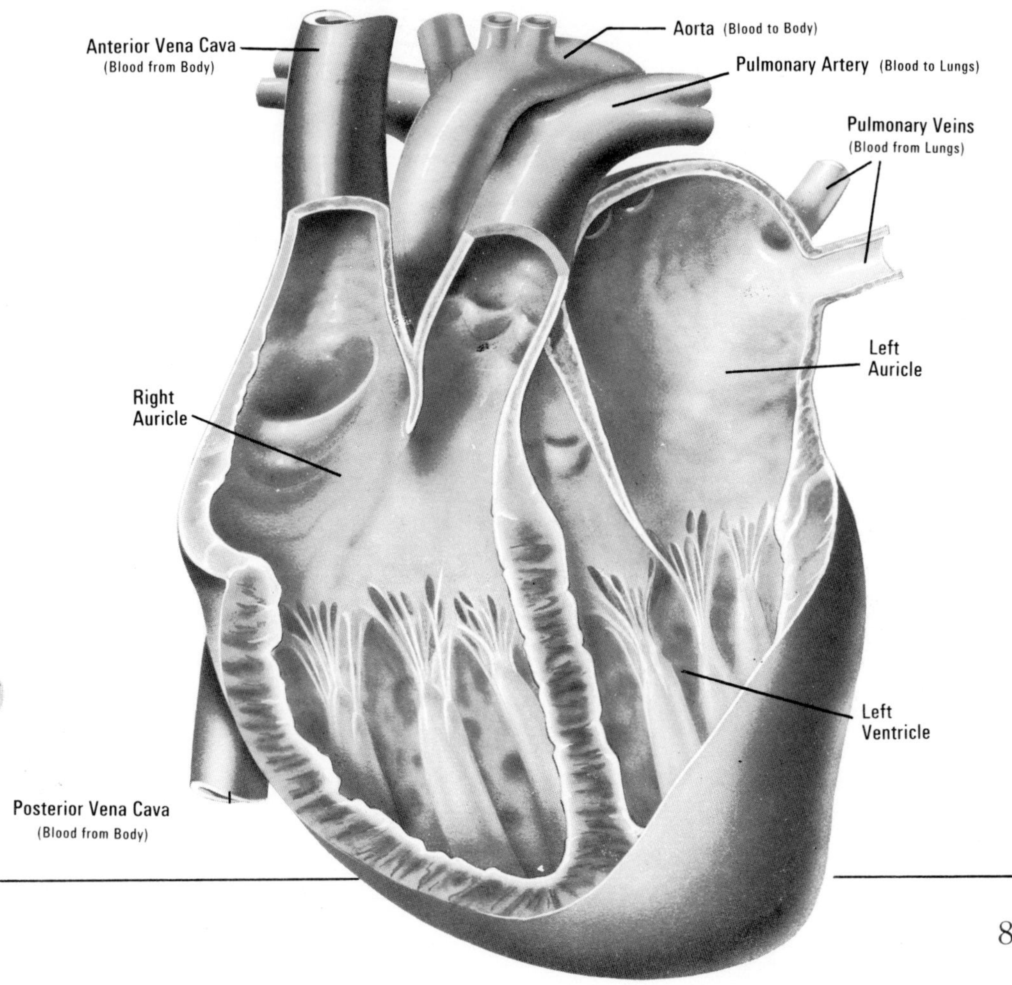

Reproduction

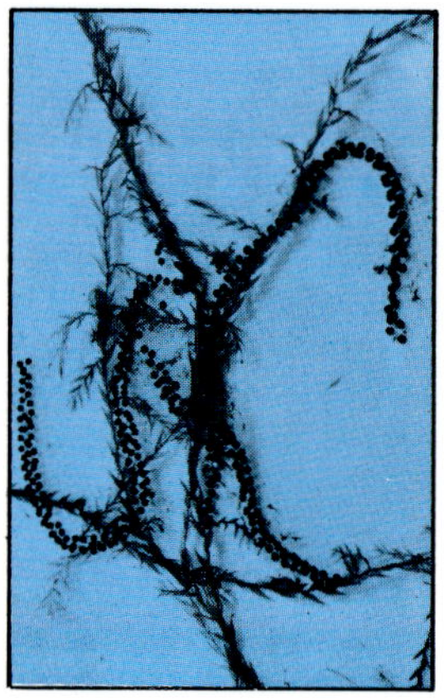

Female toads take no interest in their offspring. They lay large numbers of eggs, but only about two will ever reach maturity.

Far right: A bird's egg contains just the right amount of food.

Earthworms contain both male and female organs, but they have to pair up before they can lay eggs.

Below: Hydra has two methods of reproduction. New individuals can grow out as buds (upper pictures) or it reproduces sexually.

There are two main methods of reproduction —sexual and asexual. Sexual reproduction involves the joining together of special cells called gametes or sex cells. Asexual reproduction takes place without any joining of cells and often involves little more than the breaking of an animal into two parts. Almost all animal species reproduce sexually at some time or other, but only the simpler animals can reproduce asexually.

Splitting in Two

The simplest form of reproduction takes place in some of the protozoans, such as amoeba. These creatures consist of only one cell. The cell goes on growing until it reaches a certain size and then divides into two. Each half then starts growing again. Splitting into two halves is a form of asexual reproduction. But Amoeba can also reproduce sexually at times.

Budding

Some simple animals, notably the corals and their fresh-water relative hydra, produce new individuals by a process called budding.

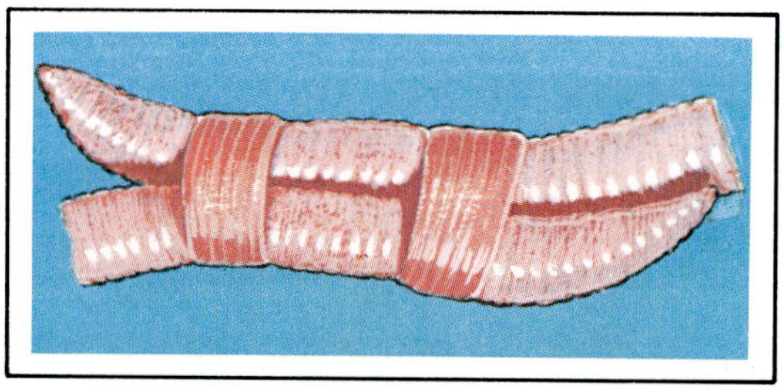

A 'bud' develops somewhere on the body and gradually grows to form a branch. This branch is a smaller version of the parent. A branch of hydra normally separates from the parent and begins an independent life. In many other creatures, however, including most of the corals, the branches do not separate. The animals form colonies. Each individual normally looks after itself, but some colonies contain special individuals which are concerned only with sexual reproduction.

Sexual Reproduction

This method of reproduction involves the joining together of special cells called gametes. The joining together of the gametes is called fertilization. In amoeba and some of the other simple animals all the gametes are alike, but the more advanced animals have two kinds of gametes. One is called a sperm and the other is called an egg or ovum. The two kinds of gametes are usually, but not always, produced by separate individuals. Sperms are produced by the male sex and eggs are produced by the female sex. A sperm must join with an egg before a new animal can be produced.

Some water-dwelling animals merely release their sperms and eggs into the water and leave fertilization to chance. In most animals, however, the two sexes have to meet before reproduction can take place. The eggs may be fertilized inside the female's body or outside it.

When an egg has been fertilized it starts to

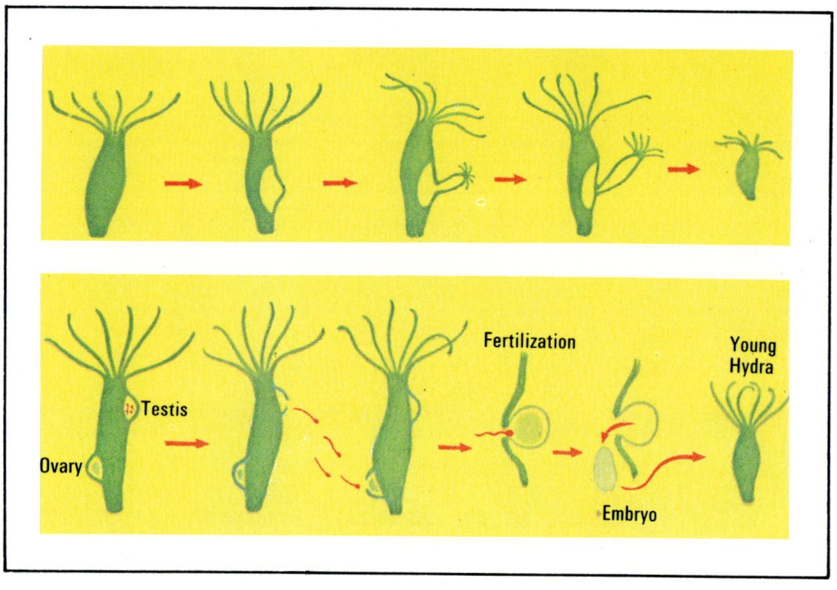

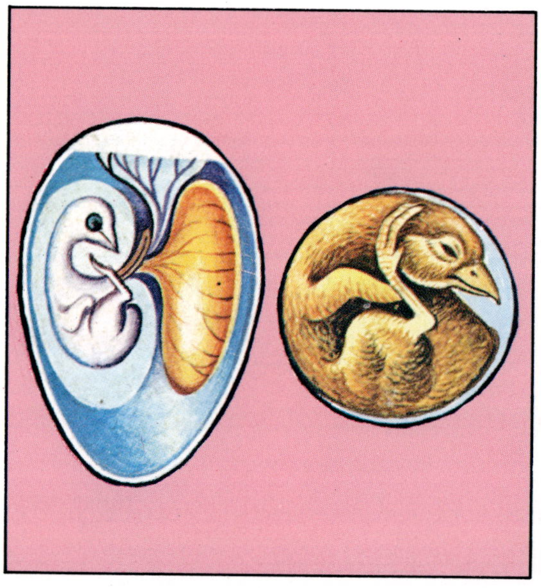

develop into the new animal. The egg contains enough food material for all the early stages of development. Eggs that have been fertilized inside the mother's body may be laid soon afterwards, or they may remain in the mother's body. Quite often they hatch before they leave the mother's body, in which case the mother gives birth to active young. In nearly all mammals the young animal remains inside its mother and obtains food from the mother's own body.

Parental Care

Some animals produce large numbers of eggs or young, while others may have only one or two babies. The number of eggs or young depends very much on the dangers that they face during their lives. Young animals are easily caught and eaten by other creatures. Animals that merely scatter their eggs and abandon them suffer the most and these animals survive only by producing huge numbers of eggs. The female cod, for example, may produce about 9 million eggs, but only two are likely to reach maturity.

Hermaphrodites

Earthworms and many snails do not have separate sexes. Each individual possesses both male and female reproductive organs and produces both sperms and eggs. Such animals are called hermaphrodites. But the animals have to pair before they can reproduce. They exchange sperms and each then goes away and lays its own eggs, fertilized by sperms from the other animal. Any adults can pair in this way.

Parthenogenesis

Many stick insects, greenflies (aphids) and other insects can lay eggs which hatch without being fertilized. The male sex is very rare or even unknown in some species and the females reproduce almost entirely by laying these special eggs. This method of reproduction is called parthenogenesis. We can think of it as a special kind of sexual reproduction.

Regeneration

A number of the simpler animals are able to regrow or regenerate parts of their bodies that have been lost or damaged. In some animals this ability amounts to a form of asexual reproduction. Hydra, for example, will not normally die if it is cut into two parts. Each part will regenerate the missing sections and become a complete animal. Starfishes can grow new arms if any are lost, and the broken arms can sometimes grow new bodies! Young insects can grow new legs and antennae if these are broken or lost, but the new ones are usually a bit smaller.

Animals with backbones cannot regenerate lost limbs. The nearest approach is in the lizards, which break off their tails when alarmed. The broken piece continues to wriggle and distracts an enemy while the lizard escapes. A new tail will grow, but it is shorter and contains no backbone.

Emperor penguins, like many other sea birds, breed in large colonies. The male looks after the single egg for about six weeks, then the female returns to look after the chick while the male collects foods.

Animal Classification

The animal kingdom can be divided quite conveniently into two large 'parcels'—animals with backbones, and animals without backbones. These groups are properly called vertebrates and invertebrates, but they are very unequal groups. The vertebrates belong to just one of about 20 major groups into which the animal kingdom is divided.

These major groups are called phyla (singular, phylum), and most of them are further divided into classes. The main phyla and classes are shown on this 'family tree' of animals. Some of the phyla are obviously related to each other. Others are more difficult to fit in because they are not clearly related to other groups.

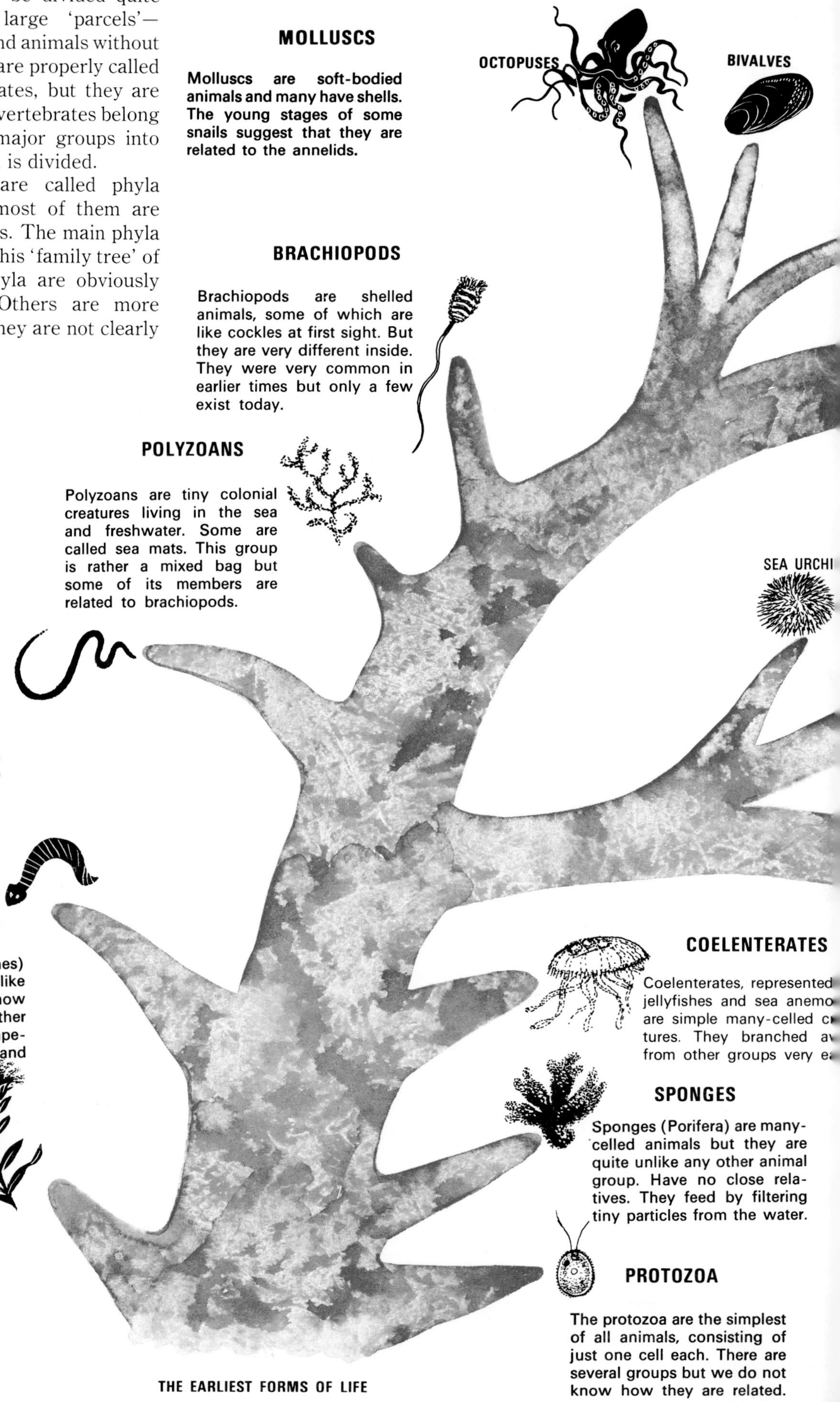

MOLLUSCS

Molluscs are soft-bodied animals and many have shells. The young stages of some snails suggest that they are related to the annelids.

BRACHIOPODS

Brachiopods are shelled animals, some of which are like cockles at first sight. But they are very different inside. They were very common in earlier times but only a few exist today.

POLYZOANS

Polyzoans are tiny colonial creatures living in the sea and freshwater. Some are called sea mats. This group is rather a mixed bag but some of its members are related to brachiopods.

ROUNDWORMS

Roundworms (Nematoda) are nearly all minute creatures. Many are parasites. Their needle-like bodies are not segmented and they are not related to earthworms.

FLATWORMS

Flatworms (Platyhelminthes) are rather flat, worm-like creatures. We do not know how they are related to other groups. They include tapeworms, liver flukes and planarians.

PLANTS

COELENTERATES

Coelenterates, represented jellyfishes and sea anemo are simple many-celled c tures. They branched a from other groups very e

SPONGES

Sponges (Porifera) are many-celled animals but they are quite unlike any other animal group. Have no close relatives. They feed by filtering tiny particles from the water.

PROTOZOA

The protozoa are the simplest of all animals, consisting of just one cell each. There are several groups but we do not know how they are related.

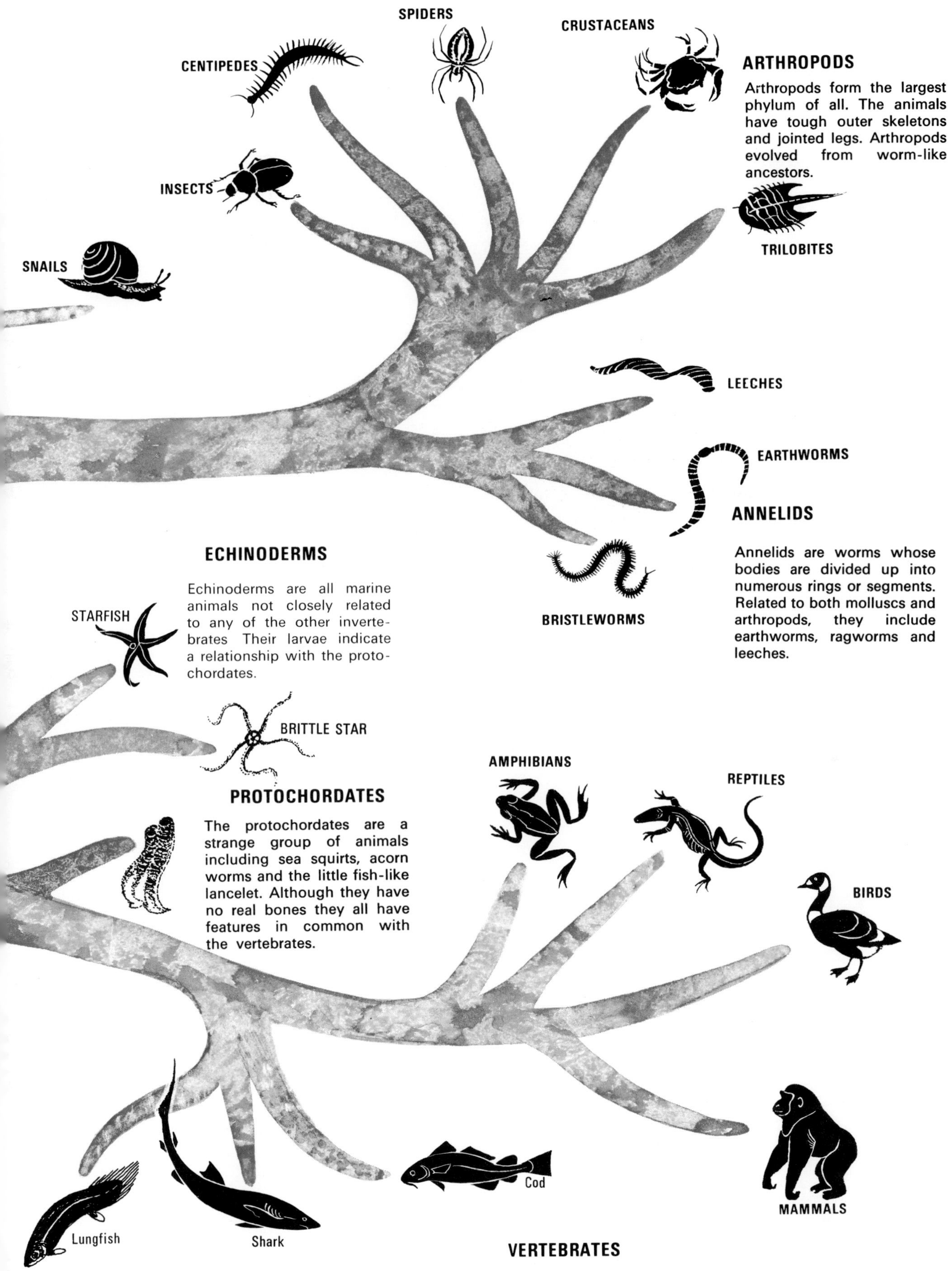

ARTHROPODS

Arthropods form the largest phylum of all. The animals have tough outer skeletons and jointed legs. Arthropods evolved from worm-like ancestors.

ANNELIDS

Annelids are worms whose bodies are divided up into numerous rings or segments. Related to both molluscs and arthropods, they include earthworms, ragworms and leeches.

ECHINODERMS

Echinoderms are all marine animals not closely related to any of the other invertebrates Their larvae indicate a relationship with the protochordates.

PROTOCHORDATES

The protochordates are a strange group of animals including sea squirts, acorn worms and the little fish-like lancelet. Although they have no real bones they all have features in common with the vertebrates.

VERTEBRATES

The vertebrates are the backboned animals and, with the protochordates, they make up the phylum Chordata.

The Microscopic World

Below right: Some interesting protozoans. Paramoecium is one of the commonest pond dwellers. Euglena is a flagellate, on the border between plants and animals. Trypanosomes are harmful protozoans, causing sleeping sickness.

Below: Amoeba merely splits into two halves when it gets too big. Each half then begins life as a new animal. It has no problem getting oxygen or getting rid of waste. Materials simply pass through the thin walls of the animal.

A jar of dirty pond water looked at with the naked eye does not seem very interesting, but if some of the water is examined under a microscope it becomes full of life.

Most of the animals will be tiny single-celled creatures called Protozoa. This name means 'first animals', for it is likely that the earliest animals were quite similar to some of today's little pond creatures. One of the animals that you are likely to see, especially if your sample contains some mud from the bottom of the pond, is amoeba. This is often described as a shapeless blob of jelly. It would be more correct to say that amoeba's shape is always changing. Finger-like projections or pseudopodia are continually being pushed out from the body and withdrawn and the animal's body moves too. As one of these 'fingers' is pushed out, living material from the rest of the body flows into it. The animal also feeds by putting out pseudopodia. They flow around small particles of food and completely engulf them. The particles then move around inside the body and are gradually digested. Any indigestible material is simply left behind as the animal flows forward.

Amoeba finds its food by a chemical sense. The whole body surface is sensitive to chemicals in the water, and the animal reacts by moving towards food materials and away from harmful materials such as acids. The animal is also sensitive to light and it moves away from bright light. This sort of reaction ensures that the animal remains in suitable surroundings.

Breathing is no problem for the amoeba because it is so small. The thin skin does, however, have one disadvantage: water can pass through it and the animal tends to absorb water from its surroundings. This extra water must be removed. Amoeba

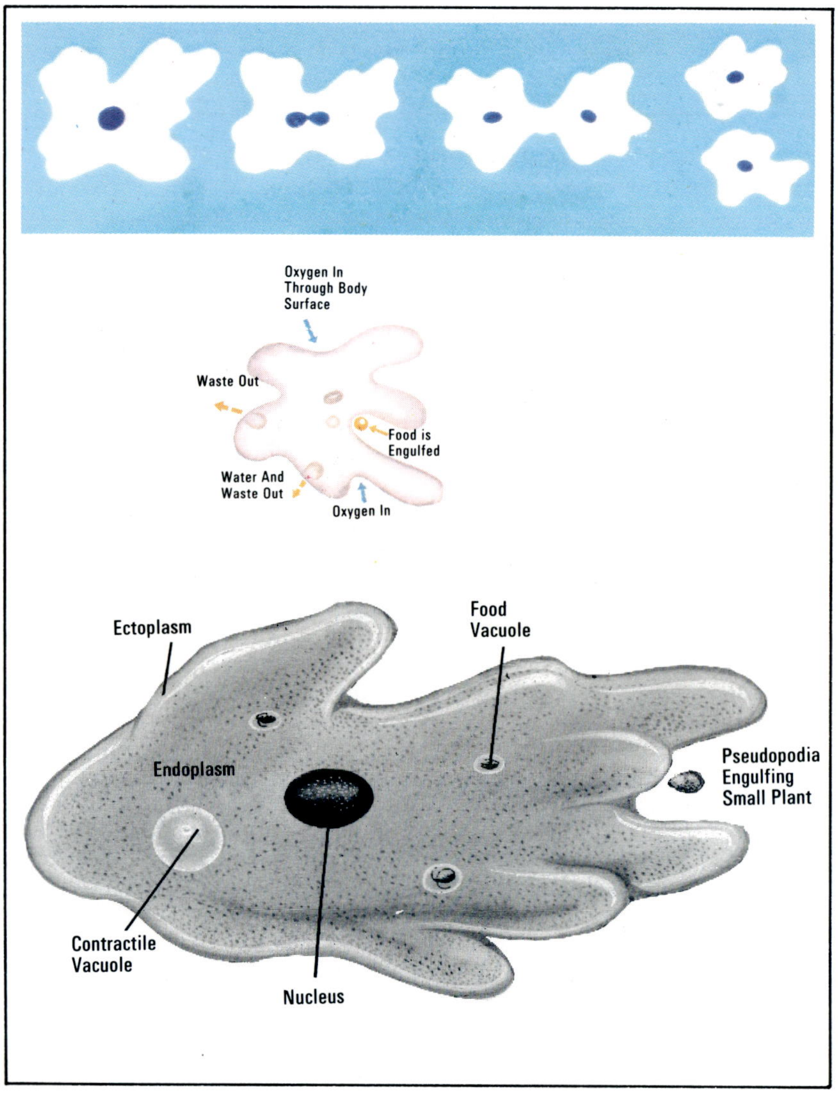

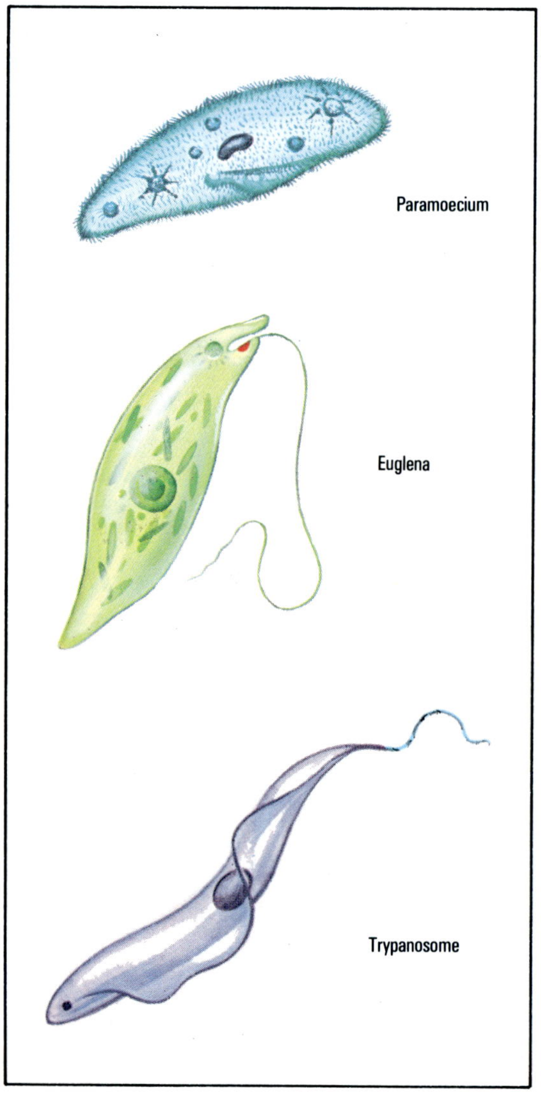

collects it in a contractile vacuole and then squirts it out through the skin. As it grows, amoeba gradually reaches a certain size and simply divides into two halves.

Plant or Animal?

Some of the simplest creatures in the world are known as flagellates. They have one or more whip-like hairs, called flagella, which help them to swim about. Some flagellates, such as chlamydomonas, are clearly plants. Some are clearly animals. But others are right on the border-line between plants and animals. Euglena is one of these border-line creatures. There are several different kinds, some of which feed like plants and some of which feed like animals. No-one knows whether these strange creatures are plants or animals. They are frequently called, in fact, plant-animals.

Marine Protozoans

Many protozoans live in the plankton of the sea. Two groups are of particular interest. These are the radiolarians and the foraminiferans. Both groups are related to amoeba, but they have shells around their bodies. The foraminiferans have chalky shells and the radiolarians have glassy shells, often with very delicate patterns. When the animals die the shells sink to the bottom, and some parts of the sea bed are covered with shell layers.

Disease-causing Protozoans

Many protozoans live inside the bodies of other animals and cause illness or disease. Sleeping sickness, a dreadful disease carried by African tsetse flies, is caused by flagellate protozoans called trypanosomes. Malaria is another serious disease caused by protozoans. It is carried by mosquitoes.

Some of the small plants and animals (not all protozoans) which can be found in the sea.

The Reef Builders

Below: Coral begins as a single polyp. New polyps branch off and the skeleton grows up around them.

Bottom: A reef with several different kinds of coral.

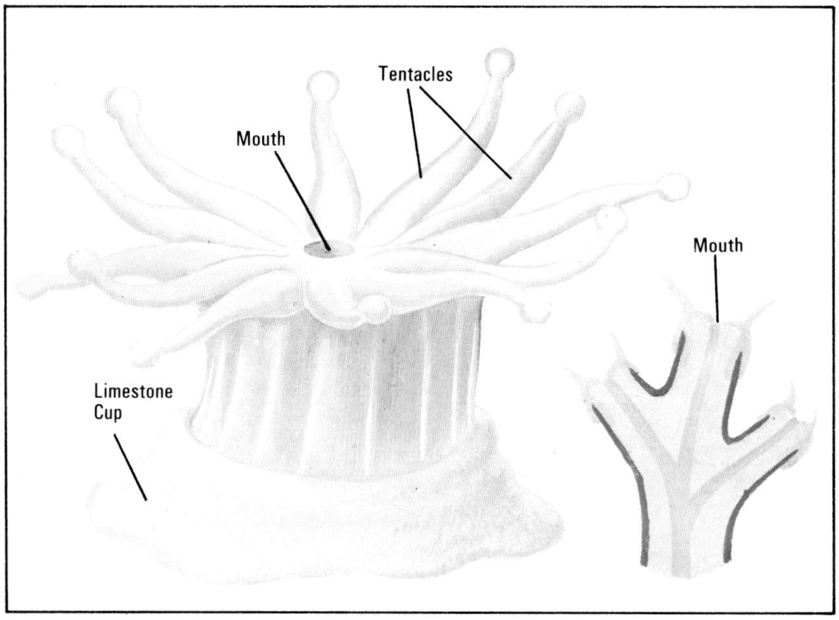

Coral reefs occur in many of the warmer seas of the world. The most famous reef is the Great Barrier Reef off the coast of Queensland in Australia. This is hundreds of kilometres long and several kilometres wide in places. It is hard to believe that such a massive structure has been built almost entirely from the skeletons of the tiny animals called corals.

Corals are coelenterate animals closely related to the sea anemones. The main difference between the two is that the corals form limestone skeletons around themselves. Some corals live by themselves, but the majority live in colonies built up by the repeated branching of one individual and its offspring. These colonies may be several metres across and they are the basis of the coral reefs.

The body of a coral animal is just like a tiny sea anemone—a hollow tube with a number of tentacles surrounding the mouth. It is called a polyp. Some polyps reach a few centimetres across, but the majority are about the size of a grain of rice. They are often brightly coloured. The skeleton is deposited around the base of the polyp in the form of a little cup. Inside the cup there are numerous vertical plates of limestone. These are easily seen when the coral withdraws into the cup or when the coral dies.

The coral polyps feed on small crustaceans and other animals, which are trapped by the tentacles. These tentacles are armed with stinging cells just like those of the jellyfish and sea anemone. They quickly paralyse small animals and the tentacles then carry the food to the mouth. Many reef-building corals contain green algae in their bodies. This is probably a symbiotic arrangement (see page 133) and it seems likely that the algae remove waste products from the polyps.

Corals and sea anemones reproduce by scattering eggs and sperms into the water. The eggs settle down to grow into new polyps. The new polyps form branches and the whole colony grows. The older polyps die, but their skeletons remain to support the rest of the colony.

The Distribution of Coral Reefs

Solitary corals are found in most of the seas of the world, but the colonial species are found only in warm waters and the reef-formers are confined to areas in which the sea temperature never falls below 21°C (70°F). Reefs are not found everywhere inside the tropics. Cold currents prevent them from growing along the west coasts of Africa and South America. Reef-forming corals also need clear water, and so they do not grow where rivers discharge mud into the sea.

The Formation of Reefs

There are three main kinds of coral reef. Fringing reefs grow close to the shore. Barrier reefs grow farther away from the shore and are separated from it by lagoons. Atolls are little coral islands, usually horseshoe-shaped with a lagoon in the centre. Fringing reefs and barrier reefs are probably just two stages in reef development. The reef would start to grow close to the shore and it would gradually rise up. Growth of the reef is most vigorous at the outer edge, where the waves bring plenty of food and oxygen. This part would rise to the surface first and the waves might pile broken coral on top of it to form a ridge. This would protect the inner region even more and sediment would begin to settle. The sediment would kill the corals and the inner part of the reef would break down. The outer part would continue to grow outwards and, especially if accompanied by a gradual sinking of the land, it would eventually form a barrier reef. Atolls could be formed in the same way if the central island sank below the waves. Alternatively, atolls could grow up on submerged platforms. They would become ring-shaped because the inner part would not receive enough food and it would die. The same would happen to the sheltered part of the ring, and it would become horseshoe-shaped.

Whatever the type of reef, living corals form only its outer coat. The rest is made of the compacted skeletons and other materials, such as shell fragments, that become cemented together. The reef is very hard and a danger to ships, although some fishes crunch up living corals as food. Dead coral is cut into blocks for building in some parts of the world.

The corals are the main reef-building organisms, but many others contribute their skeletons to the reef. Some algae are particularly important in this respect, while sponges and shellfishes also provide material. As you might expect, the reef provides food and shelter for a great many other creatures. Fishes abound around them, feeding on the corals themselves or on the other plants and animals. Starfishes also enjoy a meal of corals, and one species, known as the crown of thorns, appears to be destroying parts of the Great Barrier Reef. Once the living coral is removed, there is nothing to prevent the erosion of the coral rock underneath.

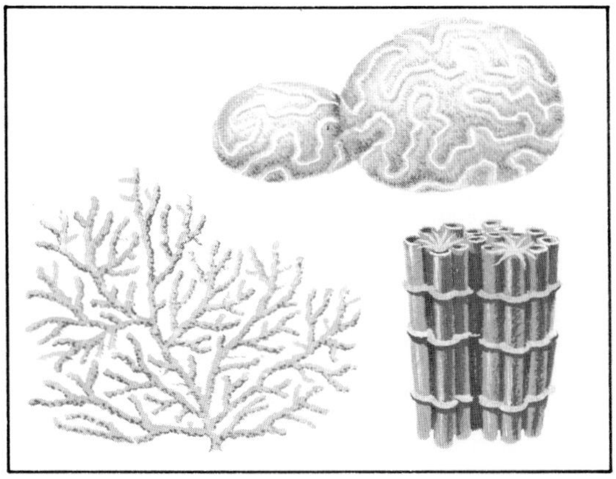

Some of the different kinds of coral.

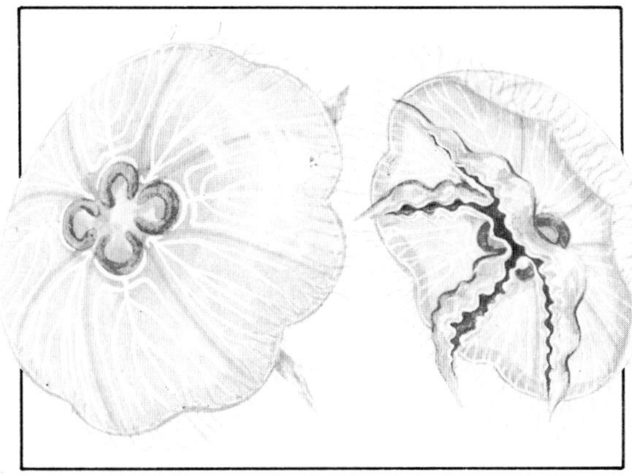

Jellyfishes are free-floating coelenterates distantly related to the corals and sea anemones. If you imagine a sea anemone turned upside down and floating freely, you will see the similarity. Jellyfishes normally have numerous tentacles and most of them have powerful stinging cells with which they catch small fishes and other animals. The Portuguese man-o'-war, however, is not a true jellyfish. It is really a colony of animals more closely related to hydra.

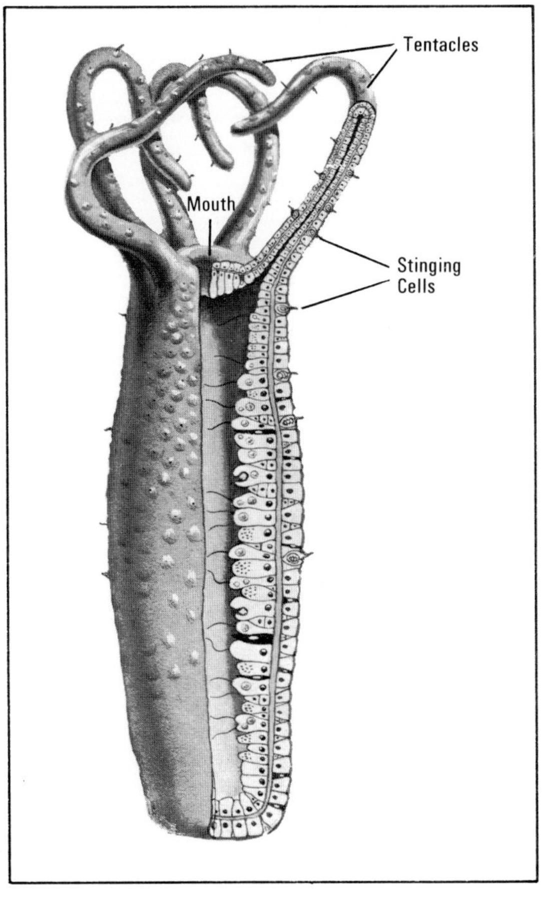

Stinging Cells
The stinging cells of the coelenterate animals are found mainly on the tentacles. Each one consists of a fluid-filled bag with a coiled thread inside. When the 'trigger' is touched, the thread is fired out. There are several kinds of threads. Some simply coil around the hairs of the small creature that touches them. Some are sticky, and some actually penetrate the animal and inject poison. The threads all combine to trap the prey and the tentacles then carry it to the mouth.

Hydra is a small freshwater coelenterate, rather similar to the sea anemones although only distantly related.

Worms and Leeches

We use the name worm for a whole range of long and slender creatures. They belong to many different groups, but the most important are the flatworms, the round worms and the segmented worms or annelids.

The Earthworm

The segmented worms or annelids get their name because their bodies are divided up into a number of little rings or segments.

The kinds of earthworms vary in length and in the number of segments. The adult worm has a thickened region called the 'saddle' in the front half of the body, but otherwise the segments are all more or less alike. The front end of the animal is normally pointed, and the hind end is often somewhat flattened. The animal has no eyes, although its whole body is sensitive to light and it quickly burrows into the soil when disturbed.

Each segment apart from the first and last has four pairs of tiny bristles on the lower surface, which you can feel. They help the worm to move.

Feeding and Reproduction

Earthworms feed on decaying matter. They will often pull dead leaves down into the soil, but they get much of their food simply by swallowing the soil as they tunnel. The undigested soil particles are passed out as worm casts on or near the surface of the soil. The worms thus perform a very useful ploughing action, bringing mineral-rich subsoil up to where the plants can use it. The depositing of worm casts on the surface means that objects are gradually buried by the worms. Rocks on the surface of the ground sink at a rate of about 15 centimetres every century and this is why we do not find stones under old lawns and meadows. Worms can swallow only tiny particles of soil and so the material deposited at or near the surface is very fine.

The earthworm has both male and female organs in its body. The animals have to pair up, however, before they can reproduce. They lie close together, surrounded by a coating of slime, and exchange sperms.

The sperms are stored in special pouches and the worms separate. Eggs develop in each individual and, when they are ripe, they pass back to the saddle. A cylinder of skin breaks away from the saddle and works its way forward with the eggs. It then receives sperms from the other worm and the eggs are fertilized. The cylinder of skin then comes right away and becomes wrapped around the eggs to form a cocoon.

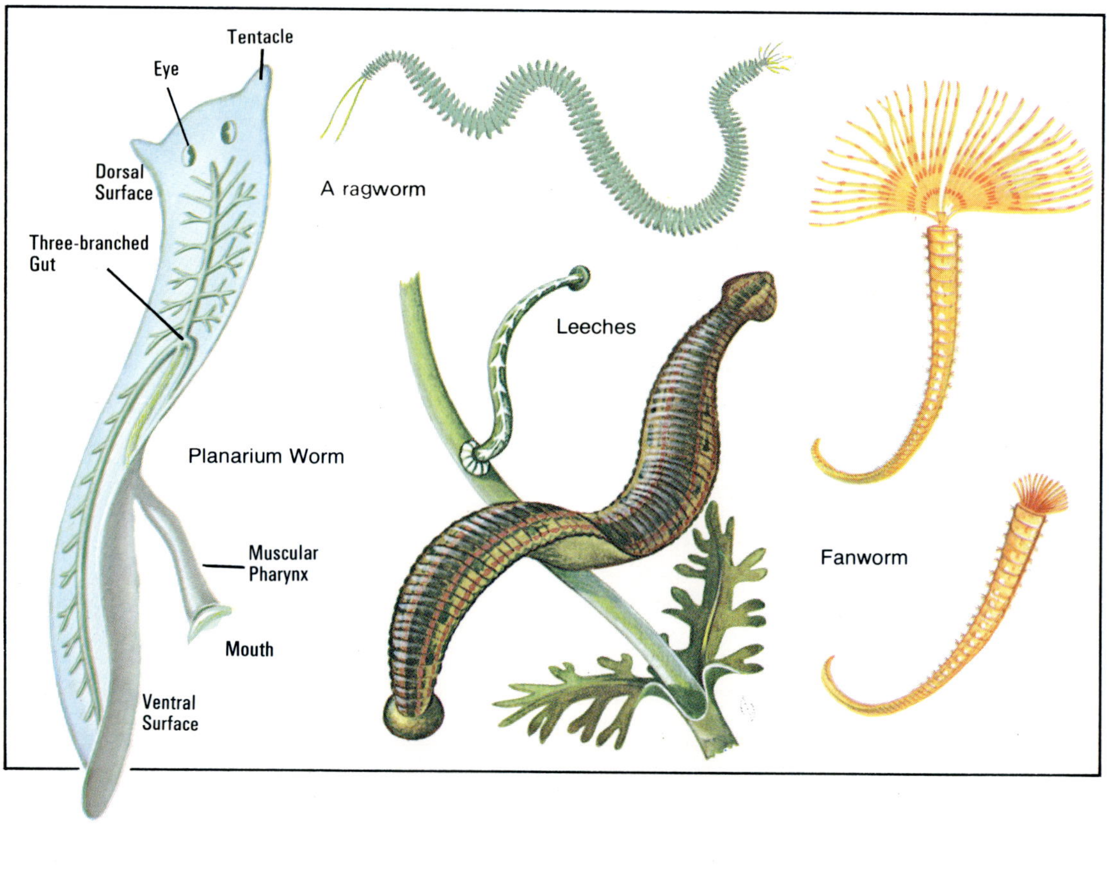

Planarian worms glide about in water, propelled by the beating of thousands of minute hairs. They have simple eyes on the head, but the mouth is near the middle of the body and is pushed out on the end of a tube. The digestive system sends branches to all parts of the body.

Leeches can be recognised by the large suckers at each end.

Fan worms are bristle worms that live in tubes. Bristles at the head end form a fan which traps food particles. The fan is quickly withdrawn if the animal is disturbed.

Bristle Worms

Bristle worms are marine annelids, many of which have long bristles on most of their segments. Ragworms are free-living creatures and they have well developed heads with eyes and jaws. Other bristle worms live buried in the mud or sand or else they form tubes of sand or limestone. The lugworm burrows in the mud and the peacock worm forms tubes of sand grains. It has a crown of special bristles around the mouth and these trap particles of food floating in the water. The tentacles are rapidly withdrawn if the animal is disturbed.

Leeches

Unlike the other annelids, the leeches have no bristles. They are readily identified by the large sucker at each end of the body. Some live in the sea and some live in damp soil, but most leeches live in fresh water. Some of them eat other small aquatic creatures. Other leeches are blood suckers, attaching themselves to various animals and taking two or three times their own weight of blood for one meal. The blood is stored in special pouches and is digested very slowly. The blood-feeding leeches can go for very long periods without a feed. Leeches reproduce in the same way as earthworms.

Flatworms and Roundworms

The flatworms include the little planarian worms that glide about the ponds, propelled by the beating of thousands of minute hairs called cilia. The flatworms also include the flukes and tapeworms, parasites that live inside the bodies of other animals.

Roundworms, or nematodes, have cylindrical bodies. Many of them live as parasites inside other animals or plants. Those living in plants often cause serious diseases and they are known as eelworms. Most of the roundworms, however, live in the soil or in water. Most can be seen only with a microscope.

The earthworm moves its body forward in stages. While one region is being extended the other parts are anchored by the little bristles sticking out from the underside of the animal. The bristles also help to anchor the worm in its burrow.

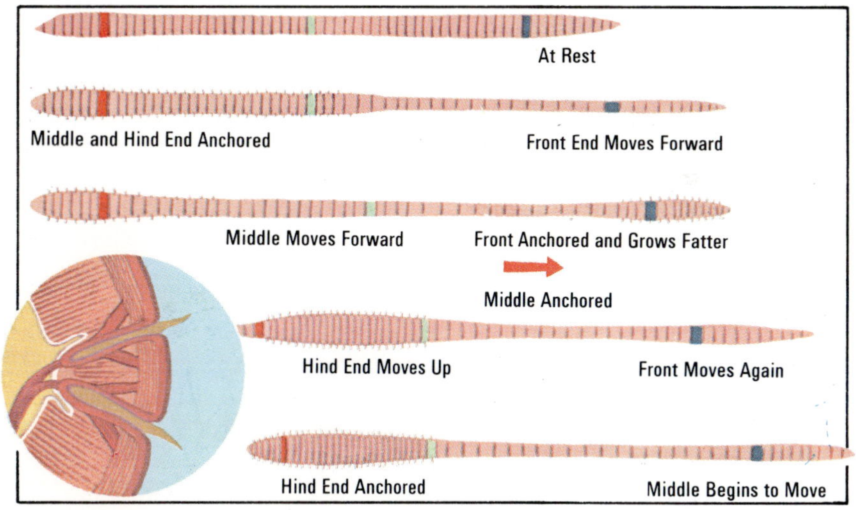

Left: Lug-worms taken out of their burrows.

Crabs and Their Relatives

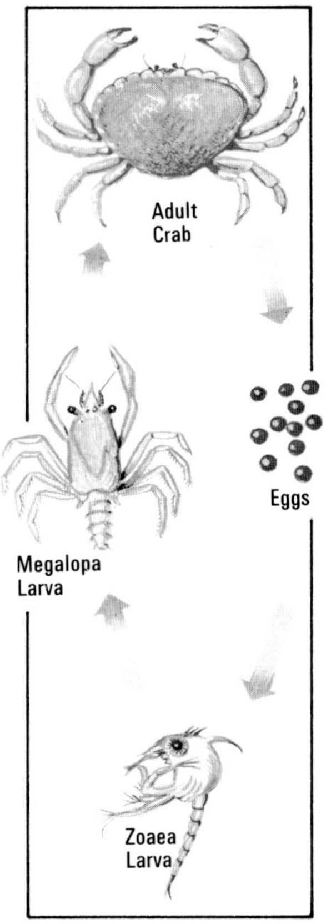

Crabs have a complex life cycle (above), involving stages that look nothing like the adult crab. If a crab's limb is broken off, it can grow another when it moults (below).

Crabs, lobsters, shrimps, woodlice and barnacles belong to the large group of arthropods known as the crustaceans. This name refers to the hard, chalky coat which covers most of the animals.

Nearly all crustaceans live in water. This fact distinguishes them from most other arthropods, but there are other differences as well. For example, the crustaceans have two pairs of feelers or antennae, although one pair may be rather small. Many have a 'shell' covering all or part of the body. It is called the carapace which becomes as hard as stone in some animals. There are usually many pairs of limbs of several different types.

The crustaceans range from minute floating creatures to lobsters weighing 13 kg and crabs with legs more than 1.5 metres long. Many live in fresh water, but the majority live in the sea. They make up a large part of the animal plankton—the drifting animals in the surface layers. Some of the crustaceans live permanently in the plankton. These include the shrimp-like creatures called krill which form the bulk of the diet of the large whalebone whales. Another important planktonic crustacean is called calanus. It is a relative of the little freshwater cyclops and it is the main food of the herring and other shoaling fishes. Many other crustaceans live in the plankton only during the early part of their lives. Crabs and lobsters all have floating larvae.

Filter Feeders

The little fairy shrimps have many pairs of broad, hinged limbs which filter food particles from the water while they 'row' the animal along. The limbs also act as gills and absorb oxygen from the water. Related to the fairy shrimps are the water fleas, the little reddish-brown creatures that are very common in ponds. The trunk limbs are enclosed by the carapace and beat to draw a current of water through the carapace. Food and oxygen are obtained from the water. The animals swim by 'rowing' with their large second pair of antennae. This produces a jerky upward movement, from which the animals get their name.

There are usually some little pear-shaped creatures called copepods in the pond. There are several different kinds, but cyclops is the commonest. Some copepods filter food from the water, but cyclops picks up individual pieces with its mouth-parts. Like the water fleas, it can swim by beating its antennae, but it also swims more rapidly by paddling with its tiny trunk limbs. Female copepods can easily be recognised by the little egg sacs they carry at the hind end.

Barnacles

The little white tent-like barnacles that we see at the seaside do not look like crustaceans. Their young stages are just like the

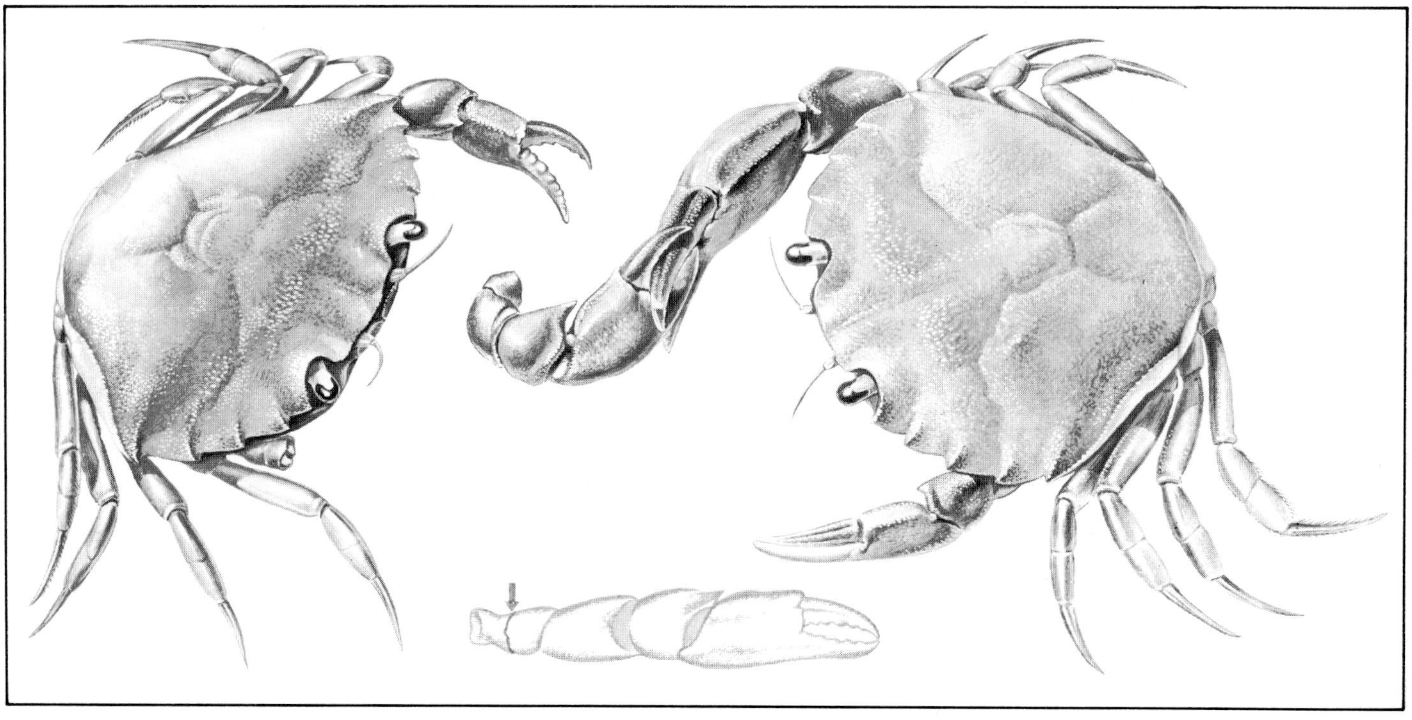

young of crabs and they show that barnacles really are crustaceans. The common barnacle of the shore closes its 'tent' when the tide goes out. It opens it again when the water returns and the animal starts to 'comb' food from the water by pushing its delicate limbs out into the water.

Crabs, Shrimps and Lobsters

These creatures are often known as decapods because they have ten walking legs. Not all of them are used for walking. At least one pair is modified to form pinchers. These are very large in some crabs and lobsters and are used for signalling as well as for catching food. The animals are mainly carnivorous and take both living and dead material. The decapods breathe by means of gills, which are leaf-like or feathery outgrowths of the body wall or the leg bases. The gills are enclosed by the carapace and they are provided with a current of water by the continuous movement of some of the limbs of the head.

Crabs are relatively short, broad creatures, in which the abdominal or tail region is small and folded tightly under the front part of the body. Most crabs walk or scuttle sideways on the sea-bed, although some have broad legs and are able to swim. The shrimps, prawns and lobsters have relatively longer bodies and their abdominal regions are clearly visible. There are several pairs of abdominal legs called swimmerets, which are used as paddles. The abdominal legs are also used to hold the eggs. If you eat shrimps or prawns you have probably seen individuals with their hind regions covered with eggs. In this condition they are said to be in berry.

Woodlice

The woodlice are the only group of crustaceans that have successfully invaded the land. They belong to a group called isopods. Woodlice are flattened, oval creatures a couple of centimetres long. Most of them are greyish in colour. They have seven pairs of walking legs and a number of leaf-like abdominal limbs towards the back. Although they live on the land, the woodlice cannot survive in very dry conditions. They need moisture to enable them to absorb oxygen through their abdominal limbs. Some species, however, have developed breathing tubes rather like the insects' tracheae. These species can survive in drier places. Some of them can roll themselves into a ball and this also helps them to survive dry periods. Most woodlice live under logs and stones. They feed on decaying material. Not all members of the group live on the land. The sea-slater lives on the sea-shore, although it is almost a land animal. Another member, known as the hog louse, lives in ponds and streams.

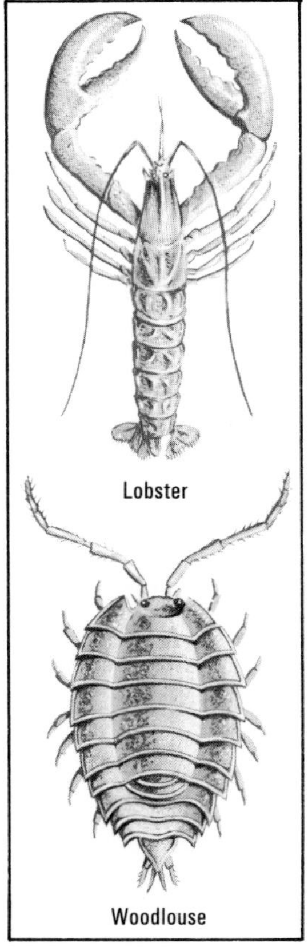

Top: A lobster, a marine crustacean with large claws for tearing up food.

Bottom: A woodlouse, the only land-living crustacean, which lives in damp places.

Left: These barnacles coating a glass float look rather lifeless out of the water, but when submerged by the tide the inner plates open up and out come the barnacle's limbs to comb food from the water.

The Insect World

Dragonflies, butterflies, bees and beetles are just four of the many groups that make up the insect world—a world with more than a million different species and untold millions of individuals. The insects belong to the group of animals called the arthropods. This name means 'jointed feet', and if you look carefully at the leg of an insect you will see that it is made up of a number of joints or segments. In fact, the whole body is made up of segments. Some segments are tightly joined together, others are more loosely connected by soft membranes. The arthropods also include animals such as spiders, shrimps and centipedes. You can see the body segments very easily in a centipede. Insects can be distinguished from the other arthropods because they have three distinct regions of the body. These are the head, the thorax (in the middle), and the abdomen. The thorax bears three pairs of legs and it usually carries two pairs of wings as well. Insects also have a single pair of feelers, or antennae, on the head.

Insects can be found all over the earth — on the land and in the water, in the deserts and around the poles, but very few insects live in the sea.

One of the features that prevents the insects from getting very large is their method of breathing. Tiny tubes carry air from the surface to all parts of the body, but the system works only over short distances and so insects cannot get very fat. The fattest insect in the world is the goliath beetle from Africa. It is about the size of a fist and weighs about 100 grammes. At the other end of the scale there are minute beetles only about 0.2 millimetre long.

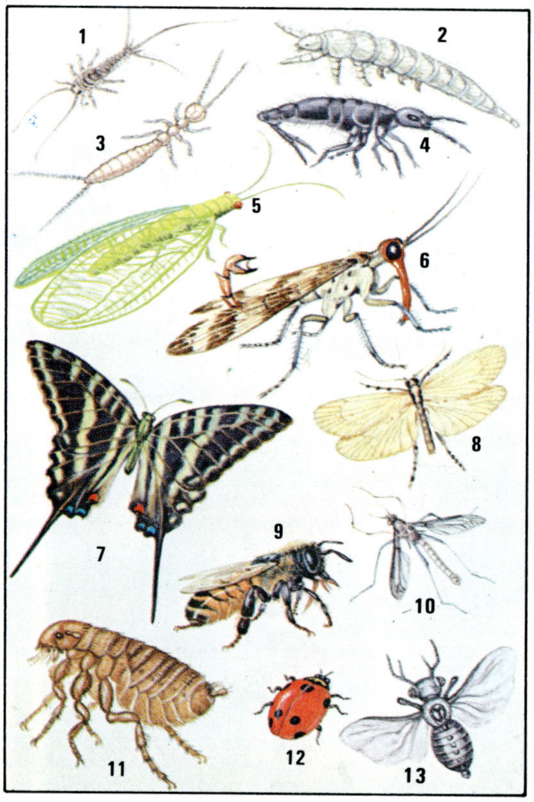

Some of the important insect groups. 1, Order Thysanura includes the bristletails and silverfish. 2 and 3, Orders Protura and Diplura contain small soil-living insects. 4, Order Collembola contains the springtails. 5, Order Neuroptera contains lace-wing flies. 6, Order Mecoptera includes scorpion flies. 7, Order Lepidoptera includes butterflies and moths. 8, Order Trichoptera includes caddis flies. 9, Order Hymenoptera includes bees, wasps and ants. 10, Order Diptera includes true flies. 11, Order Siphonaptera includes fleas. 12, Order Coleoptera includes beetles. 13, Order Strepsiptera includes internal parasites of bees.

Right: The beetle shows the major features of insect anatomy—three body sections, three pairs of legs, and one pair of feelers.

Insect Groups

There are about 30 major groups of insects, separated mainly by differences in the wings and the methods of feeding. Four groups contain rather primitive insects without wings. These include the little silverfish which is often found in dusty corners in houses. The other groups are basically winged insects although some of them have lost their wings like the fleas and lice. Some of the important insect groups are shown on this page.

Insect Life Histories

A young grasshopper shortly after it has left its egg looks like an adult grasshopper, except that it is much smaller and has no wings. It is called a nymph. It starts to eat grass and it soon gets too big for its tough outer coat or skeleton. The insect rests for a short while and then the outer coat splits. The insect then wriggles its way out. A new and larger coat has already grown beneath the old one, but it is rather soft to start with. The insect puffs itself up with air and continues to rest until the new coat has hardened. It then expels the air, leaving room for more growth. This process of skin-changing is called moulting and it takes place four times before the grasshopper is fully grown, and ready to breed.

After the first moult the grasshopper nymph begins to develop its wings. They appear as tiny flaps on the thorax. After the second moult the wing flaps are larger and after the third moult they are larger still, but they do not become fully formed until after the fourth moult. The insect is then a fully grown adult grasshopper and it does not change its skin any more. This sort of life history, in which the young insect gradually takes on the appearance of the adult, is also shown by dragonflies, earwigs, bugs and various other insect groups. The gradual change from young to adult form is called partial or incomplete metamorphosis.

Butterflies, bees, house-flies and beetles have a different kind of life history. The young stages of these insects are called grubs or caterpillars and they look nothing like the adult insects. Scientifically, they are called larvae, and they often eat quite different food from the adults. The larvae change their skins, just like the grasshopper nymphs, but there is no sign of wing flaps. Then, after two, three, four, or even more skin changes, the larvae turn into pupae or chrysalides. The pupae do not feed and they do not usually move much, but great changes are going on inside them. Instead of the young insect gradually taking on the adult form, the changes take place all at once inside the pupa. This abrupt change is called a complete metamorphosis. After a few days or a few months, depending on the type of insect, the adult

Below: The head of an aphid and (bottom) of a fly showing the compound eyes.

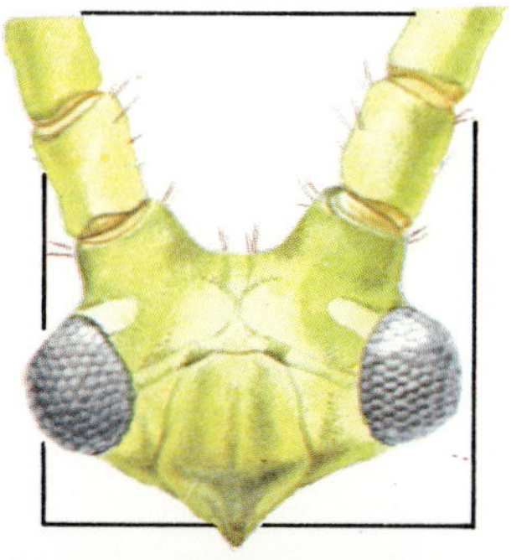

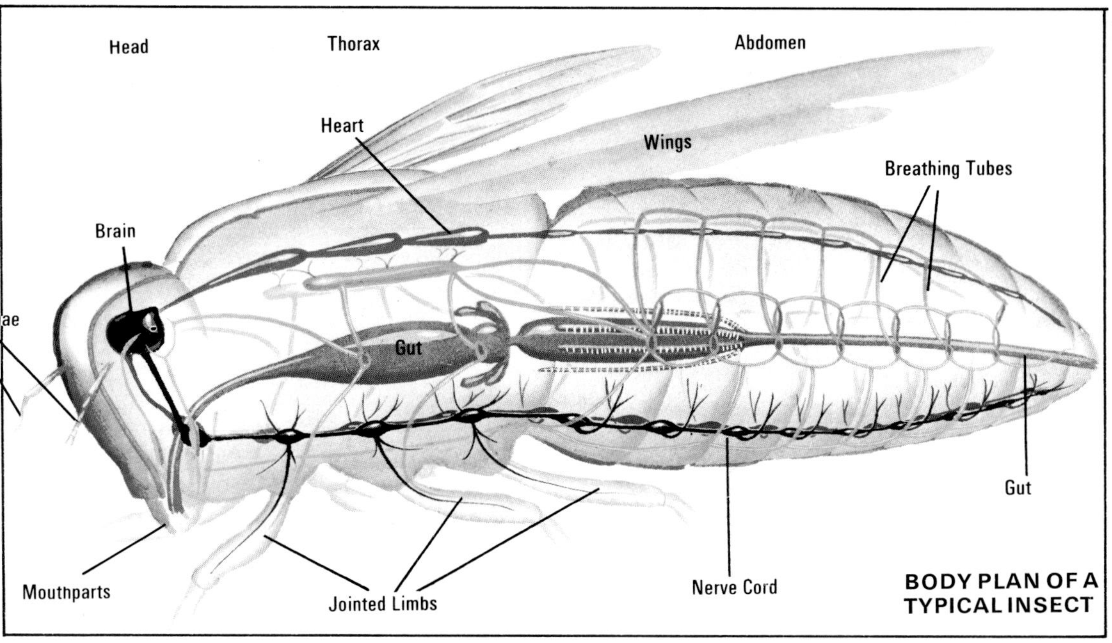

Right: Many insects, including moths and flies, have young stages which look nothing like the adults. The young stages are called larvae and they have to pass through a resting stage (the pupa) before they become adults.

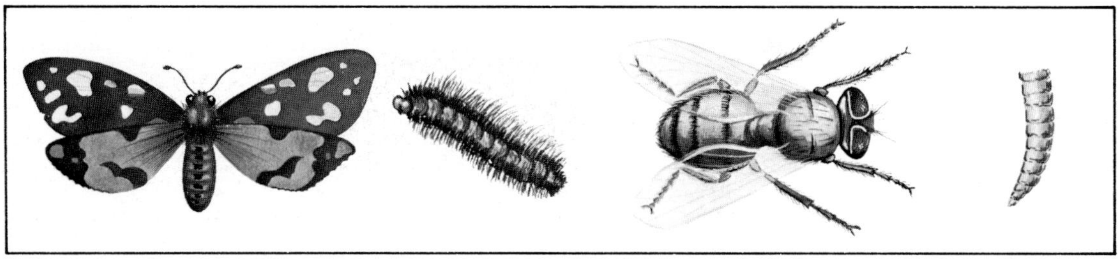

Far right: Ichneumon flies are insects whose young feed on other insects. Rhyssa, shown here, feeds on wood-boring grubs. The female has a long egg-laying tube she drills into the wood and lays an egg on the grub.

Right: Caddis flies are moth-like insects which spend their early days in water. The larvae have soft bodies (centre) but they protect themselves by building cases of sand grains or plant fragments (left).

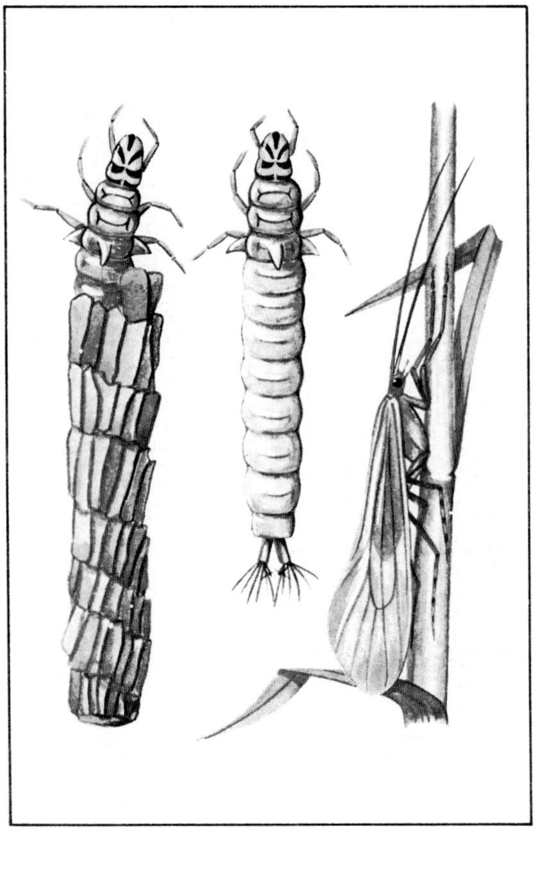

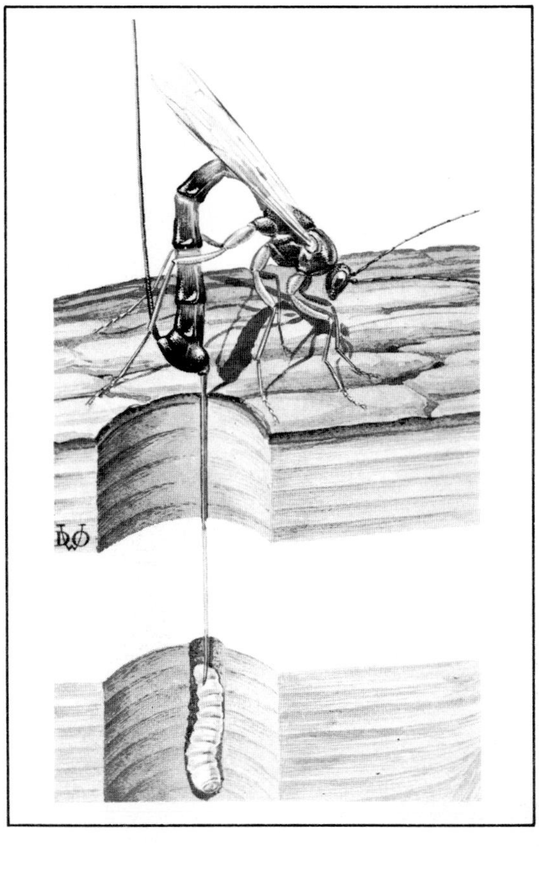

comes out of the pupa. Its wings are crumpled and its body is soft, but the wings soon expand and the body hardens.

Insect Diets

Many insects feed on plants and virtually no plant species in the world is not attacked by some insect. A whole lot more insects are carnivorous, which means that they feed on other animals. Dragonflies, bush crickets and ladybird beetles eat other insects. Fleas, bedbugs and mosquitoes all feed on much larger animals. Then there are the omnivorous insects that eat more or less anything they can find. The cockroaches are good examples. There can be few natural materials that are not eaten by one kind of insect or another.

Insect Mouth-parts

Many insects have biting jaws for eating solid food, including grasshoppers, beetles and wasps. The jaws are really very special legs just outside the mouth. They have sharp teeth and they cut the food into small pieces. Other 'legs' around the mouth help to hold the food and to push it into the mouth when it has been cut up. The jaws and the other feeding limbs are collectively known as the mouth-parts.

Butterflies, flies, fleas, bugs and some other groups feed on liquids. The butterfly mouth-parts form a long 'tongue', called a proboscis. When the insect finds a flower it unrolls its proboscis, pushes it into the flower and sucks up the nectar.

The mouth-parts of bugs and fleas are in the form of sharp needles which are sunk into the tissues of plants or other animals. The needles fit together to form narrow tubes through which the insects drink sap or blood. Many of these insects carry disease germs from one plant or animal to another.

Many flies have sharp, piercing mouth-parts which they use for sucking blood. The mosquito is a well known example, and others include the tsetse fly, the stable fly and the horse-fly. Like the fleas and bugs, many of them carry diseases from one animal to another. The house-fly and the bluebottle, however, have different kinds of mouths. Their mouth-parts form spongy pads and the insects mop up liquid food with them. Solid food can be dealt with by pouring digestive juices on to the food and then sucking up the resulting solution.

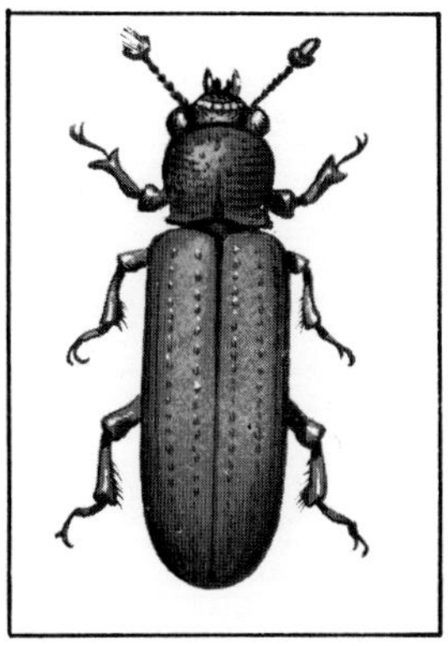

The powder post beetle is one of several species whose grubs do much damage by tunnelling into wood.

Below left: The house-fly mops up liquid food with its sponge-like tongue.
Below right: The dragonfly is a hunter throughout its life. The adult scoops flies from the air with its legs, while the larva has a clawed lower lip which it shoots out.
Left: The mosquito female is a blood sucker.

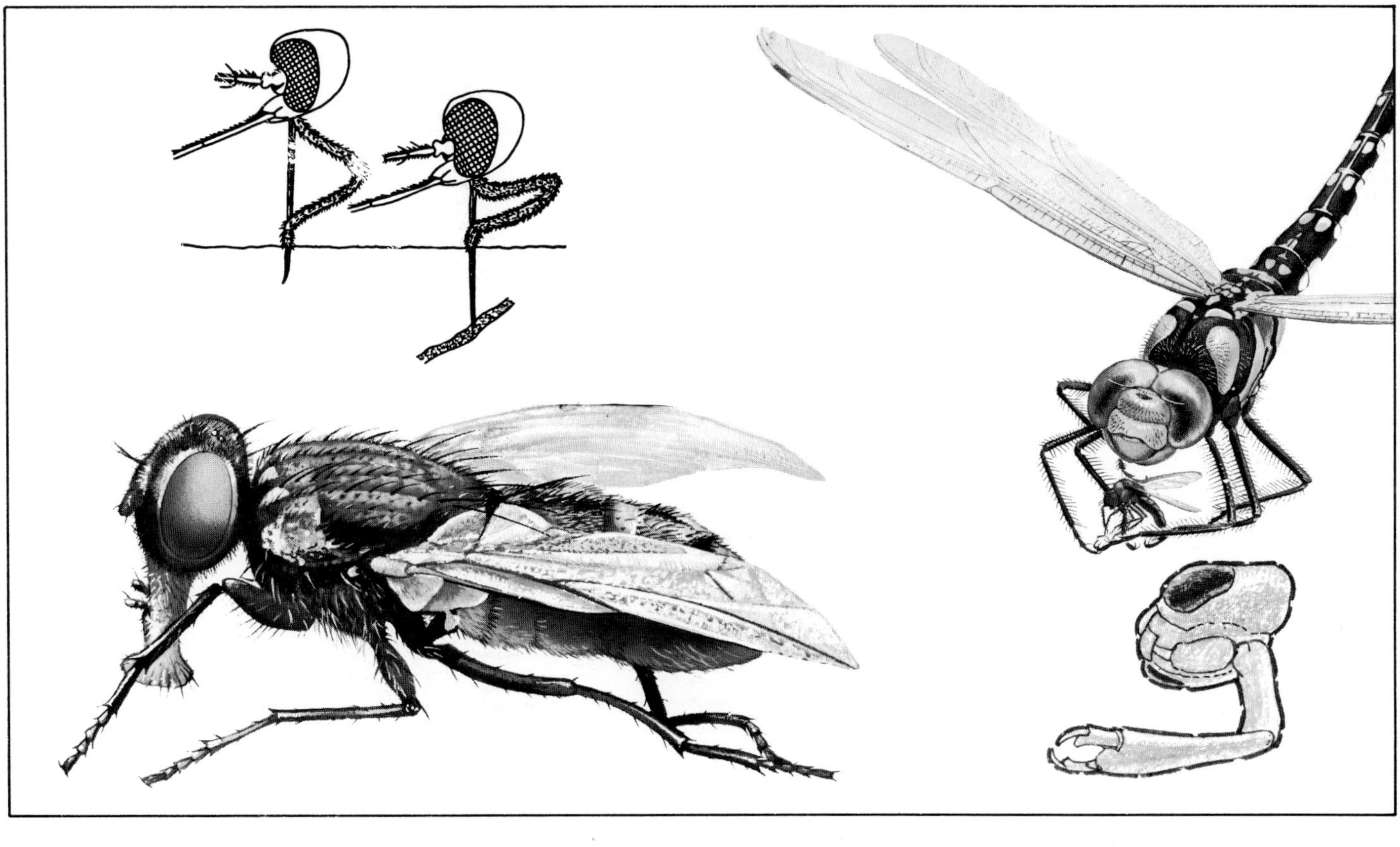

Butterflies and Moths

Above: Butterflies vary a great deal in shape and size.

Right: The colours of a butterfly's wing are produced by thousands of tiny overlapping scales which come off like dust if the wings are rubbed.

Butterflies and moths belong to a large group of insects called the Lepidoptera. This name means 'scale wings' since the whole wing is covered with tiny overlapping scales. It is these scales that give the wings their patterns. Some scales in male butterflies also give off scent which attracts the female.

The Lepidoptera is one of the largest groups of insects and contains something like 100,000 different species. The butterflies account for relatively few species out of this total, the rest belong to various families of moths. There is an enormous size range within the moths, from insects such as the giant owlet moth of South America (30 cm from wing tip to wing tip) to minute moths no more than 3 mm across.

There is not a simple distinction between butterflies and moths. It is often said that butterflies are brightly coloured and fly by day, whereas moths have dull colours and fly at night, but this is certainly not true for all of them.

The best way to distinguish a butterfly from a moth is to look at its feelers or antennae. All the butterflies have clubbed antennae. Moths have many different kinds of antennae, but rarely have clubbed tips. Those moths that do have clubbed antennae can be distinguished from butterflies by looking at the wings. The 'shoulder' of the hind wing carries a bristle, known as the frenulum, which fits into a little hook on the underside of the front wing. This arrangement holds the two wings together in flight. Butterflies do not have a frenulum. There are many moths without a frenulum, but these never have clubbed antennae and they cannot be confused with butterflies.

Reproduction

The butterflies and moths belong to that division of insects which pass through four distinct stages in their life history and undergo a complete change, or metamorphosis, during that time. The first stage, as with all insects, is the egg. The eggs are usually laid on the insect's food plant and they are often beautifully patterned. A caterpillar develops inside the egg and, when it is ready, it chews its way out. All caterpillars have biting jaws and, with the exception of a few 'clothes moths' which feed on woollen material, are herbivores. Some feed inside the stems, roots and fruits of plants, but most of the caterpillars feed on the leaves. They are generally well protected by camouflage or by hairy coats, but vast numbers are eaten by birds. Many more fall victim to ichneumon flies and other parasites but some escape and, after about four skin changes, they are ready to enter the third stage of the life history.

Many caterpillars, especially those of moths, spin silken cocoons around themselves and attach them to the branches of the food plant. Others hollow out snug chambers in the soil, while many butterfly larvae simply attach themselves to a convenient support by a pad of silk. After a short rest, the caterpillar's skin splits and is pushed off to reveal the pupa or chrysalis. Inside the pupa, the caterpillar's body is broken down and rebuilt into the body of the adult insect. This may take as little as 10 days, but it is often nine months before the adult insect emerges. When the adult first crawls out through a split in the pupal skin it is very soft and its wings are tiny crumpled objects. Its first action is to climb up some support and hang itself up to dry. It pumps blood into the veins of the wings and they gradually expand to their full size. After a few hours they are hard enough to bear the insect away on its first flight.

Sight and scent both play a part in the courtship of butterflies and moths. Among butterflies it is the male who gives out the scent, but among moths it is usually the female. Some of the male moths have extremely sensitive 'noses' on their antennae and they can smell a female's scent from more than a kilometre away.

Feeding

A few moths have biting jaws, which they use for feeding on pollen, but the rest of the moths and the butterflies have lost their jaws. Their feeding apparatus, if they have any, consists of a slender tube which they use to suck nectar and other sweet substances. One sure way to encourage butterflies into your garden is to plant aubretia, Michaelmas daisies and other plants with plenty of nectar.

The majority of butterflies and moths are quite harmless in the garden, and many are very useful because they pollinate the flowers and help them to set seed. There are some species, however, which are garden pests. This is because of the damage caused by the caterpillars which feed on leaves. The 'cabbage whites', for example, are found in most parts of the world and their caterpillars destroy large amounts of valuable greenstuff. Bufftip moth and lackey moth caterpillars do much damage to fruit trees by stripping them of their leaves. The gypsy moth, a European species, created havoc in the American forests when it found its way to North America some years ago. Another common pest is the codling moth, whose caterpillars are the 'maggots' so often found inside apples, which have not been sprayed.

Bright colours will not always distinguish butterflies from moths—the tiger moth at the bottom is just as bright as the fritillary butterfly. The antennae are a better guide: almost all butterflies have distinctly clubbed antennae.

Insect Pests

A variety of troublesome pests: house-fly, cockroach and Colorado beetle (above); cabbage-white butterfly caterpillars and grain weevils attack crops; woodworm attacks furniture and mosquitoes bite warm-blooded animals, including humans.

Clothes moths eat our clothes and carpets, furniture beetles (woodworms) tunnel through our furniture, grain weevils destroy stored grain, caterpillars eat our cabbages, mosquitoes spread malaria and house-flies contaminate our food. These are just some of the insect pests which man has to put up with.

Domestic Pests

One of the commonest household insects is the house-fly, although it is less common today than it used to be. The house-fly breeds in all sorts of rubbish but it is especially fond of horse dung. This was probably its original home, but it now finds suitable breeding sites in the dustbins and rubbish tips of human settlements. The adults lay their eggs on the rubbish and they also feed there to some extent. Then they might fly to our tea-table and contaminate our food with germs picked up on the rubbish dump. The use of insecticides, together with better methods of refuse disposal, has reduced the house-fly population in recent years.

Clothes moths are small insects whose caterpillars feed on woollen articles. There are several different kinds. Many of the clothes moths have been found in the nests of birds and rodents, where they feed on scraps of feather and fur. It is quite natural, therefore, that they should invade the homes of man in search of similar materials. Carpet beetles have had much the same sort of history.

The furniture beetle or woodworm and the much larger death-watch beetle have always made their homes in dead wood. Originally, their larvae tunnelled in dead tree trunks and helped to break them down and return the material to the soil. The beetles still do use tree trunks out in the wild, but they are also quite happy to feed on our furniture and floor-boards.

Carriers of Disease

Mosquitoes, tsetse flies, fleas and lice are all responsible for carrying disease-causing germs. They are blood-sucking insects and if they take in germs when they feed on one person they are quite likely to inject some into a later victim. The germs undergo changes in the insect's body and they are associated with just one kind of insect. Malaria, for example, is carried only by certain kinds of mosquitoes, while sleeping sickness is normally carried by tetse flies.

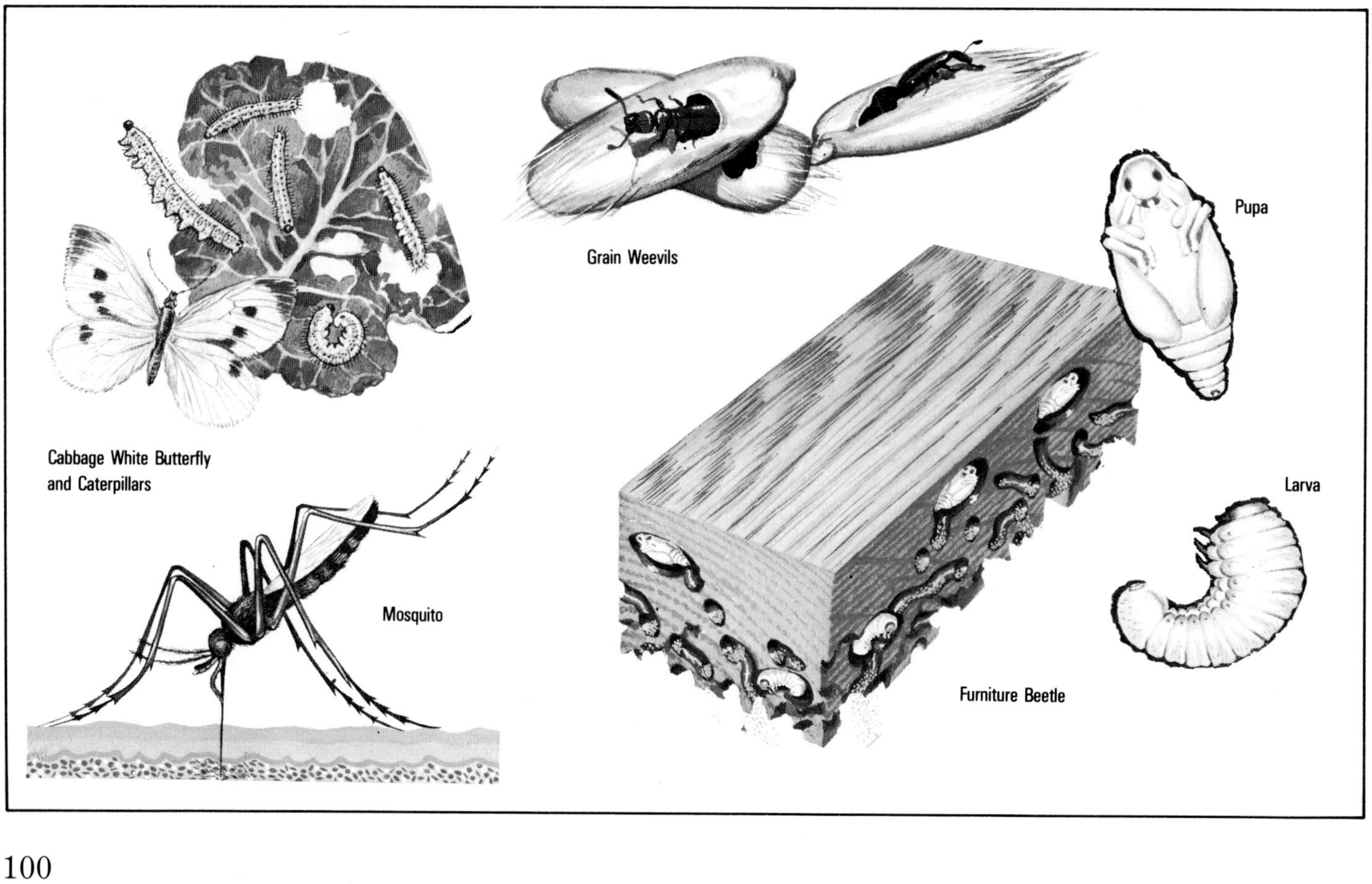

Crop Pests

A great deal of the world's food is lost every year because insects eat it or damage it while it is growing in fields and gardens. The insects existed long before we started to grow crops, and it is because we grow large amounts of crops that the insects can multiply and become pests. The Colorado beetle is a good example of this. It came originally from the western parts of North America, where it fed on wild plants and did no harm to anyone. Around the middle of the nineteenth-century, people started to grow potatoes in the region, and from then on the Colorado beetle has been a pest. The potato plant is related to the wild plants on which the beetle fed. Consequently the Colorado beetle soon transferred its attention to the potatoes. Surrounded by abundant food it was able to increase its numbers and to spread out from its original home. Potatoes were being grown over much of the United States, and within 20 years the beetle had reached the east coast of America. It got into Europe attached to some imported plants and it is now a pest nearly all over Western Europe.

Aphids—greenfly and blackfly—are probably the most serious of the insect pests. There are many different kinds and they affect a whole range of plants. They weaken the plants by sucking sap from them, but they do even more damage by carrying virus diseases from plant to plant. These diseases may eventually kill the plant.

Controlling Pests

There are two main ways of controlling insect pests. One way is to use insecticides, which are insect-killing poisons. They usually kill the pests well enough, but there is also the danger that they will kill useful insects such as bees as well.

The other way of controlling pests is known as biological control. This means using the pests' natural enemies to keep their numbers down. It is not a very practical method for large-scale use because it is not easy to rear large numbers of the natural enemies. There have, however, been some notable successes with this method. Successful pest control has also been achieved by releasing sterilized males into infested areas.

Control of domestic pests is very much a matter of keeping things clean. House-flies can be kept down, for example, by ensuring that there is no rubbish left around in which they can breed.

The locust is perhaps the most destructive of all insects. There are several species and they affect all of the warmer parts of the world. Huge swarms with millions of individuals build up in the semi-desert areas and then migrate. Large swarms will strip every leaf for kilometres when they land, and when flying they may completely blot out the sun.

The Honey Bee

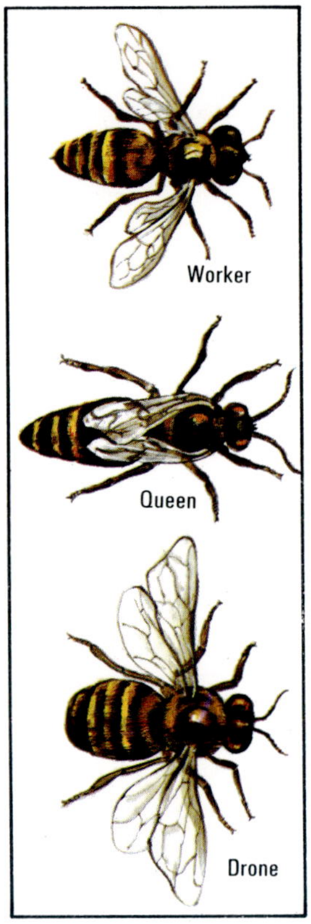

Most insects live alone but some of the bees and wasps and all of the ants and termites live in communities of many individuals. They are social insects and each individual works for the good of the whole community. A familiar social insect is the honey bee.

Ruled by the Queen

The honey bee colony is headed by the queen, who is larger than the other bees in the colony. She does nothing but lay eggs. Most of the bees in the colony are workers. They are females, but they are not fully developed and they cannot usually lay eggs. The workers look after the queen, feed and tend the young bees, build and clean the nest, and collect food. Although the workers do all the work, the smooth running of the colony is maintained by the queen. She produces an oily material called queen substance all over her body. The workers lick this off and spread it around themselves. It unites them and maintains the 'community spirit'. A third type of bee is produced in the colony during the summer. This is the male or drone bee. His job is to mate with a new queen.

Life in the Hive

The bees' nest consists of a number of 'combs' hanging vertically in the hive or tree. Each comb is composed of hundreds of little six-sided cells, all made of wax from the bees' bodies. The cells are used for storing pollen and honey and also for rearing the young. The queen wanders over the combs and lays an egg in each empty cell she finds. When the eggs hatch the workers begin to feed the grubs. For the first three days the grubs receive a substance called brood food. This is a protein-rich material made in the salivary glands of the young workers. After the first three days the grubs are fed on pollen and nectar. About six days later they turn into pupae, and the adult bees emerge about 10 days after that.

When they first emerge from their cells the

Right: The queen wanders over the combs and lays an egg in each empty cell she finds. She is always attended by workers, who lick her and touch her with their feelers to obtain queen substance.

young workers spend a few days doing 'housework' and feeding their younger sisters. Then, when their wax-making glands start to work, they take over the duties of making and repairing the combs. Not until three weeks after emerging from their cells do the young workers go in search of food.

The bees visit flowers and collect both pollen and nectar. While doing this they pollinate the flowers. This pollinating activity is more important to us than the honey that the bees provide, because without the bees to pollinate the blossoms we would be without many of the fruits and seeds that we eat. The bees carry pollen back to the hive in the pollen baskets on their back legs. Bees often can be seen almost weighed down by the yellow pollen masses on their legs. The nectar is carried back in a pouch of the food canal and it is then given up to other bees in the hive who remove much of the water from it and convert it into honey.

Bee Dances

The bees have ways of telling each other about good nectar sources that they have found. They come back to the hive and 'dance' excitedly on the combs. The type of dance tells the other bees where to find the nectar and off they go to look for it. They find their way by the sun and they even make allowances for the movement of the sun across the sky during the day.

Swarming

When the population in the hive gets too large the workers prepare for a swarm. They build special queen cells at the edge of the comb. These are larger than the ordinary cells and they look something like acorns. The queen lays an egg in each queen cell and the workers look after these eggs. The grubs in the queen cells, however, are fed on brood food for the whole of their larval life. The extra protein that they receive ensures that they become fully developed queens. The first queen to emerge from her cell kills the other developing queens and then goes on a marriage flight with one or more drones. She returns to the hive later to become queen. In the meantime her mother, the old queen, has left the hive with a swarm of workers to start a new colony somewhere else. A new queen is also reared when the old queen is becoming weak. The new queen returns to the hive and the old queen soon dies.

The queen honey bee normally lives for about three years and she lays over half a million eggs during this time. The workers live for only a few weeks during the summer, although those reared in the autumn will survive until the spring. Drones may live for several weeks during the summer, but they do not survive the winter. The workers refuse them food in the autumn and often throw them out of the hive to die. In winter the colony is quite small and it survives on the food stored up during the previous summer. Numbers build up again in spring when food becomes plentiful, and there may be 60,000 bees in the hive during the summer months.

Bumble bees are larger and more hairy insects than the honey bees. The main difference, however, is that the bumble bee colony lasts for only one year. New queens are produced in the summer and, after mating, they hibernate. The drones and the workers, however, die in the autumn.

Below: The bee keeper provides the bees with sheets of wax on wooden frames.

Bottom: The worker bees collect both pollen and nectar from flowers. The pollen is brushed into the pollen baskets on the back legs.

Ants and Termites

Above: The three castes of the wood ant.

Below left: The wood ant's nest has many galleries and chambers. The queen ant can be seen in her royal chamber at the centre.
Right: Weaver ants make small nests by sewing or gluing leaves together. They use the larvae rather like tubes of glue.
Top left: Parasol ants carrying leaf fragments.

There are more than 10,000 different kinds of ants, found in all but the coldest parts of the world. All ants live in colonies and, like the honey bee, the colony is headed by a mated female called the queen. Male ants are produced at certain times of the year, but most of the ants in a colony are wingless females, the workers. They are easily recognised by their narrow waists and by their 'elbowed' antennae. Many ant species, especially those living in warm countries, have more than one type of worker. Each type has a particular job to do. Many ant species also have an extra caste called a soldier. This is a large-headed ant whose job is to defend the colony with its large jaws. The ordinary workers help in the defence of the colony by using their stings and sharp jaws. Not all the species have stings, but some squirt formic acid at their attackers.

The typical features of ant life are shown by the little black garden ant, although this species does not have a soldier caste. Winged male and female ants are produced during the summer and, when the weather is just right, they emerge for their wedding flights. All the nests in an area release their flying ants together. The males die after the wedding flight, but the queens begin their duties as nest founders and mothers. They devote the rest of their lives to laying eggs. They may live for several years, although the workers do not live so long.

As well as building the nest, the workers collect food and look after the young ants. Plant and animal material is eaten, but many ants are particularly fond of honeydew. This is the sweet, sticky liquid given out by greenfly. You can often see ants running about on greenfly-infested roses and stroking the greenfly. This makes the greenfly give out honeydew, and the ant then takes it back to the nest. Some ants will actually take the greenfly back to their nests and install them in special chambers hollowed out around the plant roots. The greenfly feed on the plant roots and the ants 'milk' them without having to go out of the nest.

Some tropical ants make no permanent nests at all. They are called army ants. They settle down for short periods now and then to rear more young, but most of the time they are on the march. A marching colony may be several metres wide and hundreds of metres long, and kill any small animal which cannot get out of the way.

Many ants harvest seeds but some actually grow their own crops. These farming ants live in South America and they feed entirely on fungi which they grow on beds of chewed leaves in their nests. The workers go out and bring back pieces of leaves, waving them

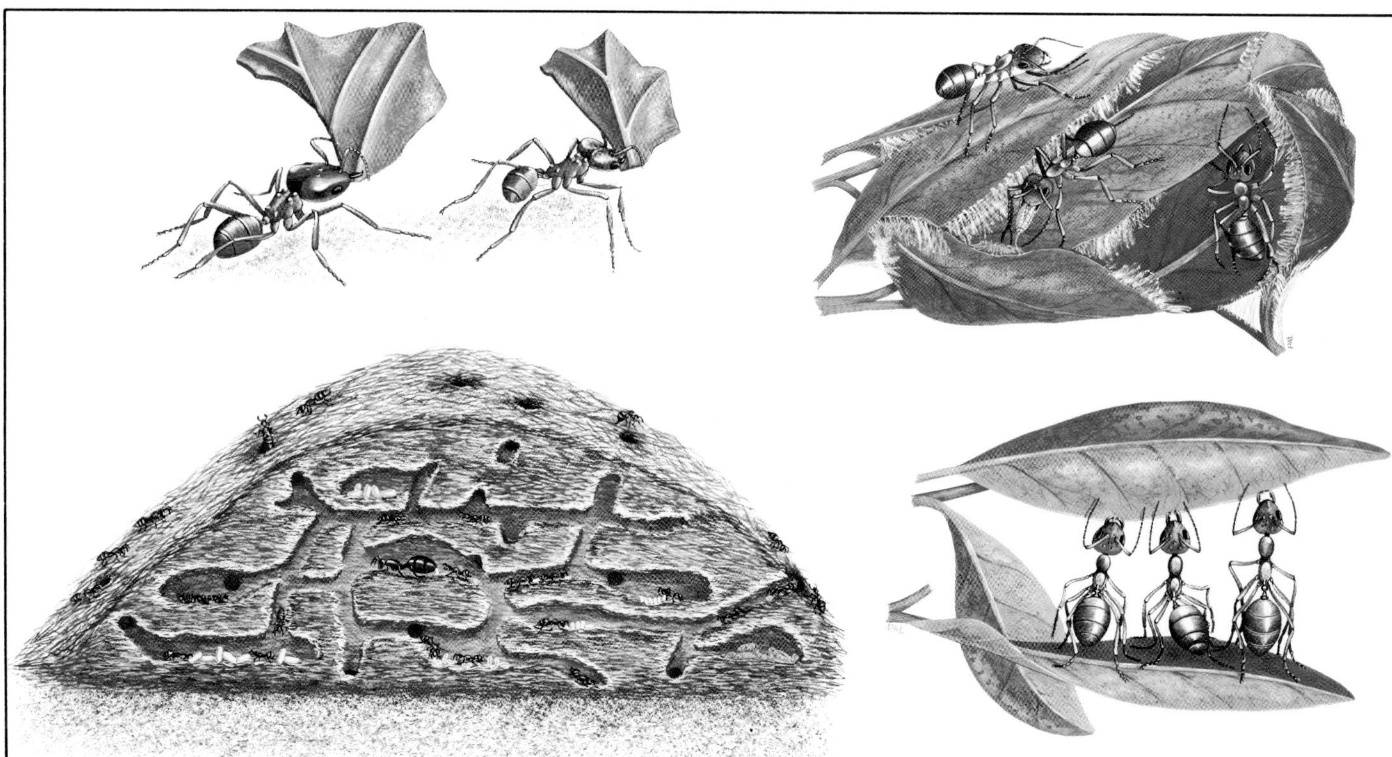

above their heads as they go. For this reason they are often called parasol ants.

Slave Makers

Some species of ants have no workers of their own. They are rather like cuckoos because they lay their eggs in the nests of other ants and rely on these ants to rear them. Other species have some workers of their own but rely on 'slaves' to do most of their work. Workers of the slave-making ants periodically raid the nests of other ants and bring back pupae. The ants that emerge from these pupae are the slaves.

Termites

Termites are often called white ants, but they are not related to the ants. Termites live in the warmer parts of the world and there are about 2,000 species. Two species live in southern Europe. They feed mainly on wood, and some species do great damage to trees and to buildings. Wood is not a very easy material to digest, and the termites enlist the help of tiny protozoans for this job. The protozoans live in the termite's food canal and digest the wood for it.

All the termites are social creatures and, unlike the ants, they have a king and a queen at the head of the colony. The workers (if any) and the soldiers are also of both sexes, whereas those of the ants are always females.

Termite colonies are started by both the king and the queen after they have had a short flight. They break off their wings and start to dig out a nest. The workers take over later and the royal couple retire to the royal chamber, where they may live for 50 years in some species. The most primitive termites make their nests in dead wood—usually in old tree trunks or logs. These termites do not have proper worker castes and the work of the colony is carried out by the young termites. They do have soldiers, however. Other termites make their nests under the ground, and the soil dug out may be heaped into huge mounds and cemented with the insects' saliva. These mounds are called termitaria and they are especially common in Australia and South Africa. They are very hard and they are full of tunnels and chambers. The termitaria not only protect the inhabitants from the climate outside, they also prevent attacks from all but the strongest animals.

Termites resemble the ants in that their workers and soldiers have no wings. The termites, however, have a much simpler life history and the young insects do not change much as they grow into adults.

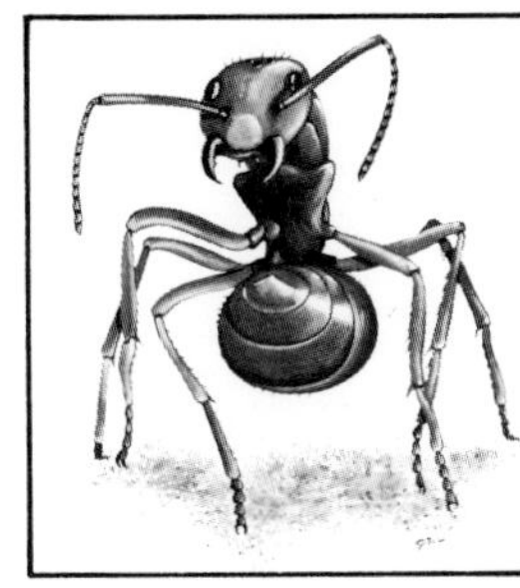

Above: Some ants can turn their hind ends forward and squirt acid at their attackers.

Below: The queen termite becomes a huge barrel-shaped creature full of eggs. The king rests on her back, while they are protected by a ring of large-headed soldiers.

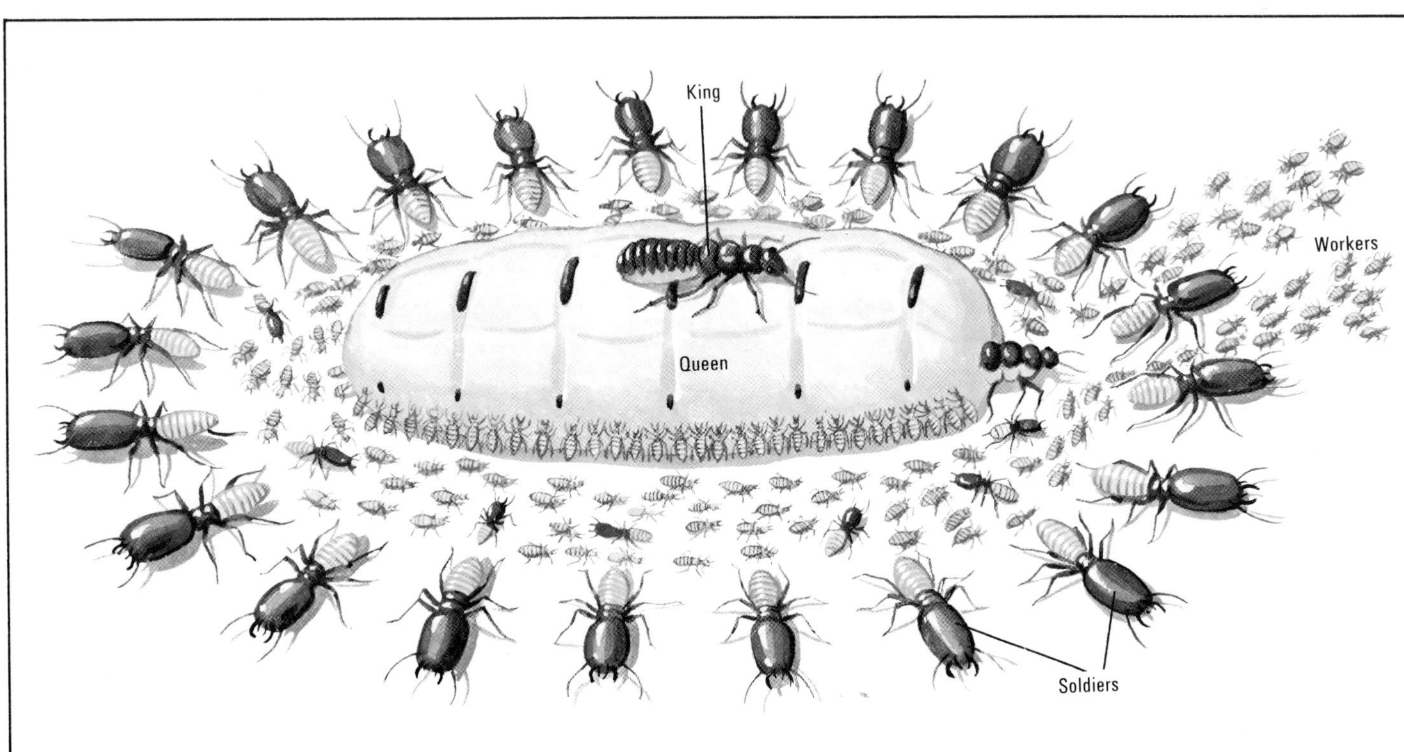

Spiders and Scorpions

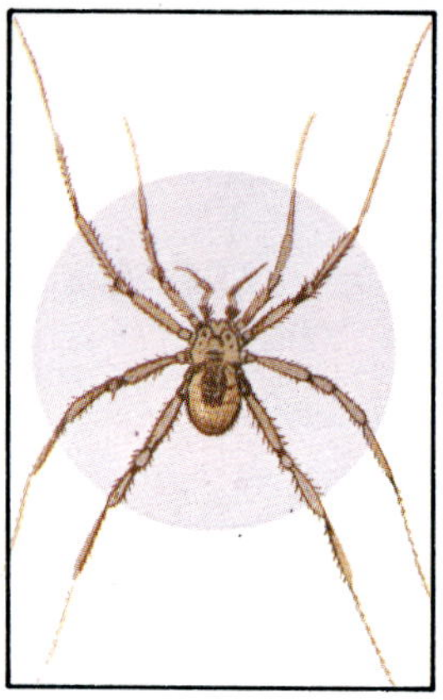

A harvestman, distinguished from spiders by the absence of a 'waist'.

Below: A selection of spiders showing the 'waist' and the four pairs of legs. What look like antennae are actually palps. They are swollen in male spiders. The black widow (bottom left) shows the 'hour-glass' mark on the underside.

Spiders and scorpions, together with mites, ticks and a few other animals, form the group of arthropods called arachnids. They normally have four pairs of walking legs and they have no antennae. These features easily distinguish the arachnids from the insects.

Spiders

The spider's body is divided into two regions. The front part bears several pairs of eyes and it also carries the legs. Around the mouth there is a pair of poison fangs and a pair of small leg-like structures called palps.

All spiders are carnivorous and they eat only freshly caught animals. Most spiders eat insects, but some of the larger ones eat birds, lizards and small mammals. The spider's venom is used to kill or paralyse the prey and digestive juices are then poured into the victim. The spider then proceeds to suck the victim dry. Spiders take only liquid food. Some are harmful to people, but most are unable to pierce human skin with their fangs.

The Spider's Web

Some spiders chase their prey, or lie in wait for it, but many of them make traps or snares. These are in the form of silken webs. There are many different kinds of webs, but the most fascinating are the circular orb-webs spun by the garden spider and its relatives. A spider starts its web by making a frame and a number of radii. The latter are threads which run out from near the centre, rather like the spokes of a wheel. The spider then moves round on the radii and leaves a rather open spiral of dry silk. Then, starting from the outside and using the first spiral as 'scaffolding', it lays down a tighter spiral of sticky silk. This is what traps the insects. The spider then retires to a little platform in the centre of the web or else it hides under a nearby leaf, ready to rush out as soon as an insect gets caught in the web.

All spiders produce silk, whether they make webs or not. It is used for wrapping up the eggs, and also as a life-line for a spider that falls from its home. It pays out a thread as it falls, and then simply climbs back up. Young spiders also use silk to help them to reach new areas. They let a strand blow in the breeze until it whisks them up into the air.

The silk is produced in the abdomen. The silk glands open through tiny pores called spinnerets. The silk is liquid to start with and it flows out like toothpaste from a tube, but it hardens as soon as it meets the air. Another gland adds the gum to make the silk sticky.

Male spiders are usually somewhat smaller than the females and they have to take great care when they go courting. They have an elaborate system of signals, such as waving

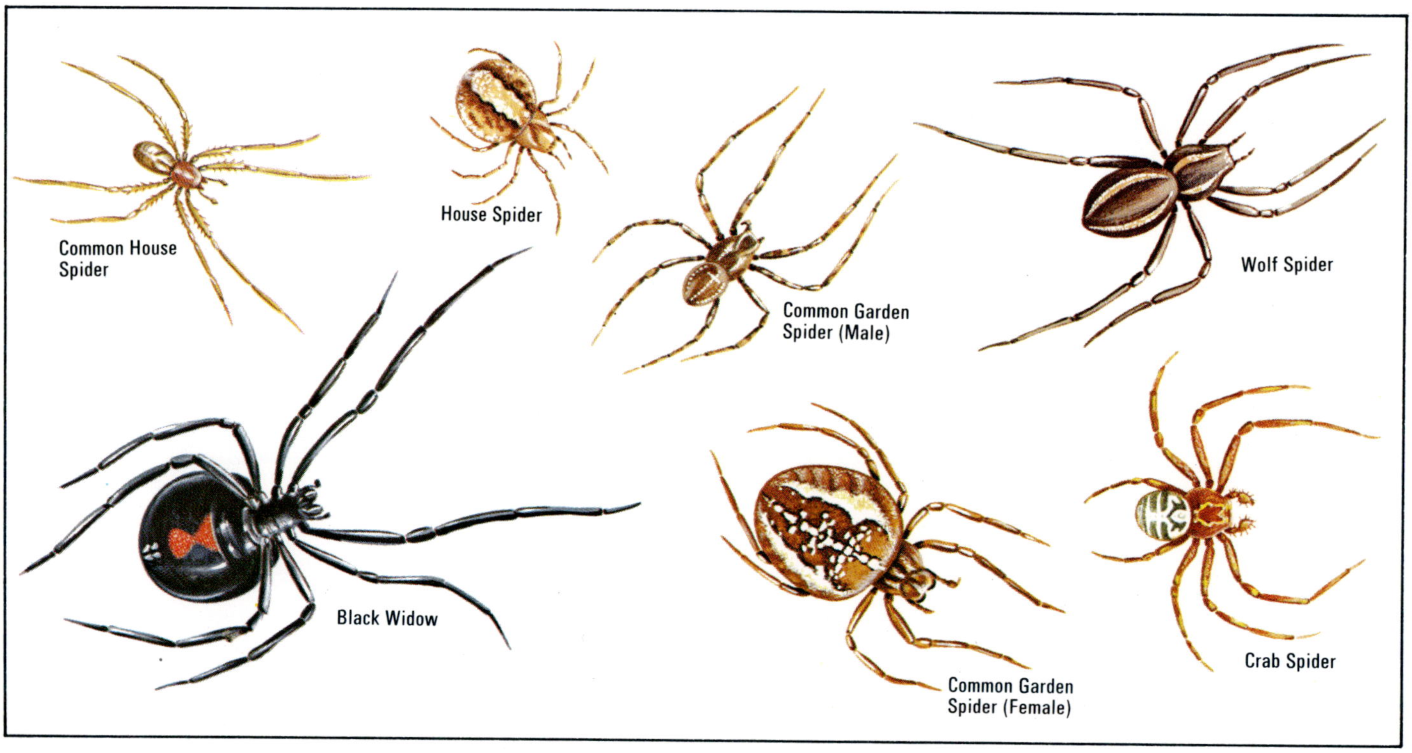

their enlarged palps or tugging the web in a special way. These signals prevent the female from rushing out and eating the male.

Scorpions

These animals are easily recognised because the palps are enlarged to form powerful pincers and because the abdomen is prolonged into a tail with a sting at the end.

Scorpions eat insects and other small animals, which they catch with their pincers. The food is then torn to pieces by the smaller pincers at the front of the head and the juices are sucked up. Scorpions, like spiders, have no jaws and they cannot eat solids. The sting is rarely used in catching food. It is mainly a defensive organ. When a scorpion is disturbed it is more concerned with getting away than with attacking. It will sting when cornered, though, and campers in scorpion country are well advised to shake out their shoes and clothing before dressing in the morning. The effect of the poison varies with the species of scorpion. Some have very little effect on a normal, healthy person, but others can be fatal.

The Water Spider

Spiders are basically land animals. Several species live around the water, and some even skate across the surface, but only one species lives under the surface. The water spider spins a little silken 'tent' under the water and then fills it with air bubbles brought down from the surface.

Harvestmen

The long-legged harvestmen are often confused with spiders. The most obvious difference is that the harvestman's body is not divided into two parts.

Below: A dew-spangled web, death-trap for unwary insects.

Bottom: The scorpion carries its sting above its body. The sting is mainly a defensive organ but it is not often used.

Slugs, Snails and Bivalves

Right: Cross-section of a marine snail.

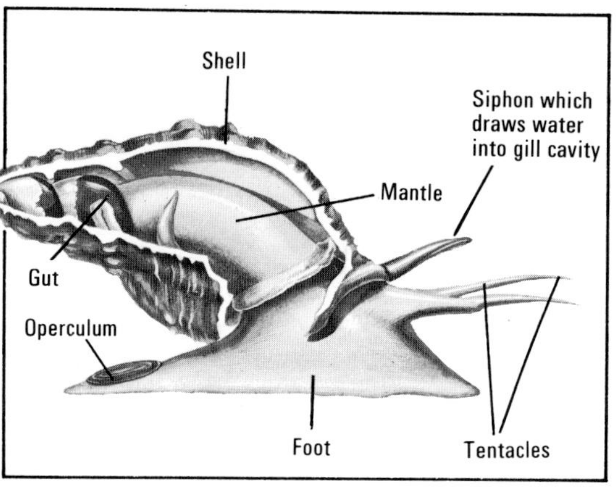

Below: The common garden snail (top) and a slug (bottom), two common garden and hedgerow animals.

Slugs, snails, cockles, mussels, oysters and octopuses are all molluscs. They are all very soft-bodied animals without backbones. Most of them are protected by a hard shell.

Snails

Snails belong to the group of molluscs called gastropods. They usually have a coiled shell into which they can retreat. Many also have a horny plate with which they can close the shell. Snails live in the sea, on land, and in fresh water, although we usually use the name snail only for the land and freshwater species. Examples include whelks, winkles, limpets, pond snails and garden snails.

The snail's body has three main regions. The most obvious is the flattened foot on which the animal glides about. It is propelled by muscular ripples. A gland near the front of the foot pours out slime which lubricates the snail's path and makes movement easier. The head bears one or two pairs of tentacles. The eyes are at the tip of the larger tentacles in land snails and at the base of the tentacles in other species. Most of the snail's internal organs are in the coiled hump, which remains inside the shell. The hump is covered by a thick 'cloak' called the mantle.

The shell is formed by the mantle. It consists of three layers. The outer layer is thin and horny and it carries the colour pattern. The middle layer consists of large rectangular crystals of calcite, while the inner layer is formed of mother-of-pearl. Only the inner layer can be replaced if the shell is damaged, and so we often see shells with pearly patches showing through. Because the shell consists mainly of lime, there are far more snails in chalk and limestone regions than in sandy areas.

The marine snails breathe with gills. The gills lie in a cavity between the mantle and the body. The snail pumps water in and out of the cavity, and oxygen passes from the water into the blood of the gills. Some pond and river snails also breathe in this way, but the mantle cavity of land snails has been converted into a lung. The snails pump air in and out of the cavity instead of water. The gills themselves have disappeared. Many water snails breathe in this way as well.

Most of the land snails are herbivores, feeding on dead plant material as a rule. Freshwater snails are also mainly plant-eaters, and so are many marine species.

Other marine snails, however, are carnivorous. The whelk, for example, feeds on other molluscs. The snail has a peculiar 'tongue' called a radula. It is covered with hundreds of horny teeth, and it is used like a file to rasp away the food.

Most snails are hermaphroditic animals. This means that each snail has both male and female organs. They have to pair up, however, before they can reproduce. Some snails lay eggs, while others give birth to young.

Slugs

Slugs are also gastropods and they are closely related to snails. They are, in fact, snails which have almost or quite lost their shells. They behave in much the same way as snails, although some of them are carnivorous and eat earthworms. The thick, slimy coating on a slug is its protection against drying up. It has no shell into which it can retreat and it would quickly shrivel in dry air without the slime. Even so, the slugs are confined to moist places.

Bivalves

The bivalves are those molluscs with two parts or valves to their shells. The two valves are hinged at one edge by little teeth and by an elastic ligament. Muscles hold the shell shut and, when they relax, the ligament opens it. All bivalves live in water, and most of them are marine. They include cockles, mussels, scallops, oysters and giant clams. The giant clams live in warm seas and may reach a weight of 225 kg. They are among the largest invertebrates.

Some bivalves are cemented to rocks or attached by threads. Others live freely in the mud or sand and use a tongue-shaped foot for burrowing. Scallops can actually swim by flapping the two halves of the shell together and shooting themselves through the water.

The animals have no head, and many of those that are fixed to the bottom have no foot either. The body consists mainly of the mantle and the large gills. All the bivalves are filter feeders. This means that they filter tiny particles of food from the water. The mantle usually forms two tubes called siphons. Water is drawn in through one siphon and it goes to the gills. Oxygen is absorbed from the water into the gill tissues and tiny hairs on the gills waft food particles along to the mouth. The water then goes out again through the other siphon. Some bivalves have a long inlet siphon and they suck up mud by moving the siphon about on the bottom.

Most bivalves have separate male and female individuals, but there is no pairing in these animals. The males scatter sperms into the water, which have to swim to the eggs. Many species release eggs into the water as well, so the fertilization takes place in the water. Other species retain their eggs until they have been fertilized by sperms drawn in with the water current. Fertilized eggs normally develop into free-swimming larvae which become widely scattered.

Pearls

Very often a grain of sand gets inside a mollusc shell and irritates the animal. When this happens the mantle pours mother-of-pearl around the sand grain. This makes it nice and smooth and it stops the irritation. The smooth, round object is called a pearl and it is eagerly sought for jewellery. The best pearls come from certain types of oyster, but many bivalves, including freshwater mussels, produce good pearls.

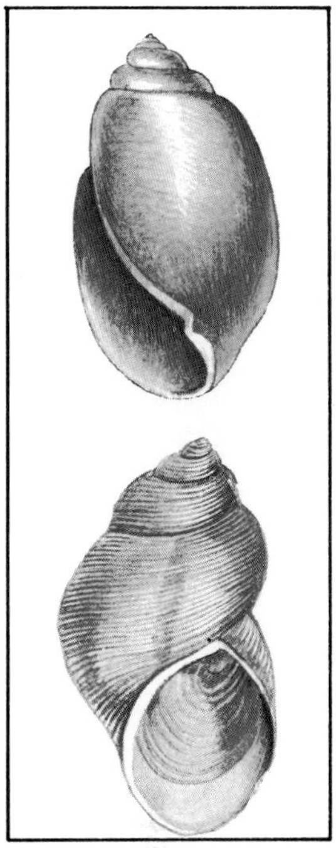

Above: Most snail shells are right-handed (as the lower shell) but a few are left-handed (like the upper shell).

Below: A selection of sea shells.

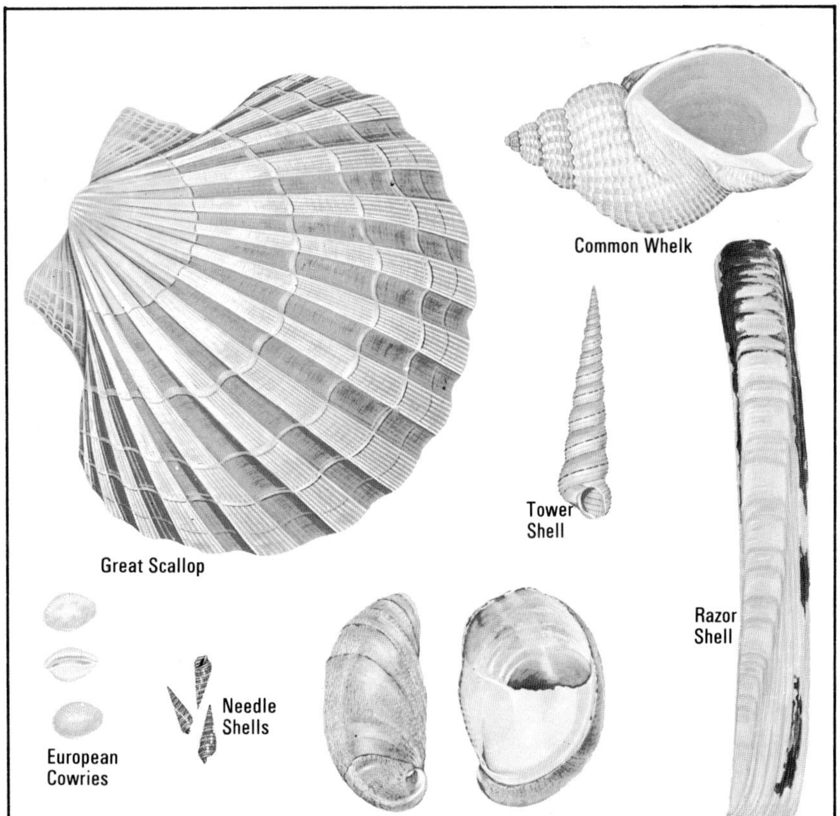

Squids and Octopuses

Tales of sea monsters with many arms and hideous eyes are recorded in many books and legends. Some of the tales are entirely fanciful, but some are probably based on fact, although they are much exaggerated. The description of the monsters suggest that most of them were squids or octopuses.

Squids and octopuses, together with the cuttlefishes and the pearly nautilus, are known as cephalopods. They live in the sea and they make up one of the three main groups of molluscs. They are thus related to the slugs and snails and bivalves, although they are much more active animals. Cephalopods have a more obvious head than the other molluscs and they certainly have a more efficient brain. They are among the most intelligent of the invertebrate animals. The most obvious features of the cephalopods, however, are the arms or tentacles that surround the head. Octopuses have eight arms, while most other cephalopods have ten. The arms are equipped with suckers and they are used mainly for catching food.

The cephalopods, like the other molluscs, are soft-bodied creatures and they are surrounded by a thick sheet of skin called the mantle. This normally secretes some sort of shell or skeleton, as it does in the snail. The pearly nautilus is the only cephalopod with an external shell. It is up to 30 centimetres across and it is composed of many chambers. The animal lives in the outer chamber, with its many tentacles exposed. The pearly nautilus lives in the warmer parts of the Pacific, spending most time near the seabed.

The shells of other cephalopods are inside the mantle. The shell of the octopus is almost non-existent, consisting only of a very thin plate or just a few chalky granules. The squid has a thin, horny plate known as a pen, while the cuttlefish has an oval chalky plate known as a cuttlebone, which are often washed up on the beach.

Jet Propulsion

Sitting on the sea-bed an octopus is continually swelling and contracting its body. These are breathing movements. The mantle is very muscular and it covers all of the body except the head. It joins the body at the 'neck', where there are a few small openings. When the mantle expands, water is drawn in through these openings and into the mantle cavity. This is a large space around the body in which there hangs a pair of gills. Oxygen is removed from the water and the water is then pumped out again, not through the inlet holes but through a short funnel called the siphon. The same mechanism is also used for swimming: rapid contraction of the mantle forces a jet of water out through the siphon and the animal shoots backwards.

The squids and cuttlefishes breathe in the same way and they can also jet propel themselves about, controlling their direction by altering the position of the siphon. More usually, however, they swim by gently flapping the fin-like edges of the mantle.

Right: The cuttlefish uses its long arms to catch a shrimp. Far right: Close-up view of mouth of cuttlefish.

Below: The suckers of the octopus (left) are simple horny cups. Those of the squids (middle) and cuttlefishes (right) have teeth or claws.

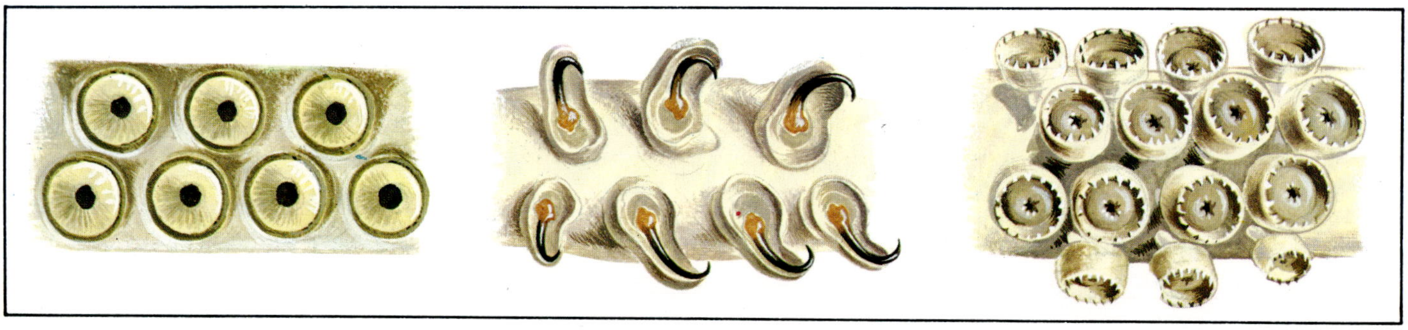

The common octopus is not an attractive animal when at rest, but it is not the dangerous animal that many people imagine. The eyes of these creatures are remarkably similar to our own eyes.

Undeserved Reputation

The octopus is the best known of the cephalopods. It is often portrayed as a fearsome monster, but it does not deserve its reputation and most are quite small creatures. An octopus with tentacles spanning 3 metres is a very large one. Most live on the sea-bed and around the coasts. They prefer rocky coasts and they tend to hide away in crevices.

The main food of octopuses consists of crabs and bivalve molluscs. These are caught by the arms and then carried to the mouth. The mouth is right in the centre of the eight arms and it has a very hard parrot-like beak which is able to crack the hard shells of the prey. The beak is also provided with poison glands.

Octopuses lay their eggs in grape-like clusters among the rocks. When they hatch, the young octopuses spend some time in the plankton of the surface layers.

The Largest Invertebrates

Squids are much more active than the octopuses. Most of them live out in the open sea and play a very important part in the economy of the sea, for they eat large numbers of fishes and they are themselves eaten by many other animals. The squid is slender with a rocket-like shape. There are some 400 species, ranging from a few centimetres to 20 metres in length. The giant squid is the largest of all the invertebrates and has inspired tales of sea monsters. Many whales bear scars showing where the squids' powerful suckers have gripped and torn their flesh. Unlike the octopuses, the squids and cuttlefishes have ten arms. Two of them are much longer and more slender than the others, but they widen out near the tip to form sucker-covered 'hands'. They can be shot out to catch prey.

Apart from the nautilus, the cephalopods all possess an ink sac. This contains a thick inky fluid which is shot out when the animal is disturbed and forms a 'smoke screen' behind which the animal disappears, or it may simply confuse the attacker for a while.

Colour Change Artists

All cephalopods can change their colours to some extent, but the best performers are the cuttlefishes. They generally live around the coasts and hunt for shrimps and other crustaceans on the sea-bed.

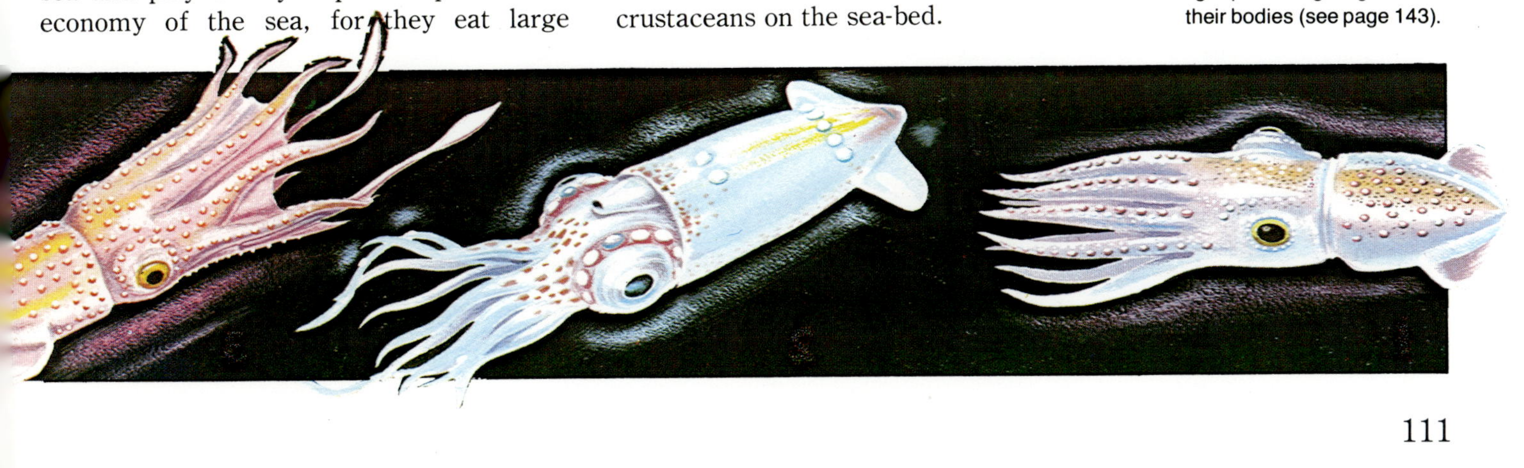

These three squids live in deep water and they have light-producing organs on their bodies (see page 143).

Spiny-Skinned Animals

Of all the animals that can be found along the shore, the starfishes are some of the most interesting. Together with the brittle stars, sea-urchins and a few others, they make up the phylum called the Echinodermata. This name means 'spiny-skinned' and refers to the rough skins of the animals. The roughness is caused by numerous chalky plates embedded in the skin. The echinoderms are all marine animals of moderate size. They are very distinct from other invertebrate animals.

Like the corals and jellyfishes, the echinoderms are radially symmetrical. This means that they are more or less circular or cylindrical creatures, regularly arranged around a central point. There is no brain nor is there a head. The nervous system consists simply of a sparse network. Sense organs are poorly developed and special breathing organs are generally absent. Oxygen is absorbed from the water through the skin.

The echinoderms possess a unique feature called the water vascular system. This is a system of water-filled canals running to all parts of the body. It is in contact with the outside through a group of little pores on the upper surface of the animal. Tiny branches of the water vascular system grow out through the general body surface of most echinoderms and form tube feet. These are muscular projections with disc-shaped ends. They help to absorb oxygen from the surrounding water and they also enable some of the animals to move about. Water is pumped into the tube feet and forces their ends out to make contact with stones or other objects. The muscles of the feet then contract

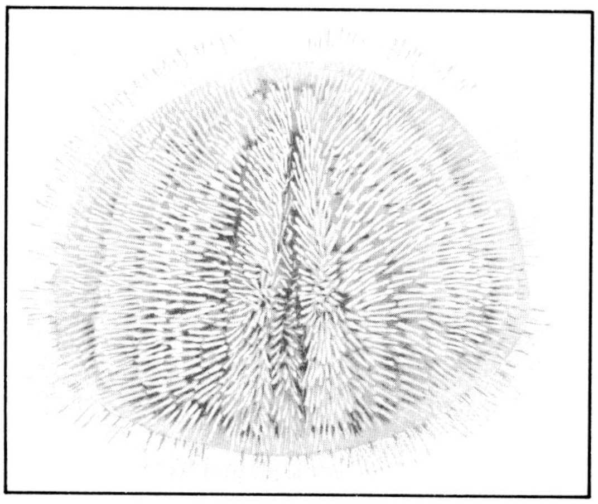

Right: An edible sea-urchin.

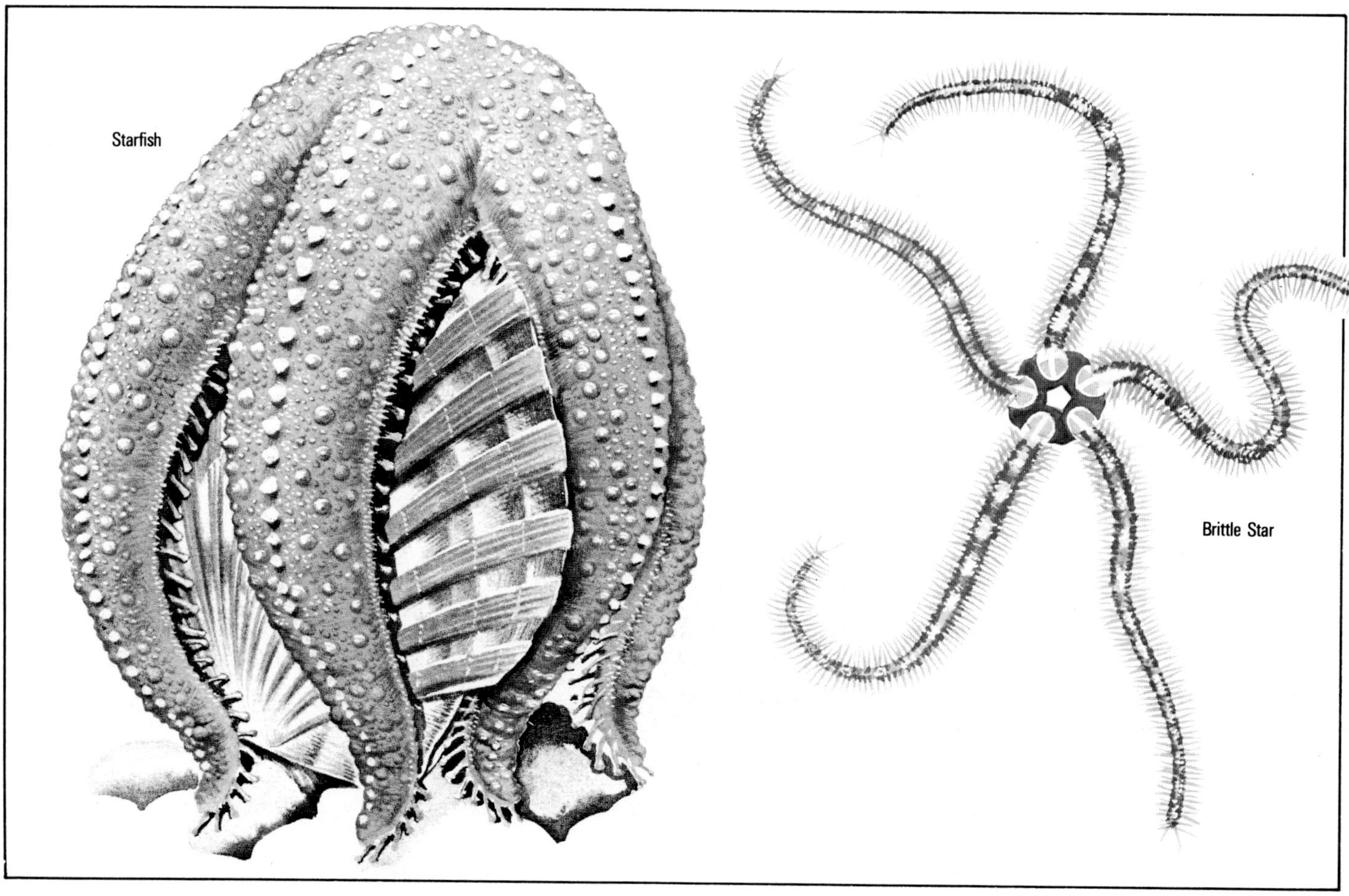

Below: The starfish is a predatory animal feeding largely on shellfish. The starfish's tube feet work in unison to exert a strong pull and open the bivalve shell. Brittle stars differ from starfishes in that the arms are quite distinct from each other and clearly separated from the central disc. Brittle stars heave themselves along by their arms.

and turn them into little suction cups. These grip very tightly and the animal can drag itself along.

Most of the echinoderms have separate male and female individuals, although some are hermaphrodite. Eggs and sperms are usually both released into the water, where fertilization occurs. Young echinoderms are very different from the adults and, whereas the adults all live on the sea-bed, the young float freely in the plankton.

Starfishes

Living echinoderms are split into five groups or classes, of which the most familiar is the starfish group. Starfishes normally have five arms radiating from the central disc. The mouth is on the underside of the body, and so are the tube feet. The latter occur along the arms. The skeleton is flexible and is made up of numerous separate chalky plates, embedded in the skin. Projections from these plates make the surface rough. Some projections develop into spines; others form tiny pincers. They pick pieces of sand from the skin, thus keeping the animal clean.

Starfishes feed on various molluscs and other invertebrates. They are often serious pests in oyster beds. Some starfishes swallow the molluscs whole and eject the shells later, but others open the shells to get at the soft parts. The starfish uses its tube feet to pull the two halves of the shell apart. Part of the starfish's stomach is then pushed out over the mollusc and digestive juices are poured out. The partly digested food is then sucked up.

Brittle Stars

These animals are often confused with the starfishes, but their arms are much more slender and they are distinctly separated from the central disc. Brittle stars move by coiling their spiny arms around stones and heaving themselves along. The animals often live at great depths and they feed on small creatures. Some brittle stars catch their prey with their arms, others shovel mud into the mouth with their tube feet and digest any creatures it contains.

Sea Urchins

Sea-urchins are globular animals with a rigid shell called a test. The tube feet grow out through the test in five distinct rays. The mouth of the sea-urchin is on the underside and it has five strong teeth, which project from the mouth. The urchin uses these teeth to browse on the seaweeds, which form the main part of its food.

Sea Cucumbers

These are sausage-shaped animals in which the skeleton is reduced to scattered little plates. There are five rows of tube feet, and those around the mouth are modified to form tentacles. The tentacles occasionally catch small creatures, but the sea cucumber obtains most of its food by scooping mud into its mouth and digesting any useful material.

Sea Lilies

Sea lilies are animals with a central disc attached to the sea-bed by a stalk. The arms bear tiny hairs (cilia) which create water currents. These water currents flow towards the mouth and carry tiny food particles to it. Some break away from the stalk when fully grown. They are called feather stars and basket stars.

A sea lily.

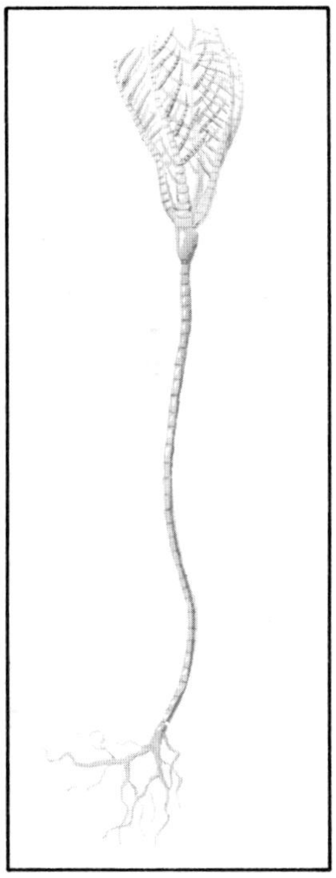

Below: Four kinds of echinoderms. From left to right they are starfish, sea cucumber, brittle star and feather star.

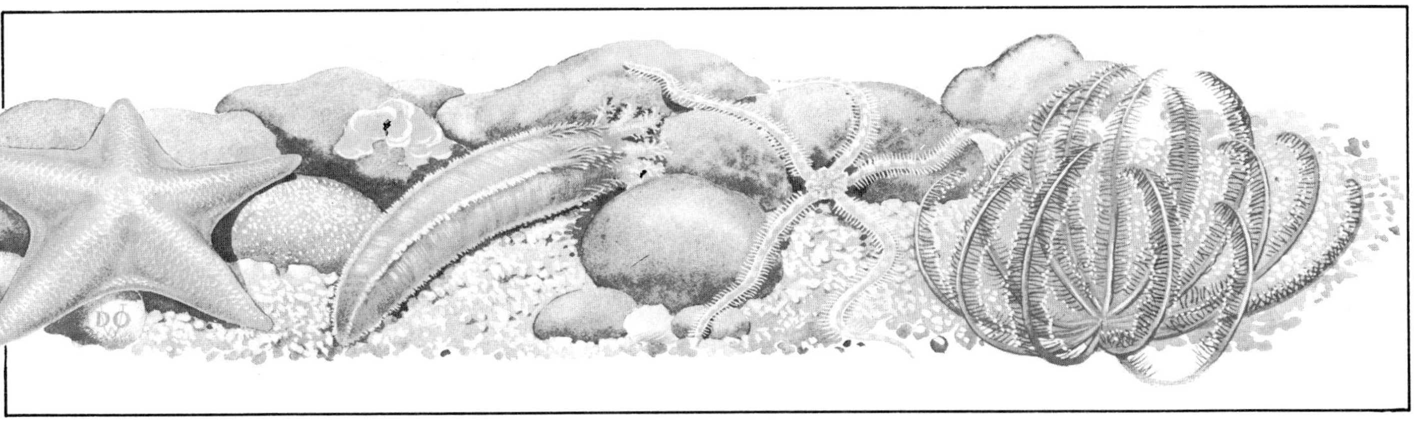

Fishes

Fishes are backboned animals (vertebrates) which, with a few exceptions, live entirely in the water. There are more than 20,000 different kinds in the world today. Most of them are beautifully streamlined, and they swim by means of their fins and tails. They get their oxygen direct from the water through their gills (see page 78). The gills lie in chambers connected to the back of the throat, and the fishes breathe by taking water in through the mouth. This is why a fish is always opening and closing its mouth. It takes a mouthful of water and then shuts its mouth and forces the water into the gill chambers. Oxygen is taken up by the gills and the water escapes through openings on the sides of the body.

The fishes were the earliest of the backboned animals to appear on the earth, but the first fishes were very different from those of today (see page 220). They were small, but heavily armoured and very clumsy. They had no jaws and they could not bite anything. They lived mainly on the bottom, sucking up mud and filtering out small animals and decaying material as food. Fishes with jaws appeared later and most of the jawless fishes died out, but a few strange jawless fishes are still alive today. They are the lampreys and hagfishes.

Cartilage Skeletons

Apart from the jawless lampreys and hagfishes, today's fishes fall into two main groups: the cartilaginous fishes, whose skeletons are made of gristly cartilage, and the bony fishes. Both groups possess two pairs of fins on the sides of the body. All the cartilaginous fishes live in the sea and they include sharks, rays, skates and dogfishes. Most of the cartilaginous fishes can be distinguished from bony fishes by looking for the gill openings. The sharks and their relatives have five gill slits on each side, but the gill slits of the bony fishes are hidden under a flap called the operculum. Cartilaginous fishes can also be distinguished by their asymmetrical tails. The upper part of the tail fin is larger than the lower part, whereas most bony fishes have symmetrical tail fins.

Despite their soft skeletons, some of the sharks grow to a great size. The whale shark is the largest of all living fishes. It reaches lengths of more than 15 metres. The cartilaginous fishes have very rough skins, which can be used as sand-paper. The roughness is due to the tooth-like scales that cover the skin. The shark's teeth, carried on the skin of the lips, are simply enlarged and razor-sharp versions of the normal body scales. It seems

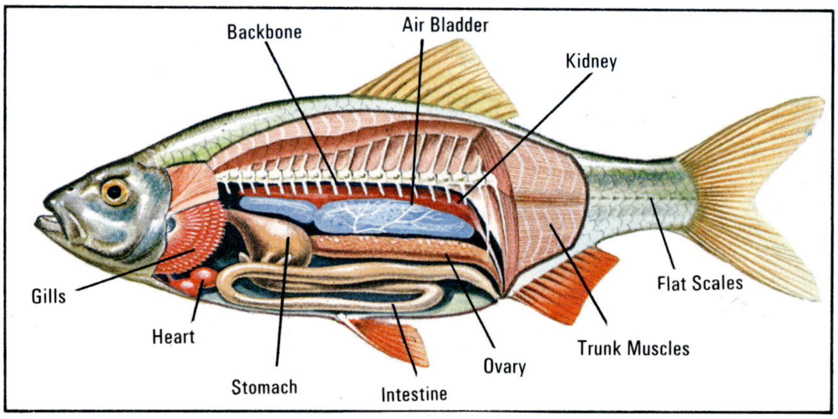

Above: A typical bony fish cut away to show the arrangement of the internal organs. The swim bladder, which helps the fish to stay up in the water, is shown in blue.

Right: Not many fishes look after their eggs or young, but tilapia is an exception. When danger threatens it gathers its young into its mouth for safety.

Thick-lipped Mullet
Cod
Neon Tetra
Rudd
Wrasse
Black Widow
Mackerel
Salmon
Tiger Barb
Norway Haddock
Bass
Yellow Dwarf Cichlid
Barbel
Sailfish
Blue Shark
Plaice
Male Enlarged
Sting Ray
Deep Sea Angler Fish
with Parasitic Male

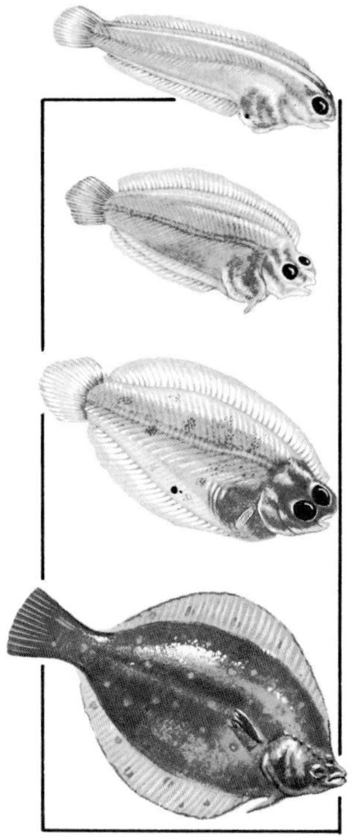

Above: The true flat-fishes, such as the plaice, lie on one side. During the fish's growth one eye moves round so that both are on the top side.

Below: A sea-horse.

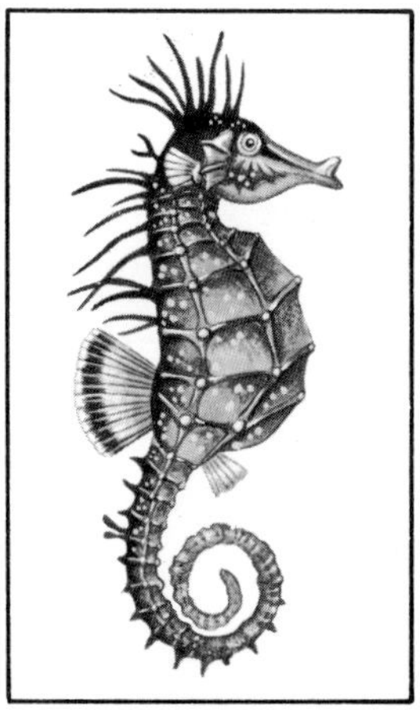

Below: The bichir is a primitive bony fish with lungs, although not related to the true lung fishes.

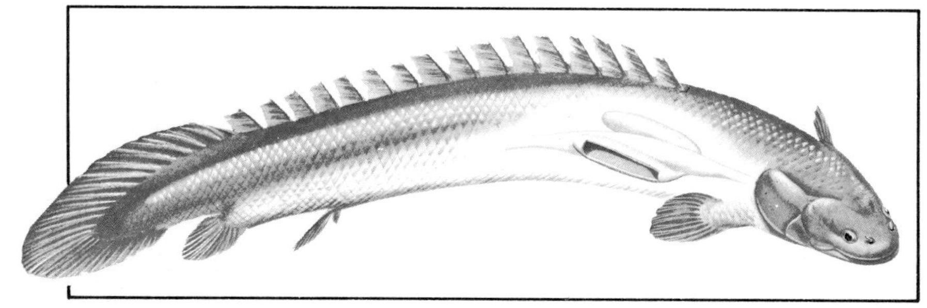

likely that all vertebrate teeth have been derived from this type of scale. Most sharks feed on other fishes, but the skates and rays are bottom-feeders and prefer shellfish. Instead of having sharp cutting teeth, the skates and rays have blunt teeth well suited to cracking and crushing mollusc shells.

Bony Skeletons

Nearly all of today's fishes are bony fishes, with skeletons of real bone. Examples include herrings, cod, perch, stickleback, salmon and plaice. A few primitive species retain the bony armour of their ancestors, but the armour is reduced in most species to a covering of flat circular scales. Some fishes have no scales at all. The body is generally flattened from side to side and much more slender than that of the sharks.

Apart from the various bottom-living species, the bony fishes have a swim bladder, or air bladder. This is a white or silvery pouch lying just above the food canal. In some of the more primitive fishes, the swim bladder has a duct connecting it with the throat. The swim bladder of most bony fishes, however, is completely closed. It contains oxygen and it acts as a buoyancy tank, enabling the fish to float effortlessly at any level in the water. As the fish swims deeper, the swim bladder produces more oxygen to compensate for the greater pressure. The gas is absorbed again as the fish rises.

Those fishes whose swim bladders are connected to their throats can gulp air into them. Some of them can stay alive for a while out of water because they can breathe in this way.

Reproduction in Fishes

The majority of fishes lay eggs, and some of them lay enormous numbers. A female cod may contain up to nine million eggs. Very few of them ever reach maturity. Fish eggs and young fishes form a very important part of the diet of other sea creatures. Not all fishes lay vast numbers of eggs. The cod simply scatters her eggs in the water and leaves them. She has to produce large numbers to ensure that at least some escape being eaten. At the other end of the scale, the little freshwater bullhead lays only a few dozen eggs. These are deposited in a hollow scooped out under a stone on the stream bed and the male keeps a watch over them until the young fishes are several days old.

The stickleback is another fish that cares for its eggs and young. The male adopts a territory and defends it against other males by displaying his bright breeding colours. He then makes a nest with water plants and twigs and he encourages one or more females to lay their eggs in it. After the eggs are laid the male stands guard over them and ensures that they get plenty of oxygen by fanning a current of water over them with his tail. He does the same for the young fishes until they are able to look after themselves.

The sea-horses—fishes, in spite of their strange appearance—have an even more unusual breeding behaviour. The male has a pouch on his belly and the female lays her eggs in it. The eggs develop in this pouch and the young sea-horses emerge a few at a time.

Fishes with Lungs

Early on in the history of the bony fishes two distinct groups developed. One group possessed fins supported by numerous fine bones or rays. The other group had muscular fins, with sturdy bones in the centre. Both groups had air bladders connected to the throat. The ray-finned fishes could move about only by swimming through the water. They could breathe with their gills and their air bladders gradually developed into buoyancy tanks, often losing their connection with the throat. Almost all of today's bony fishes have descended from this group. The fishes with muscular fins, however, could crawl about on the bottom. They could also crawl out of the water and breathe by gulping air into their bladders. These fishes gradually evolved into land animals (see page 226), but a few remained fish-like and are still with us today. They are known as lung fishes.

There are only six species of lung fishes—one in South America, one in Australia, and four closely related ones in Africa.

Amphibians

The amphibians, represented today mostly by frogs, toads and newts, were the first backboned animals to leave the water and live on land. That happened some 400 million years ago, but even today the amphibians have not completely broken away from the water. They have moist skin and they thrive only in damp places. Nearly all of them have to go back to the water to breed. The name amphibian means 'double life' and indicates that the animals live partly on the land and partly in the water. The life history of the common frog is typical of the whole group. The young stages, known as tadpoles, are fish-like and they breathe with gills. They gradually change into the air-breathing adults.

There are two main groups of amphibians living today. These are the frogs and toads on the one hand and the tailed amphibians (newts and salamanders) on the other. There is a third group, found in the warmer parts of the world, whose members look like large earthworms and spend their lives burrowing in the soil.

Frogs and Toads

These are the jumping amphibians. They use their long, webbed hind legs for both jumping and swimming. We tend to call the smooth-skinned members of the group frogs and the rougher skinned ones toads, but this is not a very scientific division. Many so-called toads are actually more closely related to the common frog than to the common toad.

Some frogs and toads live permanently in the water, especially in swiftly flowing streams. Others live entirely on the land. They lay eggs in damp soil and the tadpole stage is passed inside the egg. When the animals finally come out of their eggs they are already small frogs. In the majority of frogs and toads, however, the tadpoles live in water, but the adults return to the water only for a short time during the breeding season. Some tree frogs make use of the small 'ponds' formed in the forks of trees or between the leaves of other plants.

A few species show some concern for their young. The European midwife toad's eggs are in a string of jelly and the male toad carries them about wrapped around his back legs. When they are ready to hatch, the male enters the water and releases the eggs. A few frogs and toads build nests for their eggs, but one of the strangest habits is shown by the Surinam toad of South America. This spends almost all of its time in the water. The female lays her eggs onto her back where they sink into small hollows in her skin and the skin grows over each hollow to form a lid. The eggs hatch and the tadpoles complete their development in these little pouches.

The frogs and toads that live permanently in the water have lost their tongues and they grab their food with their jaws. They eat all kinds of animal food, both dead and live. The land-living species normally have long tongues. They are sticky at the tip and they can be flicked out remarkably quickly to pick up a fly or some other small creature, and whip it back into the mouth.

The Common Frog's Life History

Adult frogs hibernate during the winter. They awake in spring and the males return to the water. Their loud croaking attracts the females. The female carries the male about on her back and he fertilizes the eggs as soon as she lays them. The eggs are covered with jelly which swells up and protects them.

After fertilization the little black egg starts to grow, and within a few days, it develops a distinct head and tail. About 10 days after the egg is laid the tadpole emerges from the jelly and clings to a water weed or to the remains of the jelly by means of a sticky gland. It is three days before the tadpole can have its first meal of plant scrapings. By this time it has developed three pairs of feathery external gills. The hind legs start to form when the tadpole is about six weeks old, and the front legs appear a few weeks later. The diet has now changed from plant material to small water creatures. Lungs have formed

Below left: Toads usually have a thicker, rougher skin than frogs and their back legs are shorter. Toads cannot jump as well as frogs and often crawl about.

Below: The life history of a frog, from spawn to adult, showing the stages of the tadpole's development.

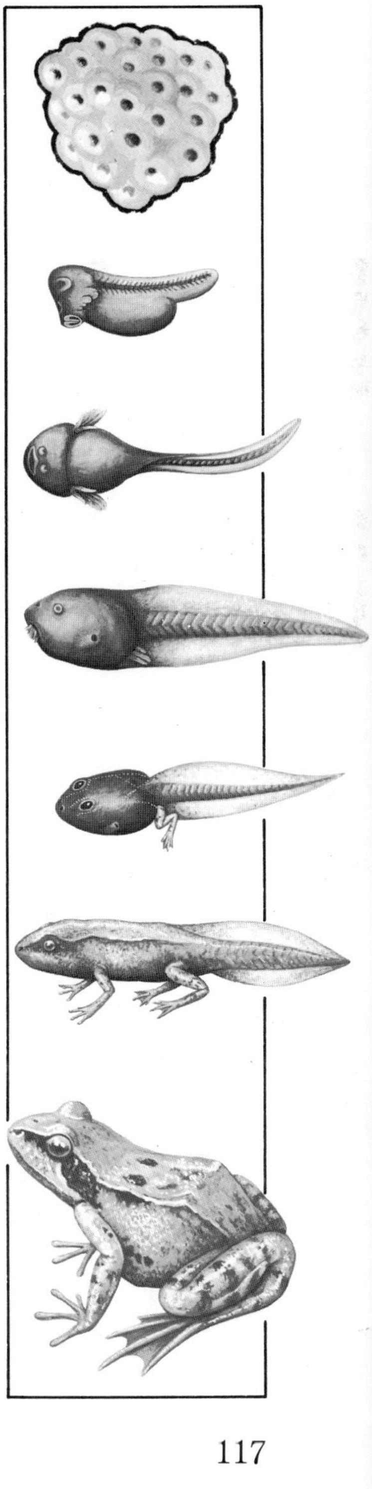

inside the body by this time and the tadpole is starting to visit the surface to gulp air. The legs continue to grow and the tail begins to shrink. The animal takes on the typical frog shape and soon leaves the water to feed on small insects among the vegetation.

Newts and Salamanders

Most of the tailed amphibians are called salamanders. They vary from a few centimetres to about 150 centimetres in length. Newts are really only a particular group of salamanders. The eggs are fertilized inside the female's body, but otherwise the life history is very similar to that of the frog.

The European spotted salamander is one of many viviparous species. This means that it brings forth active young. The eggs hatch while still in the mother's body. She then enters the water and the tadpoles are born. Some other salamanders never go into the water. Some of them lay eggs in damp soil and the tadpole stage is passed while still in the egg.

Salamanders that do not grow up

Many salamanders spend all their lives in the water and quite a number of them have no lungs, and retain their feathery external gills. This makes them look like overgrown tadpoles, although they can reproduce themselves. One of the best known of these animals is the axolotl. It is the tadpole of a Mexican salamander. It can grow up into a proper salamander, although it does not do so very often. The mud-puppy and some of the other salamanders never grow up properly.

A frog showing the moist skin which is a characteristic of frogs. Most of the oxygen it needs is absorbed through the skin.

Right: The midwife toad male looks after the eggs.

Below: A caecilian (left), one of the worm-like amphibians. Right: The fire salamander. Male newts (far right) develop bright colours and large crests in the breeding season.

Reptiles

Reptiles are cold-blooded vertebrates with dry, scaly skin. They include snakes, lizards, crocodiles and turtles. Most reptiles live in the warmer parts of the world, where their cold-bloodedness is not much of a handicap. There are some in the temperate regions, however, and the adder reaches as far north as Finland. The animals are active throughout the year in warm regions, but those of the cooler areas hibernate during the winter.

The reptiles first appeared some 300 million years ago. They evolved from some kind of amphibian. The two most important features which separated the early reptiles from their amphibian ancestors were their waterproof skins and the tough shells around their eggs. These meant that the reptiles were independent of the water.

Living reptiles fall into three main groups. These are the tortoises and turtles, the crocodiles and alligators, and the lizards and snakes. A fourth group is represented only by the New Zealand tuatara (see page 236). The lizards and snakes are very successful animals, with nearly 5,000 species between them.

Tortoises and Turtles

These animals make up a very ancient group and they have changed very little during the 200 million years. There is rather a muddle over the names of some of these animals. An individual may be called a tortoise in one country, a terrapin in another, and a turtle in a third. But there is a tendency to use the name tortoise for those living on land, terrapin for the freshwater species and turtle for the marine species.

The animals are easily recognised by their box-like shells. These shells are made of bone and they are normally covered by horny plates. There are gaps for the limbs and the neck, and the head can usually be withdrawn into the shell by bending the neck.

The land-dwelling tortoises feed mainly on plants, but the water-dwelling species are mainly carnivorous. None of them has any

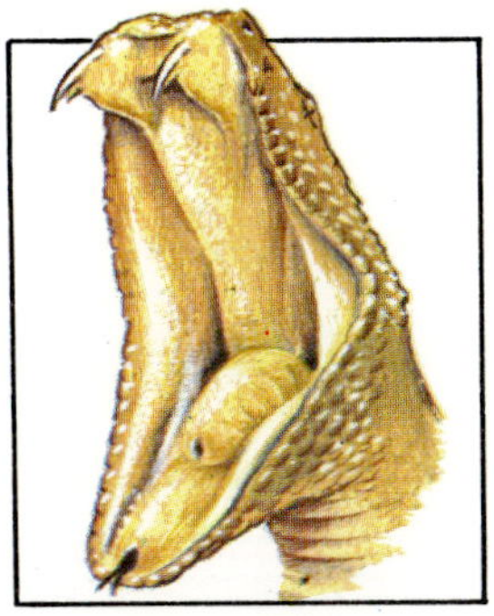

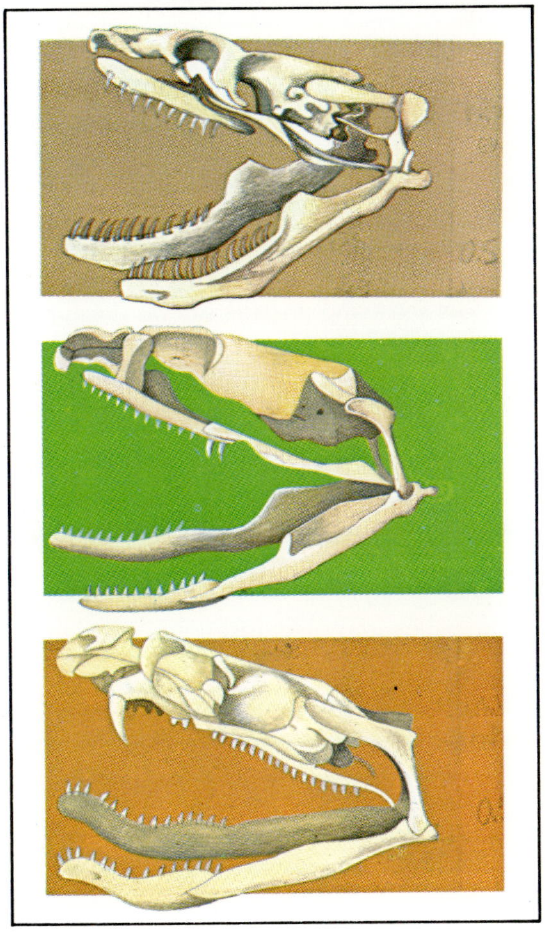

Non-poisonous snakes such as grass snakes and boas, have no fangs (top left). Some snakes have fangs at the back of the mouth (centre) but these are not usually very dangerous because their fangs cannot normally dig into a large animal. They work poison into their prey by repeatedly chewing it. The most dangerous snakes are the front fanged species, such as the cobra (left). These fangs are hollow and act like hypodermic needles to inject venom. Cobra fangs are rigid, but viper fangs (above) fold away when the snake shuts its mouth.

Below left: The thorny devil, an Australian lizard.

Many animals trick their enemies by pretending to be something else (see page 138). This frilled lizard raises a collar of skin around its neck, making itself look larger and fiercer than it really is.

Above: The cobra increases its fearsome appearance by raising a hood of skin.

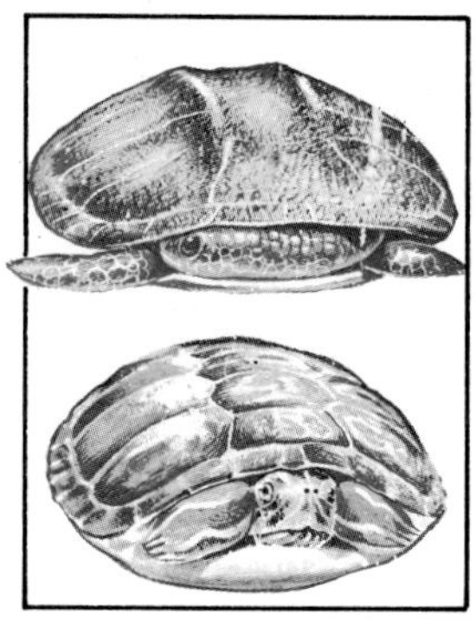

Above: Turtles can withdraw their heads into their shells by bending the neck sideways (top) or vertically.

Right: An egg-eating snake.

Below: Snakes have very many vertebrae and joints in their backbones. This is what enables them to coil up so tightly.

teeth, and the jaws are covered with a sharp, horny beak.

All the members of this group lay hard-shelled eggs. The marine turtles come ashore to lay their eggs on some sandy beach. Man collects large numbers for food and this egg-collecting has helped to make the larger turtles quite rare.

Crocodiles and Alligators

These creatures are the closest living relatives of the great dinosaurs. They are large animals, with thick skin and bold scale patterns. The skins have long been popular for ladies' handbags and the crocodile populations have suffered a great deal as a result. The animals live mainly in tropical rivers, although some species venture out into the sea. The eyes and nostrils are on the top of the snout and they just break the surface when the animal is floating. The animals swim by moving their powerful tails from side to side.

Crocodiles and alligators feed on a variety of animals. Fishes are their principal food, especially when they are young, but they also catch birds and mammals which come down to the water to drink.

Crocodiles and alligators look very much alike, but they can be distinguished by their teeth. The fourth tooth in the lower jaw is visible on the outside when the crocodile's mouth is closed, but it is hidden in the alligator. The alligator's snout is also somewhat blunter than that of the crocodile. There are only two kinds of alligator, one in the southern part of the United States and one in China. There are many different kinds of crocodiles. Other members of the group include the caimans, closely related to the alligators and the gharial. The latter animal has a very long, narrow snout and it feeds on fishes. It lives in various Indian rivers.

Some crocodiles lay their eggs in pits, but others, together with the alligators, lay them in heaps of rotting vegetation. The heat of fermentation helps to incubate the eggs. The mother of the Nile crocodile stays near the nest and, when she hears the young animals breaking out of their eggs, she helps them out.

Lizards

The lizards are a very varied group of reptiles. Most of them are only a few inches long, but some are much larger. The komodo dragon, for example, reaches a length of 4 metres. This is the largest lizard and it lives in Indonesia. The lizard's body, like that of the snake, is covered with small overlapping scales. The head is often armoured with bony plates. Most lizards have four limbs, but

some species are legless and look very much like snakes. The slow-worm is a good example.

Lizards nearly all feed on animals such as insects, but some are vegetarians. Among the most famous of the insect-eaters are the chameleons, which catch flies by shooting out their sticky tongues with remarkable speed and accuracy. Only two species of lizard are poisonous. The best known of these is the gila monster (see page 165).

Most lizards lay eggs, with rather thin papery shells, but a few species bring forth active young. The common lizard of Britain and Europe is one of these.

Snakes

Snakes are legless reptiles, although the boa constrictor and some of its relatives have small claws near the base of the tail. These claws are the remains of legs, and it is clear that the snakes have descended from lizard-like ancestors. Many people are frightened of all snakes, but not all snakes are harmful. In fact, only about 150 out of over 2,000 different kinds are at all dangerous to man.

Snakes live in all kinds of places, from the sea to the driest desert. Even though they have no legs, they manage to get about quite easily as long as the surface is rough. Many of them have broad scales along the belly and these scales can be lifted and dug into the ground. By digging in all the scales in turn the snakes can pull themselves smoothly forward. Other snakes throw their bodies into loops from side to side and they glide forward by pushing backwards against small lumps on the ground.

All snakes feed on animals. The constricting snakes catch their food by wrapping their bodies around it and squeezing it until it suffocates. These snakes include the anaconda and the python. Other snakes catch their prey with their mouths. They strike very rapidly and sink their teeth into the prey. The poisonous snakes have special grooved teeth called fangs. These carry poison into the wound. The non-poisonous snakes, such as the grass-snake, overcome their prey by strength.

The prey is swallowed whole and the snake's body is specially built so that it can swallow animals wider than its own body. The lower jaw is separate from the skull and the mouth can open very wide. The snake gradually works itself over its food by using its backward-pointing teeth. The ribs of the snake are not joined on the lower side of the body and they can open out to let the meal move down the food canal.

Most of the snakes lay eggs with leathery shells, but some species bring forth active young.

The crocodiles (below) can be distinguished from alligators (above) by the fourth tooth of the lower jaw. It is visible in the crocodile when the mouth is closed. The alligator's snout is also much blunter than the crocodile's.

Birds

It is impossible to mistake a bird for any other member of the animal kingdom because of its feathers. No other kind of animal has feathers. We do not know exactly when the first birds came into being, but they were the last great group of animals to appear on the Earth. It is believed that they arose from reptiles. Birds' legs are still covered with scales like those of the reptiles, but the scales on the rest of the body have developed into feathers.

A bird is a warm-blooded creature and its feathers help to keep it warm. The feathers also enable birds to fly. Birds probably descended from some kind of tree-living reptile which used to glide from branch to branch.

Wings have enabled the birds to spread far and wide and to reach all parts of the Earth. There are nearly 9,000 species living today, with a very wide range of sizes, shapes and habits. Many birds have now lost the ability to fly. They include ostriches, emus, kiwis and penguins. The penguins' wings have been transformed into flippers which are used for swimming, but the wings of the other flightless birds are weak and useless. There are many flightless birds in New Zealand and on other isolated islands. The birds arriving on these islands found no predatory mammals and they gradually lost the ability to fly. Many of New Zealand's flightless birds are now being killed by cats and other mammals introduced by man, and face extinction in the wild.

Ostriches and emus have evolved into large running birds, well suited to the grasslands on which they live. The ostrich is the largest living bird. A male may reach a height of about 3 metres and a weight of about 150 kg. But even the ostrich is dwarfed by some of the extinct species. The elephant bird, which lived in Madagascar until a few thousand years ago, was a large relative of the ostrich. It weighed nearly half a tonne, although it was hardly any taller than today's ostrich. The tallest birds of which we have any record were the moas of New Zealand. Some of them lived until a few hundred years ago and they reached 4 metres in height. The moas and elephant birds were unable to fly. The heaviest flying bird alive today is the mute swan. It reaches 25 kg in weight, although several birds have greater wingspans. At the other end of the scale, the smallest bird is the bee hummingbird. Found in Cuba, this bird has a body less than 2.5 centimetres long, although its beak and tail make it up to about 5 centimetres. It weighs less than 3 grammes.

How Birds Fly

Any flying object, whether a bird or an aeroplane, must have two forces acting on it. It must have thrust to push it along and it must have lift to keep it up in the air. Some birds glide and soar almost effortlessly on air currents, but most birds fly by flapping their wings. In flapping flight the wings provide both thrust and lift. Thrust is provided by the twisting movement of the feathers at the wing tips. This movement forces the air

backwards and therefore drives the bird forwards. The feathers also produce the curved, or cambered, upper surface which is responsible for the lift. Air passing over the curved upper surface of the wing is 'stretched out' a little. Its pressure is lower than that of the air pressing up on the underside of the wing. As long as the pressure difference is large enough, the extra pressure on the underside will keep the bird in the air.

The greater the area of a wing, the more lift it can provide. Large birds, such as swans, therefore have large wings to lift them. Narrow wings are best for fast flight and for birds such as albatrosses that glide through fast-moving air. Vultures, buzzards and other birds that fly slowly or soar round and round have very broad wings. These provide plenty of lift at slow speeds.

Small birds usually take off merely by jumping into the air, but larger birds often need to run in order to get the air moving over their wings. On landing, the wings are held back and the body is tilted so that it acts as a brake.

Feeding

Birds use up a great deal of energy when they flap their wings in flight. They also need a lot of energy to keep their bodies at a temperature of about 40°C. This means that birds need a lot of food. Many birds, especially the smaller ones, spend much of their time looking for food. No living bird has any teeth. The horny beak is used for

Above: A painted stork arrives at its nest.

There is a great variety of birds' beaks. They include the hooked beak of the macaw which can be used as a third leg, the sifting beak of the shoveller duck, the seed-cracking beak of the bullfinch, the dagger-like beak of the kingfisher, the stout 'all-purpose' beak of the rook and the sharp-edged hooked beak of the flesh-eating falcon.

catching and cutting up food. The birds have a wide variety of beaks, each type suited to the diet. A beak suitable for crushing hard seeds would obviously be unsuitable for catching fishes or for picking up small insects. Most kinds of food are eaten by birds although very few species feed on leaves. Many birds feed on seeds or insects. Many also eat fruit, and small animals such as worms and snails. Smaller numbers of birds eat fishes, mammals and other birds.

Sight and Hearing

The sense of smell is poorly developed in birds. They rely on the senses of sight and hearing to find food. A blackbird can actually hear a worm tunnelling just under the ground and it can peck in just the right place to catch it. Owls can pinpoint a rustling mouse in pitch darkness. Sight is extremely good in birds. Hawks hovering high in the sky can spot a tiny mouse in the grass below and swoop down to catch it. Kingfishers on their perches can see the outlines of fishes in fast-moving water and dive down to get them. The skimmers also feed on fishes, but they have a different way of catching them. They fly low over the water with the elongated lower half of the bill ploughing through the water to scoop up fishes.

Nest Building

Many animals build nests in which to rear their young, but none of them builds such elaborate nests as the birds. The nests are used only during the breeding season and they are not permanent homes, although some birds return year after year to the same nest. At the start of the breeding season the males of many species adopt territories. They stake their claims by singing all around the boundary of the chosen territory. They defend the territory against other males, but they attract females by singing and displaying their plumage. The feathers are often very bright at this time of year. When the birds have paired up they begin to build the nest. Some species make do simply with a rocky ledge or with a hollow in the ground, but others make very elaborate nests. The birds collect twigs, grass, moss, hair, mud and other materials and work it together into a cup-shaped nest. Many species add a roof as well, especially in tropical countries where monkeys and other animals might take the eggs.

When the nest is complete the eggs are laid. Some species lay only one egg but most species lay between four and ten. Some species lay as many as twenty eggs. The eggs have to be incubated—that is, they have to be kept warm. The parent birds keep them warm by sitting on them. Sometimes both parents take it in turns to sit on the eggs; sometimes only one parent sits on the eggs. The other one brings food. When the eggs hatch the little birds need almost continuous feeding. The parents are very busy at this time, often bringing insects to the nest at the rate of four every minute. If food is short the young will die.

Some young birds, especially those nesting on the ground or on the water, are able to run about right away. They are already covered with a coat of down and they can find their own food, under the protection of their parents. Most tree-nesting birds, however, are blind and naked when they hatch. The parents have to continue to keep them warm until their feathers have grown. Small birds probably rarely live more than four or five years in the wild. Larger birds live longer. In captivity, parrots and ravens have been known to live for 70 years.

Right: There are several different kinds of feathers. The most obvious are the contour feathers which cover the outside of the bird. There is a stiff, horny shaft in the centre. The shaft is called the quill. The flat part, called the vane, consists of hundreds of tiny branches called barbs. These are all hooked together.

Far right: Nests of weaver finches.

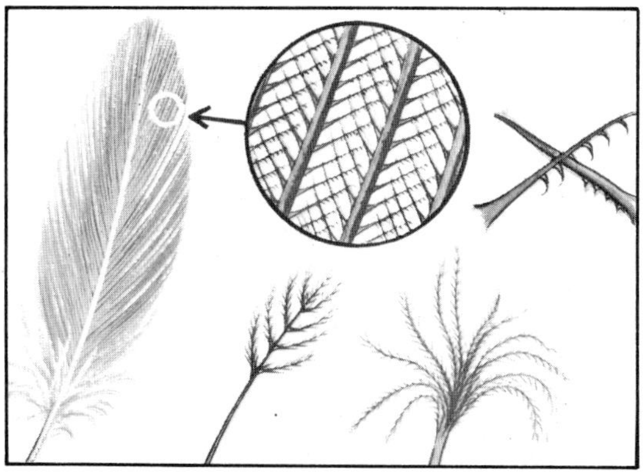

Mammals

The mammals are the dominant animals in the world today. They are not the most numerous animals, but many of them are large creatures and they live in a wide variety of habitats. They have a marked effect on other animals and on the land in general. One of the main factors which have helped the mammals to dominate the earth has been their intelligence. Mammals have large brains and they are able to learn quite quickly. Another thing which has helped them has been their ability to maintain their bodies at constant high temperatures regardless of their surroundings. This has enabled them to invade the coldest regions of the earth.

Mammals are easy to recognise by their furry coats. All mammals have some hair, although an elephant or a whale is almost naked. Other features that distinguish the mammals are the warm blood, although this is also shared by birds, and the feeding of the young on milk from the mother's body. There are also various internal features which separate the mammals from the other vertebrates. For example, the lower jaw of a mammal consists of a single bone on each side. Experts can use this fact to decide whether fossil bones come from mammals or reptiles, because it is very rare for fur to be fossilised.

The mammals came to prominence quite recently in the earth's history—only about 70 million years ago, when the dinosaurs became extinct. Thousands of different kinds of mammals have roamed the earth since then—many of them weird 'experimental' types—but there are less than 5,000 species alive today. Although they still dominate the earth, several of the orders of mammals are on the decline. The aardvark is the only member of its order; there are only two elephants, and several more orders contain only a few species. The only really large groups are the bats, rodents, carnivores and hoofed mammals. In fact, these four groups contain more than 80 per cent of all living mammals.

Living mammals are arranged in three major groups. These are the monotremes, mammals that lay eggs; the marsupials, mammals with pouches; and the placental mammals. The first two groups are almost confined to the Australian region. The world is dominated by the placental mammals, the group to which we ourselves belong.

The Monotremes

The mammals originally descended from egg-laying reptiles. Most of the mammals gave up the egg-laying habit, but one small group broke away from the others very early in their history. They did not give up laying

Representatives of each of the order of mammals. (Not drawn to scale.)

Above: The koala is one of Australia's most famous animals. It is a marsupial and it feeds almost entirely on eucalyptus leaves.

Right: Prairie dogs are American members of the squirrel family, part of the largest of all mammal orders—the rodents.

eggs and they also kept many other reptile features. Two of these primitive mammals are still alive today. They are called monotremes and they are the duck-billed platypus and the spiny ant-eaters. The latter are also called echidnas. Although they lay eggs, they feed their young on milk, so they are true mammals. They also have hair and warm blood, although they are not as good at keeping their temperature steady as the other mammals. The monotremes are found only in Australia and New Guinea.

The Marsupials

The marsupials include such well known animals as the kangaroo and the koala bear. They do not lay eggs, but the young are born at a very early stage of development. The red kangaroo may be over 2 metres tall but it gives birth to a tiny baby only a couple of centimetres long. This tiny baby is quite unable to look after itself, but it does manage to crawl into its mother's pouch. This is a large fold of skin on the mother's belly and her milk glands open into it. The baby stays in the pouch for some months and feeds on the milk. Eventually it is sufficiently well developed to leave the pouch and hop about, but it still returns to its mother's pouch from time to time until it is quite able to look after itself. The wallabies, koala bears, opossums and all the other marsupials start life in the same way, although some of the opossums have no real pouch.

Most of the marsupials live in the Australian region today, although some live in America. At one time they were found all over the world, but the placental mammals gradually replaced them in most places. Australia and South America had become separated from the rest of the world before many of the placentals reached them. The marsupials thrived there for a time. South

Below: An alert lioness (left), a member of the carnivores. The American dormouse (middle) is one of the smaller members of the rodent order. Walruses (right) are relatives of the seals. They use their tusks to rake up shellfish.

America was later connected to North America and placentals from the north wiped out most of the marsupials. A few opossums survived, however, and the Virginia opossum even managed to invade North America.

Marsupials are still quite numerous in Australia, but their numbers have dropped a great deal since Europeans introduced cats, dogs, foxes and other placental mammals. Several species, especially the smaller ones, have become extinct.

The Placental Mammals

This is the most advanced and most intelligent group of mammals. It is the group to which man belongs. The female keeps her babies inside her body for a relatively long period and she feeds them through a special organ called the placenta. This is attached to the mother's womb and the baby is connected to it by the umbilical cord. This cord carries blood vessels from the baby to the placenta. In the placenta the blood vessels from the baby lie very close to those of the mother. Food and oxygen can then pass from the mother's blood into that of her baby. The umbilical cord breaks when the baby is born and it must feed and breathe for itself.

Because they are fed for a while inside their mother's body, placental babies are much more highly developed when they are born than the babies of marsupials. But many of them are still quite helpless. The young of dogs, cats, rabbits and many others are blind and naked when they are born. Their mothers have to do everything for them. The young of horses, antelopes and other animals that normally live on the open plains are able to get up and run about as soon as they are born. This is essential for them because they have to keep up with the herd. A helpless young animal out in the open would soon be found and eaten. But even babies that can run

The black bear is a common animal in North America. Although it belongs to the flesh-eating group of mammals (the carnivores), the black bear eats a lot of berries and other plant material.

Far left: The echidna, or spiny ant-eater, one of the monotremes or egg-laying mammals.

Left: Zebras, which are close relatives of the horse.

about when they are born need milk from their mothers. During the time they are with their mother they learn a great deal about hunting or finding food. This period of learning while in the care of the mother (and father as well with some animals) has surely helped the placental mammals to outbreed the other mammals.

The placentals have managed to invade all habitats—the land, the air, the sea and the fresh waters. They have also adapted themselves to a wide variety of foods. The greatest number are plant-eaters. For instance, there are all the rats, mice and voles and all the hoofed animals, from the horse to the hippopotamus.

Rhinoceroses are hoofed mammals belonging to the same group as the horse and tapir.

Bush-babies (below right) and vervet monkeys (below left) are two representatives of the most successful order of mammals—the primates. Man is classified in this order.

Instinct and Learning

The thrush does not have to be taught how to build its nest and nor does the spider have to be shown how to make its web. The animals know automatically how to perform these tasks. Behaviour patterns of this kind, which are inborn, are called instincts.

Instincts are very common in the animal world, particularly among the lower orders of life. They account for a great deal of animal behaviour, including reaction to danger, courtship displays, rearing and feeding of the young and migration. The behaviour pattern needs something to trigger it off. The trigger is called a releaser. It might be a noise, it might be a visual signal, or it might be something that happens inside the animal.

Each kind of animal has its own types of instinctive behaviour and all members of a species will normally behave in the same way. The instincts are inherited and they are just as much part of an animal as its shape and colour. Behaviour patterns have evolved in just the same way as colours and shapes and they are just as important in adapting the animal to its surroundings and helping it to survive. The wasp beetle (page 138) has the colours of a wasp and it also moves like a wasp, to complete the deception.

Some instincts are very simple actions. Woodlice, for example, scuttle about in an agitated fashion if exposed to bright light or dry air. They keep this up until they reach a dark or damp place and then they settle down. This is a simple action, but it ensures that the animals keep themselves in the right conditions. Other instincts are much more complicated. Nest-building, for example, involves collecting various kinds of materials and joining them together to make the layers of the nest. Even more complex are the engineering feats of the beaver. This animal knows instinctively how to fell trees and to use them to build dams to make lakes where it can live safely.

Courtship behaviour is also a very complicated business for many animals. Peacocks display their fine feathers to the females. Male redstarts hold singing contests to impress the hens. Male fishes often perform elaborate 'dances' to engage the attention of females, while deer and many other animals fight among themselves. There are usually several stages to this sort of behaviour and

Below left: Blue tits soon learn to peck through milk tops to get at the cream.

Below right: The courtship of the whooping crane.

Although many animals fight, they spend more time threatening their opponents, like this elephant.

each stage normally requires a separate trigger. In courtship behaviour, for example, the female's reaction to one stage will trigger off the next stage in the male's display.

Some instincts are perfect, right from the start. For example, a silk moth only makes one cocoon in its life, but it is perfectly made. Other instincts have to be perfected by practice. Birds know how to fly by instinct, but they need a bit of practice before they master it. However, animals can often be misled. A male robin will attack a bundle of red feathers but it will ignore a stuffed robin whose breast feathers have been painted brown. The attacking behaviour is triggered off simply by sight of the red breast feathers.

Right: These baby shrikes have just left the nest. They know how to fly, but they will have to have several practice flights before they master it.

Bottom: Thresher sharks (left) rounding up the herrings on which they feed. The woodpecker finch of the Galapogos Islands (right) uses thorns to dig insects out of crevices.

Below: The male lyre bird displays his fine plumage when courting the female.

Instincts and Hormones

Some instincts appear only at certain times. They are often due to the action of hormones. These are chemical substances made in the body and released into the blood stream. A releaser is still necessary and the effect of the hormone is to make the animal sensitive to a signal which might not affect it at other times. Hormone activity is high during the breeding season and a cock bird will display vigorously when he sees a female. Out of the breeding season, when the relevant hormones are missing, the hen does not make any impression on the cock.

Learning

Mammals, birds and many other animals are able to learn to some extent. They remember things that have happened before and they can sometimes modify their instinctive reactions as a result. Much of the behaviour of adult birds and mammals is probably a combination of instinct and learning. Birds reared by themselves can sing quite well, but their songs are often quite different from the songs of wild birds. It seems that the ability to sing is instinctive, but the ability to sing the right song has to be learned. Occasionally, birds and mammals show signs of real intelligence.

Animal Parasites

On pages 47 and 48 of this book there are some pictures of parasitic plants. These are plants which 'steal' some or all of their food from other organisms without giving anything in return. But not only plants live in this way. Many animals are parasites too. They live in close association with other organisms, called the hosts, and they take food from them. They do not usually kill the hosts, but they weaken them.

Oak Apples and other Plant Galls

A soft pinkish outgrowth is a common sight on oak twigs in the summer. This is the oak apple, an abnormal growth caused by an insect. In the spring a small brown ant-like creature laid its eggs in the oak twig and when the grubs hatched out they caused the twig to swell up around them. They then started to feed on the soft tissues and they are in effect parasites of the oak tree although they do not seem to do it any harm. Growths of this kind are quite common on many kinds of plant. They are called galls. Most of them are caused by insects, but some are caused by microscopic creatures called mites. The little red pimples seen on sycamore and maple leaves are galls caused by mites.

Internal Parasites

Internal parasites are parasites that live inside the bodies of their hosts. The most important members of this group are tapeworms, roundworms and liver flukes. Some live in the blood system of the host animal, but the majority live in the food canal. Some worms merely attach themselves to the wall of the host's stomach or intestine and absorb the digested food. Other kinds of worms actually eat the host's tissues, rasping them away with sharp, horny teeth.

Nearly all animals have worms and the worms do not do much harm in small numbers. It is only when their numbers build up that they start to weaken their hosts. Farm animals are normally dosed with worm-killing medicine every so often to prevent the

Left: These strange objects on a rose leaf are galls caused by the grubs of an insect. Below: Parasites usually have some way of attaching themselves firmly to the host. The louse (top) has claws, the fluke (middle) has suckers, and the tapeworm (bottom) has both hooks and suckers.

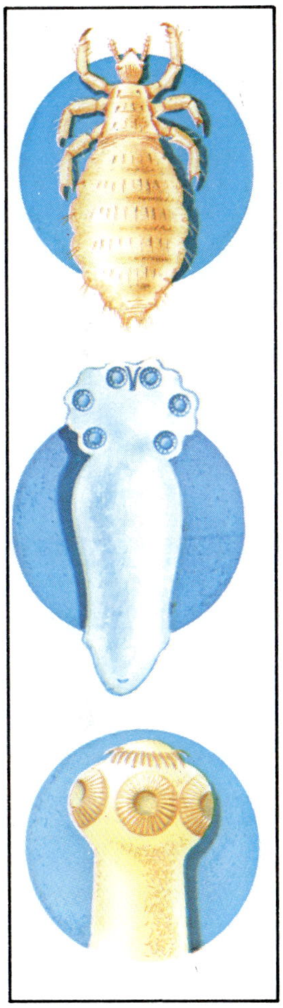

Left: The tapeworm's body consists of a small head and a string of segments containing little more than eggs. One segment with developing eggs is shown enlarged.

worm population from becoming too large.

Some parasitic worms, including the roundworms, have a fairly simple life history. Their eggs pass out with the host's droppings and they wait on the ground until another animal takes them in with its food. Tapeworms and liver flukes, however, usually have a much more complicated life cycle. The common tapeworm of dogs lives in the food canal. Its eggs pass out with the droppings and many of them end up in and around the dog's sleeping quarters. Here, there are usually a number of young fleas feeding on the rubbish. They take in some of the tapeworm eggs and the eggs hatch inside them. The young tapeworms grow in the flea and then they get back into the dog when it licks its coat and swallows the flea.

The internal parasites do not have much work to do: everything is provided for them. Like the parasitic plants, they concentrate all their efforts into reproducing themselves. Huge numbers of eggs are produced, but only a few manage to reach the right kind of host.

Many caterpillars and other insects are attacked by ichneumon flies. These are rather special parasites because they do kill their hosts, but not until they have finished with them. The female ichneumon fly, which is something like a slender wasp, seeks out a caterpillar of the right kind and lays her eggs inside it. The eggs hatch and the grubs begin to eat their host. They eat only the non-vital parts, such as muscles, to start with and the infected caterpillar becomes very 'lazy'. When the ichneumon grubs are fully grown they finish off their host and then turn into pupae themselves..

Below: A blood-sucking louse is an external parasite on warm-blooded animals.

A magnified photograph of a flea. Fleas are parasitic only in adult life.

External Parasites

External parasites live on the outside of their hosts and most of them suck blood. Examples include ticks, lice and fleas. The latter are parasitic only in adult life, for the young fleas live by eating rubbish in the nests of their hosts. External parasites often have strong claws or hooks with which they hang on to the fur or feathers of the host.

Many of the external parasites carry disease-causing germs. Fleas can carry plague, a disease of rats which they transmit to humans. Lice carry typhus fever and ticks carry many serious diseases of cattle. Ticks are related to the spiders. They attach themselves to cattle and other warm-blooded animals and bury their mouths in the host's flesh. They then suck blood and gradually swell up. Cattle in tropical countries may carry thousands of ticks and they have to be sprayed regularly with insecticide in order to keep them free of these parasites.

Brood Parasites

These creatures display a special form of parasitism. They do not parasitise an individual animal, but they take advantage of a family or a community. One of the best known brood parasites is the cuckoo. This bird simply lays its eggs in the nests of other birds such as warblers and pipits. The cuckoo is much bigger than these other birds and when the young cuckoo hatches from its egg its first action is to throw out the other eggs or nestlings. Only one cuckoo egg is laid in one nest and the young cuckoo then does nothing but take food from its 'foster parents' until it is big enough to fly away.

Similar examples are found in the insect world. Bumble bees are industrious creatures that make nests and bring up their young. There are, however, some closely related insects called cuckoo bees. These do not make their own nests and they do not have workers. They lay their eggs in the nests of bumble bees and leave the bumble bee workers to look after them and to feed the grubs until they grow up.

Animal Partnerships

The animals described on the previous two pages are parasites. They live in close association with other creatures, but the associations are very one-sided, with the parasites getting all the benefit. There are many other associations, however, in which both partners derive benefit from living together. This type of association is called symbiosis, which simply means 'living together'. It is also called mutualism.

Animal Partnerships

One of the best known examples of symbiosis involves a hermit crab and a sea anemone. Hermit crabs have soft hind parts and they protect themselves by living in old sea shells, such as whelk shells or winkle shells. As they grow they have to find larger ones from time to time to accommodate their growing bodies. A crab sometimes chooses a shell on which a sea anemone is growing, or else a sea anemone might start to grow on an occupied shell. This could be the beginning of a partnership. The base of the anemone may spread as it grows and cover part of the crab's body as well. The growth of the crab and the anemone then keep pace with each other and the crab has no need to change its home any more. As the hermit crab moves about in search of food the anemone is carried into new feeding grounds as well and it certainly benefits from the association. The hermit crab also benefits further because it is protected by the stinging cells of the anemone.

Bird Partners

There are many symbiotic partnerships between birds and large game animals. Birds called oxpeckers spend their time on the backs of animals such as buffaloes, zebras and rhinoceroses. Far from annoying the animals, they perform a useful service by eating ticks and other blood-sucking parasites. Both partners benefit from this arrangement and so it is a clear example of symbiosis. It is also said that the birds warn the animals of approaching danger.

Cattle egrets also associate with buffaloes and antelopes. The birds feed on the insects disturbed by the animals as they walk through the grass. In return, the birds warn the animals of approaching danger. This is a somewhat looser association than that between the oxpeckers and their mammals.

Perhaps the strangest partnership is that between the Nile crocodile and the Egyptian plover. This little black and white bird feeds on the leeches that infest the crocodile. It is even allowed inside the crocodile's mouth, where it removes leeches and scraps of food adhering to the teeth.

The hermit crab can get along quite nicely without an anemone sitting on top of it, and

The cattle egrets on these buffaloes feed on the insects that the animals disturb. In return, they warn the buffaloes of approaching danger.

the game animals do not really need their feathered friends. But there are animals that cannot live without their symbiotic partners. This is especially true of the termites. Wood is a difficult material to digest and termites rely on hordes of tiny protozoan animals to do the job for them. The protozoan live in the stomachs of the termites, and in return they get food and shelter.

Plant Partnerships

The most obvious partnerships between plants are those found in the lichens. These plants, described on page 32, consist of algae and fungi living in a symbiotic association.

The roots of clovers, peas and all other members of the pea family bear little swellings called root nodules. These nodules contain certain kinds of bacteria which convert atmospheric nitrogen into nitrates. Nitrates are very important plant foods. The bacteria get shelter and food materials from the plant. Farmers often include peas, beans or clover in their crop rotation because the decaying roots and nodules add nitrates to the soil. The farmer does not then have to add so much fertiliser for his next crop.

Many fungi enter into symbiotic associations with the roots of other plants. Such associations are called mycorrhizas. Most forest trees have networks of fungal threads around their roots and the threads also invade the outer layers of the roots. The fungi help the roots to absorb water and minerals from the soil and in return they get certain carbohydrates from the trees. Some fungi are very particular about the trees with which they associate. The red and white fly agaric toadstool is almost always associated with the roots of pine or birch trees. Some trees will not grow if the right sort of fungus is not present.

Mixed Partnerships

Partnerships between plants and animals are quite common. Many corals and other aquatic animals contain green algae in their bodies. These tiny plants were once believed to provide oxygen for the animals through their photosynthetic activity, but they actually produce very little oxygen. Their main role is probably in using up various waste materials produced by the animals.

Termites employ tiny animals to digest their food for them, but many other animals employ bacteria. Most grazing animals have large populations of bacteria in special pouches somewhere in their food canals. The bacteria break down the tough cellulose of the grass and other plants, producing sugars and other materials that the grazing animals can absorb.

The hermit crab carries the anemone to fresh feeding grounds. In return, the anemone protects the crab with its stinging cells.

The crocodile is quite happy to let the plovers feed on the leeches on its skin, and even lets them into its mouth.

Survival

Animals are engaged in a non-stop struggle to find food and to avoid being eaten. Those that survive best are those with the best forms of attack and defence.

Camouflage

During their long history the animals have developed many different ways of protecting themselves. Large numbers of animals rely on camouflage and blend very well with their surroundings. Camouflage helps animals to hide from their enemies but it also helps the hunting animals, such as the leopards, to stalk up on their prey without being seen. One common form of camouflage is known as countershading. The underside of the body is generally lighter in colour than the upper-side, thus tending to cancel out the shadows. This helps the animal to merge with the background, even when it is out in the open.

Irregular stripes and patterns are very effective at camouflaging an animal because they break up its outline. Many moths that sit on tree trunks during the daytime have irregular stripes. When they settle on the bark they line up their patterns with the cracks and they 'disappear'.

Some animals are able to change their colours to match the backgrounds on which they are sitting. The chameleon is the best known of these creatures, although it is not so good at changing its colour as certain other animals. One of the best colour-change artists is the cuttlefish. It can change colour very quickly. The skin of the cuttlefish (and of its cousins the squids) has three layers of pigmented cells. One layer is black, one is red and the outer one is yellow. Each pigment cell

The pale wing tips and thorax of the buff-tip moth (left) look just like broken twigs when the insect is at rest (right).

Above: The colouring of many animals blends well with their natural habitats.

Left: Many young deer are marked with white spots. These help to conceal the animals in the woodlands.

Above: Some animals with stings or poisonous bites are marked with bold colours. These are called warning colours.

is controlled by a nerve and it can contract or expand very quickly. The animal can produce a whole range of colours from black, through reds and browns, to yellows according to which cells are expanded. When the black cells are expanded the animal looks dark; when they are contracted it looks much paler. Because each cell has its own nerve the animal can expand the cells in one part of the body and not in another. Many fishes, such as the plaice, can also change colour to match either sandy or stony backgrounds. In experimental work some of these fishes have even adopted a chequered pattern matching a chess board, but animals can produce only those colours associated with the pigments in their skins. They cannot match every background.

Animal Twigs

A number of animals, especially among the insects, have taken camouflage even further. They have evolved remarkable similarities to objects in their surroundings. The majority resemble leaves and twigs, some twig-like caterpillars bearing 'warts' which look like buds. One group of bugs look just like prickles on a stem, and a number of moths even resemble bird droppings. Few birds would bother to peck at such things.

The porcupine is adequately protected by its barbed quills, which stick into the flesh of attackers.

Spines and Stings

It is usually the defenceless animals that employ camouflage to hide from their enemies. Those with some form of defence do not need to hide. One common form of defence is the possession of spines. Hedgehogs can roll up into very prickly balls when attacked and they are then safe from most of their enemies. Several spiny fishes, such as the porcupine fish and the pufferfish, inflate themselves with water when attacked and present a formidable problem to their attackers. Other animals may have a more active form of defence in the possession of stings. Bees, wasps and scorpions are good examples. The stings of bees and wasps are actually the modified egg-laying organs and it is only the females (queens and workers) that can sting. Other animals, including the skunk and ladybird, protect themselves by having an unpleasant taste or smell.

Warning Coloration

Far from hiding themselves, the animals with unpleasant tastes or stings are often marked with bold colours and they are very conspicuous. For example, many wasps are clearly marked with black and yellow. Ladybirds are also black and yellow or black and red. These bold colour combinations are known as warning colours, because they warn birds and other animals not to touch the insects. Young birds will try these unpleasant insects, but they will not eat them. They soon learn that the bold pattern is associated with something nasty.

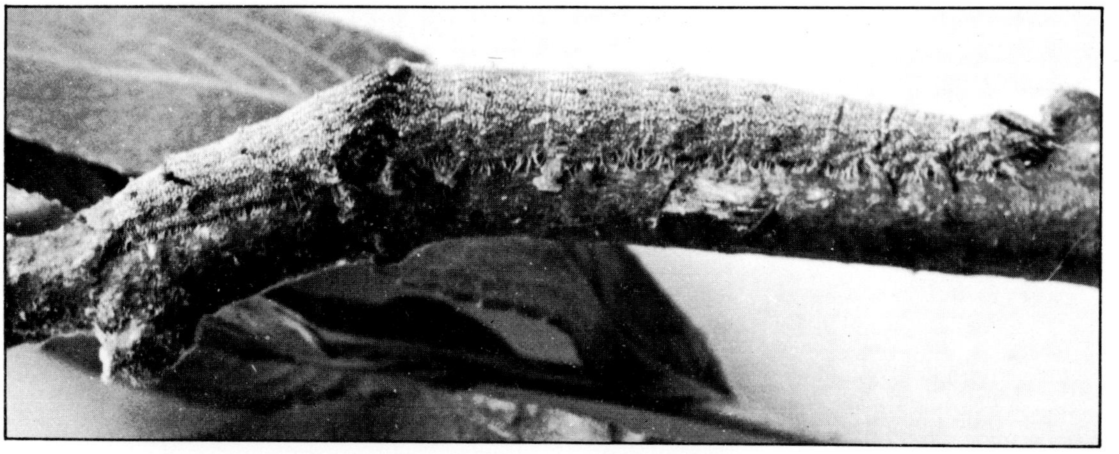

The red underwing caterpillar is almost invisible as it lies along a twig. Shadows are obliterated by a fringe of hairs along the underside.

Mimicry

Many of us have drawn back hastily from a harmless hoverfly at some time or other in the belief that it was a wasp. It certainly looks like a wasp at first glance and even birds are fooled. They avoid the hoverfly so the insect survives because it resembles a wasp. This is an example of mimicry, and we say that the hoverfly mimics the wasp. There are many examples of mimicry among insects. The boldly marked bees and wasps, which are unpleasant because of their stings, are mimicked by a variety of harmless insects. These include several different kinds of hoverflies, beetles and moths. The bees and wasps are the models and the other insects are the mimics. Young birds try to eat the models, but they soon learn to leave them alone. They also leave alone any other insects that look like these models. The mimics are therefore protected by their appearance, although they are harmless and perhaps good to eat. This rather clever arrangement will work, however, only if the unpleasant models are much more common than the mimics. If the mimics were common the young birds would associate the bold pattern with pleasant food. This is called Batesian mimicry.

Left: Prawns become lighter or darker according to the background, by decreasing or increasing the size of the red pigment cells in their skin.

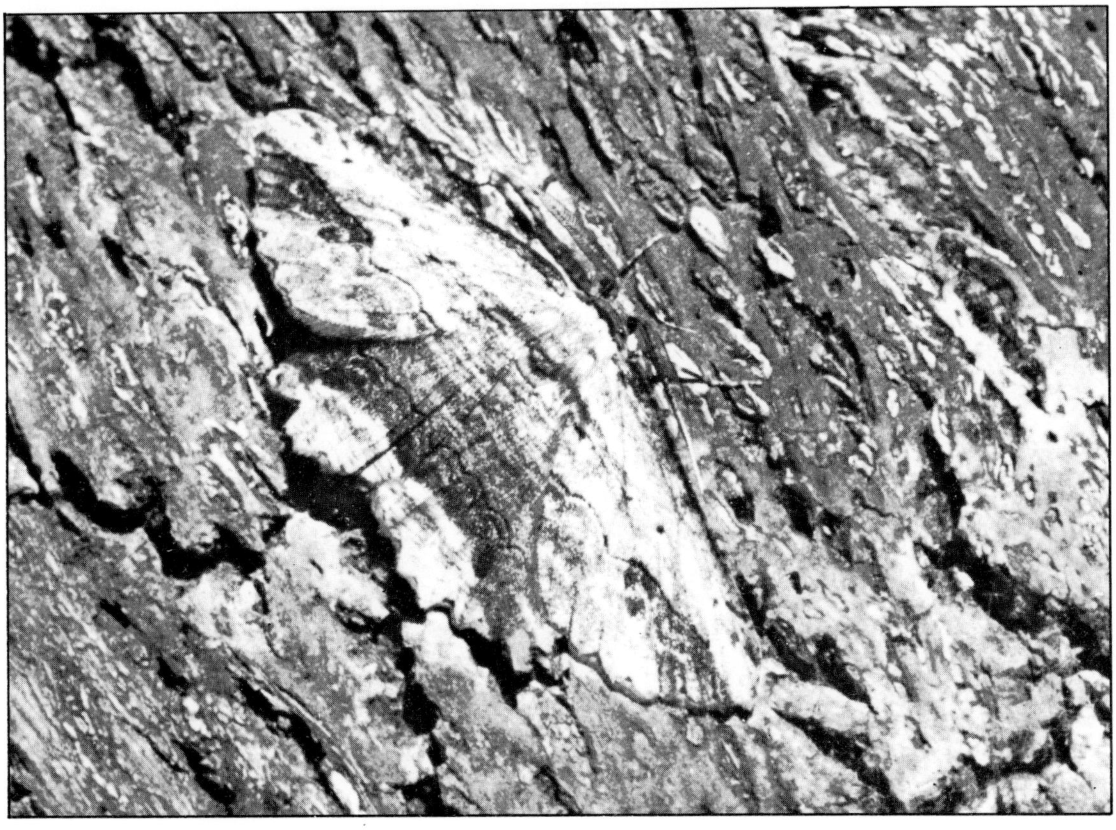

Left: The waved umber moth settles with its wing pattern lined up with the bark crevices and it almost disappears.

Right: The cinnabar moth and its caterpillar have a very unpleasant taste and they advertise their unpleasantness with bright warning colours.

Below right: In their behaviour and appearance the hoverfly (bottom) and the wasp beetle (top) mimic certain wasps. They are left alone by birds and other predators although they are quite harmless.

Below left: The eyed hawk-moth is quite inconspicuous as it rests on a tree trunk (top). But when it is disturbed, it raises its front wings and displays two large eye-spots to frighten predators away (bottom).

In another form of mimicry, called Müllerian mimicry and best shown by various tropical butterflies, two or more inedible or otherwise unpleasant species share the same warning pattern. An insect-eating bird therefore has only one pattern to learn before it avoids all such insects.

Eye Spots for Protection

A number of small animals, notably fishes and insects, are decorated with eye spots. Small eye spots near the tail of a fish or on the wings of a butterfly might deceive any enemy and cause it to strike at these relatively unimportant parts of the body. The animal then escapes without much harm. Larger eye spots are often used to frighten enemies because they look like the eyes of much larger creatures.

Cinnabar Moth
and Caterpillar

Migration

Many birds breed in the temperate regions and then, when autumn approaches, they return to the warmth of the Tropics. This regular movement between two regions is called migration. It is of great importance to the birds because it enables them to find food throughout the year. Nearly all of the birds that migrate between the Tropics and the temperate regions are insect-eating species. Well-known migrating species are various warblers, the swifts, the martins and the swallows.

Not all birds migrate between the tropics and the temperate regions. Many species move between the temperate regions and the Arctic. A good number of these species are ducks and wading birds. The lakes and marshes all freeze over during the long northern winter, and so the birds fly south in search of open water and feeding grounds.

Land Migrations

Birds are perhaps the most obvious of the migrating animals. Land-living mammals do not cover such large distances as the birds, but many of them make important migrations. The caribou, for example, spends the summer wandering over the open tundra in the far north, but it moves southwards into the coniferous forests for the winter. Mountain animals, such as the chamois and various species of sheep and goats, spend the summer on the upper slopes, but move down into more sheltered regions for the winter.

The Monarch Butterfly

Many butterfly species migrate. One of the best known of the migrating species is the monarch or milkweed. It is an American butterfly and during the summer it spreads

The migration routes of many birds have been discovered by putting little rings on their legs and recording where they have been found. Some species travel thousands of kilometres.

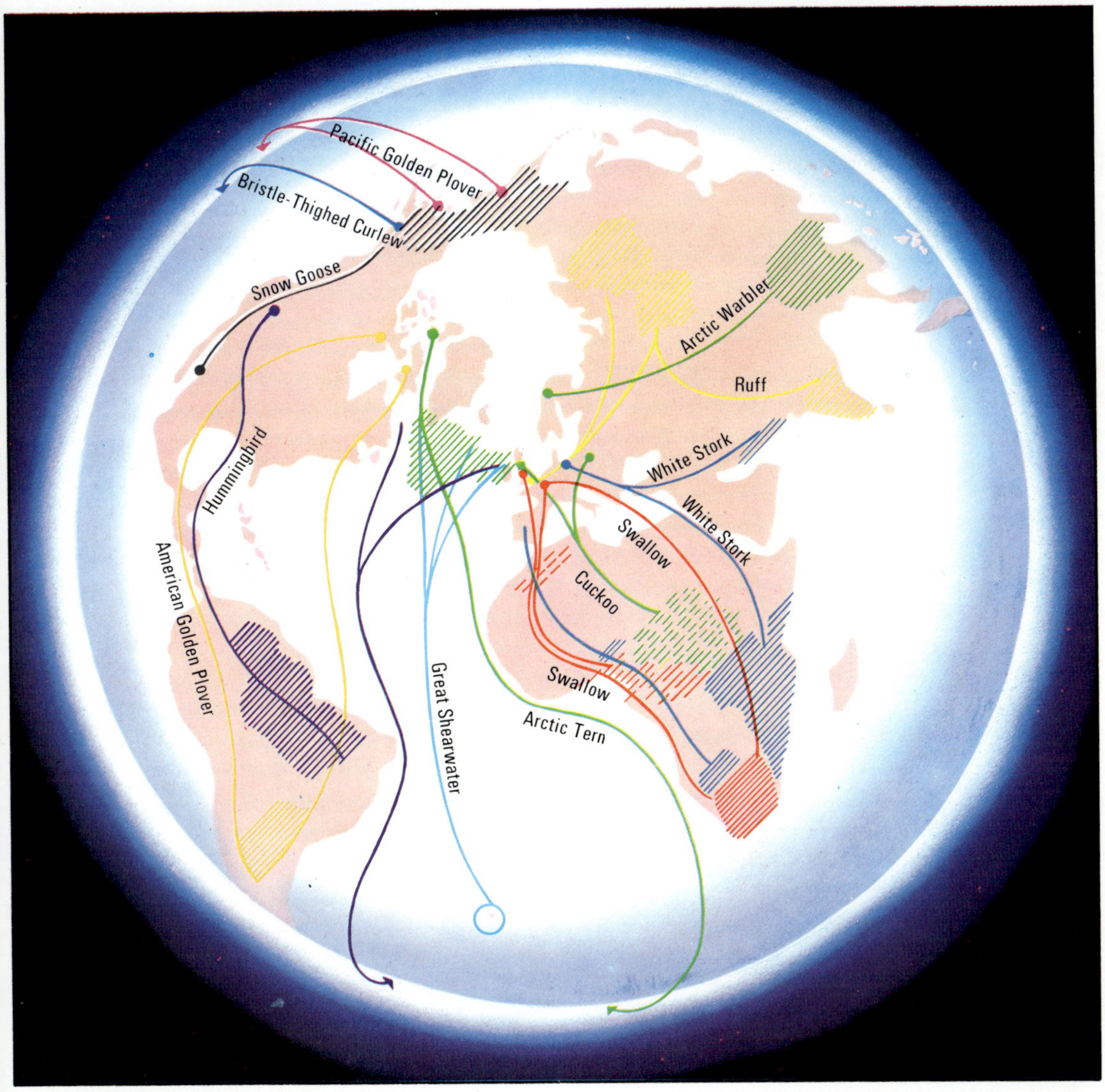

Above: The lemming is famous for its emigrations. These are mass movements in one direction. Every few years their numbers build up to such levels that they move away in hordes.

far into Canada. In early autumn the insects begin to move southwards, gradually joining up into swarms which fly down to their winter quarters in Florida and Mexico.

Migration in the Sea

Marine creatures have almost as much freedom to migrate as the birds. Many whales move from their polar feeding grounds into the warmer seas before bringing forth their young. The European eel starts its life in the Sargasso Sea in the western Atlantic. The young eels take about three years to reach the coasts of Europe. They then move up the rivers and stay there for several years while they grow up. Each year the fully grown eels move downstream to the sea and make their way across the Atlantic. They never return to the rivers again.

The life history of the salmon is the reverse of that of the eel. The fishes spawn in rivers and the young salmon make their way down to the sea, where they spend a year or two before returning to the rivers to breed.

All the migrations mentioned so far have been seasonal ones. Some creatures, however, migrate every day. The little crustaceans and other members of the plankton that float in the sea spend about 12 hours in the surface layers and then they sink down to lower layers for about 12 hours.

Finding the Way

The urge to migrate is quite instinctive in animals. Internal changes, together with changes in temperature and length of day, trigger off the movements. How the migrating animals find their way has always been a puzzle. Memory must certainly play a part in the return of birds to the same nests year after year, but it cannot explain how young birds find their way to Africa several weeks after their parents have gone. The birds navigate by the position of sun and stars and the earth's magnetic field. Butterflies and many other migrating animals use the sun to guide them. Fishes may use similar methods.

Below: Caribou on the move: huge herds of these animals move south into the forests in the autumn.

Hibernation

Many animals living in the cold and temperate regions disappear in the autumn and go into hibernation. This is a very deep sleep during which the body processes slow down almost to a stop. Very little energy is consumed and the body temperature, even in mammals, falls to within a degree or two of that of their surroundings.

Hibernation in Cold-blooded Animals

A large number of invertebrate animals pass the cold season in the egg stage but many butterflies and moths pass the winter in the pupa stage or chrysalis, often safely buried in the soil, and some species hibernate as caterpillars. A few butterflies and moths hibernate as adults. When the days grow cold they find some dry corner—perhaps in a hollow tree or a garden shed—and go to sleep until the first warm days of spring. Several species of snail hibernate under stones and logs. They seal up their shells with mucus.

Frogs, tortoises, snakes and lizards are well known hibernators. They all bury themselves away from the effect of frost. Fishes do not really hibernate, although some species become lethargic and partly bury themselves in the mud. The temperature at the bottom of lakes and rivers does not fall below 4°C as a rule and most freshwater fishes are able to remain active in winter.

Hibernation in Warm-blooded Animals

Some birds become drowsy in cold weather, but true hibernation is not known among the birds. The nearest approach to hibernation is shown by the whippoorwill, an American nightjar or goatsucker. It sleeps for much of the winter, but its temperature does not fall as much as in the true hibernators. It stays at about 20°C, compared with the 38°C of the active bird.

Many mammals, such as bears, badgers and tree squirrels, sleep for several days at a time during the winter but these are not really hibernating. True hibernation, where the body temperature falls almost to that of the surroundings, is found in only a few groups of mammals. Bats and other insect-eating mammals such as hedgehogs hibernate, and so do various groups of rodents. These include dormice, ground squirrels and hamsters. But even though they go into a deep sleep, they wake up periodically during the winter and they may feed on stored food. Before they go into their winter sleep, the animals put on weight in the form of fat.

Colder weather, shortage of food, and the shorter days of autumn probably all play a part in bringing on the winter sleep. The end of hibernation is probably brought about by the warmth of the spring, and the animals then gradually speed up their body processes until their temperatures return to normal and they can start to move about. The waking process uses up a great deal of energy, and it is likely that many hibernating animals never wake up because they have not enough food reserves to provide the necessary energy. This is likely if the animals have been disturbed during the winter.

Aestivation—the Summer Sleep

In some of the warmer parts of the world, especially where there is a well marked dry season, a number of animals hide away and go to sleep to avoid the heat and drought. This 'summer sleep' is called aestivation. Many desert-dwelling animals aestivate. They include various frogs and toads, as well as some of the desert rodents. The African lung fish also aestivates. It lives in sluggish rivers which often dry up during the summer months. When this happens the fish burrows into the mud and surrounds itself with mucus. It can breathe air, which it obtains through a narrow 'chimney' from the burrow, and it remains moist until the rains come and the river starts to flow again.

The lung fish aestivates in the mud of its dried-up river until the water returns.

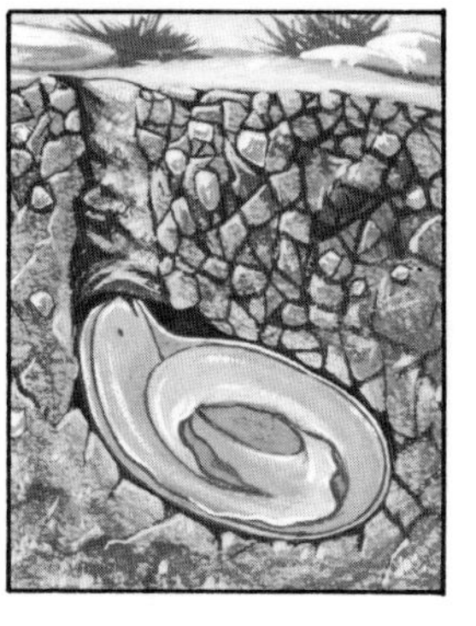

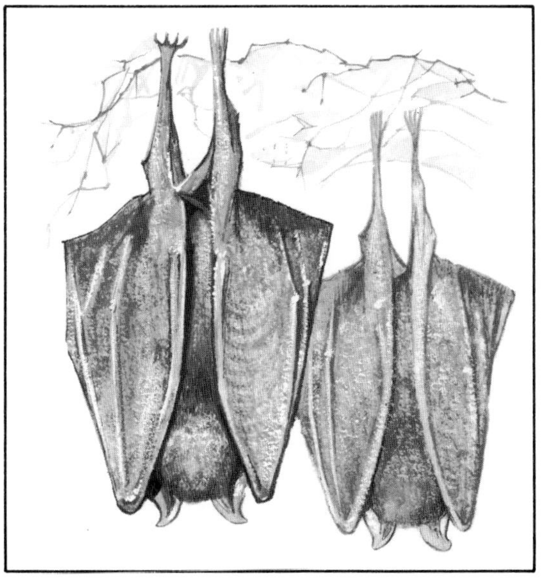

Left: The bats of cool climates sleep throughout the winter in caves and other secluded places. They hang upside down and their temperature falls to a very low level. Moisture from the air often condenses on their fur and gives them a glistening appearance.

Nocturnal Life

When night falls a great change-over takes place in the animal world. Birds, butterflies and most of the other creatures that are active by day seek their resting places. Many other animals wake up and venture out into the open.

The air temperature drops when the sun goes down, and the air also becomes damp because it cannot hold so much water vapour when it is cool. If it cools down very much, some of the moisture may condense and form dew. This is very important for small creatures such as slugs, snails and woodlice which have no waterproof coats. They can come out at night without risk of drying up, but they have to spend the daytime hidden away under stones and leaves. Most desert-dwelling creatures also come out at night and get much of their water supplies by eating dew-laden food.

The light is poor at night and many of the nocturnal animals have large eyes which gather in as much light as possible. The owl is a good example. Our own eyes are also quite good for seeing at night, although the cells which detect colour do not work at low light levels and we see everything in shades of grey. Cats, foxes and some other nocturnal animals increase the sensitivity of their eyes by having a 'mirror' at the back. You can see this if the animal passes through the beam of a torch or a car headlight. The light is reflected back through the eye. Because the light passes through the retina twice it helps to produce a brighter image.

Cats have a 'mirror' behind the eye to make the eye much more sensitive.

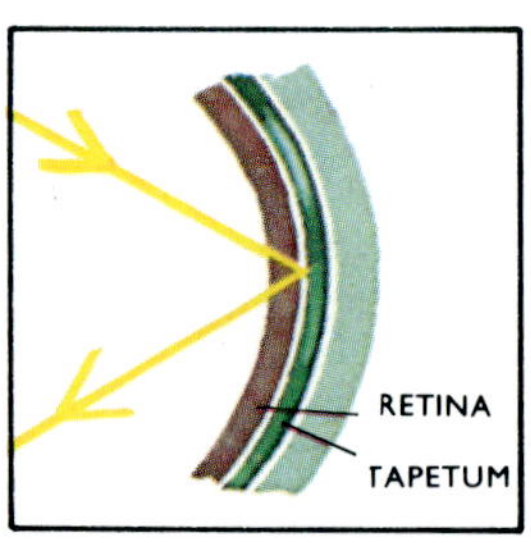

Not all nocturnal animals have good eyesight. They use the other senses for finding their way about and for finding food. The sense of touch is very well developed in many nocturnal animals. The large hairs or whiskers on the faces of cats and mice are sense organs. The sense of smell is also very important for nocturnal animals such as badgers, hedgehogs and field mice. The moist night air holds scent well.

The sense of hearing is another very important one for nocturnal animals, as well as for many creatures that are active by day. The animals hear their food and their enemies and they also hear other members of the same species. This helps them to meet and mate. Many of the sounds are beyond the range of human hearing, but the animals' ears are specially tuned to pick up the sounds that are important to them.

The Bat's Radar

Insect-eating bats fly by night. They have very weak eyes, but they hardly ever bump into anything. In one experiment, some thin wires were stretched across a darkened room and some blind-folded bats were released in the room. They flew about quite easily without bumping into the wires. This showed that the bats were not using their eyes to find their way about. They were using a system known as echo-location, which is rather similar to the radar system used for locating ships and aircraft. The bat gives out a very high-pitched sound—far too high for us to hear it—and listens for the echoes bouncing back from nearby objects. The bat can detect the direction of the echo and so avoid obstacles or catch flying insects.

Animal Lights

Many animals produce their own light. It helps them to find their way about and it also helps them to find mates. One of the most famous of the light-producing animals is the European glow-worm. This is really a beetle, but the female has no wings and she looks rather like a worm. Her light-producing organ is on the underside of her hind end, and

Below right: The bat has weak eyes and it finds its way about by sending out high-pitched sounds and listening for the echoes.
Below: The firefly and a click beetle (left), two insects that produce light.

the greenish light is produced by a chemical reaction. Man-made lights give off a fair amount of heat as well, but the glow-worm's light-producing reaction is very efficient and gives out almost no heat. The female shines her light as she sits in the grass, and the winged, lampless male flies to her. Fireflies are also beetles, but both male and female insects produce light. Their courtship involves an exchange of flashing signals. The New Zealand glow-worm is the larva of a fly that lives in caves. The luminous larvae spin sticky threads which hang from the cave roof. Mosquitoes and other insects are attracted to the lights. They get entangled in the threads and are eaten by the glow-worms.

Light-producing animals are common in the sea, especially down in the depths where there is no daylight. Jellyfishes, prawns, squids and fishes have luminous species. Eyes are well developed in some of them and the lights help them to find mates and food. Some deep-sea angler fishes have luminous 'bait' on their rods, and this lures smaller fishes to their doom. Several squids and prawns baffle their enemies by giving off clouds of luminous slime. These distract their enemies, allowing them to escape.

Left: The fox hunts mainly by night, using its keen eyes, its ears and its sense of smell.

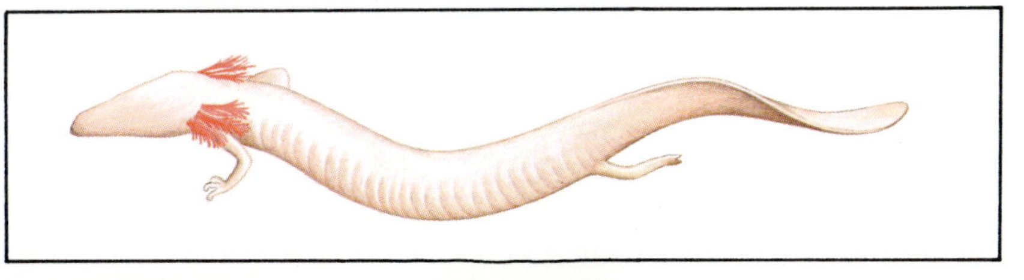

Above: Many cave-dwelling animals, which never meet the light, are blind and very pale in colour. The olm, which lives in south-east Europe, is a relative of the newts and salamanders.

More than about 600 metres down in the ocean it is completely dark, but many species of animals carry their own lights around with them. Some have luminous patterns which enable them to recognise members of their own species. Some of the angler-fishes (centre) dangle luminous 'bait' above their mouths and lure their prey with it.

Animal Electricity

Certain fishes have the remarkable ability to generate high voltage electrical energy in their bodies. This is not the simple sort of static charge produced when we comb our hair or pull off a nylon jumper. It is a powerful discharge, sufficient in some instances to stun a horse. The fishes use these electric shocks for paralysing their prey and for defending themselves. They can also use the shocks for the purposes of navigation.

An electric impulse is involved every time a signal travels along a nerve and into a muscle. The electric fishes have modified this system. Their electric organs, or 'batteries', are composed of special muscles. The modified muscle fibres are known as electroplates and large numbers of them are stacked up to form the battery.

The muscles of the electric organs cannot contract and the energy is not converted into movement. It moves on as an electric discharge. If all the electroplates are discharged together, a powerful shock can be sent through the surrounding water. The fishes can also produce less powerful discharges by firing off only part of the battery at one time.

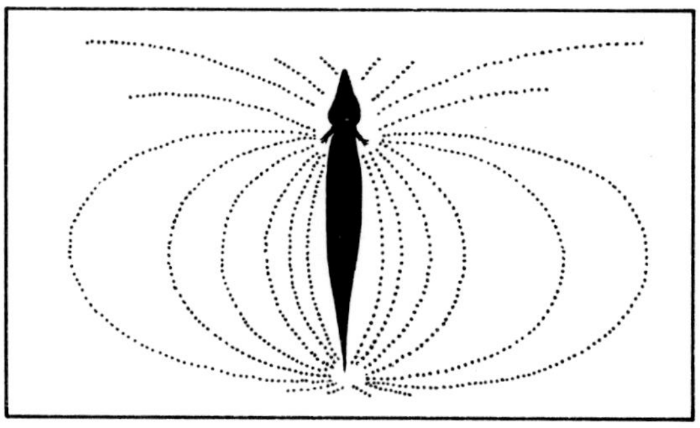

Right: The pattern of the electric field surrounding the Nile fish. The pattern is disturbed when the fish approaches an object, so the fish can take avoiding action. Below: Some of the various types of electric fishes.

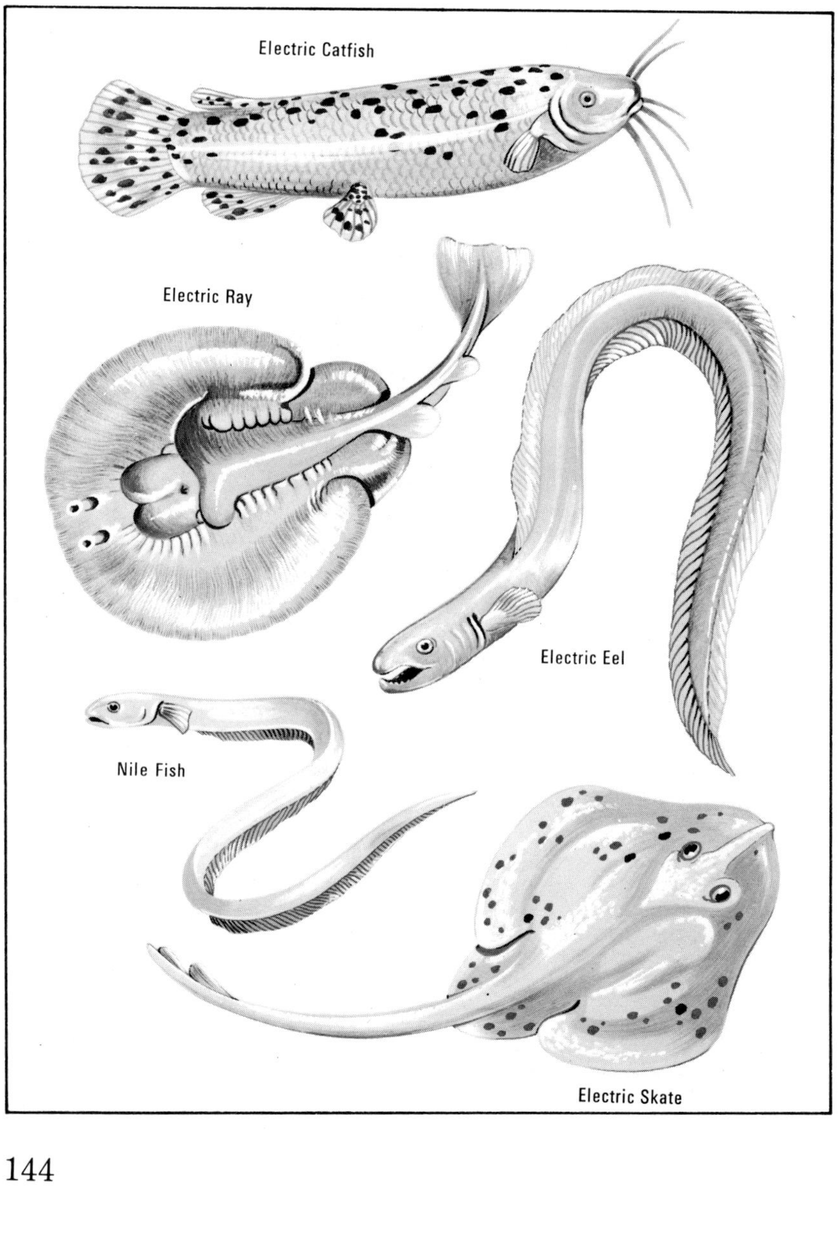

Electric Fishes

Electric organs are found in a variety of fishes, in the sea and in fresh water. One of the best known of the electric fishes is the electric eel, which lives in the rivers of the Amazon basin in South America. The electric organs can generate up to 550 volts—more than enough to kill the frogs and fishes on which the eel feeds. Larger animals coming too close to the eel are likely to be stunned by the shock. The fish can also produce smaller discharges which help it to navigate in the murky streams which are its home.

The eel-like Nile fish also finds its way about in muddy water by means of its own electricity. It surrounds itself with a weak electric field generated in its tail, and it is very sensitive to disturbances in this field. If it swims too near a rock it will detect a change in the field and take avoiding action. It can also find crevices for hiding.

Marine electric fishes normally generate lower voltages than freshwater fishes. This is because salt water is a much better conductor of electricity than fresh water. It requires a lower voltage to push a current through it. The skates and rays are the most important electric fishes in the sea. Most of the species have batteries in their tails and produce low voltages of unknown function. The various species of electric rays, however, have large batteries on each side of the head. They can produce a large current at up to 200 volts. The discharge is used for both defence and feeding. The fishes wrap themselves around their prey and electrocute it.

Dictionary of Animals

Aardvark An African mammal with no close relatives. Its bulky grey body is about 2 m long, including the tail. It has a long narrow snout. It feeds mainly on termites, which it digs out of the ground with its very powerful legs.

Aardwolf An African member of the hyena family, yellowish-grey with black stripes and a bushy tail. It is nocturnal and feeds mainly on termites, which it picks up with its long tongue.

Abalone A single-shelled marine mollusc related to limpets and also known as an ormer or earshell. The body is fringed with tentacles. The shell has a line of holes, through which water is exhaled. They live in many parts of the world but are commonest in warmer waters.

Accentor A member of a small family of birds found in Europe and Asia. The commonest species is the dunnock, also called the hedge sparrow. Accentors have slender beaks and feed on insects and small seeds.

Acorn worm An animal that lives in the mud of the sea-bed, often at great depths. The 'acorn' is the head end of the animal, which sticks out of the mud and is bright orange or red. There are several species, ranging from about 6 cm to 2 m in length. The body is rather like an earthworm, but the animal breathes by means of gills. It is a link between the invertebrates and the vertebrates.

Addax A rare whitish antelope, related to the oryx. It lives in the deserts of North Africa and can live almost indefinitely without drinking. It gets enough water from plants that it eats.

Adder A snake of the viper family, often simply called the viper. It has a fairly stout body up to about 60 cm long, and has a characteristic black zig-zag mark along the back. It lives in Asia and Europe and it reaches further north than other snakes. It feeds mainly on lizards, mice and voles.

Agouti A South American rodent looking like a long-legged guinea pig. There are several kinds, all brownish in colour. Agoutis live mainly in woods and feed on leaves, roots and fallen fruit.

Albatross A bird of the petrel family, characterised by tube-like nostrils on top of the beak. Albatrosses are large birds, with goose-sized bodies and very long, narrow wings. The wandering albatross has a wing span of 3 m or more—greater than that of any other bird. Most of the 13 species live in the Southern Hemisphere and they spend nearly all their lives at sea, gliding gracefully over the waves.

Alder fly An insect related to the lacewings. The young alder fly lives in water and the adults are never found far from ponds or streams. They have rather smoky wings with thick black veins. Fishermen often use artificial alder flies as bait for trout.

Alligator A large reptile closely related to the crocodiles, but distinguished by its blunter snout and by the fourth tooth in the lower jaw not being visible when the mouth is shut. Adults feed on fish, birds and small mammals that come to the river to drink or swim. There are two species of alligator, one in North America reaching 4.5 m or more in length, and a much smaller one in China.

Ammonite An extinct animal whose coiled shell is often found in rocks of the Mesozoic Age. There were many different kinds and they were related to octopuses.

Amoeba A member of the Protozoa. It is very small—the largest species can only just be seen with the unaided eye—and usually lives in water. The animal is continuously changing its shape as it moves about. It feeds by engulfing bacteria and other particles.

Anaconda The largest snake in the world, with lengths often exceeding 6 m. The anaconda lives in South America and spends a lot of time in the water. It feeds mainly on birds, deer and rodents. It is not a poisonous snake, but kills its prey by twining tightly around it until it cannot breathe.

Anchovy A small herring-like fish, of which there are several species. Anchovies are most abundant in warmer seas, but they are also found in the shallower regions and bays of cooler seas. The anchovy lives in huge shoals and feeds on plankton near the sea surface.

Anemone Sea anemones are simple marine animals related to jellyfishes. The body is soft and jelly-like and bears numerous tentacles. The tentacles are covered with stinging cells which are used to catch fishes and other small animals. Sea anemones live attached to the rocks.

Angler-fish Angler-fishes are bottom-dwelling fishes which catch their food with a sort of 'fishing rod'. The 'rod' is a modified fin spine, and it hangs near the mouth with a worm-like flap of skin acting as the bait. Small fishes investigating the bait are quickly snapped up. The angler-fishes have very large heads and mouths. They live in warm and temperate seas and some species go down to great depths.

Ani The anis are unusual birds. The four species live in North and South America and are related to the cuckoos, although they do not lay their eggs in other birds' nests. Their nesting behaviour is unusual, however, because they live in colonies and several pairs usually combine to build a communal nest. The birds are about 35 cm long and shiny black in colour. They feed on insects, which they usually collect on the ground.

Anole Anoles are small, slender lizards with long tails and triangular heads. They are related to the iguanas and are found only in the Americas. Most of them live in the trees and climb by means of sharp claws and adhesive pads on the toes. Males can inflate a pouch under the throat when they are excited.

Ant Ants are insects belonging to the order Hymenoptera, which also contains the bees and wasps. There are several thousand kinds of ants and they can usually be recognised by their slender 'waists' and by their sharply bent antennae. All ants live in communities and most of the work is done by wingless worker ants. Winged males and females fly off to mate. The males then die and the females or queens form nests or swell the size of existing ones.

Antbird The antbirds are a family of small birds living in South and Central America which feed mainly on insects and other invertebrates, not necessarily ants. Antbirds live mainly in the forests, but they occupy many different habitats within the forest and there are many different kinds. Some look like thrushes and others like shrikes, so we have names like ant-thrush, ant-shrike, and so on.

Anteater The three kinds of anteater live in South and Central America. The giant anteater has a long cylindrical snout at one end and a huge busy tail at the other. The whole animal is 2 m long and it lives on the ground. Its black, grey and white colours help to conceal it. The silky anteater and the two-toed anteater (or tamandua) are smaller and they live in the trees. Both have prehensile tails, with which they can grip branches. All the anteaters have long, slender tongues which they use to lick up ants and termites. They have no teeth.

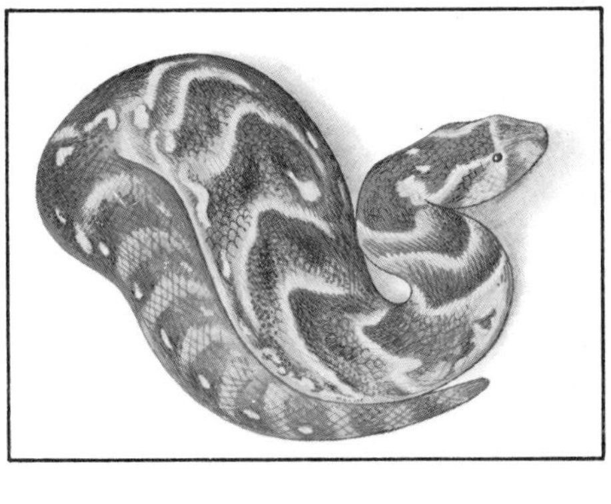

Left: The puff adder, a relative of the European adder which lives in Africa.

Right: The giant anteater, a native of Central and South America. It is also called the ant bear.

Antelope Antelopes are hoofed mammals belonging to the same family as the cows, sheep and goats. Both males and females may have horns. Antelopes live in Africa and Asia, often forming huge herds. Gazelles, oryxes and elands are all antelopes.

Ant lion An insect resembling a dragonfly but more closely related to the lacewing fly. The adults have long slender bodies and four narrow netted wings. The name 'ant lion' refers more to the young insects. They live in sandy soil and they make little pits. They lie more or less buried at the bottom of the pit and wait for an ant or some other insect to tumble down the loose sandy sides. They then pounce on it and eat it.

Aphid Aphids are better known as 'greenfly' or 'black fly', for these are two of the commonest of the many types of aphid. Also called plant lice, the aphids are sap-sucking bugs and they do an immense amount of damage to crops by sucking sap and by spreading germs that cause plant disease. Aphids are all small insects, sometimes with wings and sometimes without.

Arapaima One of the largest freshwater fishes, the arapaima is rather like a pike. It is usually two to three metres long, but some specimens grow to 5 m and may weigh over 180 kg. It lives in South America.

Archer-fish The archer-fishes, of which there are five species, get their name because they obtain insect food by 'shooting' the insects down with streams of water drops. They have been known to hit insects from a distance of two metres. Archer-fishes, which grow up to about 30 cm in length, live in the coastal waters and swamps of South East Asia.

Arctic fox A small fox with short ears and muzzle, giving it a somewhat cat-like appearance. It lives in the far north and its greyish-yellow summer coat turns white in winter. Like the polar bear, the Arctic fox has hairy soles to its feet. This helps it to get a grip on the snow and ice, as well as helping to keep its feet warm.

A Uganda Kob, an antelope related to the waterbuck

Argonaut Also called the paper nautilus, this little marine animal is distantly related to the octopus and the cuttlefish. There are six species, all living in the warmer seas of the world. They move about in the surface layers by jet propulsion, squirting jets of water out through the breathing tube. They feed on small fishes, and they themselves are eaten by larger fishes.

Armadillo There are 20 species of armadillo, distributed from the southern part of the U.S. to Argentina. The best known species is the 9-banded armadillo, which reaches as far north as the United States. The largest armadillo is the giant armadillo of the South American forests. It reaches a length of 1 m. Only the 3-banded armadillo, or apara, can roll up into a ball to defend itself. Armadillos feed mainly on ants and termites, ripping open the nests with their strong claws and licking up the insects with their long tongues.

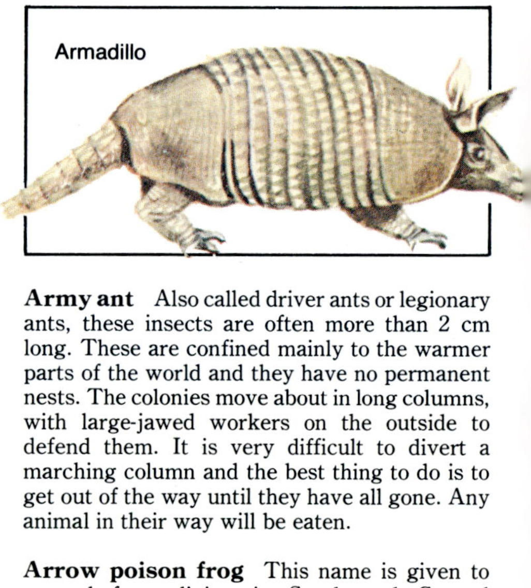

Army ant Also called driver ants or legionary ants, these insects are often more than 2 cm long. These are confined mainly to the warmer parts of the world and they have no permanent nests. The colonies move about in long columns, with large-jawed workers on the outside to defend them. It is very difficult to divert a marching column and the best thing to do is to get out of the way until they have all gone. Any animal in their way will be eaten.

Arrow poison frog This name is given to several frogs living in South and Central America. They are generally very brightly coloured and they secrete a very powerful poison which the native Indians use on their arrows. The most poisonous frog is the kokoi, which lives in Colombia. It is only 2 cm long, but it can provide enough poison from its skin to kill 50 men.

Arrow worm A little animal, up to 10 cm long, that floats in the plankton of the sea. The body is transparent except for a pair of tiny black eyes. Arrow worms have spiny jaws and they catch small animals by darting after them and spearing them.

Asp A snake closely related to the adder and distributed over the warmer parts of Europe. Its colour ranges from greyish-brown to orange or red, and it rarely exceeds 60 cm in length. It can be distinguished from the adder by its turned-up snout and by its yellow eyes. The adder's eyes are coppery-red.

Ass The ass is a small kind of horse. Two species are known—one in North Africa and one in central Asia. A race of the African species has been domesticated for a long time as the donkey. Wild asses survive in Asia.

Assassin bug There are more than 3,000 kinds of assassin bug, so called because they grab and kill their insect prey rather violently. A powerful curved beak is thrust into the prey to suck up its juices. Many assassin bugs mimic their prey and can mix with them freely without causing alarm. Most assassin bugs live in the Tropics.

Atlas moth One of the largest moths in the world, the atlas moth is found in India and other parts of South East Asia. It is mainly brown, but there is a transparent spot on each wing. The moth may reach a wing span of 25 cm. The atlas moth belongs to the same family (Saturnidae) as the European emperor moth and the Indian tussore silk moths, but it does not provide useful silk.

Avocet A graceful black and white wading bird with a long upturned beak. There are four species, one in Eurasia, one in North America, one in South America, and one in Australia. The upturned beak allows the avocet to feed on floating animals. The beak is held just under the surface and the bird then sweeps its head from side to side, scooping material from the water.

Axis deer The two species of axis deer live in India, Burma and neighbouring countries. One species, known as the chital or spotted deer, is one of the prettiest of all deer. It is a small deer, rarely more than 1 m high, and it has only small antlers, but its beauty lies in its white-spotted red coat. The other axis deer is quite different. Its squat pig-like appearance has given it the name hog deer. These deer are preyed upon by wild dogs and cats, as well as by large snakes such as pythons.

Axolotl The axolotl is a sort of Peter Pan—it never grows up. It is a brownish newt-like creature about 15 cm long and it breathes by means of feathery gills, just like the young newt or salamander. But, whereas the young newt eventually develops lungs and leaves the water, the axolotl retains its juvenile appearance, but it is able to reproduce. For a long time, scientists were puzzled to know just what sort of animal the axolotl was. The puzzle was solved about 100 years ago in Paris, when some axolotls turned into salamanders. The axolotl is therefore a form of salamander that does not normally change into the adult form. Axolotls live in Mexico.

Aye-aye The aye-aye is one of the many strange animals that live in Madagascar. It is closely related to the lemurs. It is about the size of a cat, dark brown in colour, and it has a long bushy tail. Fruit and insects make up the bulk of the aye-aye's diet. It feeds at night and uses its very long narrow middle finger to dig insects from holes and crevices. This long finger is also used for combing the fur and for picking the teeth. The aye-aye is now very rare because its forest home has been cut down to make way for agriculture.

Axolotl

Babbler Babblers are song birds related to the warblers and flycatchers. They live mainly in South East Asia, but extend into Africa and Australia. One species, the wren-tit, lives in America. The babblers are short-winged birds and they do not fly well. They live near the ground in the forests, searching for berries and insects in the undergrowth. They get their name from their almost continuous but varied song.

Baboon Baboons are Old World monkeys that live mainly on the ground, although they return to the trees to sleep at night. There are several species, living mainly in Africa, but they also extend into Arabia. Baboons live in tribes, or troops of up to 50 individuals, headed by one or more old males. They eat virtually anything. Lions and other large cats are the main enemies of the baboons, but three or four male baboons, armed with vicious teeth, are often more than enough to see off a lion or leopard.

Backswimmer Backswimmers are water bugs that get their name because they swim on their backs, using their long hind legs as oars. Like most other water bugs and water beetles, the backswimmer has to come up for air every now and then. It hangs upside-down from the water surface and renews the bubble of air that it carries on its underside. The backswimmer is often called the water boatman, but this is really a different insect. It looks like a backswimmer, but it does not swim on its back. Backswimmers have sharp beaks with which they pierce other insects and suck their juices.

Badger The badger is a short stocky animal, about 1 m long. The most striking feature is the black and white striped head. Badgers are related to the stoats and weasels. They are carnivorous creatures, but they also eat a variety of plant food. Insects, mice, berries, eggs and worms all appear on the badger's menu. The European badger is found all over Eurasia. The American badger is more carnivorous, but it lacks the black and white striped head of its European cousin. It lives on the open plains of the West.

Bagworm The bagworms are moths whose caterpillars make cases from silk and plant fragments. Most of them feed on trees, and some are considerable pests. When mature, the bagworm larva fixes its case to a twig and turns into a pupa. Some species have wingless females that cannot even crawl out of their cases. They mate where they are and lay their eggs in the case.

Bald eagle This striking bird used to be found all over North America and it was adopted as the emblem of the United States. Today it is extremely rare. It is not really bald, and it gets its name from the pure white feathers on its head and neck. The bald eagle feeds mainly on fishes.

Bandicoot Bandicoots are rat-like marsupials with long pointed snouts and naked ears. There are 19 species, ranging in size from that of a rat to that of a rabbit. They live in Australia and New Guinea. Their food is very varied and consists of roots, leaves, seeds, insects, worms, slugs and mice. Some species are more carnivorous than others. Some bandicoots dig burrows, others make untidy nests among the undergrowth.

Barbary ape This is a monkey of the macaque family. It has an extremely short tail. Barbary apes live in North Africa and a small colony lives in Gibraltar. These are the only monkeys living in Europe, although nobody knows when they were brought there.

Barber fish These fishes, which come from a wide range of families, are also called cleaner fishes. They provide a service for other fishes by cleaning them of parasites, patches of dead skin and dirt. They also clean wounds and help them to heal. While this is going on, the fish being cleaned co-operates with the barber, even allowing it to enter the mouth and gill cavities. This is a remarkable form of behaviour in which both fishes benefit.

Barbet Barbets are colourful birds related to woodpeckers. They live in the tropical forests in both Old and New Worlds and they use their strong beaks to bite out nest holes in dead trees. They feed mainly on fruit.

Bark beetle These insects include a variety of small species whose larvae live by tunnelling just under the bark of trees. The tunnelling activity eventually separates the bark completely from the wood and the bark falls. Each species has its own tunnelling pattern and this is easily seen when the bark falls. Bark beetles normally attack only weak trees, and they do some damage by carrying fungus diseases.

Barnacle Barnacles are those very common sea-shore creatures whose white tent-like shells coat rocks and pier legs. When the tide is out, the plates of the shell close up and the animal is hidden, but the plates open when the tide returns and the animal starts to feed. Feathery arms come out and rhythmically comb food particles from the water. Despite their unusual appearance, the barnacles are crustaceans. The young barnacles swim freely before settling down and making a shell.

Barnacle goose A small black and white goose, with a conspicuous white face. Flocks appear in Europe in autumn, and they disappear again in the spring. Not until 1907 did anyone discover where they spent the summer. We know now that the geese breed in the far north—in Greenland and Spitzbergen.

Barn owl The barn owl is found in all continents except Antarctica. It is very pale in colour and has probably been responsible for many 'ghost' stories. It has a very white, round face. Barn owls live in hollow trees and old buildings, such as barns, and they eat mainly rats and mice. They are very useful birds, but are less common in many places than they used to be.

Barracuda Barracudas, of which there are about 20 species, are slender pike-like fishes with vicious-looking teeth. The larger species, which may reach 2.4 m in length, can be quite dangerous and some fishermen fear them more than sharks, but there are not very many reports of them attacking men. They feed mainly on herrings and other surface-feeding fishes.

Barracudina About 50 species of barracudina live in the world's oceans. They are pale slender fishes, usually living at great depths. Very little is known about them, but they probably play a large part in the diet of other deep-sea fishes. Some barracudina species reach at least 60 cm in length when mature.

Basilisk Basilisks are lizards living in tropical America. They are up to 60 cm long and the males have a crest on the head and back. The animals always live near water and they can actually run across the surface, using only their back legs. They will also run on land in this semi-erect position. Basilisks eat plants and insects and are quite harmless.

Basket star A marine animal related to starfishes. The central disc has five major arms, but these fork many times and they tend to curl up when they are dead. This gives the animal a basket-like appearance. Basket stars live on the sea-bed and capture small creatures with their arms.

Basking shark One of the largest fishes, the basking shark is most common in the North Atlantic, but it is found in all the temperate seas of the world. Despite its great size, the basking shark has tiny teeth. It feeds on plankton, which it strains from the water with its very large gills.

Right: A beaver about to bring down a log.

A basket star

Bass A silvery-grey fish weighing up to 9 kg. The true bass lives in the Mediterranean and the eastern Atlantic, but there are other kinds of bass (not necessarily related) in other parts of the world. The stone bass, or wreckfish, likes to live in and around ship-wrecks. It is an aggressive fish, reaching a length of 2 m.

Bearded lizard This stout-bodied lizard, also called the bearded dragon, lives in Australia. The body is covered with small spines. There is a pouch under the jaw and this can be inflated so that the spines look like a beard. The animal feeds mainly on insects. It can run on its two back legs, balancing its body with its long tail.

Beaver The second largest rodent in the world, the beaver is about 1 m long, including the tail. There are two species, very much alike. One lives in northern Europe and the other lives in North America. Beavers always live near water and they make their homes in river banks or in 'lodges' built of branches in the middle of a pond. Even the pond is made by the beavers. They use their chisel-like front teeth to cut down small trees which they then use to build a dam across a stream. The dam creates a pond.

Bed bug One of the many insect pests that man has acquired during his history. It is a small flat brownish insect that feeds by sucking blood. It has no wings and it hides in crevices or among bedclothes during the daytime. It comes out to feed when we are asleep at night.

Bee-eater The bee-eaters are very spectacular birds distributed over most of the warmer parts of the Old World. They are brightly coloured and they have curved beaks. They nest in sandy banks and their nesting colonies may contain thousands of birds. They feed on insects, which they catch in flight.

Bell bird A very well named bird, of which several species live in the Southern Hemisphere. They are not all closely related and are named from the metallic ringing sound of their voices. The crested bell bird of Australia collects caterpillars in the breeding season and, after paralysing them with a nip, it stores them in its nest to provide a store of fresh food for its young.

Beluga The belugas or white whales are related to the dolphins and porpoises. The young animals are grey, but the skin gradually becomes white by reduction of the black pigment. Belugas usually grow to about 4 m in length and they are fairly slow swimmers in comparison with some of their relatives. These whales live in the Arctic Ocean.

Bichir A primitive freshwater fish of tropical Africa. It has a small, but broad head and its body is covered with an armour of scales. A series of small fins runs along most of the back. The bichir has an air bladder connected with the throat, and it is able to breathe air in addition to obtaining oxygen through its gills. The front fins can be used as props, almost like legs, and the bichir may well represent one of the stages through which land animals passed during their evolution from fishes.

Bighorn One of six species of wild sheep, the bighorn lives in the Rocky Mountains. The males have enormous horns which curve around the back of the head and come forward again to the eyes. The horns are marked off into segments, each of which represents one year of the animal's life. The domestic sheep must have arisen from one of the bighorn's Eurasian relatives, such as the mouflon or the argali. The woolly coat of the domestic sheep, however, is not shared by the wild species. They have coarse hair, rather like that of goats.

Binturong The binturong is a tree-dwelling carnivore found in South East Asia. It is about 1.2 m long and has black fur. Its tail has very long fur and it is partially prehensile and accounts for nearly half the animal's body. The animal cannot swing by its tail, but it wraps it around branches as a brake or a fifth limb. The binturong is clumsy on the ground, but it is an excellent climber. It feeds on birds and small mammals, together with a fair amount of fruit.

Bird-eating spider This is one of the largest spiders and it measures over 17 cm across the legs. It lives in the jungles of the Amazon basin. It does not spin a web, but catches birds and small mammals by dashing after them. The bird-eating spider, of which there are several species, is covered with irritating hairs. It is often called the tarantula, but the real tarantula is a different kind of spider that lives in southern Europe.

Bird of paradise The 43 species of birds of paradise live in the forests of New Guinea and surrounding islands. Four species reach the northern parts of Australia. The female birds are rather dull in colour, but the males of most species have beautiful plumes which they use in the most elaborate courtship displays.

Birdwing The birdwings are magnificent butterflies living in the forests of South East Asia and the neighbouring islands. Some of them have wingspans exceeding 25 cm. The females are a little larger than the males, but they are less colourful. The males have velvety black wings, marked with beautiful shining greens and blues. Many of the species, especially the males, are attracted to decaying meat and to damp places.

Bison Bison are massive, ox-like creatures weighing up to 300 kg. The largest stand up to 2 m at the shoulders. The hair on the head, neck, shoulders and forelegs is long and shaggy. Two species are alive today: the European bison or wisent, and the American bison. The latter is often wrongly called the buffalo and it has longer hair than the wisent. Both species were almost exterminated during the last 100 years, but numbers have now increased again due to protection schemes.

Bitterling A minnow-like fish living in the streams of central and Eastern Europe. During the breeding season the male becomes brilliantly coloured and the female develops a long pink egg-laying tube. The male guides the female to a freshwater mussel and she then lays her eggs in the mussel's breathing tube. The male releases his sperm, or milt, and this is drawn into the mussel with the breathing current. The bitterling eggs are then fertilised and they stay there until they hatch. The young fishes also stay in their safe 'hotel' until they have finished up their supply of yolk and are ready to venture out into the water.

Bivalve One of the large group of molluscs that have two parts or valves to their shell. Examples include cockles, mussels, oysters and razor shells.

Black bear There are five species of black bear, living in the Americas and southern Asia. They are much smaller than the grizzly and the other brown bears, weighing only about 225 kg at the most. The American black bear is very common in North America, especially in the national parks. Like its relatives, it is a good tree climber. The black bears eat a wide variety of food, including birds, berries and rodents.

Blackbuck Also known as the Indian antelope, the blackbuck is found over much of India and Pakistan. It is about 1.2 m long and the male has remarkably twisted horns. It is one of the fastest land animals and has been credited with speeds of 80 kph. It can also leap well. The blackbuck is one of the few antelopes in which males and females have different colours.

Birds of Paradise

Bison, back from the brink of extinction.

Barn owl

Bee-eater

Black molly

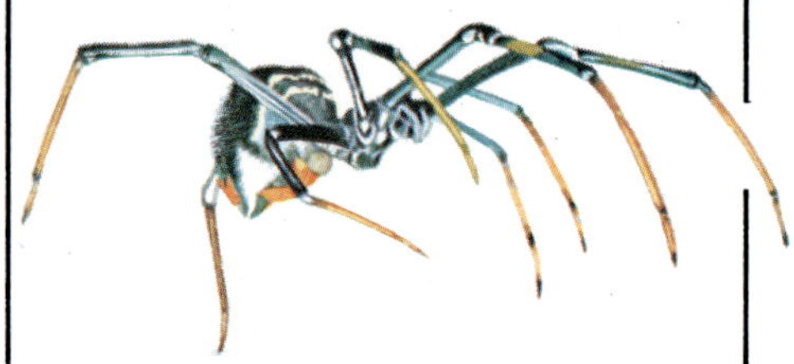
Black widow

Blister beetle

Black molly This little fish, a favourite with aquarists, is a black variety of the sailfin or some related fish (genus mollienisia) which comes from the rivers of Central America. The black varieties crop up from time to time in nature and they are bred artificially by the aquarists. The fishes can be recognised by the large sail-like dorsal fin of the male.

Black widow This infamous spider has a number of sub-species distributed over the warmer parts of the world. The North American sub-species is noted for its powerful venom which produces severe pain and paralysis in a man. It can sometimes cause death, but fatal bites are rare. The female spider—the one that does the damage—is about 15 mm long and shiny black in colour. There is a red 'hour-glass' mark on the underside of her spherical abdomen. The male is much smaller. The name of the spider comes from the belief that the female always eats her husband after mating, but this does not necessarily happen.

Blesbok These and the similar bontebok are small antelopes, related to the hartebeestes. They stand a little over 1 m at the shoulder, but they are sturdy creatures and they weigh over 68 kg. They are reddish with a white blaze on the face and a white patch at the base of the tail. The short horns diverge from each other near the base and then become more or less parallel. Blesbok and bontebok were once in danger of extinction, but numbers are now quite strong. Many live a semi-domesticated life on South African farms and, as they do not leap well, a low fence is sufficient to keep them in.

Blind snake This name applies to several hundred small non-poisonous snakes belonging to two families. They live throughout the warmer parts of the world. They are worm-like creatures, usually only about 5 cm long, although some species reach 1 m. They are not completely blind, but their eyes are very small and they can do no more than distinguish light from dark. Some scientists believe that the blind snakes might be lizards, rather like the slow-worm.

Blister beetle Blister beetles, of which there are many species, are found throughout the world although they are most common in warm dry climates. They get their name because their bodies contain a substance called cantharidin, which produces blisters on the skin of people touching the insects. The only British species has a shiny green body and it is known as the Spanish fly.

Bluefish A voracious fish living in most of the warm seas of the world. It is only about 38 cm long, but it swims in large shoals and attacks all kinds of fishes with astonishing ferocity. The bluefish occurs in exceptionally large numbers in the western Atlantic and is caught commercially for its tasty flesh.

Blue whale This is the largest animal that has ever lived. It can reach 30 m in length and nearly 150 tonnes in weight—as much as 30 elephants. It is a whalebone whale, that is it has no teeth. Inside its mouth there are plates of horny material called baleen, or whalebone. These strain the little planktonic animals from the water and the whale then swallows them, for this largest of all animals feeds on some of the smallest. During the summer, blue whales live in the polar seas, but they move to warmer seas in the winter, and their calves are born in these warmer regions. The calves are 7 m long when they are born. The species was in great danger of dying out because whalers killed so many of them. They have been protected for many years now, but the population is still very small.

Boa Boas are large snakes found in the warmer parts of America, especially in the Amazon basin. They are slow movers and lie in wait for victims at night. They kill their prey by coiling around it and constricting it. This means that the snake holds the prey so firmly that it cannot breathe. But the prey is not crushed. Large lizards and birds are eaten as a rule, but some mammals may be eaten. Best known of the boas is the boa constrictor, which generally reaches a length of about 4 m, although larger ones have been known. The anaconda is also a boa.

Bobcat The bobcat is the wildcat of America. It is actually a small lynx, about 1 m long including its short tail. Its tufted ears indicate its relationship with the lynx, and the tufts are believed to increase the efficiency of the ears. The bobcat hunts mainly at night and it is an excellent climber. It feeds mainly on rabbits (cottontails) and small rodents. It ranges from Mexico to southern Canada.

Bollworm This name is applied to the caterpillar of several moths which attack the bolls, or seed pods, of cotton. Bollworms are widespread in the cotton-growing regions of the world and do a great deal of damage to cotton and also to many other crop plants including tomatoes and tobacco.

Bonito This name is applied to several species of the mackerel family. The common bonito, found on both sides of the Atlantic in the tropical and sub-tropical zones, is a steel-blue fish about 60 cm long. It is beautifully streamlined and has a number of small finlets on the hinder part of the body. Similar species occur in other parts of the oceans. They are predatory fishes, hunting smaller species by sight. Their white flesh is good to eat.

Booby This name is applied to six species of the gannet family that are confined to the tropical regions. They are goose-sized birds with thick necks and large heads. They are clumsy on the land, but they are powerful and agile fliers. Five of the six species have white bodies, but the brown booby (the commonest species) has a brown back. The birds breed on coasts and islands and, like the gannets, they feed by diving for fishes out at sea. They keep their eggs warm by holding them in their webbed feet.

Boomslang One of the rear-fanged snakes, in which some of the back teeth carry venom. Back-fanged snakes are not generally dangerous to man, but the boomslang is an exception. Its venom is extremely poisonous, though only a small amount is produced and the snake does not bite unless handled. Boomslangs are African snakes and they live in the trees, feeding on lizards, birds and small mammals. They average 1.2 m in length and are usually green or brown.

Bower bird There are several species of bower birds living in Australia and New Guinea. Some of them are beautifully coloured, but their most fascinating feature is the bower or courtship house which is built by the male. The bower pattern varies with the species, but usually consists of a platform of twigs and grasses partly or completely roofed over. The male normally decorates it with attractive pebbles, flowers and other bright objects, and then he entices the female into it. Courtship and mating take place in the bower, but the female then makes a nest and lays her eggs elsewhere. The male's bowers normally get better each year, as he improves his technique and artistry. One species even paints its bower.

Bowfin This fish, which lives in some of the Great Lakes and several North American rivers, is a living fossil with many primitive features. The head is covered with bony plates and the rest of the body bears thin scales. A soft dorsal fin runs most of the length of the body, which may be up to 1 m, and the body ends in a rounded tail. The bowfin lives in sluggish waters and can breathe air with its lung-like swim bladder. It can live out of water for up to 24 hours. The male looks after the eggs and young in a nest, which may hold the eggs of several females at one time. Bowfins eat many kinds of small animals, such as fishes, frogs and worms, as well as dead flesh. It is sometimes destroyed as a pest, but it is also eaten.

Bream A silvery fish living in slow moving streams and lakes throughout most of Europe. It belongs to the carp family and reaches a length of about 60 cm. Its body is greatly compressed from side to side and it is very deep. Adult bream feed on the bottom of the rivers or lakes by stirring up the mud and eating the small animals they disturb. The white bream is a related fish, but the sea breams belong to quite different groups. The female lays 250,000 eggs which stick to the leaves and stems of water plants.

Brine shrimp A primitive relative of the crabs and lobsters. It likes very salty water and is found in many parts of the world from Greenland to Australia and from the West Indies to central Asia. Brine shrimps are less than 12 mm long with two pairs of antennae, two compound eyes on stalks and a third small eye in the middle of the head. It swims upside down with its underside to the light.

Bristlemouth One of the commonest fishes in the ocean, the bristlemouth lives in deep water where it preys upon small planktonic animals. They have small eyes and rows of light-organs (photophores) on their flanks. Some species are darker than others, depending on how deep in the water they live.

Bristletail These wingless insects are found all over the world, the best known being the silverfish, often found in kitchens or pantries, or among books. They are up to 3 cm long and get their name from the three slender bristle-like tails. The silverfish will eat anything but rarely becomes a pest.

Bristleworm This is the name given to a large group of marine worms in which the body carries a number of prominent bristles. Examples include the ragworms, lugworms and fan worms. The latter animals use a fan of bristles to trap food particles in the water.

Brittlestar The brittlestar, a distant relative of the starfish, is found in seas all over the world. It usually has five arms (sometimes more) joined to a central button-shaped body. These arms break off easily as the name implies, but can be regrown. Many brittlestars are delicately coloured, others light grey. They range in size from 0.5 mm to 10 cm across their bodies with a maximum spread of up to 60 cm across the arms. The arms are covered with hard plates and spines and along the underside are rows of tube feet which are used for feeding.

Brown bear The brown bear is found over a large area of the Northern Hemisphere and there are several sub-species. These include the Kodiak, Syrian and grizzly bears. They vary in size, but all are large omnivorous animals, up to 3 m or more in length and weighing up to 750 kg. They have poor sight and rely on their senses of smell and hearing, which are acute.

A brown bear.

Brush-tail opossum Also known as the vulpine or fox-like opossum, the brush-tail opossum is found in all parts of Australia, Tasmania and New Zealand. It is about 60 cm long and its fur is thick and woolly, ranging in colour from silver grey to dark brown or black. Its tail is prehensile at the tip. The brush-tail opossum is mainly herbivorous.

Budgerigar The commonest member of the parrot family in Australia, the budgerigar travels in huge flocks and, being a seed-eating bird, it is something of a pest in grain-growing areas. The wild bird is bright green with black, yellow and blue markings but many different colour varieties have been produced by bird fanciers since the 'budgie' was brought to Europe as a cage bird in the nineteenth-century. The name budgerigar is derived from an Aboriginal word said to mean 'good food'.

Bullfrog The bullfrog is a large North American frog. It is usually greenish-black on top and the underside is pale. Unlike the majority of frogs, the bullfrog is rarely found out of water. It feeds on a variety of insects caught at the surface of the pond, but will also eat other animals, including small snakes and mammals.

Bullhead Several fishes are known by this name, but the true bullhead is a small spiny fish found in clear streams over much of Europe. The basic colour is brownish, but it is usually mottled and it can alter its colour to suit different backgrounds. The bullhead is also called the miller's thumb, while its relatives in North America are called sculpins.

Burrowing owl A small owl living over a wide area in the Americas. It is a plains-dweller and hunts by both day and night. It feeds on rodents and insects. The bird gets its name from its habit of nesting in burrows. It does not normally dig its own burrow, but takes over the deserted hole of a prairie dog or an armadillo.

Burying beetle This is the name given to various beetles, mostly of the family Silphidae, which feed on the corpses of small animals. The beetles are attracted by the smell of the corpses and they usually work in pairs—one male and one female—to bury the carcase by dragging out soil from underneath it. The beetles feed on the carcase and also lay their eggs on it. The young beetles feed either on the decaying flesh or on other creatures, such as fly maggots, which they find there. Burying beetles, also called sexton beetles, play a very important role in nature.

Bushbaby The four species of bushbaby, also called galagos, are relatives of the lemurs and are distant cousins of the monkeys. They all live in the African bush or scrub regions and they move around in the trees at night, feeding on insects, fruit and even birds' eggs. They are very agile and make great leaps from branch to branch. Bushbabies are very furry creatures with large eyes and ears. They also have long furry tails. The largest bushbaby is about 75 cm long including the tail and the smallest is only 32 cm long, including a tail 20 cm long.

Bushbuck This is a smaller relative of the kudu and nyala antelopes. It is about 75 cm high at the shoulder. It is basically brown, but it has a number of white patches and stripes. Males are distinctly larger than females and have a bushy mane along the back. The sharp horns may reach 55 cm in length, but females only rarely bear them. Bushbuck are mainly browsing animals, living in the forest and bush throughout much of Africa.

Bush dog A South American dog only distantly related to the domestic dog but behaving very like it when tamed. Its legs are relatively short. It is brown in colour and, unlike most animals, it is paler on top than below. It ranges from Panama to Paraguay and hunts in small packs. Very little is known of its habits and, being nocturnal, it is seldom seen.

Left: A young bushbuck, a smaller relation of the kudu that lives in the bush.

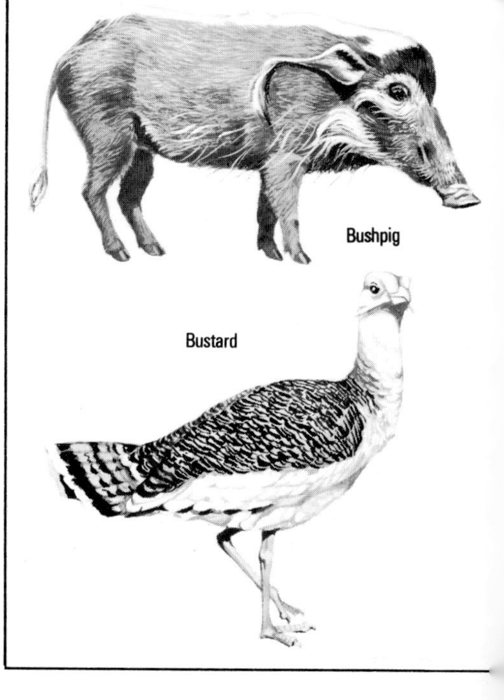

Bushpig The bushpig, also known as the red river hog, is a stout-bodied pig found over most of Africa. The head is large in proportion to the body and it bears tufted ears. The adults are reddish-brown or black and weigh up to 135 kg. Their main food is roots and fruits, and they will push against small trees to bring the fruit down. They may bring the whole tree down.

Bustard The bustards are large birds with stout legs and strong toes. There are 22 species, found in many parts of the Old World although most species live in Africa. They live mainly on the ground in open country and they take a variety of plant and animal food. The birds run well, but they can also fly in spite of their size. The great bustard is as large as a turkey.

Butcher bird The true butcher birds comprise six species of birds living in Australia and New Guinea, although the name is often applied to shrikes in other parts of the world. The name refers to the habit of impaling their prey on thorns, to form a sort of larder. The true butcher birds are stocky birds with mainly black and white plumage.

Butterfish An eel-like fish living between the tidemarks on both sides of the North Atlantic. Also known as the gunnel, the butterfish is a kind of blenny, brownish-green with darker markings. The name refers to the slippery nature of the fish.

Buzzard A large hawk with soaring flight, broad wings and a rounded tail. Many species are found in open country in the tropics but there is also a common European buzzard which ranges across northern Asia to Japan. All are large, the female being larger than the male. Rabbits and hares are the buzzard's favourite food, but it takes a variety of other animals.

Cacomistle An omnivorous relative of the raccoon, found in south-west United States and Mexico. The cacomistle has been given a variety of names including ringtail, raccoon fox and cat-squirrel. It is a small furry animal with a fox-like face and a long squirrel-like bushy tail ringed with black.

Caddis fly There are between 4,000 and 5,000 species throughout the world. The adult insects look rather like moths and fly mainly at night. Most of the larvae live in fresh water and breathe by external gills. Many of the larvae build themselves tubular 'houses' of stones, small shells or leaf fragments.

Caecilian A limbless amphibian with a long cylindrical body. The skin is smooth and slimy and has small scales embedded in it. The eyes are small and generally useless, but they have a sensory tentacle on each side of the head. Caecilians live underground in warm regions, from Mexico to Argentina, and in South and South East Asia and parts of Africa. There are about 75 species.

Caiman A close relative of the alligator, differing mainly in having the skin of the underside covered in bony plates. There are five species, the smallest being the dwarf caiman, the largest the black caiman. They are found in the north of South America and southern Mexico.

Camel There are two species of camel: the Arabian or one-humped and the bactrian or two-humped. They are desert animals, although only the bactrian camel still survives in the wild. A dromedary is a special breed of the one-humped camel used for riding. Both species are remarkably well adapted for desert life. Their humps consist largely of fat.

Canary A finch coming originally from the Canary Islands and neighbouring islands in the Atlantic. The wild bird is brownish-yellow, but many yellow varieties have been produced in captivity. The canary is a very popular cage bird, with a sweet song. It will produce hybrids with greenfinches and other finches.

Cape buffalo Reputed to be the most dangerous of the African big game animals, this bulky ox-like creature and adult males may weigh up to 1 tonne. It has large horns which sweep first downwards and then upwards. The animal lives throughout Africa south of the Sahara. Cape buffaloes are not normally dangerous unless they are unexpectedly disturbed. They then panic and charge at their opponents.

Cape hunting dog A carnivore, only distantly related to the domestic dog, that ranges over parts of Africa. It stands about 60 cm at the shoulder and has a mottled black, yellow and white coat. The animals hunt in packs to run down antelopes.

Capercaillie The largest member of the grouse family, the capercaillie is a bird of the northern coniferous forests. It is found over much of northern Europe and Asia. During the winter the birds feed mainly on the leaves of pines, but they move into more open woodlands in the summer and eat heather, grass and various berries. The male has a fine tail, which he fans out and displays to the brown hen.

Capuchin The capuchins are small South American monkeys. The prehensile tail may be nearly twice as long as the body. The monkeys live in troops of up to 40 individuals and they feed mainly on fruit and insects. Capuchins are the traditional organ grinders' monkeys.

Capybara The capybara is the world's largest rodent. It may reach over 1.2 m in length and it looks like an enormous guinea pig. The species is found over much of South America and it lives in marshland or around the banks of rivers and lakes. It swims very well and feeds mainly on aquatic plants.

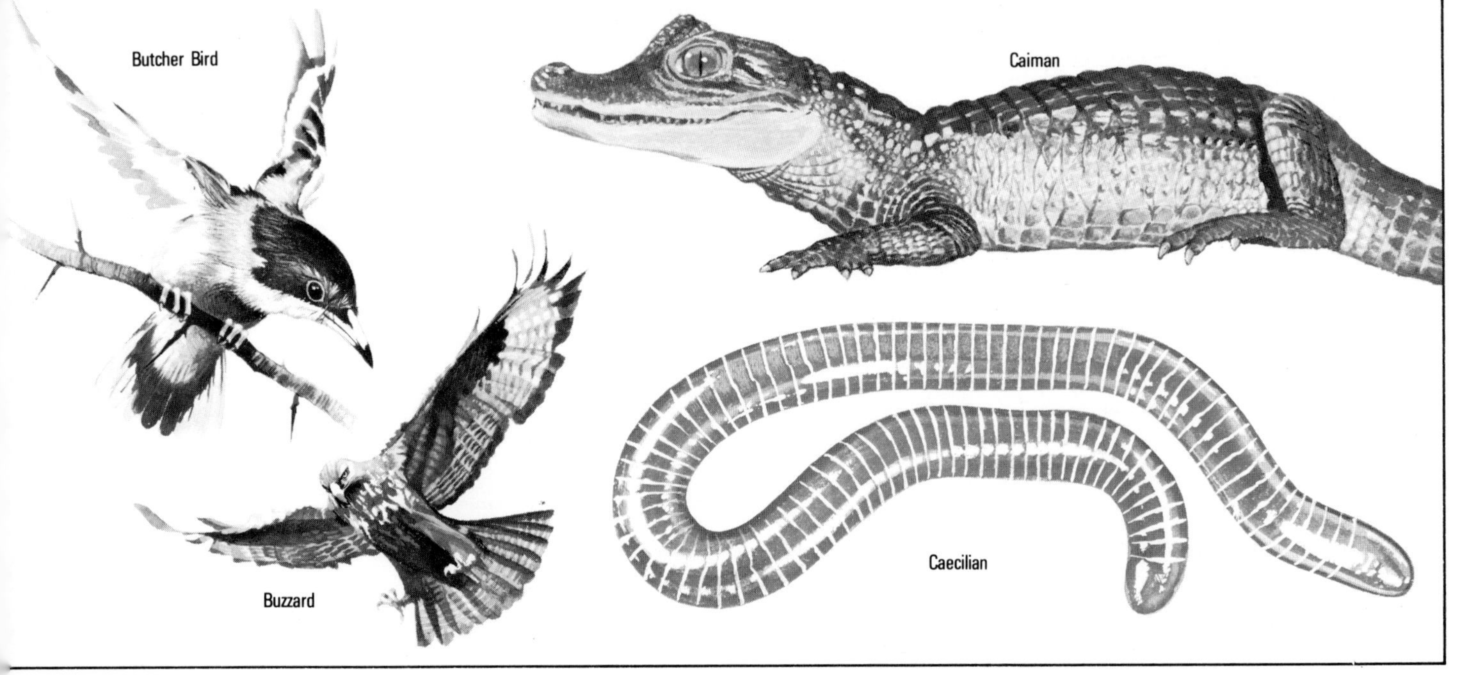

The Cape buffalo is a dangerous adversary because of its tendency to charge.

Caracal Also called the desert lynx, the caracal is a medium-sized cat. It has a short reddish-brown coat, long legs and long black ears topped by very long tufts of hair. The caracal ranges over much of Africa and extends across the Middle East to India, although it is now rare in Asia. It keeps mainly to open country and feeds on a variety of small antelopes and other mammals. It will also catch birds in flight by leaping up at them.

Caracara Caracaras are birds related to falcons, although they are unlike them in form and habits. There are several species distributed throughout the Americas. They are predatory birds, taking a variety of animals for food, but they will also eat carrion. In this respect they resemble some of the vultures. The caracaras will also chase and bully other birds until they release the food they are carrying. The caracaras then drop down and collect it.

Cardinal A familiar songbird of North America, also known as the red bird. The male has a black 'bib', but otherwise he is bright scarlet. The female is more sombre, owing to a greater amount of brown in her feathers. Both sexes have a conspicuous crest and a stout, seed-cracking beak. Cardinals, which belong to the finch family, are distributed over much of Mexico and the United States.

Caribou These animals are the reindeer of North America and Siberia. They belong to the same species as the European reindeer, but the reindeer is usually regarded as a semi-domesticated race of the species. Caribou are up to 1.8 m high at the shoulder and they weigh up to 300 kg. They are generally brownish-grey, although some individuals may be white and some may be black. They are unusual among deer in that both sexes have antlers. Caribou spend the summer on the open tundra, feeding on lichens, grasses and other plants. In the autumn most of them move back to the forests and spend the winter there feeding on lichens and browsing on the soft twigs of the aspens.

Carp The common carp is the most widely distributed fish of its family, and one of the most widely distributed freshwater fishes in the world. It is a native of Japan, China and central Asia, but it has been introduced to many other regions. It can survive for quite long periods out of water as long as it is kept moist. The carp prefers warm, shallow lakes and rivers with muddy bottoms, for it feeds on the mud-dwelling insects and worms. It is a favourite fish for ornamental pools and it can live for 50 years or more. The wild fish is olive green, but many colour varieties have been produced by breeders.

Cassowary This large impressive and flightless bird lives in the dense rain forests of New Guinea and northern Australia. The black plumage consists of coarse bristle-like feathers, but the head and neck are naked and brightly coloured. The wings are very small and are hidden from sight. The birds are very shy and are rarely seen. They can run remarkably rapidly through the undergrowth and usually have well-worn tunnels. Fruits and insects are the main foods. There are three species.

Cat-bear The cat-bear, also called the red panda or lesser panda, is the nearest living relative of the giant panda. It lives in the Himalayas. Its fur is a rich chestnut brown, with white marks on the face and dark rings on the long busy tail. Although classified as a carnivore, the cat-bear feeds almost entirely on fruit and leaves. It spends most of its time in the trees. The cat-bear sleeps by day and comes out to feed during the night.

Catfish The European catfish or wels, grows to a length of 3 m or more in the rivers of central Europe and Asia. It belongs to a large group of fishes called naked catfishes. It has a broad head and wide mouth supplied with three pairs of barbels or whiskers. One pair is very long and movable. The eyes are very small. The skin has no scales and is slimy. Although it often searches for small invertebrates by day, the European catfish normally hunts at night. It feeds on fishes, amphibians and crustaceans. Many other fishes are also known as catfishes, including a number of marine species.

Catshark Catsharks are small sharks distinguished by their picturesque patterns of stripes and mottlings. Some of the dogfishes belong to this group. One of the less well known members is the shy-eye, a South African species which curls its tail over its head when caught, as if trying to hide its eyes.

Cave fishes There are 32 known species of fishes that spend their whole lives in underground caves and lakes. They belong to several families but, because they share a way of life, they have many features in common. They have little or no pigment, and appear pinkish because the blood shows through the more or less scaleless skin. Most of the species are blind. The largest is only about 20 cm long. Cave fishes probably feed mainly on insects that fall into the water, but one species is reputed to feed on bat droppings.

Centipede Centipedes are arthropods, distantly related to spiders, crabs, insects and millipedes. They differ from all these, however, in having one pair of walking legs on almost every segment. Millipedes have two pairs of legs on each segment. Although the word centipede means '100 feet', the creatures have varying numbers of feet—from 15 to 177 pairs. They do not have waterproof skins and all have to remain in damp places. Many live under logs and stones. They are active hunters, killing insects and other small creatures with their poisonous claws. They are good things to have in the garden, although some of the large tropical species (up to 30 cm long) can give man a painful bite.

Chameleon Chameleons are lizards which are famed for their ability to change colour, which they do by altering the distribution of pigment in their skins. Other unusual features include eyes which can be swivelled around independently and the long tongue which is catapulted out to catch insect food. Chameleons are rather flattened from side to side and they are often decorated with brilliant colours, 'warts' and horns. There are about 80 species, most of them living in Africa. They range from about 5 cm to 60 cm in length.

Chamois The chamois is a goat-like mountain animal found in various parts of Europe and Asia Minor. It is a sturdy creature about 1.2 m long and weighing up to 40 kg. Both sexes have sharply pointed horns. The long coat is tawny in summer and darker in winter. The animals live mainly in the alpine forests and feed on a variety of plants. They are somewhat intermediate between goats and antelopes and their relatives include the gorals and serows of Asia.

Cheetah The cheetah is a long-legged cat with a beautifully spotted coat and a characteristic black stripe running from the eye to the corner of the mouth. Unlike other cats it cannot retract its claws. It is a very fast animal—the fastest in the world over short distances—and it catches antelopes by running them down. This contrasts with the habits of most cats, which tend to stalk slowly up on their prey and then pounce. The cheetah once ranged from India to South Africa, but it is now very rare in many places. Its main stronghold is now in East Africa.

Chevrotain Also known as mouse deer, the chevrotains are the smallest of the ruminant animals. They are rarely more than 30 cm high at the shoulder. They are not true deer and they lack antlers. Their heads are relatively small. There are four species, living in the forests of West Africa, India and the Malayan region. They eat grass and leaves mainly, but also take insects, fish and small mammals.

Chickaree This is the red squirrel of North America. It is about two-thirds the size of the grey squirrel and has a tawny-brown coat. The eyes are ringed with white. The chickaree is found throughout the coniferous and deciduous forests and a related species is found along the west coast of the United States. The squirrels are active throughout the year and actually tunnel through the snow to find food.

Chimaera The chimaera or 'king of the herrings' is one of a small group of fishes somewhat intermediate between the cartilaginous fishes (sharks and rays) and the bony fishes. They have cartilaginous skeletons, but have gill covers like those of bony fishes. The king herring has a large head and the body then tapers back to the tail. There is a poison spine on the back. It feeds mainly on bottom-dwelling molluscs and crustaceans and reaches a length of 1.5 m.

Chimpanzee One of the great apes and the nearest in intelligence to man, the chimpanzee is one of the most popular animals. The animals live in the rain forests of Africa and spend some of their time in the trees. They live in small bands, but there is little social structure and members come and go as they please. They eat mainly fruit and other vegetable food, but they also eat meat, sometimes hunting quite large animals such as monkeys and young antelopes. Occasionally termites are captured with the aid of a twig.

Chinchilla Best known for its remarkably soft grey fur, the chinchilla is a South American rodent. It is about 25 cm long and looks rather like a squirrel, although its long back legs are more like those of a rabbit. Chinchillas live in burrows in the drier mountain areas, but are now confined in the wild parts of Chile.

Chipmunk The chipmunks are a group of ground squirrels with about 18 species. They are found in North America and Asia, where they live in open country and feed on berries, grasses and a wide variety of small animals. They are great hoarders of food for the winter, although they do not actually hibernate. Chipmunks range from 10 to 18 cm in length, excluding the bushy tail.

Chough The two species of chough are members of the crow family. They are a little larger than jackdaws and have glossy black coats. The common chough, which ranges in a fairly narrow belt from Ireland to China, has a long, curved, red beak and red legs. The alpine chough has a shorter, yellowish beak and lives in the mountainous regions of Europe and Asia. The common chough is found mainly by the sea in Europe. Both species are scavenging birds and they pick up a variety of animal food.

Chuckwalla The chuckwalla is a plump lizard usually about 30 cm long and weighing between 1.3 and 1.8 kg when mature. It is a mottled, brownish-black creature and it lives in the hot desert regions of North America. Unlike most lizards, it eats plant material and shows a particular preference for flowers. When disturbed, the chuckwalla scuttles into a rock crevice and wedges itself there by digging its toes in and also by inflating its body with air. It is then very difficult to dislodge.

Cicada Cicadas are bugs related to the frog-hoppers or spittle bugs, although they are usually very much larger. The empress cicada of Malaya has a wingspan of 20 cm. There are about 1,500 species, mainly found in the tropical regions. The males (and in some species the females too) 'sing' by rapidly vibrating little membranes on the sides of the body. This makes a very shrill whistling noise which can be very unpleasant to the human ear. The insects feed by sucking sap from trees. The young cicadas feed on the roots of the trees and some species take 17 years to reach the adult state.

Cichlid The 600 species of cichlid fishes, favourites with tropical fish keepers, live in rivers and lakes all over Africa and throughout most of South and Central America. There are also two species in India. The body is flattened from side to side and many species are brightly coloured. At breeding time the male adopts a territory and defends it against other males. When a female joins the male both may help to defend the territory while they clean up a patch of gravel to receive the eggs. The eggs are continuously fanned by the parents and they are carried at frequent intervals to new quarters. The young fishes are often taken into the mouths of their parents when danger threatens.

Civet The 15 species of civet are related to the mongoose. They have long narrow bodies and pointed muzzles, but their coats are cat-like. They live in Africa and Asia and keep mainly to the forests. They eat small animals mainly, but fruit is often taken as well. They produce a musky substance widely used in perfumes.

Clawed frog Although sometimes called the clawed toad, this animal belongs to the group of tongueless frogs. The front legs are rather short and weak. The back legs, however, are very strong and carry large webbed feet. The three inner toes of each back foot have sharp black claws. The animals spend most of their time in the water and, like many amphibians, can change their colour to match various backgrounds. Having no tongue, they cannot catch food in the normal way for frogs: they use their front teeth to catch small fishes and other aquatic creatures.

Click beetle Click beetles, of which there are many species, are rather narrow insects up to about 2.5 cm long. Most of them are rather dull brown in colour, although some species have bright wing cases. The insects get their name from their ability to flick themselves up into the air if they fall on their backs. This enables them to right themselves, and in doing so they make a loud click. Click beetle larvae are known as wireworms, and several species are serious pests on farms and in gardens.

Climbing perch A greyish-green or silvery fish found across southern Asia from India to the Philippines. Part of the gill cavity functions as a lung. The fish can therefore live out of water for quite long periods. It can walk about on the land by propping itself up on its fins and spiny gill covers.

Coal-fish A member of the cod family, it gets its name from its dark back, but it is also known as the pollack. It lives in the North Atlantic and the Mediterranean and is fished commercially.

Coati A small carnivorous mammal related to the raccoons. The body is nearly 60 cm long and the banded tail adds another 60 cm or more. The forehead is flat and runs down to a long mobile snout. The general colour is reddish-brown. The three species are found in the forests of South and Central America, but they are extending their range northwards at the moment. Coatis are most attractive and industrious little animals, foraging for invertebrates and small vertebrate animals. They will also eat fruit and they often climb trees to reach it.

Cobra Cobras are poisonous snakes found in Africa and Asia. They are medium-sized snakes, some of them averaging about 2.1 m in length. There is a characteristic hood behind the head, formed by long movable ribs which swing out and stretch the skin. The snakes feed mainly on rodents, which they kill with a paralysing venom. The spitting cobra, which lives in Africa, defends itself by spitting venom for distances of up to 3.6 m. The venom causes great pain.

Cockatoo The 16 species of cockatoo differ from the other parrots by having prominent crests on their heads. Most species are white. Cockatoos live in the Australasian region, often forming large flocks. Some species are pests because they take a lot of grain and often attack fruit.

Cock-of-the-rock This is the name of two birds of South America. Both belong to the Cotinga family and are recognisable by their fan-like crests. Females are dull brown, but the males are brilliantly coloured. One species is orange and one is bright red. The birds live in the rain forests and feed mainly on fruit.

Cockroach Cockroaches are generally medium, or fairly large insects, flattened, and generally having rather leathery front wings. Females often have reduced wings and are therefore unable to fly. Most of the 3,500 species of cockroaches live in the Tropics, but some of them have become established as pests in buildings in the cooler parts of the world. The cockroaches are scavenging insects, feeding on a variety of dead plant and animal material. Our food is therefore ideal for them.

The cockatoo has a prominent crest.

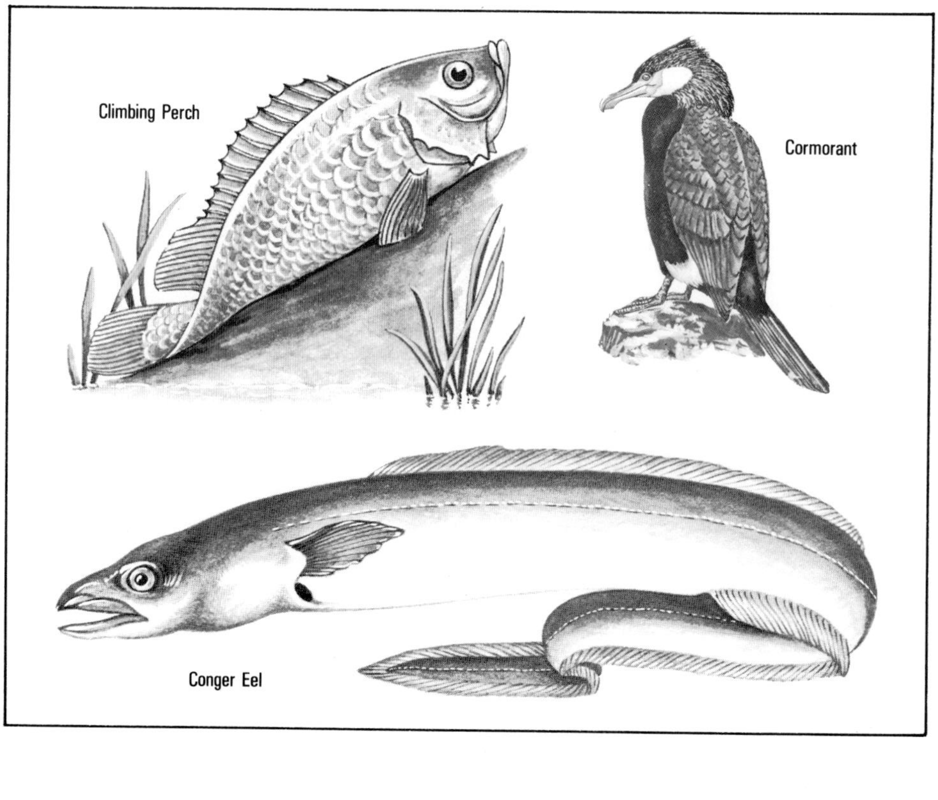

Cod The second most valuable food fish after the herring, the Atlantic cod lives on the continental shelves around the North Atlantic. It can reach 2 m in length and weigh more than 90 kg, although it is usually a good deal smaller. During the summer the cod feeds mainly on other fishes, but it is more of a bottom-feeder during the winter.

Coelacanth A fish belonging to an order whose other members have been extinct for more than 70 million years. It is a living fossil, and was discovered only in 1938. Several other specimens have been caught since. The coelacanth has fleshy lobes in its fins.

Collared dove One of the smaller doves, measuring about 28 cm. It is greyish in colour, with a clear black collar around the back of its neck. The bird originally lived in Africa and Asia, but has now spread over most of Europe.

Colobus monkey The three species of colobus monkeys live in the dense forests of central Africa. They are uncommon and rarely descend from the trees. They have long fur and reach up to 1.5 m in length. Colobus feed mainly on leaves.

Colorado beetle A native of North America, the Colorado beetle was quite harmless until potato growing reached its home. It then transferred its attention to potatoes and has since spread over large areas of America and Europe. The beetle is nearly 15 mm long and has black and yellow stripes, while its larva is dark pink with black spots.

Comb jelly Small marine animals related to jellyfishes, the comb jellies are found in all the oceans. Most species are globular and, because they bear rows of little hairs, they are often called sea gooseberries. They are usually colourless and quite transparent, and they swim about by waving their hairs or cilia. Most species live in coastal waters.

Condor Condors are large American 'vultures'. They are not related to the true vultures of the Old World, although they look very much like them. Like the true vultures, they are carrion feeders and they also attack young and wounded animals. There are two species, the Californian condor and the Andean condor. The former is very rare and lives only near Los Angeles, but the Andean condor is found in the Andes for nearly the whole length of South America. Both birds have wingspans of about 3 m and are among the largest of all flying birds.

Conger This is a stout-bodied marine eel, normally about 1.5 m long, but sometimes reaching 2.7 m. The body is scaleless. The conger lives near the coast in many parts of the world, although it prefers rocky coasts. It is a voracious animal, eating more or less any animal that it can catch. It often hides among the rocks and darts out to catch food with its powerful jaws and formidable teeth.

Coot Coots are water birds related to the moorhens and also to the cranes. They are dark in colour, but can be recognised by the brilliant white beak and the shield that extends above it. The coot does not have webbed feet, but its toes are provided with flaps which act as paddles in the water. They make floating nests of rushes.

Coral Corals are related to sea anemones and possess a hard chalky skeleton. Some corals live by themselves, but the majority are colonial creatures. Their skeletons are joined together in great masses and they often form coral reefs. All corals live in the sea and reef-forming kinds live only in warm waters.

Coral snake This name is given to many strikingly coloured snakes, with patterns of rings running around the body. The snakes are found in the Americas and in Africa and Asia. They are related to the cobras but, although they are poisonous they are seldom dangerous.

Cormorant There are about 30 species of cormorant in the world. They are large sea birds, generally with glossy black plumage although some species have white underparts. The beaks are slightly hooked. The birds live around the coasts and most species fly and swim well. They feed almost entirely on fishes, which they catch by diving after them. On land, the cormorant often stands with its wings outstretched as if it is hanging them out to dry.

Cottontail The cottontail is a small rabbit ranging from southern Canada to South America. There are about 13 species. The tail is white underneath, giving rise to the name cottontail from its resemblance to a cotton boll. The young are born in shallow depressions in the ground rather like those of the hare, but young cottontails are blind and helpless at first.

Right: The coyote is a native of the American West and is a relative of the wolf.

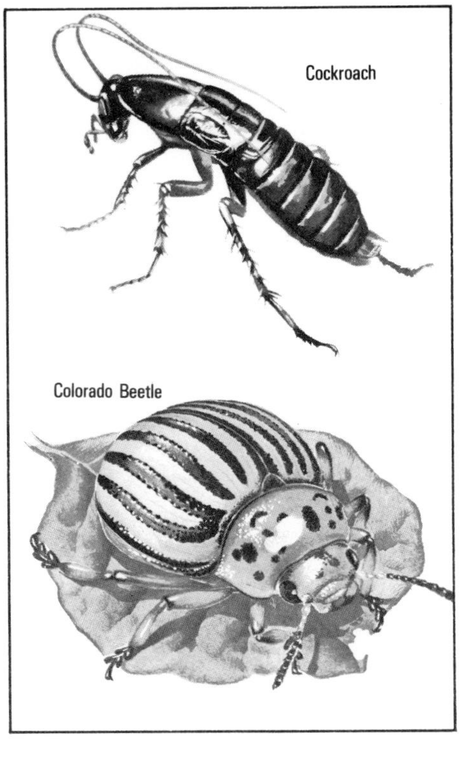

Coucal Coucals are members of the cuckoo family, with about 27 species in Africa, Asia and Australia. They are large birds compared with cuckoos. They do not lay their eggs in other birds' nests, but make their own.

Courser A long-legged, plover-like shore-bird, living in the Old World from Africa to Australia. There are about 9 species and the cream-coloured courser, that occasionally ventures north into Europe, is a small bird about the size of a starling with pale sandy colouring.

Cowbird A small American bird of which there are several species. Cowbirds get their name from the way they follow cattle to feed. Some of them have the cuckoo's habit of laying their eggs in other birds' nests.

Cowrie A carnivorous mollusc related to the sea snail but with the shell whorls enveloped during growth until only the final whorl is visible. In life, the shell is covered by the cowrie's mantle, thus keeping it from being scratched or damaged. Most cowries live in the Indian and Pacific Oceans.

Coyote A relative of the wolf, the coyote is slightly smaller. It has a bushy black-tipped tail which it carries low behind the hind legs. Coyotes used to live only in the western part of North America but, their range has increased considerably over the last century. They eat a variety of food including rabbits, small rodents, insects and vegetable stuffs.

Coypu A large rodent related to the porcupines. Its native home is in South America, but it has been reared on farms for its fur and is now established in the wild in North America and in several European countries. The coypu is well adapated for life in the water with webbed hind feet. It eats aquatic and waterside vegetation.

Crab spider So called because of the way they scuttle sideways like sea-shore crabs. They range from very tiny to not much more than 5 mm. They do not make webs but lie in wait for their prey. They are sometimes found in flowers, the colours of which they often match perfectly.

Crane Cranes are elegant long-legged birds. Most of the 14 species are now rare. They breed in lonely marshes and most species migrate long distances from summer to winter quarters. They are found in all continents except South America. Cranes feed on leaves, fruit and insects. They have remarkably loud voices, which carry for a kilometre or more.

Crayfish The crayfish is a freshwater crustacean, rather like a small lobster. There are several species, distributed widely over the world although absent from Africa and most of Asia. The largest species lives in Tasmania. Crayfishes eat a variety of small water creatures and some leave the water at night.

Cricket Crickets are insects related to grass hoppers. There are about 900 species, distributed all over the world. They have long hind legs, used for jumping, and they also have very long slender antennae. The males produce a shrill 'song' by rubbing the bases of their wings together. Bush crickets are quite similar although less flattened. The egg-layer of the bush cricket is broad, whereas that of the true cricket is slender and needle-like. Crickets eat more or less anything and are very common on rubbish dumps.

Crocodile Crocodiles are large scaly reptiles, the nearest living relatives of the dinosaurs. They are found in the warmer parts of the world, inhabiting rivers and estuaries. There are several species. Some specimens exceed 6 m in length, but large ones are now rare as a result of hunting. Young crocodiles feed mainly on insects, but they turn to fishes as they get larger. Adults more often catch birds and mammals that come to drink at the water's edge.

Crossbill Crossbills are parrot-like finches in which the tips of the beak are crossed. Male crossbills are bright red, marked with black. The three species breed in coniferous forests over most of the Northern Hemisphere and feed almost entirely on conifer seeds. The unusual beak is well suited to wrenching off the cone scales to get at the seeds.

Crow The crow family includes about 100 species of bird, including the raven, rook, magpie and jay. The carrion crow is the best known. It appears black all over, although close inspection reveals blue and purple in the plumage. It eats almost anything, from grass and fruit to small mammals or shellfishes.

Cuckoo The European cuckoo is a greyish hawk-like bird about 32 cm long. It covers thousands of kilometres each year on its migrations between Europe and tropical Africa. It is a brood parasite, laying its eggs in the nests of other birds. It eats insects, including the hairy caterpillars avoided by most other birds. There are many other birds in the cuckoo family, but not all of them lay in other birds' nests. Only the European cuckoo has the 'cuck-coo' call.

Curassow The 12 species of curassow are related to chickens. They range in size from a pheasant to a small turkey. The male is generally dark brown or black, while the females tend to be paler. Curassows are readily identified by their horny 'helmets'. They live in Central and South America and spend most of their time in the trees. They feed mainly on fruits and leaves.

Curlew The common curlew is a large wading bird, with a down-curved 13 cm beak. It breeds all the way across Europe and Asia, frequenting moorlands and marshes for most of the time. It gets its name from the two-syllable call. The curved beak is used for digging out small animals. Several other species breed in the Northern Hemisphere, and some cover huge distances in their annual migrations.

Cuscus The cuscus is an Australasian tree-dwelling marsupial about 1.07 m long including its long prehensile tail. There are over 16 species, and they fill the niches occupied by monkeys in other tropical regions. They are nocturnal and feed on fruit, leaves and insects.

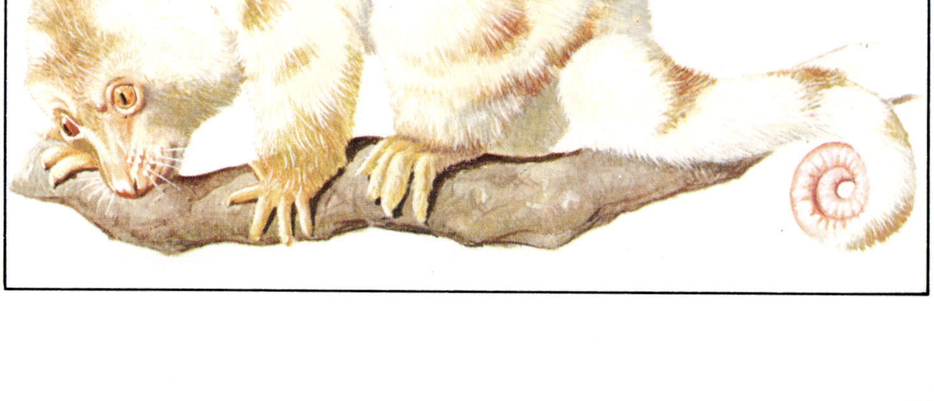

Cuttlefish Molluscs related to the squids and octopuses, the cuttlefishes live in all the seas of the world. There are about 80 species, varying from about 4 cm to 1.5 m in length. The body is shield-shaped and its margins form a continuous fin. The head bears eight arms and two long tentacles, all bearing horny suckers. Inside the body there is a chalky 'shell', often washed up on the beach as the 'cuttlebone'. Cuttlefishes feed on shrimps and small fishes, which are caught by the tentacles. The animals are famed for their ability to change colour.

Dab A small flat-fish living in the shallow coastal waters of Western Europe. It can be recognised by the sharp bend in the lateral line just behind the gill cover. The dab feeds on various bottom-dwelling invertebrates.

Daddy-long-legs The name given to long-legged crane-flies. The larvae are known as leatherjackets and they feed on plant roots. Long-legged harvestmen (relatives of the spiders) are also called daddy-long-legs.

Damselfly Damselflies are slender-bodied relatives of the dragonflies. The front and hind wings are both the same size and shape. The body is often brightly marked with blue. Ponds and slow-moving streams are preferred.

Darwin's finches These are a group of birds living in the Galapagos Islands. They are not particularly attractive, but they are famous because they helped Charles Darwin to arrive at his theory of evolution by natural selection. Several species live in the various islands, all derived from a few finches that were blown to the Galapagos from South America. Before they arrived there were few birds on the islands, so the newcomers were able to evolve into many different forms.

Dasyure The dasyure is the 'native cat' of Australia. It is not a true cat, but a pouched mammal. There are five species and they look something like civets, with short legs and long bushy tails. They feed mainly on invertebrates and small mammals.

Right: Some of the most popular breeds of dogs, all of them derived from a wolf-like ancestor.

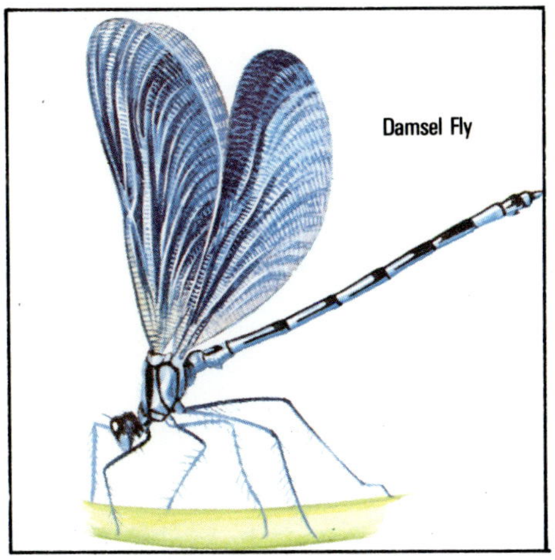

Deer mouse Deer mice are very similar to the European wood mouse, although the two are not closely related. They are found all over North America, and one species reaches south to Colombia. There are 55 species. The feet are white and the animals are often called white-footed mice. Seeds, berries and insects are their main foods.

Devil fish Related to skates and rays, these fishes live in the warmer seas of the world. The front fins are greatly enlarged as 'wings' and they also have forward-pointing extensions at the front of the head. These look like horns and give the fishes their common name. The largest of the species is the manta ray. Devil fishes swim mainly near the surface, in contrast to the other rays and skates which live on the sea-bed.

Dhole This is the wild dog of India. The fur is greyish-brown and the bushy tail is tipped with black. Dholes range from India and Malaysia to China and parts of the Soviet Union. They hunt in packs of 100 or more individuals, running down deer and other animals. They will even attack tigers and leopards, but do not seem to attack man.

Dik-dik Dik-diks are small antelopes. There are six species, distributed over most of Africa. The males have short horns, partly hidden in a tuft of hairs on the head. The tail is a mere stump, and the animal also has a longish snout.

Dingo This is the wild dog of Australia—one of the few placental (non-pouched) mammals to arrive there before the Europeans. It arrived with the Aborigines when they reached Australia from southern Asia. It is a reddish-brown. The ears are erect and pointed and the tail is bushy. Dingoes live in small packs and hunt sheep, wallabies and kangaroos.

Dipper There are four species of dipper, with short wings and tails. They live by the sides of swift-flowing, boulder-strewn streams and feed mainly on insect larvae. They walk under water and search for their food on the stream bed. They can also dive into the water. The dippers live mainly in the Northern Hemisphere, with one species in northern South America.

Diver Divers or loons are streamlined water birds with very short tails and straight pointed beaks. Their legs are set well back on the body and so, although they are good swimmers, the birds can only shuffle on land. The four species of diver live in the northern parts of the world. They feed mainly on fish.

Dog, domestic Dogs have been domesticated for at least 8,000 years. They have probably been derived from mainly wolf stock. Domestic dogs of all shapes and sizes have been bred over the centuries ranging from the St Bernard weighing as much as 90 kg to toy dogs of 0.5 kg.

Dogfish This name is given to several species of small sharks. One of the commonest, certainly around the coasts of Europe, is the lesser spotted dogfish. This fish has extremely rough skin—so rough that it has been used as sand-paper and also for scrubbing the decks of trawlers. Large numbers are caught and eaten. When fried, it is known as rock salmon.

Dormouse Dormice are rodents living in the Old World. There are several species, of which the best known is the hazel dormouse—the only native species in Britain. It is a most attractive animal with brown and white fur and a length of about 15 cm including the tail. The largest dormouse is the edible dormouse, a grey squirrel-like animal about 30 cm long. Most of the species live among the woodland under-growth, although the edible dormouse prefers taller trees and is sometimes a pest in orchards. The animals feed mainly on fruits and nuts. They hibernate during the winter.

Douroucouli This is the world's only nocturnal monkey. It is also called the owl monkey because of its large eyes and rather owl-like face. It can move absolutely silently through the tree-tops at night, but it can also make unbelievably loud calls and it has a very large range of sounds. Insects, small birds and mammals are the main items in the douroucouli's diet. The animal lives in the rain forests of South America.

Bottom: A collection of egrets and spoonbills.

Right: A young emu. Emus cannot fly but are fast runners.

Drongo Drongos are birds of the Old World tropics. There are about 20 species. They have long pointed wings and their tails often have long trailing feathers. Most of the species are black, with a bluish or greenish sheen. There are conspicuous bristles around the nostrils. Drongos live in the dense forests. They feed on insects and seem to prefer bees and wasps.

Dugong The dugong is a seal-like mammal, with flipper-like front limbs and a broad paddle for a tail. Dugongs live around the tropical coasts of the Indian Ocean. They feed on eel grass and other aquatic vegetation and they often come up the rivers. They can haul themselves partly out of the water. Dugongs are closely related to the manatees and both groups are often known as sea cows.

Duiker Duikers are small short-legged antelopes with arched backs. The tallest of the dozen or so species is only about 60 cm high at the shoulder. Both sexes have short, pointed horns as a rule, and there is a tuft of hair between them. Duikers are found throughout most of Africa, but they are very shy creatures and quickly take cover when disturbed.

Eel There are 16 species of freshwater eels, all of which spend their adult lives in rivers and lakes and then make a single long migration to sea to spawn. The skin is thick and slimy and has only very small scales embedded in it. The European eel lives in the rivers of Europe and North Africa. It feeds on almost any sort of animal food and is most active at night. It can even come out of the water and wriggle over the land to reach isolated ponds. The adults make their way to the middle of the Atlantic Ocean to spawn. After spawning they perish, but the young eels start the journey back to Europe. It takes them about 3 years.

Egg-eating snake The six species of egg-eating snakes (found in Africa and India) live almost exclusively on them and have a remarkable device to deal with them. They are active mainly at night, gliding through the tree-tops and seeking out birds' nests by smell. The eggs are swallowed whole and are then cut open by a row of teeth, or pegs, in the roof of the throat.

Egret The egrets are a group of birds related to the herons. Most of them live around lakes and marshes. Frogs, fishes and various invertebrates are eaten. The cattle egret, however, feeds on land. It often associates with cattle and other large animals and it has increased its range remarkably in recent decades.

Eider Famed for the soft warm down that it provides. There are four species, all living around the northern coasts of the Pacific and Atlantic Oceans. The male common eider is a striking black and white bird in the breeding season. The birds usually move south for the winter and tend to stay further out to sea than during the summer. They dive for shellfishes and crabs on the sea-bed.

Eland The eland is the largest antelope. It is a heavy ox-like creature and both sexes carry spiral horns. There is a short mane and there is a tuft of long dark hair on the throat. There are two species: the common eland, which lives in central and southern Africa, and the Derby eland of central Africa. The Derby eland is richer in colour and less grey. The animals live in herds of up to 100 and roam the open plains. They are now being farmed.

Elephant The elephants are the largest living land mammals. The African elephant is the larger of the two, reaching 3.5 m in height and 6 tonnes in weight. The trunk is used for carrying food and water to the mouth, for spraying water over the body, for lifting things and for smelling. It is immensely strong, and yet is also very sensitive, especially near the tip. The two species differ mainly in the size of their ears and tusks and in the shape of the tip of the trunk. The African elephant is found over most of the southern half of Africa, while the Indian elephant lives in the forests of South East Asia, from India to Sumatra. They eat a variety of plant material.

Below: A herd of elephants, usually led by a female.

Elephant seal Also called the sea elephant, this creature is the largest of the seals. The male can reach a length of 6.7 m and a weight of 3½ tonnes. Females are much smaller and weigh less than one tonne. The name refers to the peculiar drooping snout of the male. There are two species, both very much alike. The northern elephant seal lives off the coast of Mexico and California, while the southern elephant seal lives mainly in the South Atlantic and the Antarctic. They feed on fishes and squids.

Elephant shrew Elephant shrews are found only in Africa. They belong to the same order of insect-eating mammals as the ordinary shrews, although they are not closely related. They get their name from the greatly elongated snout. They range from 10 to 30 cm in length, excluding the tail, and they have long back legs.

Emu The second largest living bird, the emu stands about 2 m high. It lives in Australia in a wide variety of habitats. There were several species until the Europeans arrived, but only one now remains. It is related to the cassowary and shares its drooping, downy plumage. It cannot fly, but can run at 60 kph over short distances. It is a herbivore and is often a nuisance on farms during the dry season.

Fairy fly This name is given to various minute wasp-like creatures, not true flies at all. They belong to a group called chalcids and they spend their early lives inside the eggs of other insects. They are parasites. The name fairy fly refers to the tiny wings, little more than a couple of veins and a few hairs.

Fairy shrimp Two centimetres or more long, the fairy shrimp is transparent and almost colourless. It is a rather primitive relative of the true shrimps and other crustaceans and it turns up now and then in temporary pools. It swims on its back by means of rhythmic movements of its many legs, which also function as gills and as food collectors. The animal feeds on tiny plants and animals that it filters from the water. The fairy shrimp's eggs can survive for many years without water, and this is why the creatures can appear quite suddenly in small puddles.

Fallow deer This attractive deer is now found nearly all over the world because man has taken it about with him as an ornament for his parks and gardens, but it originally came from the Mediterranean region. The coat is reddish-brown, dappled with white spots in summer, and there is a prominent white patch on the rump, extending on both sides of the black tail. The fallow is a small deer, never more than 1 m at the shoulder, and the buck carries broad palmate antlers.

False scorpion This is a minute greyish animal only distantly related to the true scorpions. Most of the 1,500 known species live in leaf litter and other vegetable material and they feed on small insects and mites which they catch with their relatively huge pink claws. A few species eke out a living between the pages of old books or in the bodies of stuffed museum specimens. They feed on the booklice that they meet there. False scorpions often 'hitch-hike' by grabbing hold of the bristles of insects.

Fan worm This name is given to various marine bristleworms that live in tubes and filter their food from the water with a crown, or fan, of stiff bristles. Some fan worms live in little tubes made of lime, others make tubes of sand grains. One of the best known is the peacock worm, whose sandy tubes often stick out of the mud at low tide.

Featherstar A relative of the starfish, this creature has five arms, but they branch freely and it appears to have many feathery arms. The body is covered with plates of limestone and the arms are supported by little bone-like cylinders joined together like a backbone. The body is anchored by claws on the underside, but the animals can swim gracefully when they release themselves. The arms filter food particles from the water. Featherstars are related to the sea lilies, in which the body is carried on a stalk.

Fennec Also known as the fennec fox, this little animal is the smallest of the foxes, yet it has the largest ears. The head and body measure about 50 cm in length and the ears are 15 cm long. The animal lives in the deserts of North Africa and Arabia and does not need to drink. Its pale sandy colour blends well with the desert sands and its huge ears help it to pick up the slightest sound. The fennec feeds on a variety of invertebrates and small mammals.

Fer de lance A relative of the rattlesnakes, the fer de lance is found in coastal districts from Mexico to Argentina. It also lives on various islands in the Caribbean. It averages about 1.2 m long and is brownish, with a diamond pattern on the back. It is a poisonous snake and visits houses looking for rats and mice.

Ferret The ferret is a pale domesticated version of the polecat and it has been used for centuries to catch rabbits, although it is not used much now. The ferret is sent into a rabbit hole to chase the rabbits out into nets. The black-footed ferret is a rare North American animal—sometimes stated to be the rarest mammal of that continent. It feeds on prairie dogs.

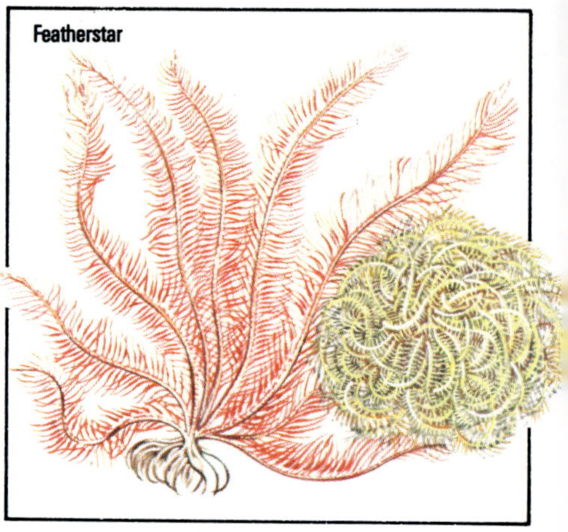

Fiddler crab This is a little crab, only about 2 cm across, found in great numbers on tropical beaches. The males have one very enlarged claw and one normal claw. They are brightly coloured and the large claw is waved about as a call sign to attract a mate. Some fiddler crabs can make sounds by rubbing their claws against a row of teeth on the shell. This stridulation produces a sound rather like that of a cricket.

Fighting fish Many fish fight, but the most famous is the Siamese fighting fish. It has been reared for its fighting ability, and fish-fighting is a traditional sport in its native Thailand (Siam). Two males will go on fighting for an hour or more before one runs out as the winner. The wild fish is yellowish-brown, but many other colour varieties have been produced.

Firebelly This is a toad with an unusual way of scaring its enemies. It is less than 5 cm long and dark grey on the back. The underside is bluish grey but spotted with red or orange. When alarmed, the animal rears up and exposes this 'firebelly'. It can also exude a strong smelling poison from its skin. The firebelly lives in Eastern Europe and Russia, extending into Germany and southern Sweden.

Firefly Fireflies are named for the brilliant light they give out when they are flying. This comes from the underside of the abdomen and is produced by a chemical reaction. The light appears much stronger than it really is because our eyes are especially sensitive to the firefly's wavelength. Fireflies are not really flies: they are beetles. The more brilliant ones live in the Tropics, but several occur in the cooler regions.

Fish eagle Described as the most handsome of Africa's eagles, this relatively small species has a white head, back and chest, together with black wings and a chestnut belly. It lives all over the southern half of Africa and is also called the river eagle. It fishes along the shores of rivers and lakes. Other kinds of fish eagle live in Asia.

Fish-eating bat This is a more or less naked bat living in America from Mexico to Argentina. It has long narrow wings and it flies low over the water, impaling fishes on its sharp claws. It is also called the bulldog bat. Two more bats also feed on fishes—one in northern Mexico and California, and one in South East Asia.

Flamingo There are four species of these strange but beautiful birds. They have extremely long legs and neck. The plumage is a delicate pink except for the flight feathers, which are black. The beak is strangely curved, and the birds feed with their heads upside down in the water filtering out plankton. They live and breed in shallow lakes and lagoons. Commonest of the four species is the greater flamingo, found in many parts of South America, Africa and central Asia. It also lives in southern Europe.

Flicker Admired for their beautiful plumage and wide variety of calls, the flickers are small American woodpeckers. There are six species, found from Alaska to Chile. Most of them feed on ants, which they collect on tree trunks or on the ground, often tearing open the nests to get at the insects.

Flounder A flat fish of the shallow seas of Western Europe, the flounder may reach a weight of 2.7 kg. It is at home in both salt and fresh water and it frequents river mouths. It is greyish-brown on the upper side and pearly white underneath.

Flying fish There are two types of herring-like flying fishes. One type has only one pair of wings—formed from the pectoral fins—and the other has two pairs of wings, formed from both pectoral and pelvic fins. They all live in the tropical seas and feed on plankton. They do not flap their 'wings' in flight: they swim quickly upwards and break surface, the fins are spread, and with a flick of the tail they take off.

Flying fox The flying foxes are large fruit-eating bats, which have fox-like faces. There are about 60 species and, unlike the insect-eating bats, they depend upon their large eyes to find their way about. They are found in India and Indonesia, Australia and many of the islands of the Indian and Pacific Oceans.

A glorious sight, a flock of flamingoes in flight.

Flying squirrel There are 37 species of flying squirrel, most of them living in southern Asia, although one lives in North America and one in northern Eurasia. All are similar in build and habits and all have a furry flap of skin stretching along the sides of the body from front legs to back legs and then on to the tail. They are nocturnal and they glide from tree to tree on their outstretched flaps of skin. They range from about 15 cm to 1.2 m long, including the tail. Some of Australia's marsupial flying phalangers are also called flying squirrels.

Flying Squirrel

Gecko

Fur Seals

Fossa This is a cat-like carnivore from Madagascar, related to the civets and mongooses. It has short soft reddish-brown fur and it measures about 1.5 m in length, half of which is the stout tail. The fossa is a nocturnal animal, feeding on lemurs which it catches in the trees.

Frigate-bird Frigate-birds, or man-o'-war birds, live around the coasts in the warmer parts of the world. Their feet have only traces of webbing and their plumage is not very waterproof. The wings are large, spanning 2.1 m in some species, and flight is good. The frigate-birds get a large amount of their food by harrying other birds until they drop the food they are carrying. They spend a lot of time in the air and they can walk only with difficulty.

Frilled lizard This is a pale brown lizard, sometimes bearing yellowish or dark patches, named from the large frill around its throat. The frill normally lies like a cape around the shoulders, but it can be raised as a warning display when the animal is disturbed. The frilled lizard lives mainly in the sandy, semi-dry areas of northern Australia and it feeds on insects and small mammals.

Fritillary This is the name given to a group of butterflies, nearly all belonging to the family Nymphalidae, which have a chequered pattern rather like that of the fritillary flowers. Most of the fritillaries have orange-brown wings marked with black and the undersides often bear silvery spots. The majority of the species live in woodland or on rough grassland.

Fruit bat The 160 species of fruit bats live in and around the tropics of the Old World. About 60 are known as flying foxes. They vary in size from a tiny 6 cm long to large bats with wingspans of up to 1 m. Although called fruit bats, some are nectar drinkers. They differ from the insect-eating bats, notably in not using sonar.

Fulmar A member of the petrel family, the fulmar's name is derived from 'foul bird'—a name based on its musky scent and its habit of spitting a foul-smelling oil at intruders. The bird swoops low over the sea and catches young herrings, squids and crustaceans. The fulmar has been increasing in numbers over the last 100 years. The cause of the increase may be the increase in fishing boats. The fulmars follow them to pick up the discarded fishes and offal.

Fur seal Fur seals belong to the eared seal family, a group which also includes the sea lions. They differ from true seals in having small ear flaps and in being able to turn their hind limbs forward when on land. This means that they can lollop along, whereas the true seals can do little more than wriggle. Most of the fur seals live in the Southern Hemisphere, but one important species lives around the shores of the North Pacific.

Gannet

Gall wasp The familiar oak apples and marble galls on oak trees, and the robin's pincushion on wild rose bushes, are known as galls. They can be produced by various kinds of insect larvae, but a large number of them are produced by the larvae of gall wasps. The gall wasps are little ant-like creatures, only distantly related to the true wasps. Most of them produce galls on oak trees and they often have a complicated life history.

Gannet Gannets are white goose-sized birds that live around the temperate oceans of the world. They are oceanic birds, coming ashore only in the breeding season. They feed on fishes which they catch by diving. Gannets tend to nest on steep cliffs and offshore rocks, and their nests are often packed tightly together—perhaps with only a metre between them.

Gar The seven species of gar, also called garpike, live in rivers and lakes of North and Central America. They are rather lazy fishes, but they can move very rapidly to snap up an unwary fish in their long-toothed jaws. Gars have quite slender bodies ranging from 60 cm to about 3.6 m in length. The body is covered with tough diamond-shaped scales like those of the early fishes. The gar is a rather primitive fish, closely related to various jurassic fishes.

Garter snake Garter snakes are the commonest snakes in the United States and Canada. There are several species, ranging from Mexico to the north of Canada. They are not poisonous. The body is slender and marked with longitudinal stripes. Worms are the major items in the garter snake's diet, but frogs, newts and mice may also be taken. The snakes often enter water and catch fishes.

Gazelle Gazelles are dainty, slender antelopes in which the males have sweeping horns that diverge from each other to form a lyre-shaped outline. The females have only short spikes or no horns at all. There are 10 species of true gazelles, most of them living in Africa. The true gazelles have a white streak on each side of the face, usually underlined by a black streak. Three other species are also known as gazelles: the Tibetan, Przewalski's and the Mongolian gazelles, living on the high plains.

Gecko The geckos form a family of lizards noted for the microscopic hooks on the toes. These hooks can hook into all but the smoothest of surfaces and so the geckos can climb up almost anything. Even window panes can be climbed. Geckos live in all warm countries and there are many species. Most of them live in trees, but a number dwell in houses. They do useful service by catching flies and other insects.

Genet The genet is a carnivorous mammal related to the mongooses and civets. The tail is about the same length as the body. Genets are elegant spotted creatures, with white marks on the face. They feed on small rodents, birds and insects. The six species are all found in Africa and one species—the feline genet—extends into southern Europe and Arabia.

Gerbil Gerbils, or sand rats, live in the desert or semi-desert parts of Africa and Asia. There are many species and two genera are more accurately known as jirds. In some respects, the gerbils resemble the jerboas, although the two groups are not closely related. The fur is fawn or brown, often tinged with black, and the underside is pale. The tail is usually long and the animals also have long back legs. Most of the species can jump, although the jirds jump less well than the others. Gerbils eat seeds, roots and other parts of plants. They will also eat insects.

Gerenuk The gerenuk is a long-necked, gazelle-like antelope, although not a true gazelle. The male carries short thick horns and stands about 1 m high at the shoulder. Gerenuks feed by browsing on trees and they often stand up on their hind legs, lifting their heads to a height of about 2 m. Gerenuks live only in Somalia and neighbouring regions.

Gharial The gharial is a long, slender-snouted crocodile living in the rivers of northern India and Pakistan. It is also known as the gavial. It can reach a length of about 6 m and keeps to the water more than other crocodiles. It feeds mainly on small fishes, which it catches with rapid movements of its slender snout.

Giant snail The giant snail is a large land-living snail native to East Africa. The pointed shell may reach a length of 20 cm and the whole animal may weigh 0.2 kg. The snail is not particularly remarkable in itself, but it is remarkable for the way in which it has spread, with man's help, to many new areas in recent decades. It is a serious pest in crop-growing areas, although it can be eaten as a nutritious food.

Gibbon Gibbons are among the most agile of mammals and the smallest of the apes. There are six species and they normally stand 1 m in height when standing upright. The arms are extremely long, perhaps 1½ times as long as the legs and they are used for swinging through the trees. Gibbons live in the forests of South East Asia and feed mainly on fruit. They will also eat leaves, insects and small birds if they can catch them.

Gila monster This is an ugly lizard living in the deserts of the south-western United States. It is one of only two poisonous lizards. The other poisonous species is the similar looking beaded lizard which lives in Mexico. The gila monster is pink and yellow, with black markings, and it has an unusually stout tail in which it stores reserves of fat. It is a rather sluggish animal, feeding on birds' eggs and young mammals. It will not bite unless handled, but the bite is very painful. The gila monster is now a protected species.

Giraffe The tallest animal in the world, the giraffe has remarkably long legs and a remarkably long neck. An old male may reach 5.4 m in height. There are many forms, differing in the pattern of the coat, but they all belong to the one species. Giraffes live in the savannah areas of Africa, mainly in the east and south. They browse the tree-top foliage with their long tongue and mobile, hairy lips. They have few enemies when adult: lions may attack them, but the giraffes have a powerful weapon in their long legs and hooves.

Right: The gibbon is the smallest of the apes, but by far the most agile.

Below: With a height of 5 m or more, the giraffe is the tallest animal.

Glass snake Glass snakes are legless lizards found in many parts of the world. They reach lengths of up to 1.2 m. All glass snakes have a deep furrow running along each side of the body. They live in open country, hiding under leaves and stones. They feed mainly on insects. Like all lizards, the glass snakes can shed their tails when attacked. The tail also breaks into pieces and so it looks as if the whole animal has broken up—hence the name of glass snake.

Gliding frog The gliding frogs of Asia belong to a family of tree frogs and they get their name from their habit of gliding from tree to tree, supported by the webbing of the large feet.

Glow-worm The glow-worm is a beetle belonging to the same family as the fireflies. The female is wingless and it is she who is responsible for the name glow-worm. All stages of the life cycle can give out light, but the female shines most brightly. She climbs up a grass stem and shines to attract the flying males. Young glow-worms, which look very much like the females, feed on snails.

Goshawk A magnificent bird of prey, the goshawk is closely related to the sparrowhawk. It has the same long tail and rounded wings when seen in silhouette, but it is much larger—the head and body measuring about 60 cm. The plumage is dark brown, with a pale underside marked with bars. The goshawk ranges over much of the higher latitudes of the Northern Hemisphere. It is mainly a woodland bird and it takes a wide variety of birds and mammals as food.

Grasshopper Grasshoppers are jumping insects which live among the grass and herbage close to the ground. They are active only when the sun is shining and they jump with the aid of the long and powerful back legs. Most of the species have wings and they can fly. They are best known for their 'songs', which are produced by rubbing the hind legs against prominent veins on the wings. Usually only the male sings. True grasshoppers have short antennae. A related group of insects, known as bush crickets, have very long antennae and are sometimes (wrongly) called long-horned grasshoppers. Bush crickets sing by rubbing their wings together and they feed mainly on other insects. Grasshoppers are herbivores.

Grass snake The common grass snake, also known as the ringed snake, extends from the British Isles (not Ireland) across all but the most northerly parts of Europe to central Asia. The snake is an olive brown or greenish colour and it can be recognised by the yellowish collar around the neck. It lives in damp places and is a good swimmer. Worms, slugs, frogs and small mammals are the main food.

Grebe Grebes are long-necked water birds, many of which have plumes on the head. The toes have horny fringes that act as paddles. There are 18 species, distributed all over the world. They live on lakes, reservoirs and slow-moving rivers. Some species migrate to the coasts for the winter. Grebes are excellent divers and they catch a variety of animal food under the water. The largest species is the great crested grebe, which is famous for its courtship dances.

Green turtle Once abundant in the tropical seas, the green or edible turtle is much rarer now because its flesh and eggs are good to eat. The

The grasshopper (left) can be distinguished from the bush cricket (below) by the length of the feelers.

Green Turtle

adult turtle has a dark brown shell marbled with yellow. It reaches a maximum length of 1.2 m, and the adult animal weighs up to 180 kg. The name green turtle comes from the green tinge of its fat. Like all marine turtles, it comes on to the shore to lay its eggs in the sand. Young green turtles are carnivorous, but the adults feed only on the vegetation growing in the shallow water.

Greylag The greylag is the ancestor of the farmyard goose. It is greyish-brown, with white markings on the wings and tail. The greylag breeds in north and central Europe and comes south for the winter. It feeds on grass and other plant material.

Ground squirrel Ground squirrels look very much like tree squirrels, but they do not have such bushy tails. The body and tail together measure between 20 and 76 cm, of which the tail may account for up to half. The animals are brownish-grey or yellowish-grey, often with stripes or rows of spots. There are 32 species, most of them living in North America. Some live in Africa and some in Eastern Europe and Asia, where they are known as susliks or spermophiles. They live in burrows or under logs and they eat seeds, fruits, bulbs, insects and many other items. Those animals living in the northern regions hibernate, but the others remain active throughout the year.

Grouper Groupers, also known as sea bass or sea perch, are heavy-bodied fishes living mainly in the tropical seas. There are about 400 species, although not all are large. The largest is the Queensland grouper, which reaches some 3.6 m in length. Groupers have many strong needle-sharp teeth and feed on a variety of other fishes. Many species lurk on the bottom, or among coral reefs and wait for food to come along. Some groupers are brightly coloured and they can also change their colours to match various backgrounds.

Ground Squirrel

Grouse The grouse family contains 18 species of game birds, ranging in size from a domestic hen to a turkey. Most of them live in the northern regions and they feed mainly on leaves, shoots and berries. Best known of the species is probably the red grouse, which is specially reared for shooting on the heather moors. Other species include the blackgrouse, the capercaillie and the ptarmigan.

Guillemot Guillemots are birds of the northern seas. They belong to the auk family and are related to puffins. They stand upright on land and look more like penguins. They fly with a rapid whirring sound. There are various species, all black and white. Out of the breeding season, the birds stay at sea, diving and swimming underwater to catch fishes and crustaceans. They breed on steep cliffs and pack their nests tightly on to the ledges.

Guinea pig Guinea pigs belong to a large family of South American rodents. The wild form is usually called a cavy, and it is eaten by the natives of South America. The Incas used to rear them specially for food and the Spaniards eventually brought them to Europe. They are now kept as pets and as laboratory animals and a large number of varieties have been reared. Wild cavies live in burrows and come out at night to eat a variety of plant material.

Gundi This is a long-furred rodent said to be the commonest mammal in North Africa. It is about 25 cm long and it looks rather like a sandy-coloured guinea pig. It lives on dry mountain slopes and other rock areas, basking in the sunshine and seeking shelter only during the hottest part of the day. It also shelters from the rain, which damages its silky fur. Gundis eat grass and other plants, getting all their water from this source.

Guppy The guppy is a small freshwater fish from the Caribbean region and the northern parts of South America. It is probably the commonest aquarium fish after the ordinary goldfish and it has also been released in many places to keep down the mosquito population. The male guppy is a colourful little fish, about 2.5 cm long, but the larger female is rather drab. She brings forth active young, but frequently eats them as soon as they are born. Fish breeders have produced many attractive strains of guppy.

Gurnard The gurnard is distinguished by its wing-like pectoral fins, in which the front two or three rays are separated off to form 'feelers'. The fish has a heavy, box-like head protected by bony plates and spines, but it can lift itself up by digging the 'feelers' into the sea-bed. It can also drag itself along in this way.

Gymnure The gymnures, of which there are five species, are related to the hedgehogs and they are sometimes called hairy hedgehogs, although they look more like shrews. They have thick underfur and a dense covering of coarse guard hairs. All five species come from South East Asia and the largest, often called the moon rat, is about 60 cm long including its almost naked tail. Gymnures are nocturnal and, like all insectivores, feed mainly on worms and insects.

Haddock A close relative of the cod, the haddock, or finnan, is an important food fish. It is greyish-brown above and it has a white belly. It is easily recognised by its three dorsal fins and by the dark patch just behind the gills. It reaches a length of about 110 cm and weighs up to 16 kg. It lives in the North Atlantic and Arctic Oceans.

Hagfish The hagfish is a degenerate descendant of the jawless fishes that lived many millions of years ago. It bears little resemblance to other fishes except the lamprey. Its scaleless body is up to 60 cm long and has no paired fins. It has a large mouth, surrounded by tentacles, but no jaws. Its powerful tongue carries many horny teeth and the animal feeds by attaching itself to some other fish—usually a dying or weak one—and rasping its flesh away. There are 15 species of hagfishes, living in all the temperate seas of the world. They are often called slime fishes because of the huge amount of slime they exude from their skin.

Hairy frog This is a greenish-brown frog, flushed with pink on the underside. It does not have any hairs and the name refers to the tufts of skin filaments that develop on the sides and thighs of the male during the breeding season. These filaments are thought to increase the breathing surface. The hairy frog lives in the fast-flowing streams of West Africa.

Hake A close relative of the cod, the hake lives in the Mediterranean and the north-eastern Atlantic. It is a streamlined fish with one short dorsal fin and one very long one. The anal fin on the lower side is also very long. The hake is brownish-grey above and silvery-white on the sides and belly. Its scales are large.

Hartebeest

Halibut This is a fish that is in some ways half way between an ordinary fish and a flat fish. It lies on its left side, but its body is not as flat as that of a plaice and its jaws are not distorted like those of the true flat fishes. It feeds on bottom-living invertebrates and also on other fishes. There are two species of halibut—one in the North Atlantic and one in the North Pacific. They are fished for food and for the oil in their livers.

Hammerhead shark There are five species of these fishes, in which the sides of the head are drawn out to form a hammer-head shape. They live mainly in the warmer seas and feed on bottom-living fishes and invertebrates. The largest species may reach a length of 6 m and span 1 m across the head from eye to eye.

Hamster There are about 14 species of hamsters, short-tailed rodents related to the voles. They range from Western Europe to China and usually live in dry regions such as sand dunes and the grassy steppes. They eat various plant materials but cereals are their staple diet and they are sometimes a nuisance to farmers. All the pet golden hamsters in the world have descended from a single family found in Syria in 1930.

Harrier Harriers are a group of hawks generally living in open country. They are usually brown, although some species are largely black. They have owl-like heads, long wings and long legs. They are found in all the continents, the hen harrier (marsh hawk in America) being the most widely distributed species. Harriers take a variety of prey, which they spot as they fly low over the ground.

Hartebeest This is a large and rather ungainly looking antelope. The head is long and narrow and the back slopes sharply down from the shoulder to the hindquarters. Both sexes bear horns. There are three species which, between them, cover most of the southern half of Africa. They are among the commonest of the antelopes.

Harvester The harvesters or harvestmen are related to the spiders. They are often called harvest spiders or daddy-long-legs. Harvesters do not have the narrow waist of the spiders, nor do they have the silk glands, but they have four pairs of long legs. Most of the world's 2,000 species of harvesters are brownish in colour and the majority live on the ground or in low growing vegetation. They feed mainly on other small animals.

Harvesting ant The harvesting ants get their name because they collect the seeds of grasses and store them in their nests. They make huge nests and they go out to forage in large bands. Small workers gather the seeds and larger workers crush them with their jaws. Harvesting ants live in the drier regions of the world, mainly in the Tropics and sub-Tropics.

Harvest mouse The harvest mouse is one of the smallest British mammals. Its prehensile tail accounts for about half its length. The animal has thick soft fur and weighs only 6 or 7 grammes. It is light enough to be able to swing about on grass stems and make its nest there. In winter the animal lives in a burrow. It feeds mainly on seeds and is found across Eurasia to Formosa. The American harvest mouse is a vole.

Hatchet fish The 15 species of hatchet fishes live in the deep sea. The crinkly, shiny body is flattened from side to side and has a sharp lower edge. This feature, together with the slender handle-like tail, is responsible for the name hatchet fish. The animals go down to 450 m during the day, but they come nearly to the surface at night when they feed on various floating creatures.

Hawkmoth Hawkmoths, or sphinx moths, are large, thick-bodied moths found throughout the world, although most of the 900 species are tropical insects. The wings are long and narrow and the moths can fly very fast. Most of them fly at night. The caterpillars are stout creatures and they usually have a curved horn at the hind end.

Hedgehog There are 15 hedgehog species, all quite similar, living in Eurasia and Africa. They feed on a variety of invertebrates and small vertebrates. They also eat plant food, especially fruits. The most obvious thing about a hedgehog is its prickly coat of numerous hardened hairs. These spines are found only on the upper surface, the lower surface being clothed with soft hair. The hedgehogs of cooler regions hibernate.

Hellbender This is a giant salamander living in North America and reaching a length of up to 75 cm. It has a flattened, brownish body and a broad head with small eyes. The tail, which accounts for one-third of the animal's length, is oar-like at the end. The hellbender lives in swift streams in the eastern part of the United States. It feeds on any animal it can catch. Similar species live in China and Japan, the Japanese species reaching a length of up to 1.5 m.

Humming Bird Hawkmoth

Honey Ant

Hedgehog

Hermit crab Hermit crabs live in empty sea shells, such as those of winkles and whelks. In place of the short squat body of the typical crabs, the hermits have a soft banana-shaped abdomen. Only the front end of the animal has a hard skeleton, and the right claw is used to close the opening of the shell. The robber crab of the South Pacific is a land-living hermit crab which does not live in a shell, although it still has a twisted abdomen.

Herring The herring has for long been the most important food fish in the world. Some 3,000 million herrings are caught in the Atlantic and neighbouring seas every year. It is a greyish-green colour on top and silvery beneath. It lives near the surface of the sea and swims in huge shoals. It feeds on tiny planktonic animals which it strains from the water with its gills.

Hippopotamus Distantly related to the pigs, the hippopotamus rivals the Indian rhinoceros as the third largest living land animal behind the two elephants. It may weigh 4 tonnes. Hippos spend most of their time wallowing in rivers and lakes, but they come on to land at night to feed. They eat large quantities of grass, but they also consume plenty of aquatic vegetation. They are found over much of the central part of Africa. The pigmy hippopotamus of West Africa is a separate species.

Hoatzin One of the strangest of all living birds, the hoatzin lives in the dense forests of the Amazon basin. It is related to the chickens and other game birds. It is basically brown and cream, with long spiky feathers forming a crest on the head. The young hoatzin has claws on its wings and it uses these to climb about in the trees. It does not fly well for it has only small flight muscles. The hoatzin feeds almost entirely on leaves and fruits.

Honey ant Honey ants belong to several species and they live in the drier regions of the world. They are famous for the development of 'living honey pots'. The ants feed largely on the honey dew exuded by aphids and much of the honey collected in time of plenty is stored in the bodies of special workers called repletes. These become greatly swollen and they hang from the roof of the nest chamber, giving out honey when stroked by other ants. The honey-filled repletes are eagerly sought by local people and are considered a great delicacy.

Honeyguide The honeyguides are birds related to the barbets. They are brown or grey above and pale beneath, sometimes with yellowish markings. The eleven species live in Africa and southern Asia and they feed mainly on bees and wasps. They seem to be immune to the stings and they even enter the bees' nests to eat the wax combs. The birds get their name because some attract honey badgers and lead them to the bees' nests. The badgers rip open the nests to get at the honey and the birds feed on the scraps.

Hornbill Hornbills are large birds—up to 1.5 m long—found in Africa and South East Asia. They have huge bills, often topped by large bony swellings called casques. Most of the species live in the forests and feed on fruit. They nest in hollow trees and, after laying her eggs, the female shuts herself in with a wall of mud and other materials. Only a small slit is left and the male feeds his mate through this.

Hornet The true hornet is a particular species of wasp living in wooded areas of Europe. It differs from the ordinary wasps in being brown and yellow, but it leads the same kind of social life. It builds its nests in hollow trees. Hornets have a powerful sting, but are less ready to use it than the wasps.

Horse-fly This name is given to certain large flies. The females feed on the blood of animals, especially cattle and horses, and the males suck nectar from flowers. The eyes have beautiful rainbow colours in life. Cleg-flies are related to the horse-flies and cause great distress because they fly so silently that we rarely notice them until they have sunk their sharp beaks into our skin.

Hoverfly Hoverflies are true flies, belonging to the family Syrphidae. They are wonderful aeronauts and they can move in all directions as well as hover. Many of them mimic bees and wasps, but the hoverflies can always be distinguished by their single pair of wings. Adult hoverflies take nectar, while many of the larvae help us by eating greenfly and other pests.

Howler monkey The largest of the South American monkeys, the howlers are named from their loud calls which are produced in a large echo chamber in the throat. The monkeys have a thick and heavy neck to accommodate this apparatus. There are five species, ranging from red to black in colour. They live in the forests and feed mainly on leaves and fruit.

Humming bird There are over 300 species of these little birds, distributed throughout the New World. The smallest has a body no bigger than a bumble bee. They get their name from the noise made by the wings as the birds hover in front of flowers. Most of them feed on nectar, sucking it up through the tubular tongue and narrow, pointed beak. Some humming birds migrate from Alaska to South America.

Hyena There are three species of hyena: the spotted or laughing hyena, the brown hyena and the striped hyena. The latter extends from North Africa to India, but the other two are found in the southern half of Africa. The back slopes sharply down to the hindquarters. The head is large and the jaws are very powerful. Hyenas feed mainly on carrion, although they often kill weak animals. Their strong jaws and teeth can even chew up the bones.

Hyrax The dozen species of hyraxes or conies are so unlike any other animals that they are given an order to themselves. They are greyish-brown, tail-less mammals with short muzzles and small rounded ears. It is thought that the elephants are probably the nearest relatives of the hyraxes. Hyraxes live in Africa and south-west Asia, some in the forests and some in rocky country. They feed on vegetation.

Ibex This name is given to several species of goats that live on high mountains. They range from Spain to Mongolia. Ibexes are sturdy animals, usually with long backward-curving horns.

Ibis Ibises are birds related to the herons and flamingos. There are about 25 species, found in all the continents. They all have long legs, fairly long necks and long curved beaks. Many are brightly coloured, such as the scarlet ibis of tropical America. Ibises live in marshes and around shallow lakes.

The koala, a pouched mammal.

Iguana Iguanas are lizards. There are many species, including the basilisk, the ground iguana, the green iguana and the marine iguana. Many of the species are eaten by man.

Impala The impala is a graceful antelope about 1 m high at the shoulder. It is chestnut brown, with a sharply defined white belly. The male has horns up to 75 cm long, but the female is hornless. The species can be recognised by a tuft of black hair on the 'heel' of the hind leg. It inhabits a large part of eastern and southern Africa, usually keeping near to water.

Australian kookaburras.

The kiwi, one of New Zealand's flightless birds.

Indri The largest of the lemurs, the indri reaches 75 cm in length. It has very long hind limbs, but its tail is only 2 cm long. The fur is basically black-and-white. The indri lives only in the northern parts of Madagascar, where it dwells in the trees and feeds on leaves.

Jacana Also called the lily trotter, the jacana is a water bird related to the curlew, although it looks more like a long-legged coot. It walks over the floating leaves, supported by its long spreading toes, and feeds on plants and small animals. There are seven species, spread throughout the warmer parts of the world.

Jackal Jackals belong to the dog family. Two species live in Africa and a third lives in North Africa, Asia and south-east Europe. They range from black to dirty yellow in colour and stand about 40 cm at the shoulder. They feed on the left-overs from lion kills, but also hunt gazelles and other small animals.

Jackdaw A member of the crow family, the jackdaw is well known for its habit of stealing bright objects. It is about 32 cm long and has black plumage shot with blue on the back and head and a grey nape. It has a short strong bill and feeds on insects, small vertebrates and fruits and seeds. It ranges across Europe and central Asia.

Jaguar The largest of the American cats, the jaguar is about the same size as a leopard but more heavily built, weighing up to 130 kg. The coat is yellow with black spots arranged in rosettes of 4–5 around a central spot. It is a carnivorous animal ranging from the southern United States to Patagonia. It lives mainly in the dense forests.

Jaguarundi Although a member of the cat family, the jaguarundi is more like a large weasel in shape and habits. Its body is long, up to 1.3 m, but with a shoulder height of only 30 cm. It has short, rusty-red or grey fur. It is found in grasslands or dense brush on the edge of forests from the southern border of the United States to northern Argentina.

Jay Colourful members of the crow family, jays make up a varied group of over 40 species, 32 of which are in America. The common jay ranges over Europe and Asia and has reddish-brown plumage, darker on the back, with black and blue barred wings. It lives in woods and forests but feeds in open scrubland on a variety of foods including seeds, fruits and insects.

Kagu An unusual bird found only in the forested highlands of New Caledonia, the kagu has no very close relatives, the nearest being the cranes and rails. The kagu is somewhat larger than a domestic fowl and has pale grey plumage. Its head bears a loose crest that it can raise in anger or display. It eats mainly snails, worms and insects, coming out to feed at dusk. Like the domestic fowl, the kagu seldom flies, running fast with wings outstretched when alarmed. Kagus are becoming increasingly rare and may soon be found only in zoos.

Kakapo The kakapo is an extremely rare, owl-like parrot living in the rain forests in parts of New Zealand. It is a flightless bird about 55 cm long with greenish upper parts streaked with black, brown and grey. It is nocturnal and feeds on fruit and grass.

Kangaroo rat This is a rodent, named for its long hindlegs and tail, short forelegs and leaping gait. It resembles a jerboa and, like the jerboa, it lives in deserts. There are several species in North America, ranging up to about 55 cm in length, including the long tufted tail. They hardly ever drink and get all their water from the seeds and plants they eat.

Katydid This is the name given to various American bush crickets. They have a remarkably loud 'voice' which sounds like 'Katy did'. (See Grasshopper.)

Kestrel Kestrels are small falcons, noted for their hovering flight. There are several species, distributed almost all over the world. All are brown and grey, with black spots. The common kestrel lives in Eurasia and Africa. It nests and roosts in open woodland, but hunts over open country. It hovers in the air while watching the ground beneath, and drops down on various small animals which it takes for food.

King crab This marine creature is not a crab, but a 'living fossil' more closely related to the spiders. It is also called the horseshoe crab because of its horseshoe-shaped body. The front end is covered with a horny brown or olive green shield and the hind end bears a long movable spike. The whole animal may be up to 60 cm long. There are five species, one on the east coast of North America and four in east and South East Asia. They live in shallow water and feed on other small animals.

Kingfisher There are over 40 species of kingfishers, living mainly in the tropics. They are stocky birds with long beaks and short tails and often with brilliant plumage. Not all of them actually catch fishes. Many of the species sit on perches and dart after lizards and insects on the ground. The kookaburra or 'laughing jackass' of Australia is a kingfisher.

Kinkajou A relative of the panda, the kinkajou or honey bear ranges from South America to southern Mexico. It has large eyes, small ears and is about 30 cm long with a 55 cm prehensile tail. It lives in the tree-tops and uses the tail for extra support. The kinkajou has soft woolly fur coloured dark gold to brown. It feeds mainly on fruit, also insects and small mammals.

Kite The kite is a bird of prey with long pointed wings and a forked tail. There are two main species—the common or red kite and the black kite. The red kite lives in Europe and the Mediterranean region. The black kite also lives in Europe, but its range extends to South Africa and Australia. Kites live mainly in wooded valleys and they feed on fishes as well as on many other animals and on carrion.

Kiwi The three species of kiwis are small flightless birds of New Zealand. They are about the size of a chicken, but they have long beaks with the nostrils at the tip. Kiwis live in the forests and come out at night to search for worms and insects. The eyes are small and the ears and nose are their main sense organs.

Koala The koala, Australia's most famous animal, is a pouched mammal related to the opossums. It looks like a small grey bear, with a prominent beak-like snout and tufted ears. It is about 60 cm high and weighs up to 15 kg. It has only a stump for a tail. Koalas are nocturnal creatures and eat only the shoots of eucalyptus trees. They rarely come down to the ground. They live mainly in eastern Australia.

Krill This is a Norwegian word, used to describe the food of the whalebone whales. It refers especially to the little shrimp-like creatures called euphausia that float in millions in the colder seas of the world. They are about 5 cm long, but they feed the world's largest animal—the blue whale. The krill might be one source of food for the world's growing human population.

Kudu The kudu are among the largest of the antelopes. There are two species—the greater and the lesser kudu—and both have long twisted horns in the male. The greater kudu stands up to 1.5 m at the shoulder, while the lesser kudu is up to 1.06 m. Both have white stripes on the flank. The greater kudu ranges from the Sudan to South Africa, but the lesser kudu is found only in East Africa. Both live in the open bush.

Lacewing Lacewings are delicate insects with two pairs of thin, netted wings. The best known ones are the green lacewings, or goldeneyes, but there are also many brown species. Both adult and larva feed on aphids and they are therefore very useful insects. The larvae suck the juices from the aphids and then often cover themselves with the empty skins as a form of camouflage. Many lacewings lay eggs with stalks on them.

Two male greater kudu, notable for their magnificent twisted horns.

The female greater kudu.

Ladybird Ladybirds are small, brightly coloured beetles, most of which are oval or circular in outline. They nearly all have red and black or yellow and black patterns, warning birds that they are unpleasant to taste. When handled they often exude a bitter fluid. The adult and larva both consume greenfly and other pests.

Lammergeier This is a graceful vulture found from the Mediterranean region to South Africa and China. It has a wingspan of up to 2.7 m and, unlike other vultures, it has feathers on its neck. It is greyish-black on the back and rusty-brown underneath. The tail is long and diamond-shaped. Lammergeiers usually have to make do with the scraps after other vultures have finished with corpses. They will eat small bones and will carry large ones up in the air and drop them until they break.

Lamprey This is an eel-like creature, but it has no jaws and its nearest relative is the hagfish. It is not a true fish, therefore. There are about 30 species, in fresh and salt water, in the temperate parts of the world. Young lampreys, and some adults, feed by sucking up debris from the sea- or river-bed. Others are parasites and feed by rasping flesh from fishes.

Lancelet The lancelet is a small marine creature about 5 cm long. It looks like a fish, but it has no paired fins and it is not a backboned animal. It has some similarities with the vertebrates, however, and is probably close to the origin of backboned animals. It feeds by straining food particles from the water. There are several species, found all over the world. Most live near the coasts.

Langur Langurs are brightly coloured monkeys with crests of hair on the head and patches of naked skin. There are 20 species in South East Asia and Indonesia. Most are slender animals, about 60 cm long and sporting a tail of about the same length. With one exception, they all keep to the trees and they feed mainly on leaves. Some species are rare now because the forests are being cut down. The proboscis monkey, with its long drooping nose, is a langur.

Leathery turtle The leathery or leatherback turtles are the largest of the sea turtles, growing to a maximum of 2.7 m. The fore-flippers are also very large and a leathery turtle of 2.1 m may have flippers spanning 2.7 m. Unlike other turtles, the shell is made up of hundreds of bony plates covered with a leathery skin. The animals are usually dark brown or black and are found mostly in the warmer seas of the world. They feed on jellyfishes and other soft-bodied animals.

Above: The best-known lemur, the ring-tailed lemur of Madagascar.

Right: Although called the 'king of the jungle', the lion actually lives in open country.

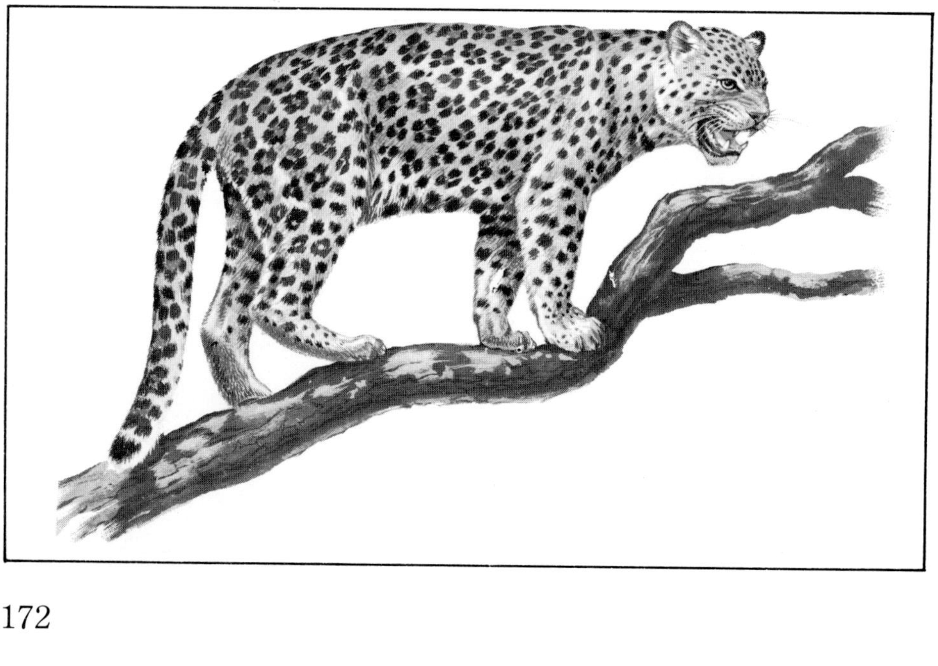

The leopard, a solitary hunter.

Leech Leeches are relatives of the earthworms, but they have a strong sucker at each end of the body. Most of them live in water and many live as parasites on fishes and snails. They suck blood and often attach themselves to people who enter the water. Some leeches eat whole insects and other small creatures.

Lemming Lemmings, of which there are 12 species, are small rodents up to 15 cm long. They live in the cold regions of the Northern Hemisphere, where the vegetation consists mainly of lichens and stunted shrubs. They continue to live under the snow during the winter. Like the related voles, the lemmings periodically build up to huge numbers. They then emigrate in all directions.

Lemur Lemurs are primates—relatives of man and monkeys—confined to Madagascar. There are several species, ranging from 15 cm to 100 cm in length. In addition, they have long bushy tails. Leaves, fruit and insects are the main foods of the lemurs. One of the best-known species is the ring-tailed lemur, which runs about with its black and white ringed tail held vertically.

Leopard One of the big cats, the leopard is a handsome animal up to 2.4 m long, including the tail. The fur is basically tawny yellow, with black spots. Black individuals, known as panthers, are quite common. Leopards live in Africa and southern Asia and feed on a wide variety of antelopes and other animals. They often catch fish.

Limpet This name is given to various water-living snails in which the shell is more or less tent-shaped. Some live in the sea, some in fresh water. When covered by water the animals glide about on a broad foot and they scrape algae from the rocks and stones. When the tide goes out the sea-shore limpets return to their own spots on the rocks and pull their shells down tightly around them. The rock and the shell are gradually worn so that they fit perfectly and a waterproof seal is made.

Linsang This is a very slender relative of the mongoose. There are two species, both living in South East Asia. They have long bodies and short legs. The fur is short and velvety, brownish-grey with darker bands or spots. Linsangs are active at night, preying on a variety of small animals. They are excellent climbers.

Lion Once found all over Africa and southern Asia, and parts of Europe, lions are now restricted to Africa south of the Sahara and a small area north of Bombay in India. Lions feed chiefly on zebra and antelopes. Unlike most cats, lions are sociable and live in groups called prides. Members of a pride frequently hunt together and share the kill.

Llama This is a South American relative of the camel. It is a domesticated descendant of the guanaco. The alpaca is another domesticated animal, probably derived from the same ancestor. The llama has a long coat and has long been used as a beast of burden in the Andes, especially in Peru. The alpaca has been bred more for its fine wool.

Lobster Lobsters are large crustaceans, weighing as much as 18 kg. Lobsters live on the sea-bed and feed on a variety of living and dead animals. They are active mainly by night and fishermen catch them with baited pots.

Locust Locusts are large grasshoppers whose populations periodically build up to plague proportions. At such times the insects fly out in great swarms and do a great deal of damage to crops. Africa suffers particularly from locusts, but various species are found throughout the warmer and drier parts of the world.

Above: The llama is a common beast of burden in the Andes.

Lorikeet Lorikeets are colourful little parrots found from Malaya to Australia and the South Pacific. There are 31 species, some of them with several sub-species. They are mainly green, with other bright colours on the head and breast. They range from 15 cm to 40 cm in length. Lorikeets live in flocks and feed mainly on nectar. They are also called honey-parrots.

Loris The three species of loris are slow-moving relatives of the lemurs living in South East Asia. They are nocturnal animals, with large forward-looking eyes. They have grasping hands and feet, which can cling tightly to branches for long periods. They eat fruit, leaves and insects.

Lovebird These are six species of small colourful African parakeets. They eat fruit, nectar and insects. Lovebirds pair for life and the pairs spend much of their time 'kissing' each other—hence their common name.

Lugworm This is a large worm living in U-shaped burrows in the sand of the sea-bed. Its coiled castings are a familiar sight at low tide. The animal looks rather like an earthworm. The central part bears tufts of reddish feathery gills. Lugworms swallow sand and extract food particles from it. A current of water passes through the burrow, bringing oxygen to the gills.

Lung fish There are only six living kinds of lung fishes, one in South America, one in Australia and four in Africa. All live in fresh water. They have air-breathing lungs as well as gills and they can live in very stagnant water. Apart from the Australian species, they have to gulp a certain amount of air even when in well-aerated water. The Australian species has strong fins which allow it to walk about. The African and South American species can survive when the rivers dry up. They burrow into the mud and aestivate, surrounded by slime which keeps them moist.

Lynx Lynxes are short-tailed, long-legged members of the cat family. They have tufted ears. The European lynx, up to 1.06 m long, lives in the forests of northern Europe and Asia. It has a sandy coat and black spots. The Spanish lynx is a little smaller and more heavily spotted. The Canadian lynx, found all over Canada, is larger and has few spots.

Lyrebird The two lyrebird species are the largest of the perching birds or song birds. The male has a body about the size of a bantam and, when he is three years old, he grows the distinctive tail which gives the birds their name. The tail is 60 cm long and its two outer feathers are very broad. It is used in courtship displays. Lyrebirds live in the mountain forests of Australia. They feed on seeds and small invertebrates which they collect on the ground.

Macaw The 18 species of macaws include the largest and the most colourful of the parrots. They live in tropical America. They have hooked beaks and tails up to 60 cm long. Macaws live in large flocks, except at the breeding season. They feed on fruit and seeds, cracking hard nuts with their strong beaks and cleverly extracting the seeds with their tongues.

Mamba The mambas are among the most dangerous snakes in the world. The black mamba is about 2.7 m long, occasionally more, while the green mamba is usually only about 1.8 m long. They are the fastest of snakes. Green mambas live in the trees and are less aggresive than the black species. Both snakes live in Africa and feed mainly on small mammals.

Manatee The three species of manatees are related to the dugongs. Both groups are known as sea cows. Manatees are seal-like mammals. One species lives around the West African coast, one around the Caribbean and the third lives in the Amazon and Orinoco rivers in South America. They all feed on aquatic vegetation.

Mandrill This is a forest-living baboon with a sturdy body up to 0.9 m long. The male's face and rear end are decorated with naked patches of pink and blue. The rest of the body is dark brown, with a golden collar and beard. Mandrills live in central and West Africa and are mainly herbivorous. They spend most of their time on the ground, but sleep in the trees.

Mantis Mantises, often called praying mantises, are insects related to cockroaches. They feed on other insects which they catch with their large spiny front legs. The mantis sits on the vegetation with its front legs held up in front of its face—almost as if it were praying. When another insect approaches, the legs are shot out and the insect is trapped by the spines.

Marabou This is a rather large and ugly stork of central and East Africa. It stands 1.2 m high and has a wingspan of over 2.4 m. The back, wings and tail are dark grey, while the underparts are white. The head and neck are pink and more or less naked, with a fleshy pouch dangling from the throat. The bill is large and heavy. Marabous eat carrion and other rubbish.

Markhor This is a wild goat of the Himalayan region. Males stand about 0.9 m at the shoulder and have fine spiralled horns. The hair is sandy coloured in summer and grey in winter. Both sexes have a long beard and heavy mane. Most markhors live between 1,200 m and 2,400 m.

Marmoset These South American animals are the smallest of the monkeys. There are several species. They have claws instead of the more usual nails and these help them to get a grip as they scurry through the tree tops. Like most monkeys, they feed mainly on leaves, fruit and insects.

Marmot Marmots are mountain-dwelling rodents living in North America and Eurasia. There are about a dozen species. One of the best known is the alpine marmot of Europe. It is about 60 cm long and may weigh 8 kg. It has coarse brown and grey fur and lives near the tree-line in the Alps. Marmots feed on grasses and other plants. They hibernate in burrows during the winter.

Marten Martens are relatives of the badger and stoat. They have long bodies and short legs. There are several species in North America and Eurasia. The largest is the fisher, or pekan, about 0.9 m long. This species hunts mainly on the ground, but pine martens live more in the trees and hunt squirrels and birds. Most of the species are brown or black.

Mayfly Mayflies are rather primitive insects whose nymphs live in water. The adults have one or two pairs of delicate wings and two or three long filaments on the end of the body. The adults do not feed and live for only a short time—a few hours in some species. The nymphs, however, live for about a year before they mature. There are about 1,000 known species.

Merganser Mergansers are colourful ducks with saw-edged bills. They are closely related to the smew and the goosander. There are several species, breeding in freshwater and spending the rest of the year around the coasts. The commonest species, the red-breasted merganser, breeds throughout the northern latitudes and moves south for the winter.

Midwife toad This small toad, under 6 cm long, gets its name because the male assists the female when she is laying the eggs and then carries them around attached to his back legs. When they are ready to hatch, he takes them to the water. The upper surface of the animal is greyish or light brown and it is covered with warts. The feet are only partly webbed. Midwife toads live in Western Europe and, like other toads, feed mainly on slugs, snails and insects.

Millipede The millipedes are arthropods in which nearly every segment of the body carries two pairs of legs. Most of them are long and slender, but some species, known as pill millipedes, are short and fat. They look more like woodlice and they can roll themselves into a tight ball. Millipedes live in the soil and leaf litter, eating the decaying vegetation as a rule, although some species attack growing crops. They are often found under stones.

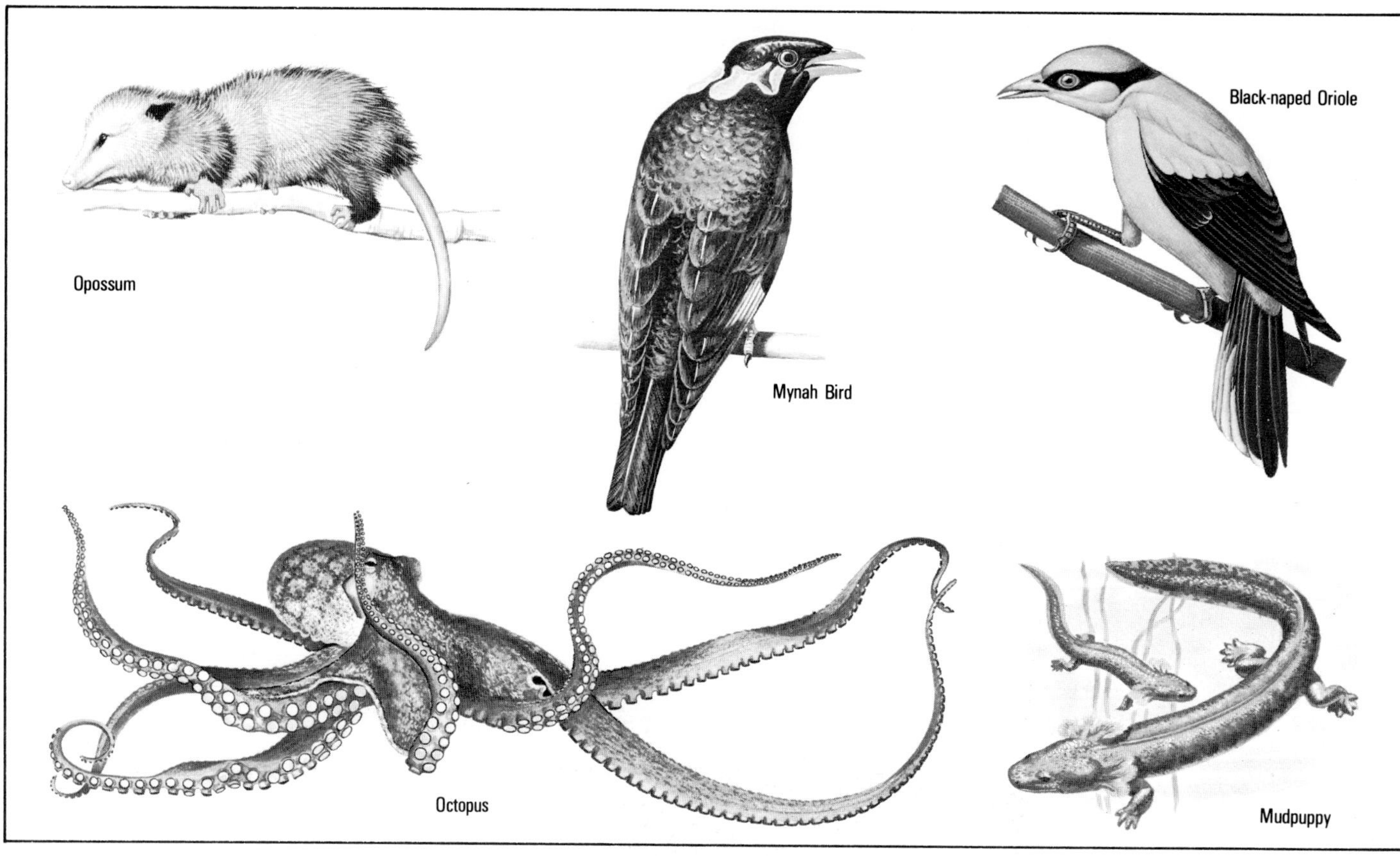

Mink The mink is a relative of the stoat and weasel. There are two species: the American mink and the European mink. The two species are very similar. Wild mink are brown, but many colour varieties have been produced in captivity, for the mink has a valuable fur and is reared on large farms. Mink feed on small mammals and ground birds. They will also dabble in streams for fishes, for they normally make their homes in river banks.

Mitten crab The three species of mitten crabs are natives of the rivers and estuaries of China and Japan. They get their name because the pincers are clothed with short hair and look as if they are wearing gloves. Mitten crabs reached Europe early in this century and now live in most of the rivers of Western Europe. They interfere with the fishing industries by taking bait and they have also damaged river banks by burrowing.

Mocking bird There are several mocking bird species in the Americas. They are related to the catbirds. Mocking birds are popular in the United States because of their ability to mimic other birds' songs. They can also make passable imitations of human voices and other man-made sounds. They eat mainly fruit and insects. They defend their nesting territories with violent pecking attacks against intruders.

Mole The several species of moles are related to hedgehogs and shrews. They spend almost all their lives under the ground and have very strong front limbs with which they excavate their tunnels. Their eyes are almost useless and the animals rely on the senses of smell and hearing. They feed mainly on earthworms, but also take insects. When worms are abundant the mole will collect large numbers, bite their heads off and store them in underground chambers. The worms are not killed, but they are paralysed. They form an important larder because the mole cannot go for more than a few hours without food.

Moloch The moloch is an Australian lizard which is covered with sharp spines. It is also called the thorny devil, although it is quite harmless. The animal is about 15 cm long and it lives in the dry parts of the continent. It eats almost nothing but ants.

Mongoose Mongooses are carnivorous mammals living in Africa and Asia. They are long-bodied creatures with short legs and sharp muzzles. The largest of the 48 species is about 1.2 m long, including nearly 60 cm for the tail. Most of the species have a uniform brown or grey coat. They are very alert and quick animals and they are well known for their snake-killing abilities. They are immune to the venom of many snakes. Mongooses severely interfered with the wildlife of the West Indies when they were taken there to combat the rats that were destroying the sugar cane.

Monitor lizard The monitors include the largest of all living lizards. The komodo dragon reaches a length of 3 m. Monitors live in the warmer parts of the Old World, from Africa and Arabia to Australia. They have lost the ability to shed their tails when attacked. Monitors spend a lot of time basking in the sun. They can be nasty opponents if disturbed. They lash out with their long tail and bite with their powerful jaws. They feed largely on small vertebrates, but some species take insects. Some live in deserts, while others never go far from rivers.

Moose The moose is the largest of the deer, standing nearly 2.4 m at the shoulder. The male carries flattened antlers more than 2 m across. The moose lives in the northern forests of North America and also ranges from Scandinavia to Siberia. In Europe it is known as the elk. It is found mainly in the wetter regions, where there are plenty of ponds and lakes and plenty of willows for it to feed on. The animals also feed on water plants and often wade into the lakes.

Moray eel There are about 120 species living in the warmer seas of the world, especially around coral reefs. Some reach lengths of 3 m or more. The head and front part of the body are usually more bulky than the rest. They hide by day and come out at night to feed on any kind of animal that they can catch. The mouth has numerous sharp teeth, which can inflict a nasty wound, but the morays are not normally aggressive fishes.

Motmot Motmots are related to kingfishers. There are eight species, all in Central and South America. Their beaks have saw-like edges and most species have two long racquet-shaped tail feathers. Motmots live in wooded country and perch on branches while scanning for large insects or lizards.

Right: The rare orang utan, a native of Borneo and Sumatra.

Mouflon This is the only wild sheep in Europe. It is about 68 cm high at the shoulder and reddish-brown in colour, with a whitish 'saddle'. The males usually have large curving horns, but the females are usually hornless. Truly wild mouflon are probably confined to Corsica and Sardinia, but flocks exist in the mountains of several countries.

Mudpuppy This is a North American salamander that never really grows up—it retains its gills throughout life and lives permanently in weedy ponds and streams. It is usually about 30 cm long and it feeds on invertebrates and small fishes.

Muntjak Muntjak are small deer, 40–63 cm high at the shoulder. Male muntjak have short antlers and long tusk-like canine teeth in the upper jaw. Muntjak come from South East Asia, but several species have been introduced to other countries.

Musk ox This creature, more closely related to sheep and goats than to oxen, lives on the bleak tundra of Canada and Greenland. The bull is a bulky creature. The cow is nearly as large and both sexes have thick shaggy coats. They stay out on the tundra throughout the year, nibbling at the sparse vegetation to keep alive.

Musk rat This is a large vole, not a rat at all. It is up to 30 cm long, with a tail of about the same length. The fur ranges from silvery-brown to black and, under the coarse guard hairs, there is a dense layer of soft hair. This is an important item in the fur trade and is known as musquash. Musk rats are natives of North America and they live in and around streams, feeding on various water plants. When introduced to Europe they did great damage to river banks.

Mynah Mynahs, or mynah birds, are large starlings of southern Asia. The Indian hill mynah, 38 cm long, is a popular cage bird because it can mimic human voices. It is also known as a grackle. It is a glossy black bird with a yellow bill and yellow wattles behind the eyes. Most of the mynah species live in the forests and eat fruit and insects.

Narwhal This is a smallish whale, reaching about 3.5 m in length excluding the long tusk. The tusk is found only in the males and it is formed from one of the upper teeth. The narwhal lives in the Arctic Ocean and often forms great herds. It feeds mainly on cuttlefishes and squids.

Natterjack The natterjack toad is easily recognised by the yellow line running down the centre of the head and back. Natterjacks are found only in Europe. They are very local in the British Isles, but common in France and Spain. They live mainly in sandy places. They have very loud voices.

Nightjar The common nightjar, or goatsucker, is a nocturnal bird about 25 cm long. It is grey, brown and black and very difficult to see as it sits on the ground during the daytime. It produces a churring noise throughout the night as it flies about catching insects on the wing. It is a migratory bird, spending the summer in Europe and Asia and going to Africa for the winter. There are about 70 species of nightjar altogether. All are much alike and they are found nearly all over the world. The whippoorwills are American nightjars.

Nilgai This is the largest Indian antelope, the males being nearly 1.5 m high and weighing up to 270 kg. The male's horns are only about 20 cm long and the female is hornless. The male is bluish-grey and the female is tawny. They may be recognised by the white 'garter' below each fetlock. Nilgai live in hilly country and open plains, feeding on trees and grasses.

Noddy Noddies, of which there are five species, are terns living in the warmer parts of the world. The white noddy or fairy tern is white, but the others are brown or grey. They nest on remote islands, but spend most of their time at sea. They catch small fishes at the surface.

Numbat This is a termite-eating marsupial, often called the banded anteater. It has brownish fur with white bands around the body. It has prominent ears and 52 teeth—more than any other land mammal. The numbat lives in south-west Australia.

Nuthatch Nuthatches, of which there are 18 species, are small birds with bluish-grey or bluish-green plumage above. They have strong feet and claws and run up and down tree trunks with ease. They do not use their tails to support them. The birds eat insects for much of the year but in autumn and winter they eat nuts, often wedging them into bark-crevices and then hacking them open with their sharp beaks.

Oarfish This marine fish, also called the ribbon fish, has a body up to 6 m long yet it is only 5 cm across. It is about 30 cm deep at the front, but tapers to a point at the tail. It is silvery-grey, with darker markings and deep red fins. The dorsal fin runs the whole length of the body and the front few rays form a spectacular crest over the head. The pelvic fins are long and slender but broaden at their tips, rather like oars—hence the fish's name. Oarfishes live in nearly all parts of the oceans and feed on tiny planktonic animals.

Ocelot This is one of the most beautiful members of the cat family. Its colour ranges from grey, through yellow, to deep brown, and it is decorated with spots and streaks. Ocelots live in the warmer parts of America from the southern United States to Paraguay. They are forest-dwellers mainly and feed on birds and small mammals.

Octopus The octopus is a marine cephalopod with eight arms. These creatures range in size from a few centimetres across to more than 9 m. They feed mainly on crabs and shellfishes which they catch with their tentacles, poison with venom, open with their beaks and scoop out with their tongues. Octopuses are found in all oceans of the world. They live on the sea-bed in nooks and crannies.

Okapi This African mammal is the only close relative of the giraffe but the neck is not so long. The top of the head is only about 2 m from the ground. Its coat is a rich reddish-brown and it is marked with white on the legs and haunches. Okapis live in the rain forests of the Congo and were not discovered by Europeans until less than 100 years ago. They eat leaves and fruit.

Olm The olm is a blind, white amphibian that lives in underground rivers and lakes. It is related to the newts and salamanders but it does not grow up completely. It retains its red gills throughout its life. It has an eel-like body up to 30 cm long. Olms live only in the limestone caves of Yugoslavia and Italy.

Opossum Opossums are American marsupials. The best known species is the Virginia opossum, common in many parts of the United States and South America. Like the other opossums, it forages for invertebrates and small vertebrates on the ground. The young are carried in the mother's pouch for about 10 weeks and for a further month they are carried on her back.

Orang utan This ape lives in Borneo and Sumatra and is in real danger of becoming extinct. The animals live in the forests, swinging from branch to branch with their arms. Orangs feed mainly on fruit.

Oriole Orioles are forest birds living in the Old World. Only the golden oriole is found in Europe. This is a very striking black and yellow bird. Orioles eat fruit and insects, being among the few birds to accept hairy caterpillars. The Old World orioles, of which there are 28 species, belong to a quite different family from the 'American orioles'.

Oryx The three species of oryx are antelopes, with long slender horns. They all live in the desert areas of Africa and Arabia, the Arabian oryx being extinct in the wild. The scimitar oryx lives in the Sahara. The gemsbok lives in south-west Africa, but there is also a northern race, known as the beisa oryx, in Somalia.

Osprey The osprey, or fish hawk, is a fish-eating bird of prey. It fishes in the sea and in lakes, diving from a height of up to 30 m and scooping up the fish with its talons. Its toes have spiny scales, which help it to grip the prey. The osprey is found in all continents except Antarctica.

Ostrich The ostrich is the largest living bird. The males have black plumage with white plumes on the wings and tail. The females are brown. Ostriches cannot fly, but they can run very fast. They live in the dry bush and desert. They are now found mainly in East and South Africa. The Asian race has not been recorded for many years.

Otter The otters are water-dwelling carnivores related to the weasels. There are several species, all much alike. They have slim bodies and short legs. The head is broad and flattened, and the ears are almost hidden in the sleek brown fur. Otters are wonderful swimmers and they catch most of their food in the water. They eat a variety of animals including eels and other fishes, crayfishes, frogs and small mammals.

Ovenbird Ovenbirds are South American birds named from the domed clay nests that some species make. The birds are between 12 and 28 cm long and most of them are dull brown. Most of the species live in the pampas and the mountain regions of Argentina and Chile and most of them eat insects. The North American ovenbird is not a true ovenbird and belongs to the wood warbler family. It makes an oven-shaped nest, using grass not mud.

Pack rat Pack rats are large voles living in North America. They are about 45 cm long, half of which consists of the tail. There are 22 species, found in almost every kind of habitat from woodland swamps to deserts. They are nocturnal animals and they collect all kinds of brightly coloured and metallic objects to hoard in their nests. Some of the species make houses of twigs and the desert-dwelling pack rats use pieces of prickly cactus. These homes provide safety from all enemies. Pack rats are mainly herbivorous, eating fruit, leaves and roots.

Paddlefish This is a large and rather primitive freshwater fish related to the sturgeon. It has a long shark-like body with few scales and a long flattened snout looking rather like a canoe paddle. The snout may account for half of the fish's length. There are two species, one living in the Mississippi region of America and the other in the Yangtse basin of China. The American species is about 2 m long, but the Chinese species is reported to reach a length of 7 m. Both feed on plankton.

Panda The giant panda is probably the most famous of all animals. It is a black and white bear-like creature, up to 2 m long and weighing up to 135 kg. It lives in the cold damp bamboo forests of Tibet and south-west China and is rather rare. Pandas eat mainly bamboo shoots, but also other plants and small animals.

Pangolin Pangolins are strange mammals in which the hair of the back has been converted into large brown overlapping scales. The seven species—four in Africa and three in Asia—are placed in an order by themselves. They have slender bodies and short legs, with long tails and snouts. The eyes are very small. Pangolins live in the forests and feed on ants and termites. They use their strong claws to rip open the nests and they pick up the insects with their long tongues. They are often called scaly anteaters.

Right: Pipefishes are related to the seahorse.

Below: Pelicans, among the biggest of birds.

Paradoxical frog The paradoxical frog lives in South America. It is greenish-brown, with darker markings on the back and yellow and black markings on the hind legs. Its outstanding feature is the great size of the tadpole. When fully grown, the tadpole is more than 25 cm long, but then changes into a tiny froglet less than 5 cm long, and even the adult frog is only 8 cm long.

Parrakeet Parrakeets are small brightly coloured parrots with long tails, but the name has been given to a wide variety of species and does not refer to any clearly defined group.

Parrot The parrot family contains more than 300 different species, but only 107 of them are strictly called parrots. The others are macaws, cockatoos, lorikeets and so on. Parrots have large heads and strongly hooked beaks. One of the best known is the African grey parrot, which is a favourite pet because of its great ability to 'talk'—that is to mimic human voices. It is a remarkably intelligent bird. Parrots are forest-dwelling birds. They feed mainly on fruits and seeds.

Parrot fish Parrot fishes are brilliantly coloured fishes in which the teeth are joined together to form beak-like structures around the mouth. There are numerous species living around the coral reefs of the Tropics. They feed mainly on seaweeds, but they also nibble corals with their sharp beaks.

Peccary Peccaries are the South American equivalents of the Old World pigs. The collared peccary lives in deserts, woodlands and rain forests from Argentina to Mexico. It feeds mainly on fruit and roots, together with some invertebrates. The white-lipped peccary lives in the rain forests, never far from running water. It feeds as much on animal material, including carrion, as on vegetable food.

The long-tailed macaw.

Pelican The pelicans are among the largest living birds. They are rather ungainly birds on the ground, but they are expert swimmers and fliers. The birds have long necks and the large beak carries an extending pouch which is used for catching fishes. The bird swims on the water and dips its head under the surface, using the pouch as a net. The brown pelican is a sea bird, but the other species, which are mainly white, live around inland lakes. They are found in the warmer parts of the world.

Père David's deer This deer came originally from the plains of northern China, but it no longer exists in the wild. There is a herd at Woburn Park in England, and quite a number in zoos. The male carries large antlers which fork near the base into two more or less equal arms. The hooves are large and spreading, and it is believed that the animals originally lived in swampy areas.

Peregrine The peregrine is a large falcon. The upper surface is slaty-blue and the underparts are white. Peregrines are most numerous in rocky areas, especially around the coast. They are swift birds and feed mainly on other birds, especially pigeons. They have been used to frighten birds away from airfields to prevent damage to aircraft. Peregrines live in all continents except Antarctica.

Phalanger Phalangers are tree-dwelling Australian marsupials. They fill the niches occupied by monkeys and squirrels in other parts of the world. They feed mainly on fruit and leaves, although some take insects.

Piddock This is a marine bivalve mollusc that bores into stone and wood. It has a rather delicate long white shell which is decorated with numerous spines and ridges, especially at the broad front end. The hinge is so arranged that the two halves of the shell can rock backwards and forwards, and it is this motion that gradually bores a hole into the stone. The animal can make quite a long burrow and it is well protected there. It feeds like most other bivalves by drawing a current of water in through a siphon and filtering out food particles.

Pika Pikas are small mammals related to rabbits and hares. There are two species in North America and 12 in Asia. They look like rabbits except that they have short rounded ears and all four legs are about the same size. There is no tail. Pikas are generally greyish-brown and they live in a variety of habitats. One species even lives more than half way up Mount Everest. The animals cut grass and dry it in the summer, and then store it for winter use.

Pike The pike is aptly nicknamed the freshwater shark. It is a long-bodied fish, sometimes reaching 1.5 m in length, with a flattened head and large jaws. The latter bristle with teeth. The fish is greenish and it blends well with the weeds among which it hides. When another fish swims close enough the pike will dart out and snap at it. Pike have been known to swallow fishes almost as large as themselves. The common northern pike, which can weigh more than 15 kg, is a fine game fish and good for eating.

Pilot fish Pilot fishes are small black and white striped fishes that swim about in the company of whales, sharks and other large fishes. They do not guide their larger companions in any way and they do not even feed on the scraps left by the sharks. It is a mystery why pilot fishes should associate with the larger animals.

Pipefish The pipefish is a long, thin fish with a long snout. It has an unusual way of swimming. Sometimes, instead of swimming headfirst through the water it swims upright. The male pipefish keeps the eggs and the young in a pouch on his body. Slow swimmers, the pipefishes depend upon bony armour for protection.

Piranha A ferocious fish found in South American rivers. It travels in schools and has been known to attack and devour large animals within a matter of minutes. Piranhas are between 5 and 20 cm long and have extremely sharp teeth.

Pocket gopher This is a small hamster-like rodent living in North America. There are about 30 species. They get their name from the fur-lined external pouches on their cheeks. These are used for carrying food. Pocket gophers are burrowing creatures with small eyes and ears and powerful front legs. They feed on bulbs and roots, often pulling whole plants down into their burrows.

Polar bear One of the largest and most carnivorous of the bears, the male polar bear may reach a length of 2.7 m. Females are a little smaller. The animal has a long head with small ears. It has powerful legs, with broad feet and hairy soles which help it to grip the ice and snow. Polar bears live along the southern edge of the Arctic pack ice and occasionally venture as far south as Japan. They eat seals and fishes and will also take vegetable food when they come on land.

Polecat A member of the weasel family, the polecat is about 50 cm long, including the tail. The upper surface has a dense golden underfur with coarse dark brown guard hairs. The underside is blackish. The animal prefers wooded country, but lives more or less anywhere that it can find small mammals and birds to eat. Polecats are found throughout most of Europe, but do not extend far into Scandinavia. In the British Isles they are confined mainly to Wales.

Pond skater The pond skater is a small bug with a flat narrow body and two pairs of long legs. These have hairy tips which enable the insect to rest on the water surface. The legs also 'row' the insect about. The front legs are short and are used for catching small insects that fall on to the water surface.

Poorwill The poorwill (whippoorwill) is an American nightjar about 20 cm long and mottled brown in colour. Like the other nightjars, the poorwill is nocturnal and it catches insects on the wing. It is the only bird known to hibernate.

Porbeagle This is a shark living in the Atlantic Ocean. It has a sharply pointed snout and a large dorsal fin. It feeds mainly on other fishes and is a rather aggressive creature.

Porcupine fish This animal looks much the same as any other kind of fish when it is relaxed. It is normally about 30 cm long, with numerous

Rabbit

spines lying flat on the body. When alarmed, the fish swallows water and puffs itself up. The spines stand out from the body then and the fish is very difficult for any enemy to swallow. Porcupine fishes live in tropical seas and feed on corals and shellfishes.

Porpoise Porpoises are small whales, never more than 2 m long. They have blunt snouts and broad rounded flippers. These features distinguish them from the other major group of small whales, the dolphins. There are several species, generally found in coastal waters. They swim in the surface waters, catching herrings and other small fishes.

Portuguese man-o'-war This is a marine animal—actually a colony of minute animals—related to the jellyfishes and sea anemones. There is a gas-filled float at the surface and below it are numerous long tentacles with stinging cells. These have a venom almost as powerful as that of a cobra and the man-o'-war is something to be avoided. It lives in the warmer seas of the world and is often brought to British waters by the Gulf Stream. The tentacles catch and digest fishes.

Left: A polar bear family.

Potto

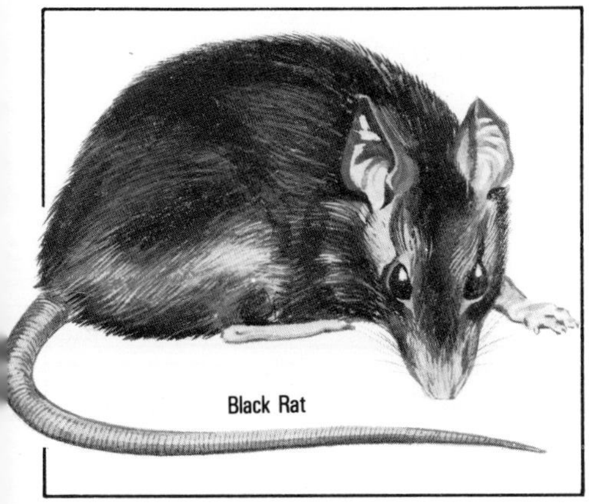

Black Rat

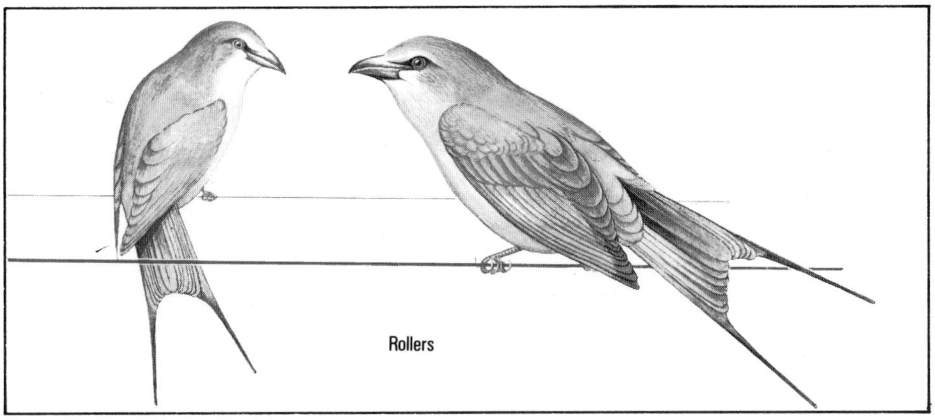

Rollers

Potto This is a slow-moving relative of the lemurs and lorises, up to 40 cm long with an 8 cm tail. It lives in the forests of west and central Africa. It has thick brown fur and large round eyes, enabling it to see as it moves around at night. It grips the branches tightly and never lets go with more than one foot at a time. Pottos eat fruit, invertebrates and small birds.

Prairie dog This is a hamster-like, short-tailed ground squirrel which has a barking call. It is about 30 cm long, yellowish-brown or grey. The five species live on the plains of North America. They are burrowing creatures and they live in 'towns' of many individuals, with numerous burrows for each family group. Prairie dogs feed on grass and other plants.

Pronghorn This is an antelope-like creature living on the grasslands of western North America. It stands about 100 cm at the shoulder. The upper parts are reddish-brown, with a black mane and white underparts and rump. Both sexes bear horns covered with a sheath of hair. The horns have a short prong at the front—hence the name—and they are shed each year.

Ptarmigan This game bird is distinguished from its grouse relatives by its white wings and underparts. It ranges right across the northern parts of the world. The birds have a brownish mottled colour in spring and summer. In autumn they become greyish and in winter they are white except for the black tail and the black eye-patches of the male. They eat berries, leaves and insects.

Puffin This is a small black and white sea bird about 30 cm long, with a triangular bill of red, blue and yellow. These colours develop only during the breeding season. The birds eat small fishes and they swim under the water scooping up the fishes as they go. The Atlantic puffins live around the North Atlantic and breed on cliffs. Outside the breeding season they may go far out to sea. Other puffins live in the North Pacific.

Puma Also called a cougar or mountain lion, the puma is a large cat looking rather like a lioness. The body is generally some 1.2 m long. The animal is found throughout the Americas, especially in the mountains and plains. It also lives in forests. It feeds mainly on deer, but may also take domestic animals. It is famous for its loud scream.

Python Pythons are the Old World equivalents of the American boas. They are large constricting snakes, of which the African rock python is the largest. It reaches a length of over 9 m. Pythons live in various habitats, but the larger ones prefer to be near water. Many climb trees. They eat all kinds of small mammals and birds.

Quail Quail are game birds rather like partridges in many ways. There are nearly 100 species, living all over the world. They do not fly much and keep within a few metres of the ground when disturbed. They keep to open ground, feeding on seeds and insects.

Quelea The quelea, or red-billed quelea to give it its full name, is a sparrow-like bird with a stout red beak. It lives in vast flocks on the grasslands and savannah of Africa and does immense damage to grain crops. Whole fields of grain may be eaten.

Quokka This is a small wallaby, looking like a large rat. It is only 1 m long, including the tail, and it is greyish-brown with a reddish tinge around the front part. The quokka lives in the swamps and brush of south-west Australia, feeding on grasses and other plants at night.

Rabbit The rabbit can be distinguished from the hare by its shorter ears and limbs. Rabbits live in extensive burrows or warrens with several exits. Their diet includes a wide variety of plant food such as grass, corn and kale. During the summer the female may have a number of litters at intervals of 5–6 weeks. There are over 50 varieties of domesticated rabbits.

Raccoon Raccoons are carnivorous mammals related to pandas and coatis. There are seven species all living in the Americas. They are between 60 and 100 cm long including the tail. The fur is generally greyish with dark marks on the face and tail. Raccoons originally lived in the forests, especially around streams, but they have adapted themselves to the changes brought about by man and they often come into towns in search of food. They will eat more or less anything and even raid garbage bins in the towns.

Ragworm This is a marine relative of the earthworm, living in shallow coastal waters all over the world. There are many species. Each segment bears broad lobes and tufts of bristles and, unlike the earthworm, the ragworm has a fairly distinct head with eyes and jaws. Ragworms range from 2.5 cm to 0.9 m in length. Most of them are carnivorous.

Rail Rails are long-legged, short-tailed birds, most of which live in and around water. Coots and moorhens are rails. They are generally rather shy birds and they run for cover when disturbed. They do not fly very strongly. Many species have loud and quite eerie calls. They eat a variety of plants and small animals.

Rain frog This very rounded brownish frog lives in the dry regions of southern Africa and sleeps for much of the year. It comes out after the rains and feeds for a couple of months or so on worms and termites. The eggs are laid under the ground and the tadpole stage is passed entirely in the egg. When the egg hatches, a tiny frog emerges.

Rat Black rats originated in central Asia but are now found all over the world. They feed almost exclusively on plant food. Brown rats are larger and omnivorous. They are a serious agricultural pest in many parts of the world and spread infectious diseases.

Male rattlesnakes in a combat dance.

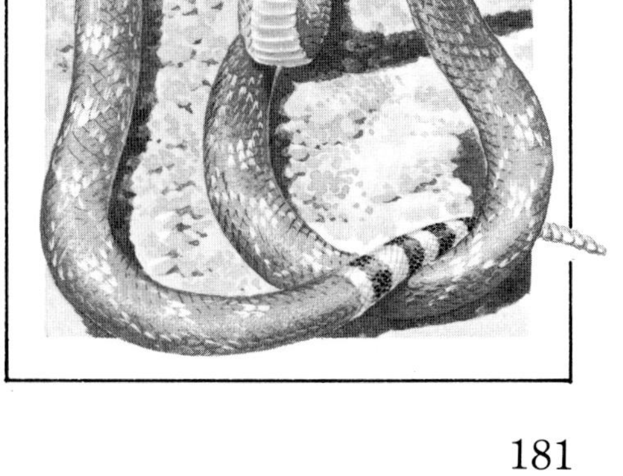

Rattlesnake The rattlesnake is a rather heavy-bodied snake, named because of the horny rings on the tail. These are the remains of cast-off skins and they rattle when the snake is disturbed. There are 29 species in North America, most of them very poisonous. Some species may exceed 2.7 m in length. They feed on a variety of small mammals. They all give birth to live young.

Raven This is the largest member of the crow family. It ranges over much of Eurasia and North America. Similar species live in Africa and Australia. They feed largely on carrion and small mammals.

Razorbill This is a black and white sea bird related to the puffins and guillemots. Razorbills are confined to the North Atlantic and spend much of the year out at sea. They breed on cliff ledges in the spring. They feed mainly on small fishes and swim after them underwater.

Reed frog There are more than 200 species of reed frogs, all living in Africa. Many species are beautifully coloured and marked. The markings often vary from individual to individual and depend to some extent on the background. The animals generally bask in the sunshine, although they are always ready to leap back into their ponds. They feed on flying insects, especially mosquitoes.

Reindeer The reindeer of northern Europe and Asia is a semi-domesticated race of the American caribou. They are true deer, but both sexes bear antlers. They have been domesticated for hundreds of years. Some Siberian tribes merely herd them and kill some for meat. Others, including the Lapps, use the reindeer for meat, milk, transport and clothing.

Remora This is a fish in which the dorsal fin has been converted into a large oval sucker. The remora attaches itself to the undersides of other fishes and gets a free ride, and sharks commonly carry remoras. The remora does no harm to the shark and often moves away to feed on passing small fishes.

Rhea This flightless ostrich-like bird is the largest bird in America. The long, powerful legs have three toes, compared with only two in the ostrich. There are two species of rhea: the common rhea and the slightly smaller Darwin's rhea. Both live on the grasslands of South America and eat plants and small animals.

Rhinoceros The rhinoceros is a bulky, thick-skinned mammal related to the horse. Both animals bear their weight on the central toe of each foot, although the rhino does have two extra toes on each foot. Rhinoes bear one or two horns on the snout, composed of densely compacted fibres like hair. There are five species: two in Africa, one in India and two more in South East Asia. The last three are very rare. All are herbivores.

Rice rat Rice rats are voles. There are about 100 species. Rice rats live in the Americas in all kinds of habitats. They are pests because they eat rice and other crops, but they are less of a pest than the true rats.

Right whale Right whales are whalebone whales. There are five species and they got their name because they were the right whales to catch when men first started whaling. None of them is common today because they have been over hunted.

Roadrunner This is an American member of the cuckoo family, famed for its speedy running and its ability to catch snakes. Its wings are short and it rarely flies, but it has a long tail which helps to balance the bird as it runs. The roadrunner is mottled brown. It lives in the deserts of North and Central America and catches a variety of animals as well as snakes.

Roller Rollers are attractive birds related to kingfishers and bee-eaters. They have long curved beaks and long tails. Most rollers live in Africa, but one breeds as far north as Scandinavia. They get their name from their rolling courtship flight. Rollers feed mainly on insects, but they also eat lizards and small snakes.

Rorqual Rorquals are a family of whalebone whales. There are six species—blue whale, fin whale, sei whale, Bryde's whale, minke whale and humpback. Bryde's whale is found in warmer seas; the others also live in polar seas.

Rove beetle Rove beetles have very short wings and wing covers which reach only part way down the back. Most are very small, but some, such as the devil's coach horse, may exceed 2.5 cm in length. Many are black or black and red. Most live in damp places, feeding on decaying matter and smaller insects.

Ruff The ruff is a sandpiper in which the male has an ornate ruff or collar of feathers around the neck. The female is the reeve. Most of the birds are mottled brown. They breed in northern Europe and Asia, inhabiting damp meadows and marshes. Out of the breeding season they migrate as far as South Africa and Australia. They feed mainly on insects.

Saiga The saiga is an antelope with a noticeably swollen snout. It has features of both sheep and gazelles. The male has lyre-shaped horns about 30 cm long. The saiga lives on the cold steppes of central Asia and feeds on wormwood and other low-growing shrubs.

Salamander The salamanders belong to the group of amphibians with tails. They are found in most parts of the Northern Hemisphere in brooks and ponds and in moist spots on land. The giant salamander of Japan reaches a metre from tip to tail.

Sand dollar This creature, also known as a cake urchin or sea biscuit, is a flattened form of sea-urchin. The flattened shell is purple or black and is about 10 cm across. It is strengthened by internal pillars. There are several species, found mainly in the warmer seas, especially in the Pacific. The animals live buried in the sand below low tide level and feed by trapping food particles in mucus produced by their spines.

Sapsucker This is a North American woodpecker, so called because of its habit of drilling holes in trees and sucking the oozing sap. There are two species: the yellow-bellied sapsucker and Williamson's sapsucker. The birds also catch the insects that are attracted to the sap.

Sawfish Sawfishes are large fishes, occasionally up to 9 m or more, with a long drawn out snout flattened into a blade with a row of strong teeth sticking out of each side. There are 6 species, found in all warm coastal waters and sometimes venturing up rivers into fresh water. They feed on molluscs and crustaceans, using the saw to search in the mud.

Saw-fly Saw-flies are related to ants, bees and wasps, but do not have the narrow 'wasp waist'. Their name is derived from the fact that they have a saw-like edge to the ovipositor with which the female cuts holes in plants to lay her eggs. Some saw-flies are called wood wasps.

Scale insect Scale insects are small bugs distantly related to greenfly. They are among the most serious of crop pests. The males normally have one pair of wings and they fly freely, but the females are wingless and they merely sit on plants and suck sap. They are covered with waxy or resinous secretions and many are also protected by a horny scale which makes them look like tiny limpets.

Scallop Scallops are bivalve molluscs. The valves are ridged and they bear 'ears' near the hinge. Scallops are among the few bivalves that can swim. They do it by opening and closing the shell quickly and shooting water out. They thus move about by jet propulsion. The mantle edge, just inside the shell, bears numerous tentacles and many small but beautiful blue eyes. Scallops live mainly around the coasts.

Salamander

Scarab Scarab beetles are stoutly built beetles. The head and the thorax often bear ornamental spines. Most scarabs feed on the dung of mammals and they are called dung beetles. They usually bury lumps of dung and feed on it underground. They also lay their eggs on it. Some species, such as the sacred scarab of Egypt, roll balls of dung until they find a suitable place to bury them. Scarabs belong to the same large group as the stag beetle and the huge hercules beetles. There are hundreds of species.

Scorpion-fish Scorpion-fishes include some of the most beautiful, the most ugly, and the most poisonous of fishes. They nearly all live in the temperate seas. Their fins are normally broken up into numerous ribbons and spines, the latter often being very poisonous. Striped colour patterns add to the strange appearance of the fishes. Members of the group include the highly poisonous stone-fish and the Norway haddock.

Scorpion-fly Scorpion-flies belong to a small group of insects. They get their name because the males of many of the species have turned-up abdomens rather like those of scorpions. They are quite harmless and they generally feed on small insects or decaying material.

Scrub-bird The two scrub-birds look like wrens, but they have their own family and they live in Australia. They live in the dense scrub and are rarely seen. They feed on worms, snails and insects. Nests consist of grass and twigs lined with 'papier mache' made from wood.

Sea-hare Sea-hares are molluscs, halfway between a sea slug and a sea-snail. They have a soft body and a thin transparent shell. The foot has a crinkly flap on each side and these flaps are folded up over the shell. They wave gently in the water and force a current of water over the gills. Similar species are found in temperate or tropical parts of the world but are much larger. They feed on sea lettuce and other seaweeds.

Sea-horse The sea-horse has a large head with a tubular snout and a very long tapering tail. It is almost entirely covered with bony bumps which give it the appearance of a wood carving. Despite its name the sea-horse is a fish. There are about 20 species. They are found almost all over the oceans, except for the colder regions. They eat small fishes and crustaceans.

Sea lily The sea lily is an animal related to the starfishes. In most species the body has five arms and is carried at the top of a slender stalk. At the bottom of the stalk there are branching tentacles which anchor it to the sea-bed. Sea lilies are found in deep water. They feed on particles of decaying matter that float down from above.

Sea-lion Sea-lions are relatives of the fur seals. Both groups have small external ears and in this respect they differ from the true seals. The most familiar sea-lion is the Californian sea-lion, which is seen in zoos and circuses. It lives around the coasts of California and Mexico and also on the Galapagos Islands and the Japanese coast. Sea-lions are beautiful swimmers. They feed almost entirely on fishes and squids.

Sea-mouse This is a stout marine bristle worm, related to the ragworms. It looks rather like a mouse, hence the name, and moves over the sand with the creeping movements of a mouse. The animals live in shallow seas and those found around the coasts of Europe are about 18 cm or more long. The sea-mouse burrows in search of food which consists of decaying animal matter.

Sea slug Sea slugs are marine snails of various kinds that have lost their shells at some time during their history. They are rather flattened, but the upper surface bears numerous flaps and filaments which act as gills. They feed on seaweeds, sponges, sea anemones and other small sea creatures. Most sea slugs crawl on the sea-bed, but some swim freely, often by 'rowing' with the flaps on the sides of the body.

Sea snake Sea snakes are reptiles that have returned to the sea from the land. Sea snakes still have to rely on air for breathing and will drown if held under water too long. There are about 50 species and they are found in tropical waters, mainly in the Indo-Pacific region. They live mainly near sandy shores and river mouths. All sea snakes are venomous with cobra-like fangs at the front of the mouth. They feed on eels and small fishes.

Sea-squirt Sea-squirts are marine animals which, in the adult state, live permanently fixed to the sea-bed or to rocks. They look little more than bags of jelly and they feed on tiny particles which are drawn in with water currents. Many live in clusters or colonies. The young sea-squirts are tadpole-like creatures with a primitive backbone. They are so called because they squirt out water after eating.

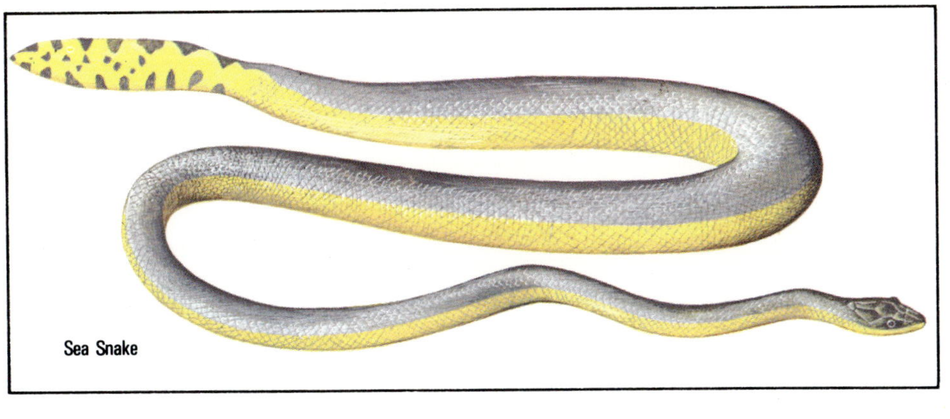

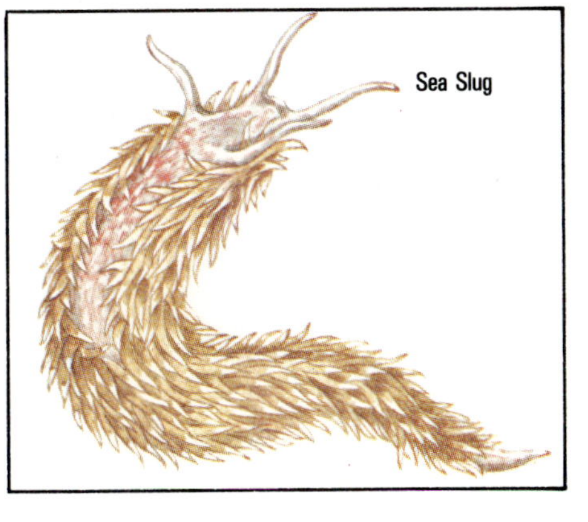

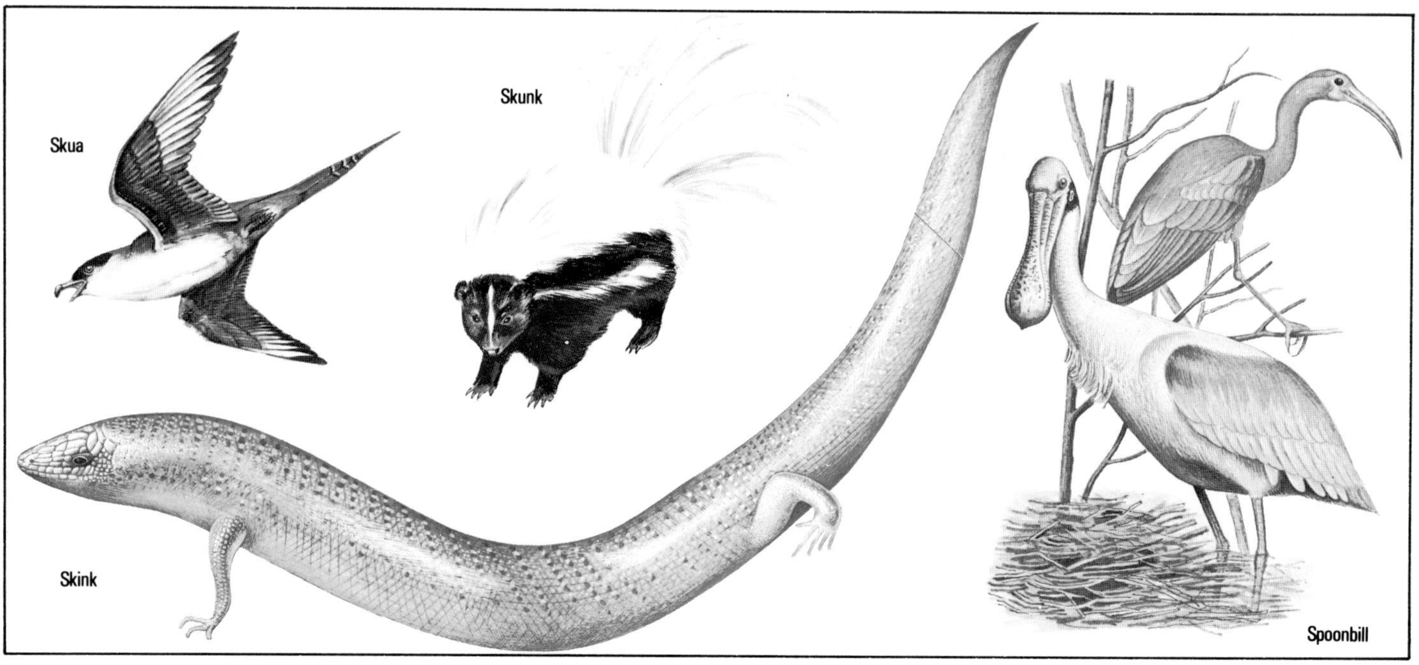

Sea-urchin A small round animal with a spiny shell. The shell or test of a sea-urchin is made up of hundreds of interlocking plates. These chalky plates carry little knobs to which the spines are attached. The sea-urchin moves about on small water-filled tube-feet which stick out through pores in the test. The test is covered with a layer of skin. Some urchins have poisonous spines. Sea-urchins feed mainly on decaying matter and algae which they scrape up with an apparatus called Aristotle's lantern. This consists of five bony teeth which act like the jaws of a grab. There are many species, including the purple sea-urchin, the heart urchin and the helmet urchin.

Secretary bird The secretary bird is a bird of prey. Its name comes from the crest of black-tipped feathers which hang down behind the head in the way 18th century clerks carried their quill pens stuck into their wigs. Adult male secretary birds stand about 1.2 m high at the shoulder. The plumage is grey, with black on the wings and legs. They are found in Africa, south of the Sahara. They feed on insects, small mammals and snakes.

Serval The serval is one of the most beautiful members of the cat family. It is a slender animal, 36–50 cm at the shoulder and up to 90 cm long with a 25–30 cm tail. The serval is long-legged, with large pointed ears. It has smooth, short hair and is a yellowish-brown colour with a pattern of bold black spots and stripes. The serval is found in most of Africa, south of the Sahara and lives almost entirely on rodents.

Shearwater The 15 species of shearwater are petrels, related to the albatross and fulmar. They are medium-sized sea birds mostly between 25 and 40 cm long. The plumage is dull, usually black or brown above and whitish underneath. Outside the breeding season shearwaters live out at sea and are found in many parts of the world excepting the polar seas. They feed on fishes and squids.

Shelduck The shelduck is a brightly coloured, rather goose-like duck common in estuaries and on coasts. The plumage is white with bold patterns of chestnut and black. The shelduck ranges from the British Isles, across Europe and Asia to China. The shelduck's main diet consists of small shore living animals such as winkles, whelks, crabs and sandhoppers.

Shrew Shrews are the smallest of the mammals. There are 170 species, found everywhere except Australasia and the polar regions. The common shrew of Europe and Asia is about 10 cm long, including 4 cm for the tail. It is a mouse-like animal, but it has a much more pointed snout, full of sharp teeth. Shrews live in undergrowth and leaf litter. They feed on insects, slugs and worms, with some vegetable matter. They have to feed every few hours.

Sidewinder This is a rattlesnake living in the deserts of western North America. It gets its name from its peculiar method of moving along the sand. It throws its body into curves, but only two points are in contact with the sand at any one time. The only tracks left in the sand are unconnected parallel grooves. Sidewinders are up to 60 cm long, with stout bodies. They are brownish in colour and they feed mainly on small rodents.

Siren The three species of siren are North American amphibians. They are related to newts and salamanders, but they are eel-like with no back legs and only weak front ones. There are feathery external gills behind the head. The sirens are thus amphibians that have not properly grown up, because they still have some of the features of young amphibians. There are three species. They live in shallow streams and eat plants and small animals.

Skate Skates are cartilaginous fishes, related to sharks and rays. There are several species and they are flattened from top to bottom. The body is more or less diamond-shaped, with a slender spiny tail. The eyes are on the top of the head, but the nostrils and mouth are underneath. Skates reach a length of 2.4 m. They live in most temperate and tropical seas, especially in the Northern Hemisphere, and feed mainly on crustaceans.

Skimmer The three species of skimmers are relatives of the gulls and terns, but they have very long beaks with the lower half much longer than the upper. They are up to 50 cm long, with stout bodies and long wings. They are black (or brown) and white. Skimmers fly low over water and scoop up fish with their beaks. The black skimmer lives around the coasts of the Americas. The other two species live in Africa and South East Asia and feed mainly inland.

Skink Skinks are lizards with very few frills or decorations. They are perfectly ordinary lizards and most of them are burrowing creatures. The largest of the 600 or so species is about 60 cm long, but most species are much smaller. They live in a variety of habitats and feed mainly on insects.

Skipper Skippers are butterflies with a very rapid darting flight. They are very distinct from other butterflies and some people think they are more like moths, although the antennae are clubbed. Some have very dingy colours and rather thick bodies. Many skippers rest with the wings half closed, especially in bright sunshine. Most of them are small butterflies.

Skua Skuas are sea birds related to gulls. There are four species and they often feed by attacking other sea birds and forcing them to give up the fishes they are carrying. They will catch fishes for themselves, however, and they also catch and eat smaller birds. The beak is hooked and the toes have sharp claws. The great skua breeds on the North Atlantic coasts and also around Antarctica. The other skuas nest around the Arctic. All are brownish and between 50 and 60 cm long.

Skunk This animal, related to the weasel and badger, is famed for its ability to squirt foul-smelling fluid at its enemies. Its bold black and white pattern acts as a warning to these enemies. There are several species, all with long shaggy fur. They live in the Americas and feed mainly on insects. They also take birds and mice and they eat nuts in autumn.

Sloth Sloths are strange South American mammals related to ant-eaters and armadillos. They spend most of their lives hanging upside down in the trees by means of their huge curved claws. The hair runs from the belly to the back, so that water runs off easily. The hairs are clothed with tiny algae and the animals thus look green. There are seven species, between 60 and 90 cm long. They move slowly and feed on leaves and fruit.

Slow-worm This creature is not slow and it is not a worm. It is a legless lizard. It is also called a blind-worm, but it is not blind either. The body is brownish, often with a bronzy sheen and with a black line down the back of the female. Adults are generally about 30 cm long, although they often lose their tails and appear much shorter. Slow-worms eat slugs and insects. They are found over much of Europe and western Asia.

Snipe Snipe are short-legged wading birds with long straight beaks. The plumage is mottled brown. There are several species. They live in marshes and other wet places and use their beaks to probe for worms and other creatures in the mud.

Sole Soles are tongue-shaped flat-fishes usually up to about 30 cm long. They lie on their left sides and are almost completely surrounded by a fringe formed by the fins. Most species live in shallow seas in the warmer parts of the world.

Solenodon The two species of solenodons are shrew-like mammals found only in the West Indies. They are about 30 cm long with a tail nearly as long. The head is relatively large and bears a long snout. The animals are brown and have remarkably large front feet and claws. They are rather clumsy creatures and feed on a variety of invertebrates and plant food. Both species are now very rare.

Spadefoot Spadefoots are toads in which there is a horny projection on the side of each hind foot. This is used for digging burrows. They have rather moist skin. Spadefoots are widely distributed in the Northern Hemisphere, the best known species living in the North American deserts. They start to breed as soon as the rains come; the tadpoles grow rapidly.

Sparrowhawk This handsome bird of prey lives in Europe, Africa and Asia. It has short, rounded wings and long legs. The bird lives mainly in woodland and feeds on small birds. It has a characteristic flight consisting of bursts of rapid wingbeats alternating with long glides.

Spectacled bear Named from the whitish markings around the eyes, the spectacled bear is the only South American bear. It stands 75 cm at the shoulder. It has a dark shaggy coat much less dense than that of bears from the temperate regions. The animal lives in the forests of the Andean foothills from Panama to Bolivia. It feeds mainly on plants.

Sperm whale This is the largest of the toothed whales, the males being about 18 m long and the females about half the size. The head is huge and contains up to 56 conical teeth. Sperm whales are found in all the oceans, but are most common in the warmer seas. They live mainly on squids and many of them carry scars where giant squids have gripped them in a struggle.

Spider monkey Spider monkeys are South American monkeys with slender bodies and sparse, rather wiry fur. The tail is remarkably prehensile and is used as an extra hand. There are two species—the common spider monkey and the woolly spider monkey. The latter lives in southern Brazil. It is more robust than the common species and has woolly hair. Both species eat nothing but fruit.

Spiny ant-eater Also called the echidna, this creature is one of the egg-laying mammals. It looks rather like a large hedgehog. There are several species found in Australia and New Guinea. Their strong front feet and claws are used for ripping open termite nests. The animals feed almost entirely on termites, picked up with their long tongues.

Spoonbill Spoonbills are long-legged wading birds related to ibises. The beak is flattened and broadens out at the tip to form a 'spoon'. The six species are found in all continents, but not in the northern regions. They live in marshes and other damp places and feed on small aquatic creatures.

Spider Monkey

Sloth

Spadefoot toad

Stork The name given to a family of large black or white birds that inhabit marshes and plains in most parts of the world. Adult storks have no voice but they clap their beaks. They hold their long beaks downwards when resting but extended horizontally when in flight. Storks feed chiefly on snakes, lizards, frogs, fishes and worms.

Sun bear Also called the honey bear, this animal is the smallest of the bears. It has short black hair, with a grey muzzle and a distinct white or yellowish crescent across the chest. The sun bear lives in the forests of South East Asia and spends most of its time in the tree-tops. It eats both fruit and small animals and is very fond of honey.

Surgeon-fish Surgeon-fishes are colourful fishes that get their name from the razor-sharp bony keels at the base of the tail. These are used as weapons by the fishes. The fishes are found around coral reefs of the Indian and Pacific Oceans and they browse on the algae and other creatures. They grow to lengths of about 60 cm and have deep bodies flattened from side to side.

Surinam toad This very flat toad is about 10 cm long and it is covered with small warts. It lives in Brazil and spends almost all of its time in the water, eating any creature (dead or alive) it finds on the stream-bed. It has neither teeth nor tongue. The female has a long egg-duct which grows out and over her back. Eggs are pressed into the spongy skin of her back. A pouch and lid develops around each egg and the whole larval development takes place in the pouch. After about 4 months tiny toads crawl out of the pouches and swim away.

Swallow The name given to a group of birds including the martins, numbering some 100 species found in all parts of the world. The commonest species is the European swallow which is called the barn swallow in North America. The tree swallow is a North American species.

Swan The six species of swans are long-necked water birds closely related to geese. Most familiar is the mute swan, a native of parts of Eurasia but taken to various other parts of the world. Whooper swans and Bewick's swans also occur in Europe and northern Asia, and the latter in North America. They have black or black and yellow bills. Black swans live in Australia and black-necked swans live in South America. Swans feed on water plants and small aquatic animals. They rarely visit deep water.

Swift Perhaps no other bird is so well adapted to life in the air, for the swift feeds, mates, bathes and even sleeps in the air. Their legs are short and weak and they rarely land on the ground. All swifts have dark plumage. Most of them live in the Tropics and feed on flying insects. Some species migrate to cooler regions for the summer.

Right: The maribou stork, a large bird that lives mainly on carrion.

Below: The attractive saddlebill stork, fishing in the shallows.

Swordfish The swordfish is a striking blue and silvery fish in which the upper jaw is carried forward to form a sword-like beak. The fish is normally between 1.8 and 3.3 m long, including the sword which is up to about 1.2 m long. Swordfishes live mainly in the warmer seas and feed on smaller fishes. The prey is snapped up or else stunned by rapid blows with the sword.

Sword-tail This is a popular and brightly coloured aquarium fish related to the carp. The sword is an extension of the lower part of the male tail fin. Sword-tails live in fresh water in Central America and feed on a variety of small animals and plants. They bear their young alive.

Tailor-bird Tailor-birds are warblers living in southern Asia and Australia. They are small birds with inconspicuous plumage. Their nests are made by stitching leaves together to form a pouch, which is then filled with soft fibres.

Takahe This is a flightless bird of New Zealand and it is very rare, only about 300 birds being known. It is related to the coot. The wings and body are green and blue and the beak is pink and scarlet. The bird lives in swampy regions and feeds entirely on the leaves and seeds of a plant called snow grass.

Takin This is a heavily built mammal, half goat and half antelope. The male is usually yellowish, with a dark stripe along the back. Females are greyish and the young are black. Takins are browsing animals living in the mountains of western China. They feed mainly on bamboo.

Tanager There are over 200 species of tanagers. Most are brilliantly coloured and they nearly all live in the forests of tropical America, although five species live in North America. They feed on fruit and insects.

Tapir This is a stoutly built mammal related to both the rhinoceros and the horse. The snout is prolonged into a short trunk and the body is covered with short, bristly hair. Tapirs live in the wet tropical forests, one species being found in South East Asia and three in South and Central America. They are browsing animals, feeding on young shoots and leaves including aquatic vegetation. The animals spend a lot of time in the water.

Above: A family of mute swans, among the most graceful of birds.

Below: These black-necked swans are native to South America.

The tiger is the largest and perhaps the most handsome of the big cats.

Tarantula This name is popularly applied to almost any large spider, especially to the hairy bird-eating spiders. The true tarantula, however, is a wolf spider found in southern Italy. It has a painful, but not particularly serious bite.

Tarpon This is a marine and freshwater fish with many common names. It is up to 2.4 m long and feeds mainly on crabs and fishes. It lives along the tropical and sub-tropical coasts of the Atlantic. The tarpon reacts violently to being hooked and it is a big-game fish for the sea angler.

Tarsier The three species of tarsiers are found only on certain islands in the East Indies. They are small primates, with thick woolly fur and enormous eyes. They have large rounded sucker-like discs on their fingers and toes and they spend much time clinging to vertical tree-trunks and branches. Tarsiers are carnivorous animals.

Tasmanian devil This is a carnivorous marsupial now confined to Tasmania. It is stockily built and rather bear-like. Its coat is black with white patches on the throat, shoulder and rump. Its powerful teeth give it a rather fierce expression. It feeds on any flesh, dead or alive, but mostly on small mammals and birds.

Tenrec Tenrecs are small insectivorous mammals related to the shrews and hedgehogs. They live only in Madagascar. There are 20 species, some looking like hedgehogs and the others looking like shrews or moles. They eat a wide variety of invertebrates. They also eat some vegetation. Tenrecs are not common.

Tern Terns are rather slender sea birds related to the noddies and gulls. There are over 30 species. Their wings are narrow and tapered and their tails are forked. The bill is narrow and the legs are short. Most of the species are black and white. Most terns live in the Tropics, but there are terns in all parts of the world.

Terrapin This name is loosely used for more or less any tortoise or turtle living in fresh water. More strictly, however, it means the diamond-backed terrapin found in the coastal waters and estuaries of the United States and Mexico. This animal gets its name from the diamond-shaped pattern on its shell.

Thresher Thresher sharks, also called fox sharks, are found mainly in the warmer seas of the world. The sharks feed on small fishes such as herrings and pilchards, which they 'round up' and then stun by fierce lashing of the long tail.

Thrip This is a tiny black insect with a narrow body and narrow fringed wings. They fly about and often get in our eyes and hair. They hibernate for the winter and often come into houses where they hide behind picture frames, loose wallpaper and in other crevices. Thrips feed by sucking plant juices and some are real pests.

Thylacine This is a dog-like flesh-eating marsupial, also called the Tasmanian Wolf. Although the front half is dog-like, the hind quarters and tail are much more like those of a kangaroo. The fur is light brown, with darker stripes across the hind part of the back. Thylacines were once common in Australia, but are now likely to be extinct. They feed mainly on small wallabies and birds.

Tick Ticks are small blood-sucking creatures related to mites. There is a small head and a larger, leathery body. The head carries mouth-parts which pierce the host—usually a mammal—and withdraw blood. The tick stays put for long periods and gradually swells up as it sucks blood. More serious than the blood sucking is the spreading of disease.

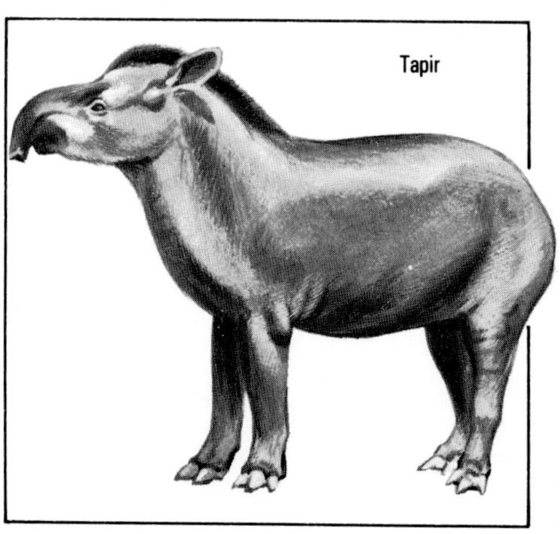

Tapir

Tiger The largest of the cats, the tiger is a magnificent striped beast ranging from Bali in Indonesia to Iran and Siberia. There are several races, differing in colour, pattern and size. Tigers live in a variety of habitats, from mountains to dense forests. They do not climb well, but they are good swimmers. They eat a variety of animals, from insects and fishes to pigs and antelopes.

Tilapia This name is given to about 100 kinds of freshwater fishes in Africa and the Middle East. They belong to the cichlid family and have large heads and deep laterally compressed bodies. They live in lakes and sluggish rivers. Tilapias eat mainly plant food and they themselves are eaten by man in many places. Most species carry their eggs and young in their mouths.

Toucan Toucans are large birds of tropical America with bright colours and huge bills which may be as long as the rest of the bird. The birds live in the forests, usually going about in small flocks. They feed almost entirely on fruit, supplemented by some insects.

Trapdoor spider Trapdoor spiders lie in wait for their prey. They construct silk-lined tunnels on the ground and fit them with lids of silk and soil particles. The spiders then sit peering out of the doors waiting to pounce on passing insects. Trapdoor spiders live only in the warmer regions of the world. They are not dangerous, although some species can give a painful bite.

Tree frogs The name given to a family of tree-dwelling frogs widely spread over the Old World with many different species. Some have suckers on their toes and some have webbed hind toes.

Tree shrew There are about 20 species of tree shrews, small squirrel-like mammals living in South East Asia. They are 20–40 cms long, about half of which is tail, and generally brownish. They live mainly in woodland and feed on a variety of plant and animal food. Tree shrews used to be included with the primates. They are now classed separately, although they resemble the first primates.

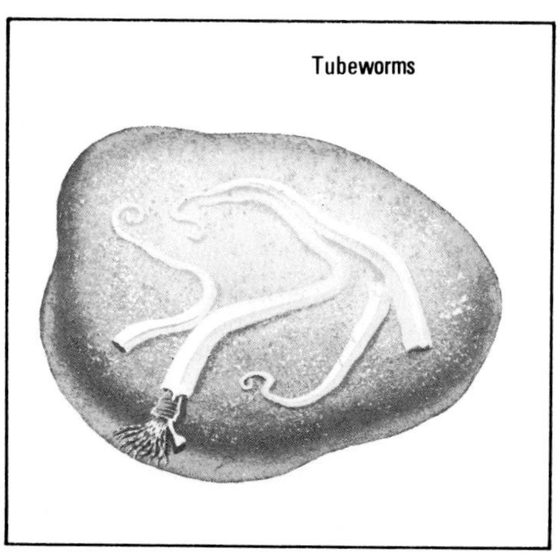

Tubeworms

Tree squirrel Many squirrels live in trees, but the true tree squirrels are members of the genus sciurus—the grey and red squirrels and their relatives. They live in most parts of the Northern Hemisphere. They differ from the ground squirrels in having bushy tails about as long as the head and body, although the tail is sometimes more feathery than bushy. They are remarkably agile in the trees, although they often wander over the ground as well. They feed mainly on fruit and buds, but also eat birds' eggs and fungi.

Tropic bird Tropic birds are graceful sea birds with two very long tail feathers. They look rather like terns, but are related to cormorants and pelicans. They are white with black markings. The three species all live in the tropical regions and come to land only in the breeding season. They fly over the oceans and dive for fishes and squids.

Trunkfish Also known as boxfishes, the trunkfishes are almost completely encased in bony boxes. The head is more or less conical and has a small mouth armed with strong crushing teeth. The eyes are large and placed near the top of the head. Trunkfishes live in the warmer seas of the world and generally live on or near the bottom. Many of them feed by nibbling at coral reefs.

Tsetse fly Tsetse flies are African insects which carry the disease called sleeping sickness. The flies also carry a disease of cattle and horses. It is called nagana and it prevented man from keeping cattle in many parts of Africa. Tsetse flies look rather like house-flies, but they suck blood. Both male and female suck blood. The female gives birth to fully developed maggots.

Tubeworm Tubeworms are bristle worms that live in tubes. They are buried in the sand or attached to rocks and weeds on the sea-shore. Chalky white tubes on the surface of stones are made by tubeworms.

Tuna Tuna are large oceanic fishes of which there are several species including the bluefin tuna or tunny of the Atlantic and Mediterranean. Tuna are very streamlined, deep-bodied fishes, dark blue above and silvery beneath. The hind part of the body bears a number of small finlets on the top and bottom surfaces. Tuna swim near the surface and feed on smaller fishes such as herrings. They are an important food.

Turaco Turacos are lively fruit-eating birds related to the cuckoos. They have strongly curved bills and all but one species have large crests on the head. Turacos live only in the African forests. Some species are called plantain-eaters.

Turbot This is one of the flat-fishes that lie on their sides on the sea-bed. It lies on its right side, whereas most other flat-fishes lie on their left sides. Its broad, diamond-shaped body has no scales, but the upper surface is covered with small bony lumps. The turbot lives in shallow water around the coasts of Europe, especially in the North Sea. It feeds on smaller fishes.

Turnstone Turnstones are small wading birds that get their name from their habit of turning stones over in their search for food. The common turnstone, which breeds all around the Arctic regions, has a 'tortoiseshell' colouring in summer—black and white and chestnut. The black turnstone, which breeds only in Alaska, is nearly all black. Both species migrate far south for the winter.

Vampire Vampires are bats. They live only in tropical and sub-tropical America and they feed on the blood of birds and mammals. They have razor-sharp teeth which can puncture the skin without the victim feeling anything. The lower lip and the tongue then form a tube through which the animal sucks the blood. There are three species and they are quite dangerous because they can carry rabies.

Velvet ant The velvet ant is not an ant but a kind of wasp. It gets its name because the female is wingless and looks like a large, hairy ant. There are hundreds of species, mostly living in the warmer regions. Velvet ants lay their eggs in the nests of bees and wasps and the young velvet ants eat the larvae and pupae.

Viperfish The deep-sea viperfishes are slender pencil-like fishes. The lower jaw is relatively huge and both jaws carry long fang-like teeth. There are three species and they live in all the oceans except the Arctic and Antarctic. They live down to depths of 2,700 m and feed on smaller fishes and crustaceans. The viperfishes are equipped with light organs.

Viscacha Viscachas are South American rodents related to the chinchilla. The plains viscacha is up to 60 cm long. It is dark grey, with black and white markings. The four species of mountain viscachas are only about half as long as the plains species. They are paler in colour. All viscachas live in colonies, with the plains viscacha digging extensive burrows. Mountain viscachas live among rocks and boulders. They all feed on grasses and other plants and they can be pests in farming areas.

Vulture Vultures are scavenging birds of prey. True vultures live only in the Old World, but the name is also applied to the condors and their relatives in America. All the vultures have more or less naked heads and most have naked necks as well. This is a useful asset because the birds plunge their heads and necks into carcases when feeding. Vultures rarely kill and they have rather weak talons. They soar around until they find a dead or dying animal and then swoop down.

Wallaby Wallabies are kangaroo-like marsupials living in Australia and New Guinea. Most of the two dozen or so species are about the size of hares. They are all herbivores and feed mainly on grass. Since the Europeans introduced foxes and other carnivores to Australia many wallabies have become rare and some have become extinct.

Walrus The walrus is a heavily built seal in which the upper canine teeth are enlarged to form long tusks. It feeds on shellfishes which it digs out of the sea-bed. Walruses live in the North Pacific and North Atlantic.

Wapiti This is a large North American deer, very closely related to the red deer. It reaches a height of 1.5 m at the shoulder. The antlers may be more than 1.8 m long. The wapiti was once an abundant animal, found right the way across the continent, but numbers have been much reduced by hunting.

Warbler There are about 300 species of warblers, named after the melodious song of many species. They have fine-pointed beaks. The plumage is rather dull, with greens, browns and greys predominant. Warblers are found throughout the Old World, from Europe to Australia. Many of them migrate. The American wood warblers belong to a different group.

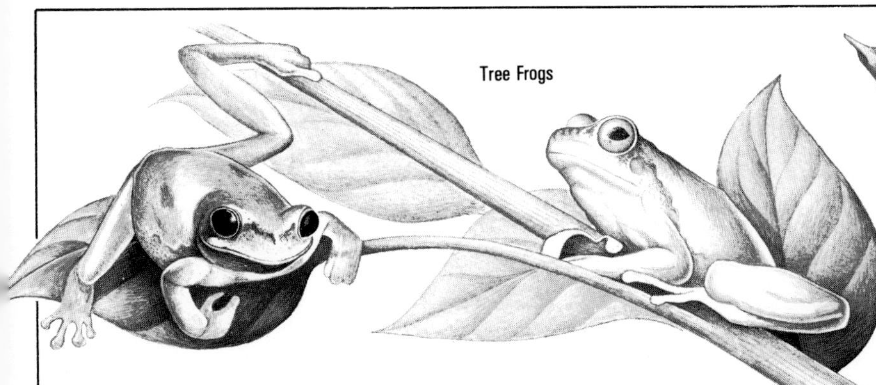

Tree Frogs

The matamata, a South American terrapin

Wart-hog One of the ugliest of animals, the wart-hog is a relative of the domestic pig. The head is long and armed with warts and a pair of upward-curving tusks. The tail is carried erect when they run. Wart-hogs are found in open country thoughout much of Africa south of the Sahara. They feed mainly on grass, but also eat berries and occasionally take a meal of carrion.

Waterbuck This is a large antelope always found near rivers, although it does not live in marshy ground. It has a coarse brown coat. The males have long, slender horns which produce a horseshoe-shape when viewed from the front. There are two subspecies, one with a white patch on the rump and one with a white ring round the rump. Waterbuck range over much of Africa south of the Sahara.

Water scorpion This is a flattened aquatic insect, in no way related to ordinary scorpions. The front legs are hinged for grasping prey. The tail end of the insect is drawn out into a long breathing tube which can be pushed up to the surface of the water. Water scorpions live on the bottom of shallow muddy ponds. They eat insects and other small creatures.

Water spider Many spiders can live temporarily under water, supported by the film of air trapped around the body, but only one species lives permanently under water. The male is normally larger than the female—the reverse of the normal situation. It lives under water by constructing a silken diving bell into which it releases bubbles of air collected at the surface. The water spider ranges through temperate Eurasia.

Wattlebird Wattlebirds have rounded wings, long tails and long hindclaws, with wattles at the corner of the mouth. They feed mainly on fruit leaves and insects. There are two species, both living in New Zealand.

Waxwings Named after the red tips of their secondary flight feathers, which look like blobs of sealing wax, the three species of waxwings are found in the northern half of North America and northern Eurasia. Waxwings are about the size of starlings. Their main diet is berries and insects.

Weasel The weasel is found throughout Eurasia. It is similar in form to its near relative the stoat, although somewhat smaller. It has a slender body, short limbs and long neck. The fur is reddish-brown with white throat and underparts. Weasels are carnivorous animals, sometimes killing animals larger than themselves, although they feed mainly on voles and mice.

Weaver bird The weavers are mainly seed-eating birds which live in Africa and Asia. There are about 70 species and many of the males have bright plumage during the mating season, reverting to drab streaky plumage outside it. Weaver birds make flask-shaped nests by weaving leaves and grasses together.

Weevil Weevils are beetles in which the head is drawn out into a snout. Weevils are found all over the world and usually feed on some particular species or genus of plant, a notable example being the cotton 'boll weevil' of American cotton plantations. There are already 40,000 species of weevils known to man.

Whale shark The largest of all sharks, the whale shark grows to a length of 15 m. The animal is dark grey, with whitish spots all over the upper surface. The head is broad and flattened and the huge mouth contains hundreds of tiny teeth. Although the mouth could easily engulf a man, the whale shark is harmless. It lives in tropical seas and feeds on plankton.

Whelk This name is given to many kinds of sea snails, but the true whelk is a widely distributed species. It lives on the sea-bed below low tide level and has long been used as food. It has a long breathing siphon, which draws water over the gills and it feeds by rasping away at various living and dead creatures. Whelk egg cases are often washed up on the shore. They look like sponges.

Whirligig beetle This is a small, shiny beetle that lives on the surface of water. It skates round and round searching for small insects that fall on to the water. The eyes are in two parts, one part being used for seeing on the surface, and one part for looking down into the water.

White-tailed deer These deer were almost exterminated in North America through years of slaughter by settlers. Now they are so abundant that their numbers are thought to be greater than prior to the arrival of Europeans in North America.

Whiting An important food fish, this is a member of the cod family. It is easily distinguished by its silvery sides and the black spot on the front fin. The whiting is found in the North Atlantic and the Mediterranean.

Whydah Whydahs or widow birds are African birds that lay their egg in the nests of weaver finches. The males have striking plumage, often with very long tail feathers.

Wild cat The European wild cat resembles a heavily built tabby cat. The tail is thick and bushy and distinctly ringed. Wild cats live in the upland regions of Europe and Asia Minor. Their numbers are increasing in the Scottish Highlands. Grouse, rabbits and hares are the main food.

Wobbegong Also called carpet sharks, the wobbegongs have stout flattened bodies and broad heads, with a rough mottled skin. They rest on the sea-bed and look like seaweed-covered rocks. There are five species around Japan, China and Australia.

Left: White-tailed deer. Below: Wallabies. Top right: Waterbuck. Bottom right: Male wapiti.

Wolf The ancestor of the domestic dog, the wolf once covered almost all of the Northern Hemisphere. Today it has disappeared from all but the wildest parts of Western Europe, Asia and North America. Wolves live in forests and in open country and they hunt by day, usually in small packs. Their endurance allows them to wear down all kinds of animals and wolf packs have been known to bring down a moose.

Wolf spider These spiders are so-named because they run down their prey like wolves. Females carry their eggs in spherical sacs of silk which are attached to the hind end of the abdomen. Wolf spiders are very widespread. The tarantula of southern Europe is a wolf spider.

Wolverine The wolverine or glutton is the largest of the weasel family, although it looks more like a badger or a small bear. It has a shaggy coat of dense dark brown fur, powerful limbs and strong claws. It lives in the coniferous forests of the Arctic and sub-Arctic regions and feeds on any animal it can catch. It will also drive other carnivores away from their kills.

Wombat This marsupial is a stocky, short-legged creature and has strong claws. The two species live in southern Australia and behave like badgers, hiding in their burrows by day and coming out to feed at night.

Wood ant This large reddish-brown ant is noted for the great piles of pine needles that it builds over its underground nest. Wood ants are carnivorous, feeding on a wide variety of other insects.

Woodchuck The woodchuck is a large North American rodent related to the squirrels. It is golden- or reddish-brown and lives in deep burrows in woods and farmlands. It is a solitary creature and feeds mainly on grasses and other low-growing plants. It will also eat fruit and it does some damage to crops.

Woodcock This is a wading bird related to the snipe. There are two species: the Eurasian woodcock, which extends from the British Isles across to Japan, and the American woodcock, which lives in the eastern half of North America. Woodcock live mainly in woodland undergrowth. They feed on earthworms and other ground-living invertebrates.

Woodlouse Woodlice, also called sowbugs, are crustaceans. They are the only group of crustaceans that have successfully invaded the land. They have a small head and abdomen, but the thorax is large and makes up most of the body. It has seven segments, each with a pair of legs and a hard shield on the upper side. Some species can roll into a ball when disturbed. They live in damp places.

Woodpecker There are about 200 species of woodpeckers, spread over most parts of the world except the Australian region. No birds are better adapted for life on tree trunks and branches. The legs are short and the tail is made up of stiff feathers which act as supports when the bird clings to a trunk. Woodpeckers spend most of their time searching for insects on tree trunks. The bill is used to prise up pieces of bark and the long tongue is then used to pick up the insects. Nearly all woodpeckers nest in holes which they drill with their bills.

Woolly monkey A relative of the spider monkey, the woolly monkey lives in South America. It is covered with close, woolly fur and it has a black, rather human face. The rest of the body is greyish-brown. There are two species, but one is very rare. The monkeys live high in the trees and eat leaves and fruit.

Wryneck This bird is a relative of the woodpecker, but it looks more like a thrush, especially when feeding on the ground. Wrynecks feed on insects and are particularly fond of ants. They nest in holes in trees, but they have to find ready-made holes as they cannot drill their own. There are two species, one breeding in Europe and Asia and one breeding in the southern half of Africa. The Eurasian species migrates south for the winter.

X-Ray fish This little fish from the equatorial rivers of South America is almost completely transparent. Much of its skeleton can be seen from the outside. It is an attractive fish and popular for aquaria. It is fiercely carnivorous and is closely related to the piranha.

Yak This is a large member of the cattle family that lives high in the mountains of Tibet—one of the most inhospitable regions of the world. The animals have long, thin horns which extend sideways and may reach 1 m in length. They also have long, shaggy black coats which reach almost down to the ground. Yaks graze on the sparse grasses and other plants of the mountains. They have been domesticated as beasts of burden and also to provide milk. Domestic yaks, smaller and paler than the wild ones, are found in the Himalaya regions.

Zebra Closely related to horses and asses, zebras are easily distinguished by their stripes. There are three species, all living in Africa. The commonest species is Burchell's zebra, in which the stripes reach under the belly. In the mountain zebra and Grevy's zebra the stripes do not extend under the belly. A fourth zebra, known as the quagga, was common until about 150 years ago, but it is now extinct. Like horses, the zebras are grazing animals. They are a favourite prey of lions.

Zorille The zorille looks and acts like a skunk and is related to the weasels. It is a slender black and white animal about 60 cm long, the bushy tail accounting for nearly half the length. Like the skunk, it ejects a foul-smelling fluid when disturbed. The zorille lives in most parts of Africa and feeds on small rodents and insects.

The Australian wombat

Homes and Habitats

Plants and animals are not scattered haphazardly over the surface of the Earth. Each species has its own preferred habitat. Habitat is another way of saying surroundings. Environment is another word meaning much the same thing. The habitat is made up of the climate, the soil, the air or water and the other plants and animals. The climate and the soil are the most important factors because they control the vegetation. The vegetation in turn affects the distribution of the animals, because animals will go where they can find food and shelter. The study of habitats and of the plants and animals that live in them is called ecology.

Some of the earth's major habitats are described in the following pages, together with examples of how the plants and animals are adapted for the various conditions found in each habitat.

The Earth provides a variety of homes for living things ranging from the cold, bleak wastes of the tundra (above), through forest retreats (far left) and grasslands (left) to sun-scorched deserts (below). In all types of environment plants and animals are adapted to the prevailing conditions.

Life on the Grasslands

Above: The sable antelope, a rather rare animal of the African grasslands.

Below right: The coyote, or prairie wolf (top), lives on the American prairies, feeding on hares and rodents. Lions (bottom) live together in a pride, spending much of the time lying lazily in the shade.

Below: The elephant is found over much of Africa in both grassland and forest. It is entirely vegetarian.

The major grasslands of the world occur on each side of the desert belts, in regions where there is a certain amount of rain but not enough for the growth of forests. There are two main types of grassland: temperate and tropical.

Temperate Grasslands

The temperate grasslands are outside the tropics and most of them are found in the inner regions of the continents, where rainfall is low throughout the year. The summers are generally very hot and the winters are generally very cold. Among the major temperate grassland areas are the prairies of North America, the pampas of South America, the veld of South Africa, and the steppes of Eurasia. Smaller areas are found in eastern Australia.

The nature of the grassland depends upon the amount of rainfall. Where the rainfall is moderately high, the grasses are tall and lush. Areas with less rain support shorter grasses and fewer of them. A large proportion of the temperate grassland has been taken over for farming.

Tropical Grasslands

Tropical grasslands, also called savannah, are found in and around the tropical areas, between the tropical forests and the deserts. The largest areas are in Africa and South America and smaller areas occur in India and northern Australia. Rainfall is markedly seasonal and falls only for a short period during the summer. The rain and the high temperature produce rapid growth and the land quickly becomes covered with lush grass. Some of the grasses reach heights of 3 metres. Then, as the dry season progresses, the plants die down and the land takes on a rather barren appearance for several months. Acacia and baobab trees are dotted here and there over the savannah. They get more common towards the forest regions and rarer towards the deserts.

The Animals of the Grasslands

Grasses are very hardy plants, able to withstand or recover from grazing, trampling, fire and drought. They produce abundant leaf and they can therefore support a large number of animals. The dominant animals of the grasslands are the large grazers. These include horses, antelopes, zebras, bisons and kangaroos. Not all of them live in the same place, of course. The savannah lands, where there are trees and bushes, also support elephants, giraffes and rhinos. Grasslands do not provide much cover for the animals and we find that most of the large grazers are fast runners. This is their way of escaping from their enemies.

Most of them also live in herds, allowing some individuals to feed while others keep a watch for enemies.

The grasslands also support many smaller mammals, such as voles and prairie dogs. These feed largely on leaves and seeds. They escape from their enemies by hiding in burrows instead of running away. There are also many insects, notably the grasshoppers and locusts. These feed directly on the grass and other plants and they themselves are eaten by birds, lizards and small mammals.

Best known of the carnivorous mammals of the grasslands are the various large cats—the lions and leopards and tigers. The lions and leopards of Africa feed mainly on the antelopes and zebras. Another famous hunter is the cheetah. The fastest land animal over short distances, the cheetah can reach 100 kph as it bounds after its prey. It cannot keep this up for long, however, and it gives up if it does not catch its prey within about 400 metres. Other well known hunters include the coyote or prairie wolf of North America and the hunting dog of Africa. The grasslands also have their full complement of scavengers waiting to pounce on a dead or dying animal or to clear up after another carnivore. These scavengers include the jackals and hyenas of Africa and the various kinds of vultures.

Water is always a problem to animals living in the grasslands, especially those in the tropical grasslands where rain falls for only a short time each year. Water holes, formed where water-bearing rocks come to the surface, are very important in the grasslands. Many of the animals come to drink daily and they often come at definite times, each species or group of species coming in turn. When the water holes eventually dry up, as they often do towards the end of the dry season, the herds move on to other regions. One hundred years ago there used to be mass migrations of antelopes in herds many kilometres long. There are far fewer animals now and the need to migrate is not so pressing, although one can still see migrating animals. The smaller animals often burrow down into the ground and sleep for the driest part of the year. In the temperate grasslands, where the winters are very cold, many of the smaller animals hibernate.

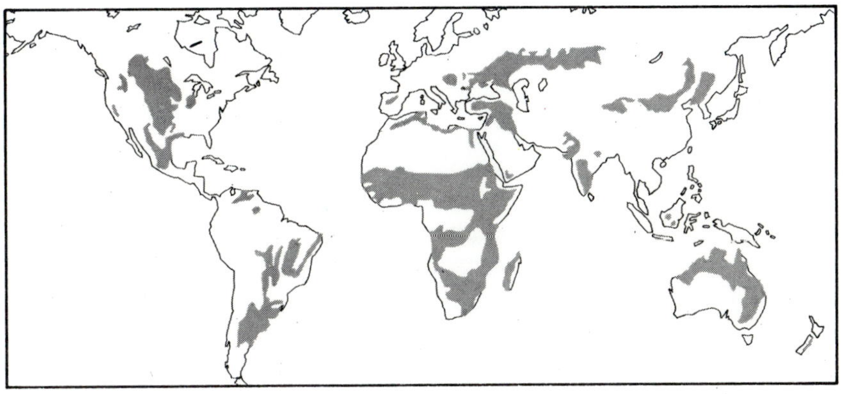

The distribution of the major grasslands of the world.

Below: The water hole is very important for the grazing animals. Zebras and wildebeests have come to drink but some individuals are always on the look-out for danger.

Life in the Rain Forests

The African grey parrot, a popular pet from the forest.

Some equatorial regions of the Earth have high temperatures and heavy rainfall throughout the year. Such conditions are ideal for plant growth and we find here the richest of all habitats—the tropical rain forest. Rain forests develop where the temperature is always above 18°C and where the rainfall is at least 200 centimetres per year. Most rain forest regions actually receive between 250 and 270 centimetres of rain each year, and it generally rains every day. These figures compare with about 100 centimetres of rain per year for most parts of the British Isles.

Hundreds of Species

Because there is no cold season, the rain forest plants can grow throughout the year and they are all evergreens. The abundant moisture means that the plants grow rapidly. A great many kinds of plants are able to grow in the rain forests. The woods and forests of Europe and North America contain relatively few kinds of trees and they are usually dominated by one or two species. Rain forests are much more variable, however, and there may be as many as 300 different kinds of trees in one square mile of forest.

Although the rain forests in different regions contain different species of trees, all rain forests look much alike. The main roof, or canopy, of the forest is generally about 30 metres high. There are scattered taller trees, reaching 60 metres perhaps, and there is also a lower layer at about 15 metres. Many of the trees bear glossy, oval leaves rather like those of the laurel. They usually have sharply pointed tips, called 'drip-tips', which allow the water to run off easily. The flowers tend to look alike, most of them being small and rather pale in colour.

Some trees in the swampy rain forests have roots which push above the wet ground and take in oxygen (right). These are called pneumatophores. Other trees are lifted into the air on stilt roots (centre). The large trees have buttress roots to support their great weight.

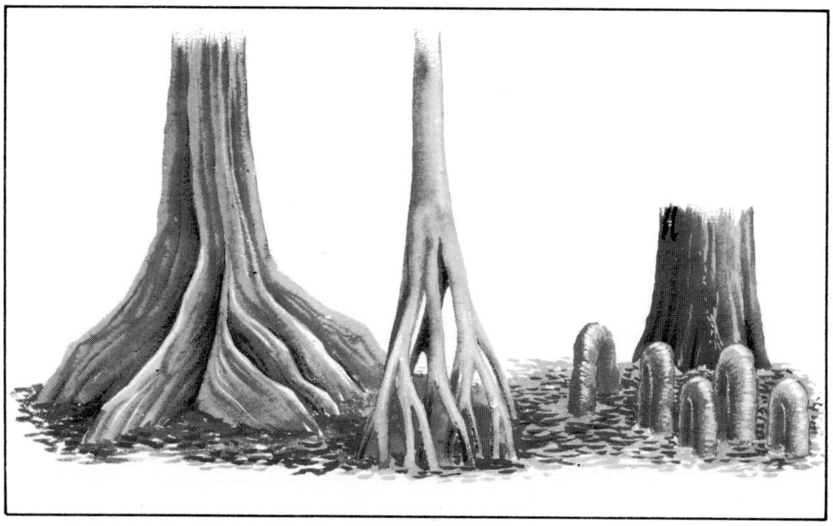

A Gloomy Place

Along the banks of rivers, or where man has interfered by cutting down trees, the rain forest is thick and often impenetrable. This is the 'jungle' that we often hear about. Further into the forest, however, much of the undergrowth disappears. The dense overhead canopy cuts off almost all the light and only a few large-leaved plants can survive on the ground. This is the true rain forest. One can walk through it without much trouble. There is not even a layer of dead leaves to kick about; the leaves decay as soon as they fall.

Treetop Orchids

Most of the rain forest's abundant life is to be found in the branches of the trees. As well as the leaves and flowers of the trees themselves, there are thousands of small herbaceous plants growing on the branches. These plants have their own leaves and they make their own food. They merely use the trees as perches to enable them to get some sunlight. Plants which grow in this way, without taking any food from the trees on which they live, are called epiphytes. These include ferns, bromeliads (related to the pineapple), and the orchids, whose beautiful flowers festoon all the tropical rain forests.

The roots of many epiphytes are thick and spongy and they absorb water directly from the moist air. Other epiphytes, such as the bromeliads, trap water in their funnel-shaped leaves. These water traps provide water for the plants, and they are also homes for mosquito larvae and for the tadpoles of various tree frogs. The epiphytes get their mineral requirements from the droppings of the many birds and other animals that live in the canopy.

Another very common type of plant in the rain forest are the lianas, climbing plants which reach the light by twining up tree trunks.

Animals of the Rain Forest

Although the visitor to the rain forest is usually struck by the quietness of the place, it does support an abundance of animal life, especially among the upper layers of the vegetation.

Each layer of the forest has its characteristic animals. Large birds of prey, such as the South American harpy eagle, live in the uppermost branches and swoop down to catch smaller birds and monkeys. The latter live in the main canopy, but they wander through most of the layers in their search for fruit and other food. The brilliant colours of the birds, together with the epiphytic flowers, make a vivid contrast with the lower levels of the forest. Snakes, such as the boas, also live in the trees and so do many amphibians. Small antelopes and deer live on the ground, together with various cats. The latter are also very good at climbing the trees. Rain forests are the homes of the largest insects, including huge beetles and cockroaches, stick insects 30 centimetres long, and the beautiful morpho and birdwing butterflies. It may never be known just how many kinds of plants and animals there are in the rain forests.

Temperate Rain Forests

Several parts of the world experience very high rainfall without the high temperatures that are found in the Tropics. As long as the temperatures are not too low, these areas will support temperate rain forests. The best examples of this type of vegetation are found on the west coast of North America, the west coast of New Zealand and along the coast of southern Chile. Like the tropical forests, the temperate rain forests are largely evergreen, but the trees are nearly all cone-bearing species. They include the largest of all trees—in fact, the largest of all living things. These are the giant redwoods and sequoias, which reach well over 100 metres in height. Epiphytes are abundant in these forests, but they are mainly ferns and mosses. They reach further down the trunks than the tropical epiphytes, and the whole forest looks much greener than the tropical rain forest. Evaporation is not rapid because of the lower temperatures, and so the forest literally drips with water. The low temperatures also slow down the rate of decay, and the forest floor is littered with dead trunks and branches, all covered with ferns and mosses. The temperate forest is much more difficult to walk through than the tropical rain forest.

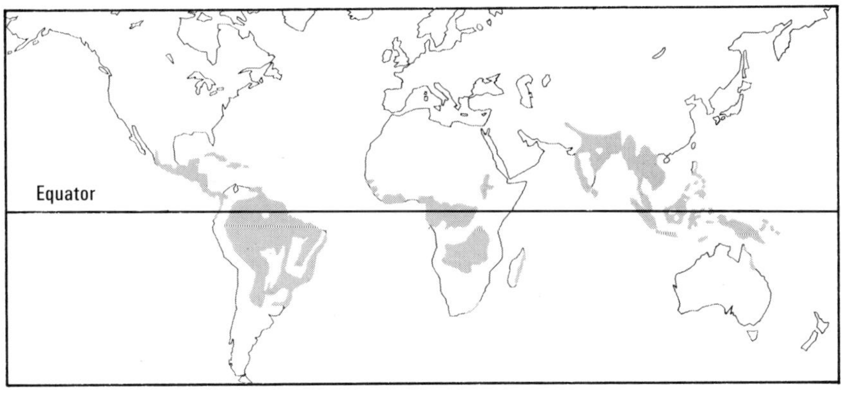

The distribution of rain forests.

The jungle fowl is a native of South East Asia. It is probably the ancestor of domestic chickens.

Below: Tapirs are shy plant-eating forest-dwellers of South America and South East Asia. They live near to water and are excellent swimmers.

Desert Life

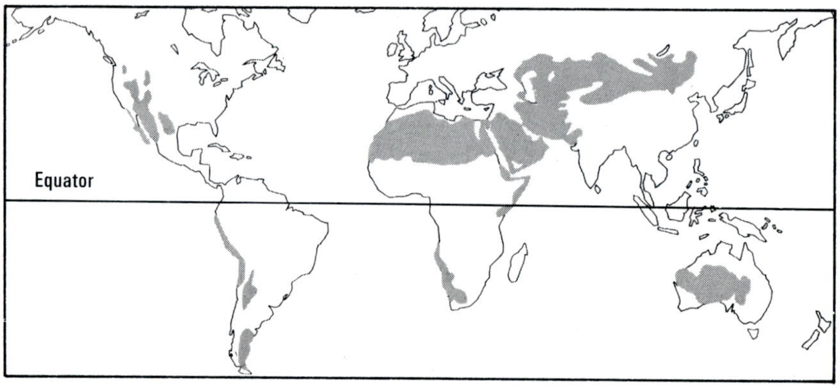

Above: Major desert regions of the world.

Right: The cactus wren.

Below right: A two-humped camel of Central Asia. Camels can go for long periods without water.

Below: A giant saguaro cactus towering above other cacti on the desert floor.

A desert is an area which receives very little rain—less than 25 centimetres per year on average. Some desert areas may go for several years without any rain. Although there are some deserts in the colder parts of the world, in Siberia for example, most deserts are found in and around the Tropics. Because there is so little cloud to absorb the sun's heat, these desert areas get extremely hot during the daytime, but they cool down rapidly at night and there may even be frosts from time to time.

The plants and animals living in the deserts therefore have two main problems—shortage of water and great heat. We tend to think of the deserts as rather lifeless places, but a surprising number of plants and animals manage to make a living there.

Desert Plant Life

Desert plants solve the water problem in several different ways. Many of the smaller plants are known as drought evaders, because they avoid the dry periods altogether. The dry season, which may be as much as 11 months of the year, is passed in the seed stage. When the rain eventually comes, these seeds start to grow very rapidly. They produce leaves and flowers and, by the time the dry season sets in again, they have already scattered a new crop of seeds. One small plant living in the Sahara scatters its seeds only 10 days after growing from seed itself.

Other desert plants are drought resisters. A few plants, such as the creosote bush of the American deserts, can actually survive being shrivelled by the sun, but most of the plants need a supply of water. The mesquite tree

has very long roots that reach down to the water. These plants are never short of water and they do not need special features to help them to live in the desert. Cacti and many other desert plants have shallow, spreading roots which absorb large amounts of water as soon as the rain falls. The water is stored in juicy leaves or stems and it is used sparingly during the dry season. Plants that store water in this way are called succulents and they are covered with waxy deposits which cut down the evaporation of water. Some also have hairy coverings which reflect away some of the heat as well as reducing water loss.

A plant loses most of its water through its leaves, and many desert plants cut down the loss of water by having very small leaves or no leaves at all. Some desert plants, such as the ocotillo, produce leaves only in the wet season and drop them again as soon as it gets dry.

Desert Animals

The desert may seem quite empty of animals if it is visited during the heat of the day, but it 'comes alive' towards evening as its inhabitants venture out into the cooler air.

As well as bringing forth the shortlived annual plants, the periodic rains bring out the insects. Bugs, beetles, butterflies and other insects emerge from their eggs or pupae. The adult insects help to pollinate the flowers, while their young make rapid growth at the expense of the leaves. Within a short time the cycle is complete and another generation of eggs and pupae is left in the ground to await the next rain. Many of these young stages will never develop any further for they will be found and eaten by the many lizards of the desert. The lizards, in turn, may be eaten by snakes or scorpions, or by some of the carnivorous mammals.

Frogs and toads are usually associated with damp places, but even some of these creatures have managed to adapt themselves to the desert. The spadefoot toad, so called from a spade-like projection on its hind feet, digs itself down into the desert sand and spends up to 11 months in sleep. Woken up by the rains, it makes its way to a temporary pond where the eggs are laid. The eggs hatch almost at once and the tadpoles grow so quickly that they turn into little toads within three or four weeks. They then bury themselves away when the dry season starts. Unlike the other animals, birds do not burrow into the ground to get away from the hot sun. There is a burrowing owl in the American deserts, but it uses the old holes of other animals and does not make its own burrow. Several other birds such as the cactus wren, make use of the shade provided by cacti.

Among the desert mammals, the most abundant are the little rodents—the mice and voles and their relatives. They feed on seeds, insects and occasionally leaves. Many of these rodents never drink. They get all the water they need from their food. Insects provide quite a bit of water, but seeds contain very little and the rodents have to be very careful about conserving water. Hiding by day and coming out at night helps to conserve water because the air is cooler and damper at night. The animals do not then lose water by evaporation. They sweat very little, if at all, and they pass very little urine. Several of the desert rodents go to sleep in their burrows during the hottest and driest part of the year.

Top: A prickly pear cactus in flower.

Above: The spiky yucca, a native of North American deserts, which holds water in its thick leaves.

Bottom left: Date palms are very important plants in the desert oases of Africa and the Middle East.

Below: The jerboa is a long-tailed jumping rodent. The rattlesnake lives in American deserts.

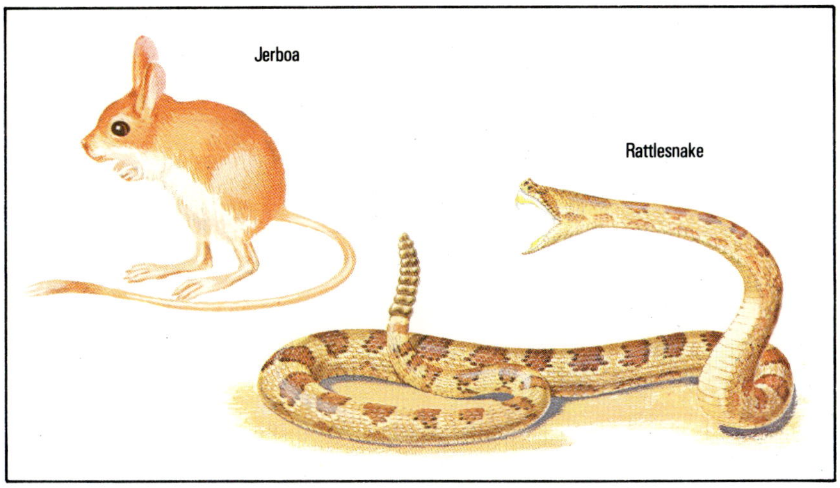

Life in Northern Forests

Below: The distribution of coniferous forests and broad-leaved forests.

Bottom: Woodpeckers (left) feed on insect larvae. They drill holes in the bark and scoop out the larvae with their tongues. Nuthatches (middle) wedge hazel nuts in bark crevices and hammer them open. Squirrels (right) are ideally adapted to forest life. They have sharp, curved claws that enable them to climb trees rapidly, and their powerful back legs help them leap from tree to tree.

Cool forests occur mainly in the Northern Hemisphere—in Europe, northern Asia and the northern half of North America. The equivalent latitudes in the Southern Hemisphere are generally too dry to support forests. Small patches occur in South America and Australia, but most of these areas are covered with grassland.

The northern forests are of two main types: deciduous and coniferous. The deciduous forests grow in the warmer regions—the temperate zones. Coniferous forests, which are mainly evergreen, grow in the colder parts. The two types of forest differ a great deal in the animal and plant life that they support.

The Deciduous Forests

Deciduous forests are forests composed mainly of trees that drop their leaves in the autumn. These include oak, beech, hickory, ash and maple. They require fairly even rainfall throughout the year and winters that are not too severe. Such conditions are found in Europe, in the eastern half of the United States and in eastern Asia. The central regions of Asia are too dry for deciduous trees and the grasslands merge northwards into the coniferous forests.

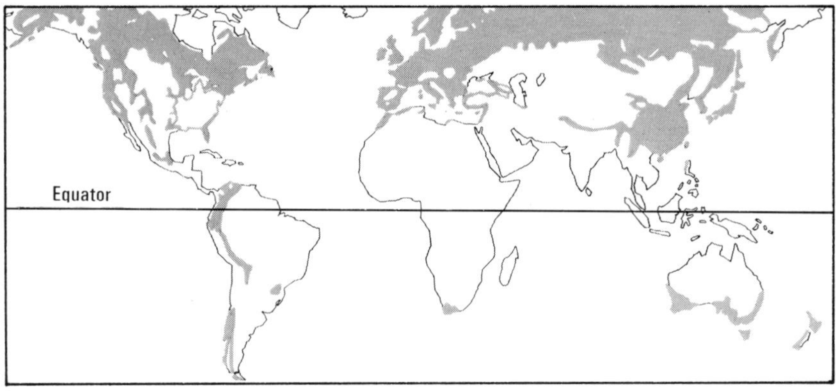

There is plenty of light in these woodlands in the spring, before the trees have spread their leaves. The light allows a rich variety of plants to grow beneath the trees. The types of plants vary from place to place, according to the soil, but they include primroses, bluebells, lesser celandines, wood anemones and many other attractive flowers. There are also many ferns.

The moist conditions allow dead leaves and twigs to decay quite rapidly. The layer of decaying material, known as the leaf litter, is full of small animals. There are worms, mites, spiders, insects, slugs, snails and centipedes. Shrews are very common and so are hedgehogs. Both find plenty of food in the shape of worms and insects in the leaf litter. Mice and voles are also plentiful. They feed on seeds and other plant material, together with some small animals.

Up in the trees there is a different community. Hordes of caterpillars and other insects feed on the leaves. Bark beetles and other wood-borers eat into the wood. These insects are snapped up by the birds that live in the woods. The insect-eating birds include titmice, warblers, flycatchers and woodpeckers. Other birds eat the buds and seeds of the trees. These birds include wood pigeons, finches and nuthatches. The latter wedge hazel nuts into bark crevices and hammer them open with their beaks. Then there are the predatory birds, including

sparrowhawks and owls, that feed on the smaller birds and mammals. The trees also support plenty of squirrels, which feed on seeds, fruit and insects. Among the larger mammals, there are deer, bears, badgers, foxes and beavers.

The Coniferous Forests

The coniferous forests grow in the colder parts of the world, extending far into the Arctic Circle. They consist mainly of pines, firs, spruces and larches. Most are evergreens, although the larch is deciduous. The cold soil does not allow decay to proceed very rapidly and so there is a deep layer of dead leaves and peat on the forest floor. The rain water becomes acidic as it drains through the peaty deposits. It removes useful minerals from the surface layers and the soil becomes very poor.

The poor soil, together with the low level of light in the coniferous forests, means that few plants can grow under the trees. There are some mosses and lichens and there are plenty of fungi, but there are few flowering plants. The forests are therefore relatively poor in animal life, although they are not as poor as some people suggest. Quite a number of insects feed on the leaves and many beetle grubs tunnel into the bark and the underlying wood. These insects attract birds, such as goldcrests, titmice and woodpeckers. A few birds feed on the seeds of the trees. The best known of these birds are the crossbills, whose strange beaks are adapted for tearing open the cones. Owls and other birds of prey are also plentiful in the forests.

Small mammals are less common than in the deciduous forests because there is not so much for them to eat in the leaf litter. There are some shrews and voles, however. Larger mammals include many squirrels, some ground-living and some living in the trees. Also in the trees there are martens and wild cats. Both prey on birds and squirrels as well as on other small mammals. Deer are common and they sometimes do much damage by browsing on the young trees, and their numbers have to be kept in check.

The badger is a shy woodland-dweller in Europe and Asia. Badgers build a large den with many entrances called a set. They search at night for worms, frogs and mice which form their main diet. They also eat bulbs and roots.

Mountain Life

In the year 1802, the German explorer Alexander von Humboldt climbed up Chimborazo, a volcano in Ecuador to a height of 5,760 metres. No man had ever climbed to such a height before.

But Humboldt's achievement was more than a mountaineering triumph. Throughout the climb he had taken detailed scientific readings. He found that as the height increased the temperature and the air pressure fell. What is more, he noticed how the changes in physical conditions were reflected in the plant life. Luxuriant tropical rain forest at sea-level gave way to forests of broad-leaved deciduous trees. The deciduous forests in turn gave way to the coniferous forests of pines and firs. Higher still it became too cold for even the conifers to survive. Here there were only stunted shrubs and small plants. Finally, a region of permanent snow and ice was reached. There were no plants growing here.

These different belts of plant life on a mountainside are just like those we find if we make a journey from the Equator to the polar regions. The similarity is due to the fall in temperature towards the poles and towards the summits of mountains.

Some of the world's largest birds live in the mountains. The golden eagle has a wing span of 2 metres or more.

Alpine Plant Life

Like the Arctic tundra, the mountain peaks experience long and bitterly cold winters, punctuated by brief summers. In addition, the slopes are exposed all the year round to strong gusts of wind. These severe conditions allow only very specialised plants to grow on the upper slopes of the mountains. Lichens are common, for they can grow almost anywhere. Grasses are common, too, and there are also many broad-leaved flowering plants which are known as alpines.

The alpine plants belong to many different flower families but, living under the same conditions, they tend to evolve along similar lines. They are small plants, generally forming mats or cushions very close to the ground. In this way they avoid the full blast of the wind, and they also gain some heat from the earth. Despite their very short stems, they have long roots. These are necessary for secure anchorage on the sloping ground and also draw up water, which drains rapidly from the stony ground.

The densely packed leaves of the alpines act rather like the fur of a mammal and they trap moist warm air around the plant. Coatings of wax and hair also help to cut down water loss and to protect the plants from the cold. The alpines cannot make food in the winter, when they are covered with snow, so they must make the best of the sunlight they receive in the summer. They tend to have large amounts of chlorophyll in their leaves, making them rather dark in colour. The flowers also tend to have deep colours. Both features help the plants to absorb warmth from the sun.

Nearly all alpines are perennials. The conditions on the mountains are generally too severe for plants to complete their life cycles in one year. Growth is very slow because of the low temperatures and short growing season. Ten years may pass before a plant has stored enough food to flower.

Mountain Animals

A few insects, such as the apollo butterflies, are found on the higher mountain slopes. Spiders are found there too, but only the warm-blooded animals—the birds and mammals—are really successful in this cold habitat. They maintain their bodies at a

Right: The Rocky Mountain goat (left) is a North American relative of the chamois. The Alpine ibex is a wild goat found in the alps. The argali (right) of central Asia is the largest of the wild sheep.

constant high temperature, regardless of the outside temperature.

The most conspicuous of the upland creatures are the large grazing animals, such as the yak, the chamois and the various kinds of sheep and goats. During the summer they wander high on the mountains, but most of them move down into the forests for the winter. Their large size and their shaggy coats are a protection against the cold. These animals, especially the goats and their relatives, move about on the rocky slopes with remarkable ease. They are helped by pincer-like toes and also by 'suction cups' formed by pads under the feet.

As well as the larger grazing animals, there are also numbers of rodents, including ground squirrels, marmots, pikas and voles. They are all preyed upon by wild cats, including the snow leopard and the puma or mountain lion.

Some of the world's largest birds live in the mountains. The Andean condor has a wing span of about 3 metres and it soars around the mountains on the many upcurrents of air. Like the vultures, it is a carrion feeder and it eats animals that have died.

Man in the Mountains

Mountaineers climbing the highest peaks—more than 6,400 metres above sea-level—take oxygen with them to help them to breathe. The air is very thin (rarefied) at high levels and there is not enough oxygen for man to work properly. Even at a height of 3,000 metres a lowlander would find it very difficult to move quickly. But some races of man live and work quite normally at heights of up to 5,500 metres. These races have lived in the mountains for generations and their bodies have become adapted to the conditions. They have barrel-shaped chests and large lungs, taking in more air and oxygen at a time. Their blood is also different from that of a lowlander in that it has more red corpuscles to carry the oxygen around the body. Mountain peoples, typified by the Sherpas of the Himalayas, tend to be fairly short and stocky. This cuts down the loss of heat from the body surface. Climbers from other parts of the world have to acclimatize to high altitude by building up more red corpuscles.

Ice Age Remnants

Many of the plants found in the European Alps are closely related to plants in the Caucasian Mountains and in the Arctic tundra. These regions are hundreds of kilometres apart and we have to look back to the great Ice Age for an explanation of the peculiar distribution of these plants. During the Ice Age there were sheets of ice over all of northern Europe and glaciers also spread out from the mountainous areas. Large areas to the south of the ice sheets must have been rather like today's tundra, and alpine plants must have been widely distributed. As the ice melted and the land warmed up, the alpine plants shrank back to the far north or to the mountain tops where we now find them. The alpine plants are therefore survivors from the Ice Age. They have been driven out by other plants which outcompete them.

Below: Vegetation changes with altitude.

Bottom left: Rocky Mountain goats.

Bottom right: The mountain avens is a typical alpine plant, forming mats or cushions of tough leaves on the rocky ground.

Polar Life

Below right: A nesting skua shrieks a warning in Antarctica. Skuas are rapacious birds. In the Antarctic their diet consists mainly of fishes and the eggs and young of penguins.

Below: The snowy owl hunts over the Arctic tundra. Small animals such as lemmings form its diet.

The polar regions occupy the extremities of the Earth's surface, bounded by the Arctic Circle in the north and the Antarctic Circle in the south. Because the Earth is tilted on its axis, the polar regions experience at least one day in summer when the sun never sets. They also experience at least one day in winter when the sun never rises.

Polar winters, with little sunlight, are intensely cold. Temperatures of $-88°C$ have been recorded in the Antarctic, and temperatures of $-50°C$ have been recorded in the Arctic. Even in the summer the temperature may remain below freezing point because, although the sun may be shining, its rays strike the Earth at a low angle and much of the heat is reflected. This is especially so if there is snow and ice on the ground.

The main difference between the Arctic and the Antarctic regions is that the Arctic region is nearly all ocean, whereas the Antarctic region contains a continent considerably larger than Europe. Land does not hold heat as well as water, so the Antarctic is colder and less hospitable. The Arctic Ocean absorbs a lot of heat in the summer and retains some of it during the winter.

Life in the Arctic

Although the Arctic Circle is a fixed boundary at 66½° North, biologists make use of another boundary—the line beyond which no trees will grow. This is partly within and partly outside the Arctic Circle. Between this tree line and the shores of the Arctic Ocean lies the tundra—a vast expanse of flat land which is frozen and bare for most of the year. During the summer the surface layers thaw out, but the deeper soil remains frozen. Drainage is impossible and the melt water is trapped in little pools. This is the tundra's major water supply, for the snow and rain that falls each year amounts to only about 20 centimetres. The tundra is in fact a cold desert.

The most abundant of the Arctic plants are the lichens. They encrust bare rock surfaces and, nearer the tree line, they cover large areas of ground. Reindeer moss, the main food of the reindeer, is one of these lichens. Dwarf species of birch and willow creep about on the tundra surface. They can survive for hundreds of years, but they grow very slowly and are rarely more than 30–60 centimetres high. Between them in the summer there are numerous flowering herbs which, for a few short weeks, turn the tundra into a colourful landscape. These herbaceous plants generally grow in little clumps or cushions very close to the ground. Here they escape the icy winds and obtain a little heat from the ground. The long hours of daylight during summer help to counteract the shortness of the growing season, but even then there is not much time for plants to store up food and produce flowers. Many flower but do not set seed and they reproduce vegetatively by means of runners. Shortage

of water is, however, a problem for plants in many places.

Animals are rarely seen on the tundra in winter, but musk oxen, hares, foxes and ptarmigan spend the winter there. Others reappear when the snow melts. Insects are soon on the wing and lemmings appear from the burrows where they have spent the winter. Ducks, geese and waders fly in from the south to nest.

Life in the Antarctic

Most of the Antarctic continent is permanently covered with ice. Only the coastal regions thaw out during the summer. Summer temperatures rarely rise much above freezing point, however, and fresh-water pools are less common than they are in the Arctic. There are some 150 kinds of lichen in the Antarctic, together with a few mosses, but there are only three species of flowering plants. These flowering plants are confined to the Antarctic Peninsula, a narrow strip of land that reaches north and just manages to cross the Antarctic Circle. Such sparse vegetation can support very little animal life and the largest truly terrestrial creature is a wingless fly less than one centimetre long. Various other insects, mites and crustaceans live in the pools or among the lichens.

The ptarmigan is white in winter and brown in summer, its colours matching the changing landscape.

The more characteristic animals of the Antarctic region are sea creatures. They include various seals and several species of penguins. These animals come on to the land to breed; but with the exception of birds that scavenge around the penguin rookeries, they get all their food from the sea. The Southern Ocean is very rich in planktonic animals (page 206), especially a shrimp-like animal called krill. These form the main food of seals, birds and whales. The penguins eat fishes and crustaceans as do seals. During winter the emperor penguin has the frozen shoreline to itself. The females each lay a single egg, which the male then picks up and supports on his webbed feet. His thick feathers surround the egg and keep it warm until it hatches eight or nine weeks later. During this time the male stands exposed to the bitter winds and snows and takes no food. This must surely be one of the strangest of all breeding habits.

A Weddell seal surfaces at a blow-hole in the frozen sea. Like all aquatic mammals, seals have to come up to the surface to breathe at regular intervals between dives.

Life in the Sea

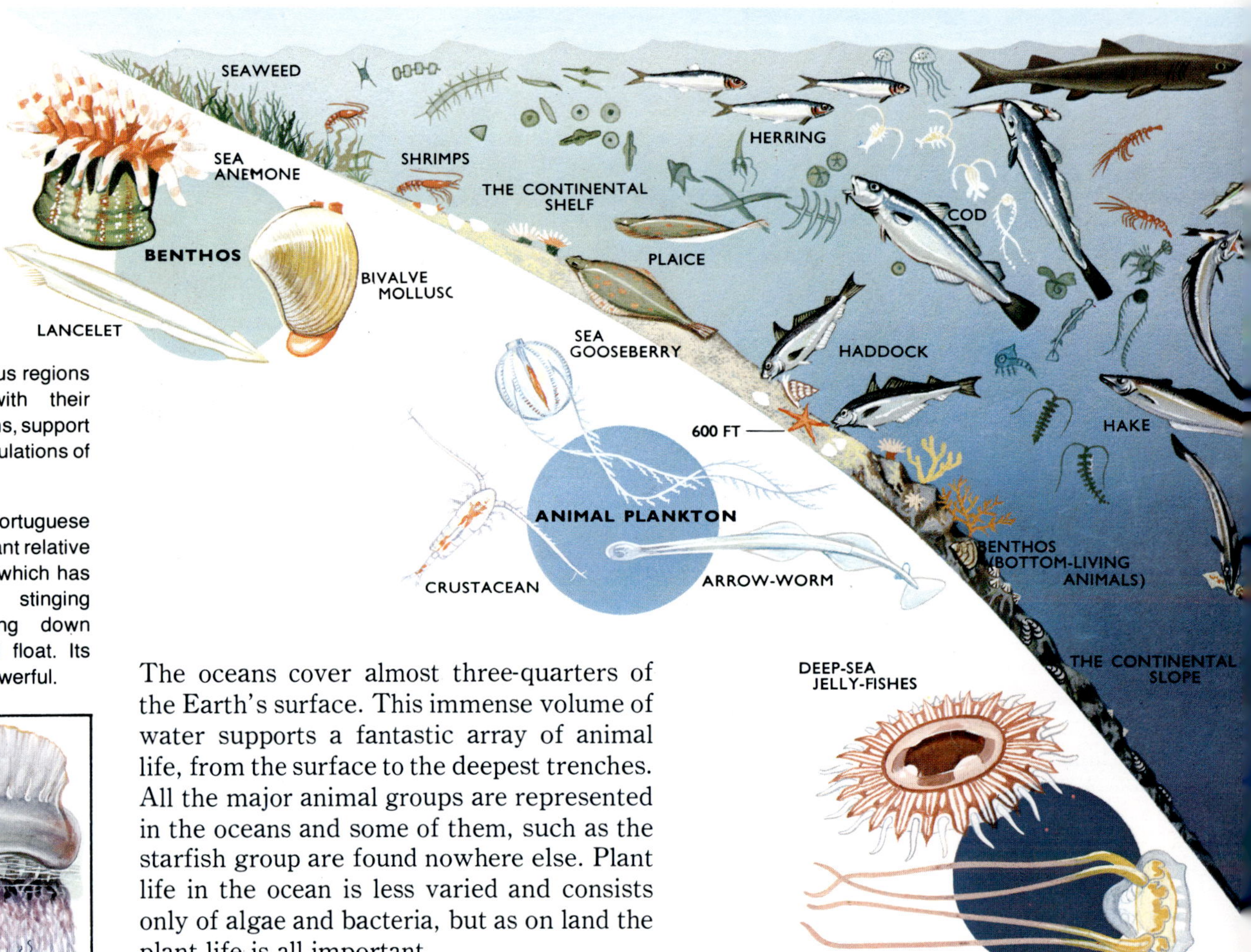

Above: The various regions of the sea, with their different conditions, support very different populations of animals.

Below: The Portuguese man-o'-war, a distant relative of the jellyfishes which has numerous long stinging tentacles hanging down from a gas-filled float. Its poison is very powerful.

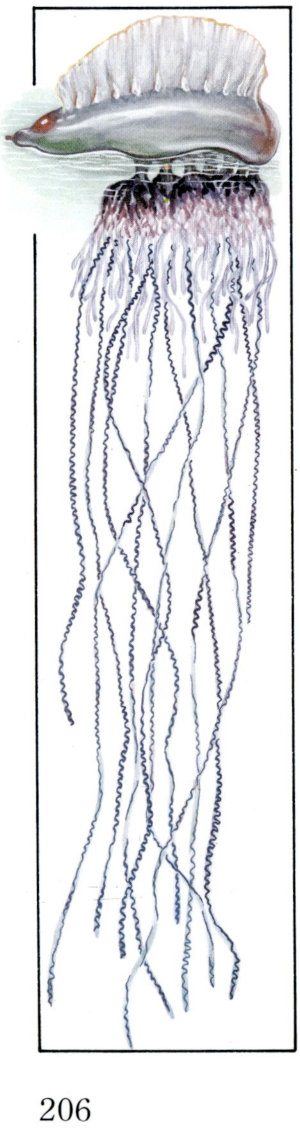

The oceans cover almost three-quarters of the Earth's surface. This immense volume of water supports a fantastic array of animal life, from the surface to the deepest trenches. All the major animal groups are represented in the oceans and some of them, such as the starfish group are found nowhere else. Plant life in the ocean is less varied and consists only of algae and bacteria, but as on land the plant life is all important.

The Pastures of the Sea

Except in the coastal regions, where seaweeds can grow on the bottom, all life in the ocean depends upon the tiny plants that float in the surface layers. These plants, together with the little animals that float with them, make up the plankton. The planktonic plants are confined to the uppermost 39 metres of the ocean, where there is enough light.

The planktonic plants—collectively called phytoplankton—carry out photosynthesis just as land plants do, and they provide food for all the animals in the sea. Because of this, the surface layers are often called the pastures of the sea. These pastures are incredibly rich, and a given area can produce far more plant life than a similar area on land.

More than 60 million tonnes of fish are taken from the sea every year, and this is only a fraction of the animal life in the sea. All of it depends on the plants. It has been estimated that for every tonne of fish produced, the ocean must produce 1,000 tonnes of planktonic plants.

The phytoplankton consists entirely of minute plants called algae. There are several different kinds, but all of them are under one-tenth of a millimetre across. The most common kinds are called diatoms. Each diatom is a single-celled plant, and it lives inside a glassy box. Diatoms are generally brownish-green or yellowish in colour.

The animals of the plankton include a great many different types. Most of them are crustaceans, but there are also arrow worms, jellyfishes and sea gooseberries. Many of these live permanently in the plankton, but others spend only part of their lives drifting at the surface. These include the young stages of many crabs, barnacles, snails, bivalves and starfishes. In common with the phytoplankton, many of the animals possess strange spines or feathery outgrowths. These help to keep the creatures afloat by increasing the resistance to the water.

The planktonic animals feed upon the

phytoplankton and upon each other. They in turn are eaten by larger creatures, such as herrings and other fishes.

The Swimmers

In contrast to the plankton, drifting with the currents, there are many active swimmers, and they include fishes, squids, whales,

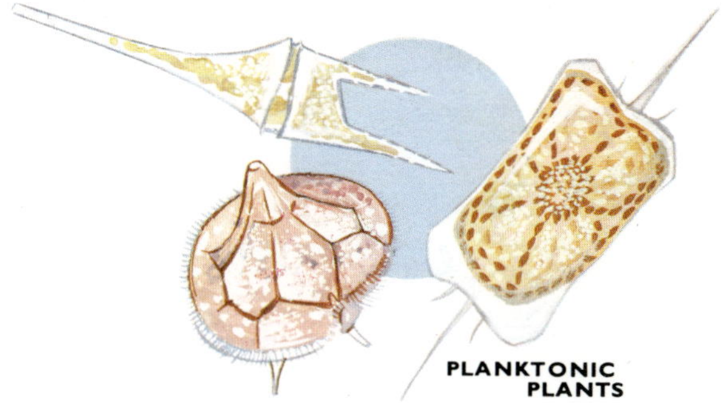
PLANKTONIC PLANTS

prawns and a few other creatures. Some live on the surface and feed directly on the plankton, while others live lower down and get their food second hand. The whalebone whales feed directly on planktonic animals. They filter them from the water with plates of baleen or 'whalebone' which hang in their mouths.

The Ocean Depths

The deeper we go into the water, the darker it becomes. Below about 600 metres it is completely black and these deep waters contain a number of very strange fishes, squids and prawns. Many of them have light-producing organs (see page 143). Most of the deep-sea creatures are carnivorous. Many of the fishes have huge mouths and formidable teeth and they have been described as 'floating fish traps'.

The Ocean Floor

The worms, starfishes, sea anemones and other creatures that live on the sea-bed are collectively called the benthos. The bottom-dwelling creatures extend from the shore right down to the ocean depths, but their numbers get fewer as they get deeper. This is because food gets scarce. Most of the bottom-dwelling animals feed on the decaying matter that falls like rain from above. In the deep sea little material falls to the sea bed. It is either eaten or completely decayed before it reaches the bottom.

SOME DEEP-SEA FISHES

Life on the Sea-shore

Conditions on the sea-shore are constantly changing. For part of the time it is covered with salt water. At other times it is exposed to the air and to fresh rain water. Many of the plants and animals on the shore cannot move about and they have to put up with the changing conditions. They also have to put up with the battering they receive from sand and pebbles hurled at them by the waves. Despite all these problems, many kinds of plants and animals do make their homes on the sea-shore. Nearly all the major groups of plants and animals are found there.

Shores vary enormously and depend very much on the rocks and the geography of the area. Exposed coasts with hard rocks will form craggy cliffs and rocky shores. Softer rocks, such as sandstones, will yield sandy beaches. Sandy beaches also develop in sheltered areas because the sea deposits the material that it has removed from somewhere else. River mouths have muddy shores. The rocky shores support the most varied life because only on the rocky shores can the seaweeds get a hold. The seaweeds provide food and shelter for the animals.

The Tides

The true sea-shore is the region between the highest and lowest tide levels. Most parts are uncovered by the tide twice every day. The tides are caused by the pull of the Moon and, to a lesser extent, the Sun. When the Sun and Moon are in line their combined effect is stronger and the resulting spring tides are of greater extent than normal tides. Spring tides occur every fortnight. Neap tides also occur every fortnight, between the spring tides. They are rather weak tides, produced when the Sun and Moon are pulling at right angles to each other. The range of tidal movement varies from place to place. There are only a few centimetres between high and low tide levels in parts of the Mediterranean, but in some parts of the world the tide may rise and fall as much as 12 metres.

The Zones of the Shore

Many animals only visit the sea-shore. Fishes come into the shallow-water when the tide is in and birds flock down to the shore to feed when the tide is out. The tides do not worry these animals because they can move about easily. The seaweeds, barnacles, molluscs and other creatures that live permanently on the shore have to be able to live in the water and out of it. They are basically sea creatures and their main problem is to survive exposure to the air when the tide goes out.

Some plants and animals can withstand exposure better than others and these creatures are usually found on the upper parts of the shore which are exposed for relatively long periods each day. Creatures which are less able to stand exposure are found lower down on the shore. The sea-shore therefore has a number of zones, distinguished by the length of time exposed to the air and each supporting its own collection of plants and animals. These zones occur on all shores, but they are most obvious on rocky shores.

The Splash Zone

The splash zone is not strictly a part of the shore because it is never really submerged, except perhaps during storms. It is above the high-water mark, but it is continually splashed by the spray. There are no seaweeds in the splash zone, but many lichens and several flowering plants grow there. Among the flowering plants, we can mention the thrift (sea pink), which usually grows on rocks, and the sea campion, which usually grows on shingle. Animals of the splash zone include the sea slater, a little woodlouse-like creature, and some of the periwinkles. Both are found lower down the shore as well, but they can survive for long periods without water.

The Upper Shore

The upper shore is the region between the high-water marks of the neap tides and the spring tides. There are days when the region is never submerged. The commonest seaweeds are the green ones that clothe the rocks and make them very slippery. The animals include the sea slater that we saw in the splash zone and several kinds of periwinkles. They hide in cracks at low tide.

The Middle Shore

This is the region between the low- and high-water marks of the neap tides. It is covered and uncovered every day and it supports much more life than the upper shore. The main seaweeds are brown. They protect the many animals that live among them. These include more periwinkles, top shells and whelks. Limpets and barnacles are also common animals of the middle shore. The limpets are snails with tent-shaped shells. They move about and scrape food from the seaweeds when the tide is in but they go back to their own resting sites when the tide goes out again. The shell is pulled down tightly and the animal remains quite safe until the tide returns. The barnacles have shells of plates which close up when the tide is out, but open when they are submerged and the animal 'combs' food from the water with its limbs. Barnacles are related to the crabs and, like the crabs, they have free-floating young. These young barnacles settle down eventually, but only those in a suitable place will survive.

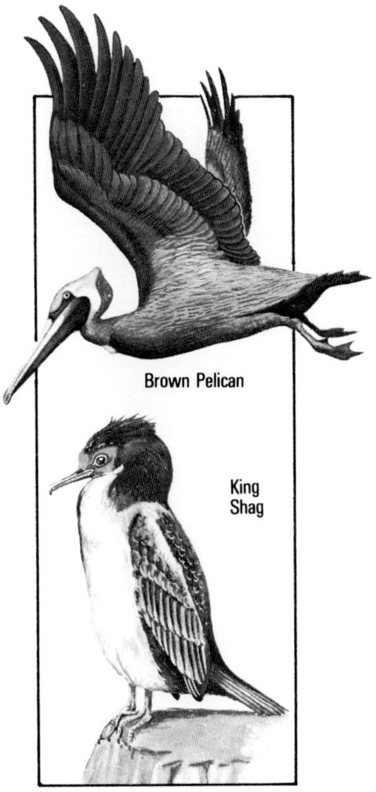

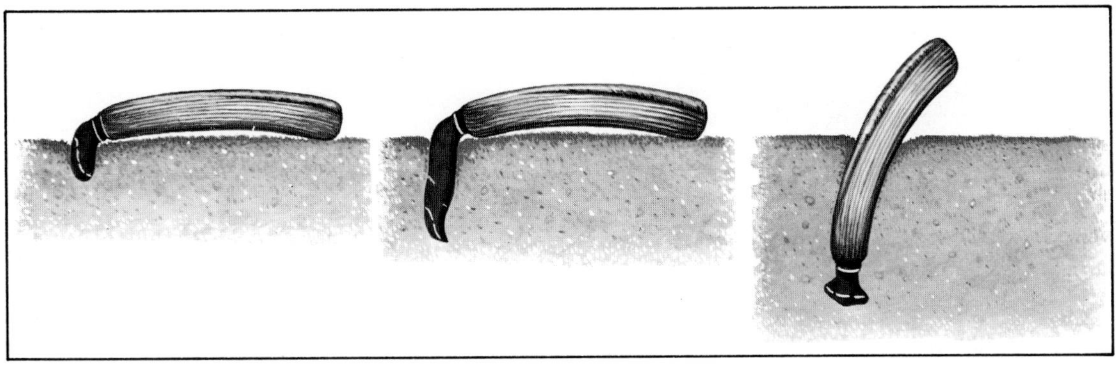

Left: The razor shell has a very muscular foot with which it burrows through the sand. The whole shell can be buried in a few seconds.

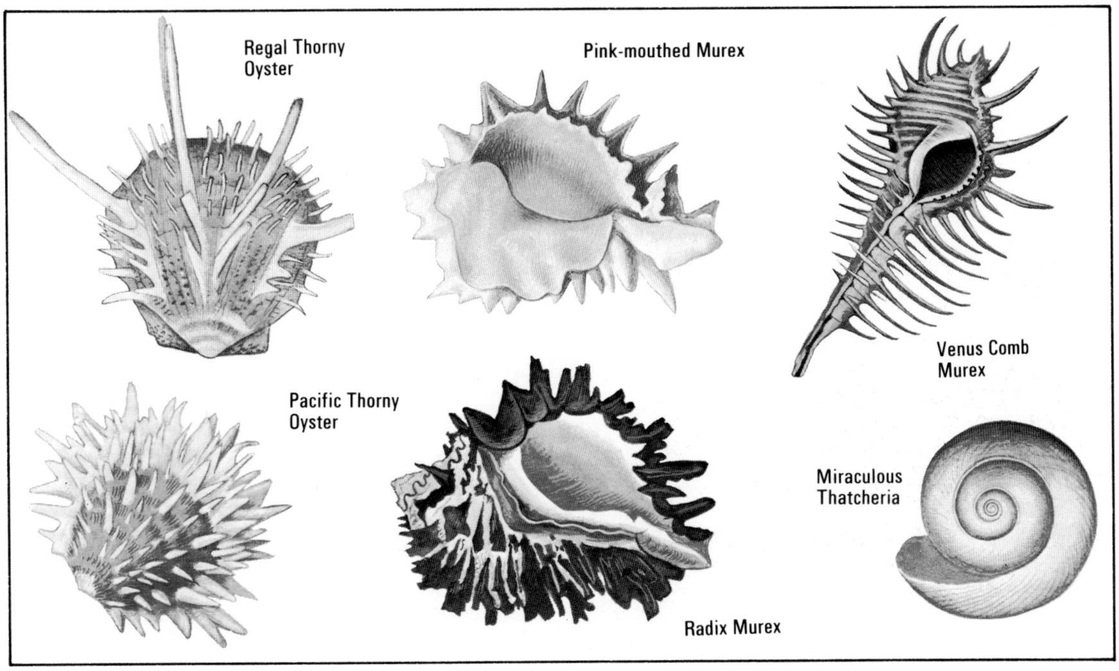

Far left: Wave-battered rocks do not shelter very many animals, but they make good vantage points for pelicans and other sea birds.

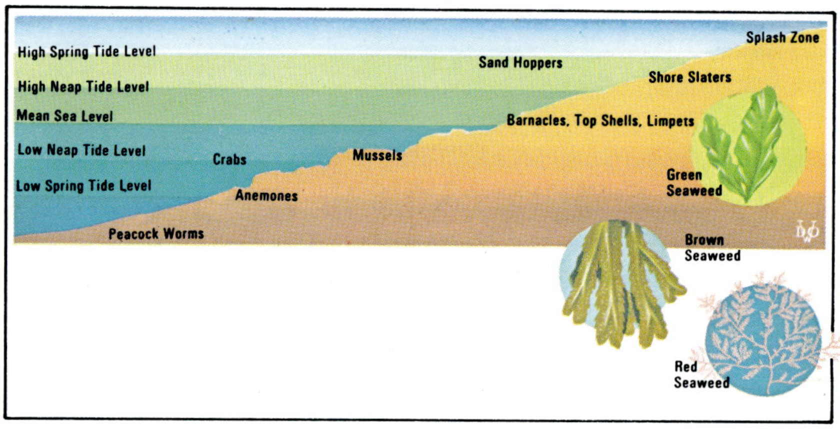

The Lower Shore

This is the region below the low-water mark of the neap tides. It is under water for most of the time and many kinds of animals make their homes here. The main seaweeds are the brown ones again, especially the long oarweeds and bootlace weeds. There may be some red seaweeds at the lowest levels, but most of these grow below the shore where they are always covered. Sea anemones cling to the rocks shrinking to little blobs of jelly when uncovered. There are also mussels, whelks and many tube-dwelling worms.

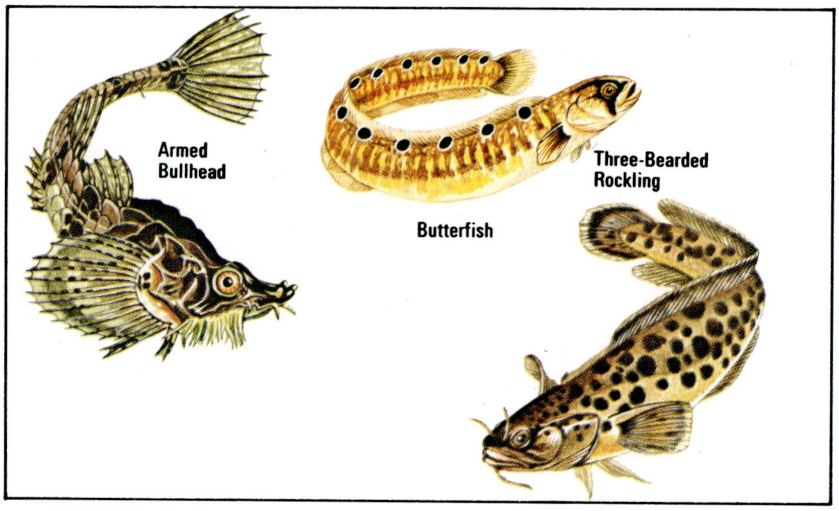

Sandy Shores

Sandy shores look very empty when the tide goes out because there are no rocks or seaweeds. The animals that live there have to bury themselves in the sand when the tide goes out. There are not so many different kinds of animals on a sandy shore, but there may be huge numbers of individual animals. For example, there may be more than 3,000,000 cockles under a hectare of sand. Worms and bivalves are the commonest animals of the sandy shore and they mainly feed by drawing in currents of water and filtering out the organic particles. Sea-urchins and starfishes are also common.

Top: The major zones of the sea-shore.
Above: Fishes generally move in and out with the tide but where rocky pools exist one can often find some of the shallow water fishes after the tide has gone out.

Right: Many tropical shores are fringed with coral reefs. Coral reefs do not occur where cold currents wash the shore.

Life in Fresh Water

Fresh water has been colonized or invaded by plants and animals from two directions: some species entered the rivers from the sea and others entered the water from the land. One major problem of living in the water is to obtain oxygen, either from the water or by coming to the surface to breathe. Animals coming from the sea had already solved this problem. For them the difficulty lay in adapting to the very different chemical conditions of fresh water.

Pond Plants

A pond is a relatively small body of still water. There is no clear distinction between a pond and a lake, although we usually use the word lake to describe a larger stretch of water. Lakes and ponds present animals with the same sorts of problems and they contain the same sorts of living organisms. The pond community depends in the first place on the surrounding rocks. Ponds surrounded by acidic sandstones or granites are much poorer than ponds in chalk or limestone regions. Rocky shores provide little foothold for plants, but a pond resting on clay or river deposits will be completely surrounded by lush vegetation. This may consist of yellow flags, various rushes and reeds and the splendid reedmace which is often called the bulrush or cattail. Some of these plants extend a fair way into the water, although they are not truly aquatic plants. The real aquatic species live farther out in the water. They may be rooted, with floating leaves (e.g. water lilies) or with submerged leaves (e.g. Canadian pondweed) or with both kinds of leaves. Duckweed, frogbit and some other plants float freely at the surface. The most important of the plants—the tiny floating organisms that form the plankton—feed many of the small animals.

Pond Animals

The plants provide food and shelter for the animals and they also provide oxygen. This is most important, both for the living animals and for the decomposition of dead material.

The kingfisher is a very striking bird of pond and stream. It sits on a branch overhanging the water and dives in after small fishes.

Below: A pond showing some of its inhabitants. Above it are plants of the marshy ground around the pond.

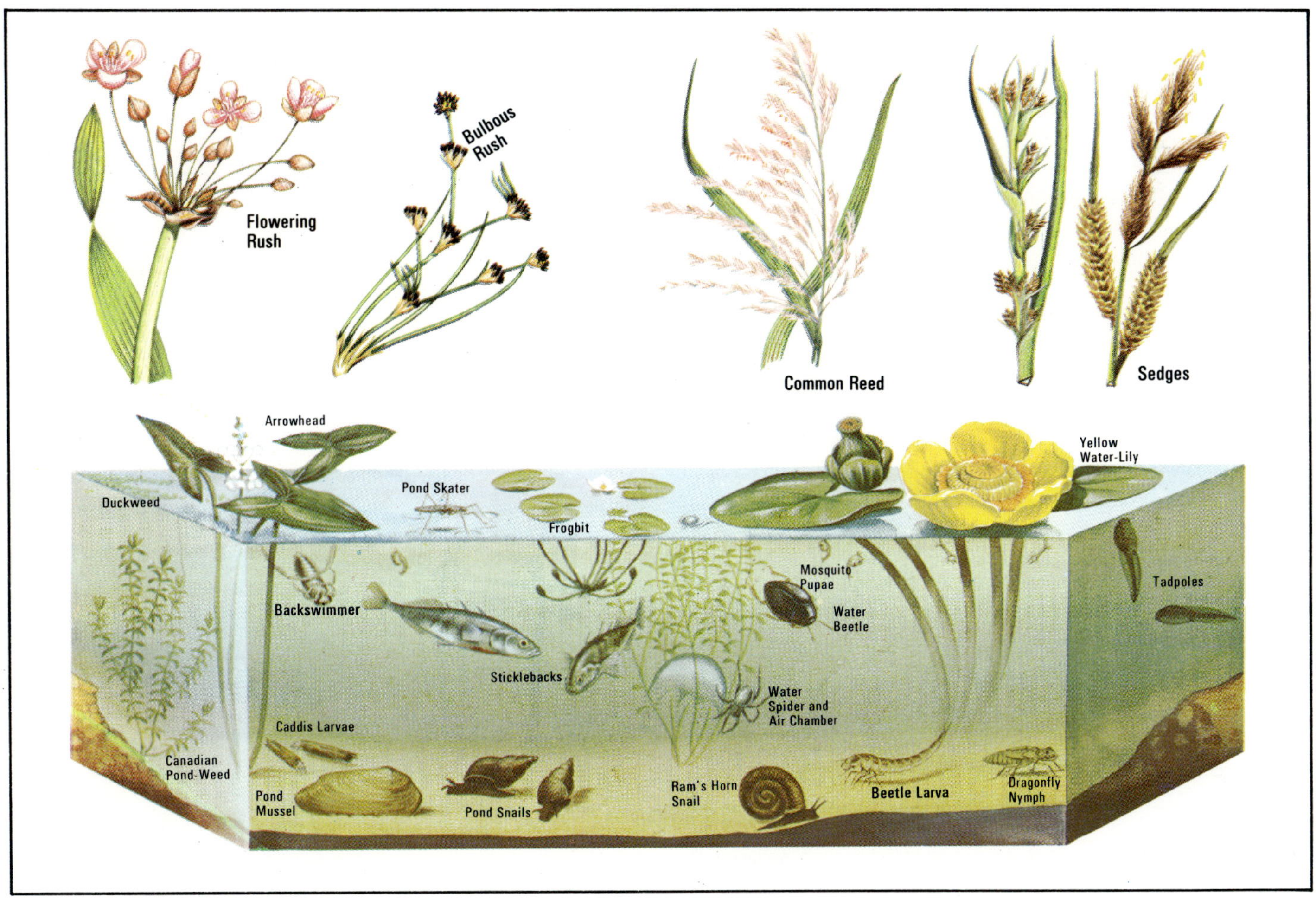

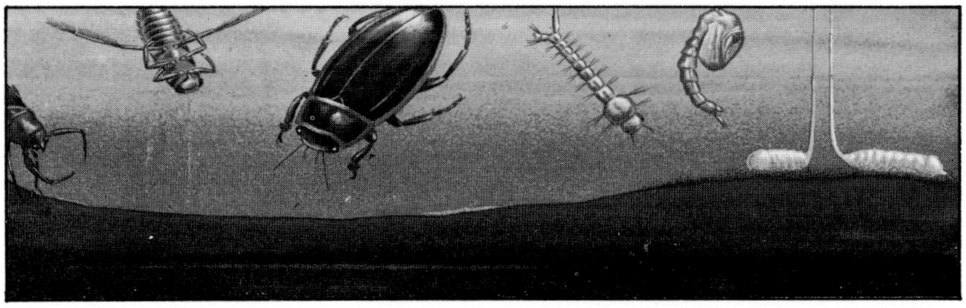

Above: Many young insects and some adult bugs and beetles live in the water. Most of them breathe air. Some have special breathing tubes which they push up to the surface. Others come to the surface to renew their air supplies.

Nearly every group of animals can be found in fresh water and every region of the pond has its characteristic inhabitants. The surface of the water, although no different in composition from the rest, acts as a very thin skin and can support various small animals. Pond-skaters skim across the surface, often accompanied by shiny, black whirligig beetles. Both feed on flies and other small creatures that fall on to the surface. The whirligig's eyes are divided into two parts, so that they seem to have four eyes. The upper parts look across the surface, and the lower parts look down into the water.

Among the free-swimming creatures there are fishes, water beetles, water bugs, such as the backswimmers and water boatmen, water spiders and mites and a horde of little crustaceans. The latter include the water fleas and cyclops which live mainly in the surface waters and they feed by straining minute plants and other organisms from the water.

Living in or on the mud at the bottom of the pond, or crawling on the water plants, we find another group of animals. These include snails and mussels, together with the young stages of dragonflies, water beetles and caddis flies. There will also be various worms and fly larvae. One of the interesting worms is a little red creature called tubifex. It is often sold in pet shops as fish food. The animal lives half buried in the mud and its tail sticks up into the water. By waving the hind end, the worm creates water currents which bring oxygen to it. Oxygen is never abundant near the bottom of the pond and the worm contains the red pigment haemoglobin which helps it to absorb enough oxygen.

Below: The dipper, a bird of the troutbeck which walks on the stream-bed in its search for insects. The grey heron and the moorhen, two common birds of pond and stream.

Breathing under Water

Small creatures, such as hydra and the water fleas, get enough oxygen through their body surfaces. Larger creatures, however, need special breathing organs. The fishes, and the water snails which arrived directly from the sea, breathe by means of gills. These absorb oxygen directly from the water and the animals therefore need well-aerated water. They cannot live in stagnant ponds. Other gill-breathing creatures include the young dragonflies and caddis flies.

The insects have invaded the water from the land and, although some young insects can get their oxygen direct from the water, the adults still have to breathe air. So do many water snails which have entered fresh water from the land. You will often see water boatmen and water beetles hanging upside down at the surface. They are renewing their air supply. They carry a bubble of air about with them, trapped under their wing cases or trapped by a coat of fine hairs on the body. The air bubble is in contact with the openings of the breathing tubes. Some water snails come to the surface every now and then to take a fresh air supply into their lungs. You

can see them open the entrance to the lung as they hang upside down at the surface.

Some insects get their oxygen without coming to the surface. We have already mentioned the rat-tailed maggot. Another interesting example is the water scorpion—a flattened insect, unrelated to real scorpions and quite harmless. It has a long breathing tube at the hind end.

Life in Streams

The moving waters of streams present quite different living conditions from those found in the still waters of ponds. What is more, the conditions vary as one moves up or down the stream. It is possible to divide a stream into several regions according to its animal and plant life.

The upper reaches of a river form the headstream. This is usually on high ground and it is a shallow, fast-flowing stretch. There is plenty of oxygen here and the main problem is to avoid being swept away. The only plants that manage to grow here are little algae that attach themselves to the rocks. A few small snails crawl on the bed of the stream, but the main animals are the young stages of various insects. Flattened nymphs of some mayflies and stoneflies cling to the stones and nibble away at the algae. There are also some caddis larvae, which make themselves little cases of sand grains.

The headstream gradually merges into the troutbeck region. The slope is not so steep here, but the bed is still rocky and the water still runs quickly. A few patches of water crowfoot may grow on the stream-bed, but there is little vegetation apart from the algae. The flattened insect nymphs from the headstream also live in this region, together with various snails and the river limpet. The latter has a conical shell, but it is not closely related to the limpets of the sea-shore. Fishes make their appearance in the troutbeck. They are either strong swimmers, such as the trout, or they hide among the stones and boulders. The loach and the bullhead are among these bottom-dwelling species. They feed on the insect nymphs or on adult insects that fall on to the water surface.

The next stretch of the river is usually called the minnow reach. The current is slower and a certain amount of sand and gravel covers the bottom. There are plenty of water plants and animal life is also abundant. There are many different kinds of water snails, dragonfly nymphs, mayflies and other insects. The minnow is the typical fish, but there are also sticklebacks, lampreys, dace, grayling and salmon. The fishes of the troutbeck are found here as well. Another common creature is the freshwater shrimp, which darts among the plant stems.

Below the minnow reach, the river gets deeper and slower. This is the carp reach, characterised by fishes of the carp family and others such as roach, rudd, perch, pike, chub, bream and carp. The slow-moving water deposits plenty of mud, and plants are able to grow along the edges. Water lilies may grow further out in the river. Worms, water snails and mussels are common in the mud. There is a certain amount of floating plankton in this stretch of the river, especially in the weedy parts, but it is never as common as it is in the still water of a pond.

Above: The pond snail (top) and the ramshorn snail, two common pond-dwelling species.

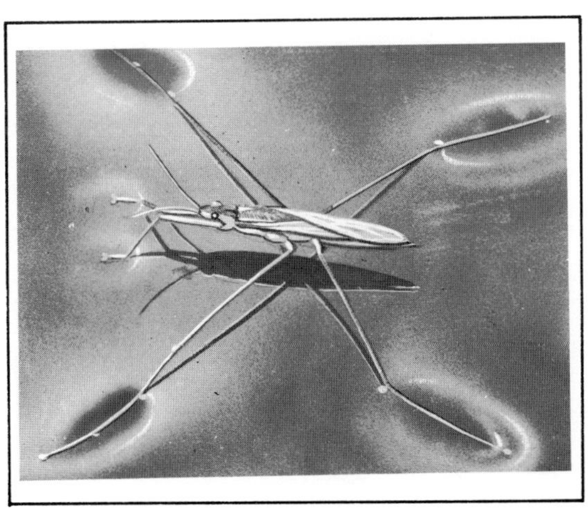

Left: The pond skater 'rows' itself over the water surface with its long legs.

Most fishes feed on insects and other small invertebrates. The pike, however, eats other fishes.

Fossils

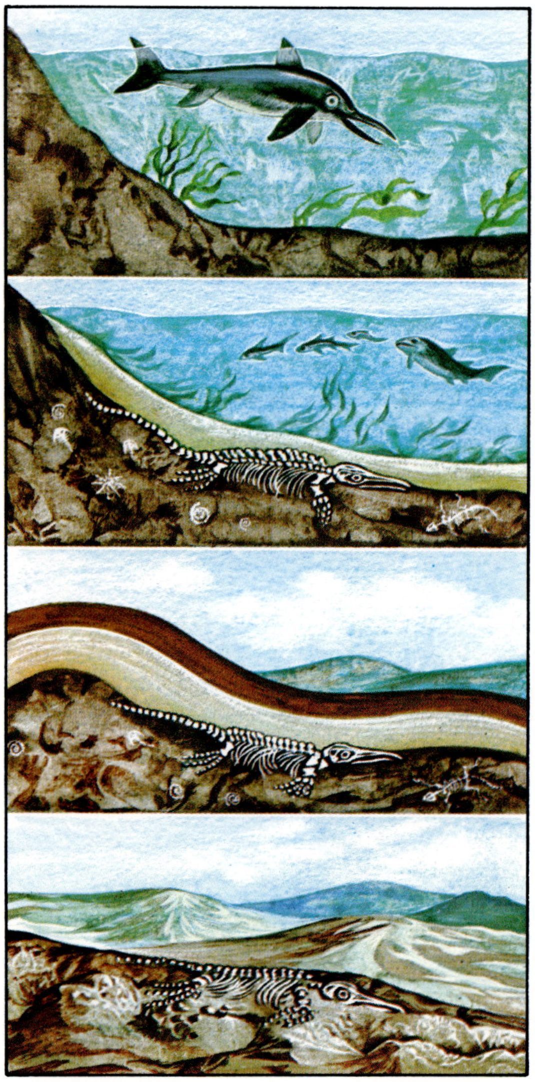

Diagram showing how an animal may be fossilized. A sea-dwelling ichthyosaur dies and sinks to the sea-bed. Soon its skeleton is covered with mud which gradually settles into solid rock. At a much later date earth movements buckle the sea-bed and cause it to rise above sea-level. Erosion then strips away the rock covering until the fossil is exposed.

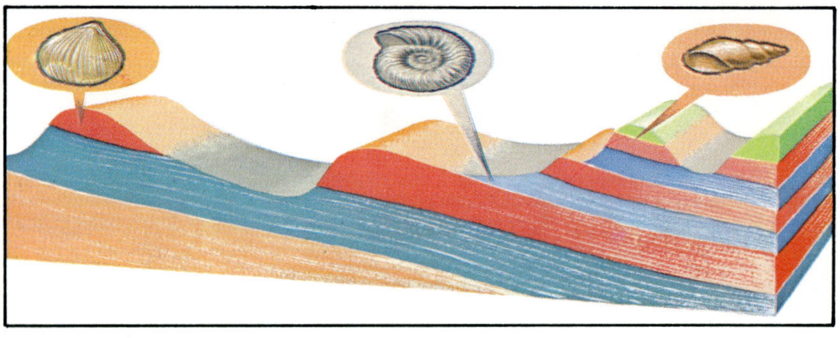

Rocks laid down at different times tend to contain different collections of fossils which enable the rocks to be recognised wherever they are found.

Fossils are the traces and remains of animals and plants which have been naturally preserved in the rocks, sometimes for many millions of years.

When an animal dies its body usually decomposes or else it is eaten by other animals. But the hard parts—the teeth and the bones or shell—are not so easy to destroy and if they are buried quite quickly they stand a good chance of being preserved or fossilised. Most of the fossils that have been discovered are of marine creatures. This is because the best conditions for fossilisation occur in the sea. The majority of the sedimentary rocks in the Earth's crust were actually formed under the sea.

The story of a typical fossil can be followed by imagining some animals living on the sea-bed millions of years ago. Imagine also the sand and mud settling around the animals. When the animals died their shells or skeletons became buried by this rain of sand and mud. In time the sediment became compressed and hardened into rock and the animal remains became converted into fossils. At a much later date, movements of the Earth's crust lifted up these new rocks to form land. Wind and rain began to wear down the rocks and the fossils eventually came to light.

Fossils take on a number of different forms. Very occasionally the skeleton may be preserved. This has happened where animals have been trapped in bogs or tar pits and buried very rapidly. The Californian tar pits, for instance, have yielded a wealth of animal skeletons including those of several birds. Under certain very unusual conditions an entire animal may be preserved. Mammoths (relatives of today's elephants) have been preserved almost intact in the ice of Siberia and Alaska. The flesh of some has been found fit to eat, after perhaps more than a million years in 'cold storage'.

More often, however, the buried remains

A mould of a trilobite (left), the impression that may remain after the animal has disappeared. A cast (centre) formed by the deposition of minerals in the original mould. Fossil track (right) left by a prehistoric animal.

undergo a certain amount of change. The skeletons and shells are most commonly petrified, or converted into stone. Water percolating through the rocks gradually dissolves the original material and deposits mineral matter in its place. If the original material is dissolved away and not replaced it leaves a hollow in the rock. This hollow is called a mould and it is a very common form of fossil. If mineral matter is deposited in the mould it forms a natural cast. This type of fossil shows all the external features of the object, just as a jelly follows the shape of the mould it is made in, but it does not tell us anything about the internal structure of the object. It is possible to make artificial casts of fossils by filling the moulds with modelling wax or some similar substance.

The ammonites are among the best-known fossils. They were marine creatures related to today's squids and cuttlefishes. The original shell has almost always disappeared and, as a rule, the fossils we find are either moulds or internal fillings. The internal fillings were formed when the shells became filled with sediment and then dissolved away, leaving the filling with a detailed pattern of the inside of the shell. Ammonites are very common in the Jurassic limestones and clays formed about 150 million years ago. Some of the fossils in the clays are composed of iron pyrites and they sometimes shine like gold.

Many plant fossils are simply residues of

Sometimes the fossilized skeleton of an animal may be surrounded by a film of carbon showing the outline of the animal's body.

Left: A petrified tree trunk. Each particle of wood has been replaced by mineral matter.

Below left: Amber is fossilised resin. It often contains well-preserved insects. Fossil ammonites have been found over 2 metres across.

Below: A fossil dragonfly.

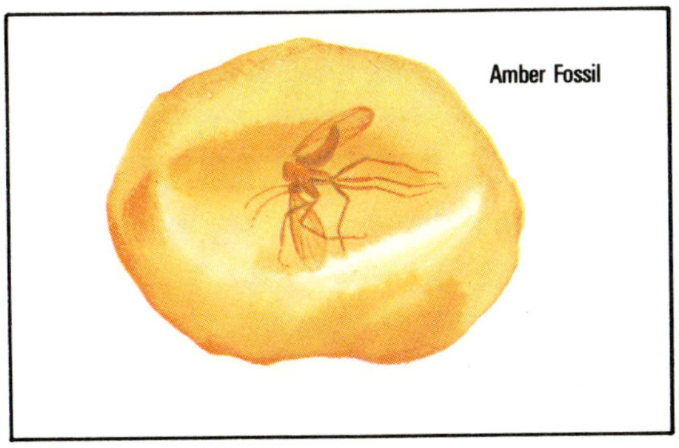

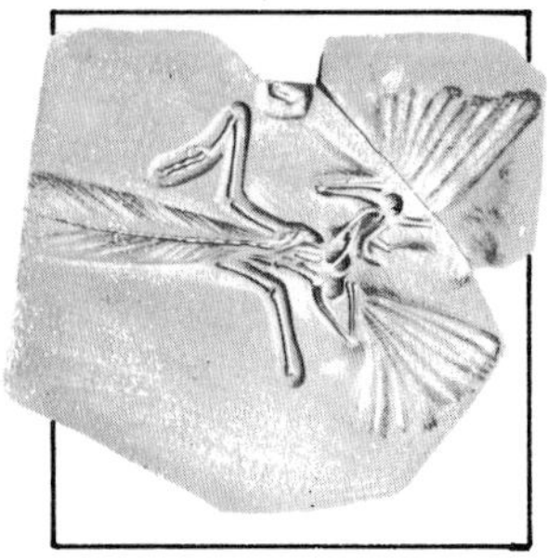

Above: Archaeopteryx, the first known bird from fossils found in a Bavarian limestone quarry.

carbon, which give the actual shapes of the leaves and stems. Some animals may be preserved in this way, too. Pieces of amber, which is a hardened or fossilised resin from coniferous trees, sometimes contain the remains of insects which had become trapped.

Ancient animals often left tracks and footprints in mud that became baked hard. Although a footprint is not actually a part of an animal, it is a true fossil and it tells us quite a lot about the animal that made it.

Looking for Fossils

Fossils are quite easy to find if you know the sort of places in which to look for them. You can often pick them up in fields and gardens. Better specimens are obtained from freshly exposed rocks. If you want to find fossils you must look at the sedimentary rocks, which formed in the seas and lakes. Sandy rocks are not very good for fossils, and limestones, clays and shales are the best rocks to examine. Railway cuttings, roadworks, quarries and seaside cliffs are also very good places to look.

The fossils are not usually scattered haphazardly through the rocks. More often they are concentrated in bands or layers. These layers of rock and fossils were laid down at times which were particularly favourable for the preservation of the remains. The best example of this concerns the formation of coal. Coal consists of the remains of giant fern-like plants that grew in coastal swamps some 250 million years ago. At that period the sea-level was unsteady and it kept flooding the forests. This killed the plants and buried them with sandy and muddy sediment. When the sea retreated again, a new forest sprang up on the deposits and the remains of the earlier forests gradually turned into coal. This happened many times, producing numerous coal seams separated by beds of sandy rock.

Many limestones also consist almost entirely of fossils. Some are made up of old coral reefs, while others contain little but the remains of crinoids, or sea lilies. These were animals related to the starfishes and they had skeletons composed of little limestone discs. Chalk is made up of microscopic fossils.

The rocks are like the pages of a history book to a geologist: they tell the story of the Earth. But they are far more difficult to read than the pages of an ordinary book because they are frequently torn, bent, or upside-down. Some of the pages are scattered over a wide area and some are missing altogether. The key to the pages and their order lies in the fossils contained within the rocks.

If we take an undisturbed sequence of rocks it is fairly obvious that the oldest rocks will be at the bottom and the newest rocks, which were laid down most recently, will be at the top. If we look at the fossils in such a sequence of rocks we will find that the fossils at one level are not exactly the same as those at another level. As one goes higher up the sequence, some of the fossils disappear and new kinds come in to take their place. Each layer of rock thus has a characteristic collection of fossils.

This is of great importance to the geologist because if he finds the same groups of fossils in rocks from different regions he can safely say that the rocks are of about the same age. This helps him to piece together the jig-saw of the Earth's long history. The Earth's history is, in fact, divided up into a number of

Below: Mammoths have been found preserved in the frozen wastes of Siberia and Alaska. Right: Fossil crinoid or sea lily.

periods which are separated mainly on the basis of the fossils they contain. The fossils in the rocks also show us how the plant and animal life of our planet has changed. Five hundred million years ago there were plenty of shelled creatures related to today's crabs and cuttlefishes. There were also many other kinds of animals that are now completely extinct, but there were no animals with backbones as far as we know. Then, about 450 million years ago perhaps, the first fishes appeared. Only fragments of these early fishes have been found, but the fossil record tells us that a great number of different kinds of fishes were in existence. Soon after this a new sort of creature began to live on the Earth. It was called an amphibian and it was one of the early forerunners of today's frogs and newts. Still later, about 300 million years ago, there appeared the animals that we now call reptiles. Birds and mammals did not appear until much later.

The fossils in the rocks therefore show us roughly when the various groups of animals (and plants) came into being. But they do more than this. There are some rare fossils that do not fit easily into any of the main groups. Some of them look partly like fishes and partly like amphibians; others look partly like amphibians and partly like reptiles. These fossils show us that fishes gradually changed into amphibians and that amphibians changed into reptiles. In other words, the fossils show us that life evolved.

THE AGES OF THE EARTH

Geological Periods	Plant and Animal Life Forms
Quaternary Period Began 2–3 Million Years Ago	Great Ice Age. Coming of Man.
Tertiary Period Began 70 Million Years Ago	Modern Mammals Appear.
Cretaceous Period Began 135 Million Years Ago	Dinosaurs Decline. Mammals Increase. First Flowering Plants.
Jurassic Period Began 180 Million Years Ago	Dinosaurs Abundant. Birds and Mammals Appear.
Triassic Period Began 225 Million Years Ago	Early Dinosaurs.
Permian Period Began 270 Million Years Ago	Reptiles Increase.
Carboniferous Period Began 350 Million Years Ago	First Reptiles.
Devonian Period Began 400 Million Years Ago	Age of Fishes. First Amphibians.
Silurian Period Began 440 Million Years Ago	Earliest Land Plants.
Ordovician Period Began 500 Million Years Ago	First Fishes.
Cambrian Period Began 600 Million Years Ago	First Abundant Fossils. All Invertebrates.

Formation of Earth About 4,500 Million Years Ago

Fossil of paradoxides, the 50 cm giant trilobite of the Cambrian seas.

The First Animals

Some Ordovician graptolites preserved in shale. The horny skeletons have been completely flattened.

A somewhat magical line in the geological time scale separates the Cambrian period from the vast expanse of Pre-Cambrian time. The first Cambrian rocks were laid down about 600 million years ago and they contain a wide variety of fossils. Nearly all the major animal groups were in existence at that time, but the Pre-Cambrian rocks contain very few fossils. It is almost as if life suddenly started up about 600 million years ago. But we know that this cannot be true because many of the Cambrian animals were quite advanced creatures. Life must have been in existence for a very long time before the opening of the Cambrian period. Why then are there so few fossils? The most likely answer is that the earliest plants and animals had no hard parts which could be preserved. The early animals were probably soft creatures like worms.

Interest in the Pre-Cambrian rocks has increased in recent years and intensive searching has brought a number of fossils to light. In 1947 rocks formed from a late Pre-Cambrian mudflat were discovered in the Ediacara Hills of South Australia. Pressed into these ancient deposits were the shapes of numerous soft-bodied animals, including worms, jellyfishes and sea-pens.

The First Signs of Life

The earliest signs of life so far discovered are various lumps of limestone found in Zimbabwe. There is little to suggest that it was formed by living organisms, but its appearance is very similar to that of some of the limestones formed today by algae living on coral reefs. They are believed to be about 3,000 million years old. Unfortunately, there is still a very big gap in our knowledge concerning the rather sudden appearance of the many shelled creatures in the Cambrian rocks. The development of shells must have taken millions of years and shelled animals must have been living in Pre-Cambrian times. But the uppermost layers of the Pre-Cambrian rocks are missing in most places and we have yet to find fossils that show how the shelled animals evolved.

Trilobites

The most abundant of the Cambrian fossils are the trilobites. These creatures were distantly related to crabs and other arthropods and they looked rather like woodlice. They probably lived on the sea-bed and fed on the debris that accumulated there. Trilobites had several pairs of legs, but these are rarely preserved and the most common type of trilobite fossil is a mould of the body. This shows three distinct regions: a triangular or semi-circular head-shield, a thorax made up of several segments, and a tail section, or pygidium, which often looks like another head. The animals frequently broke up when they died and the head and tail sections are often found separately. The trilobites were mostly small, averaging less than 2.5 cm in length, but one species reached nearly 50 cm. Trilobites lived for about 400 million years, before becoming extinct.

Brachiopods

Also very common in the Cambrian seas were shelled creatures called brachiopods.

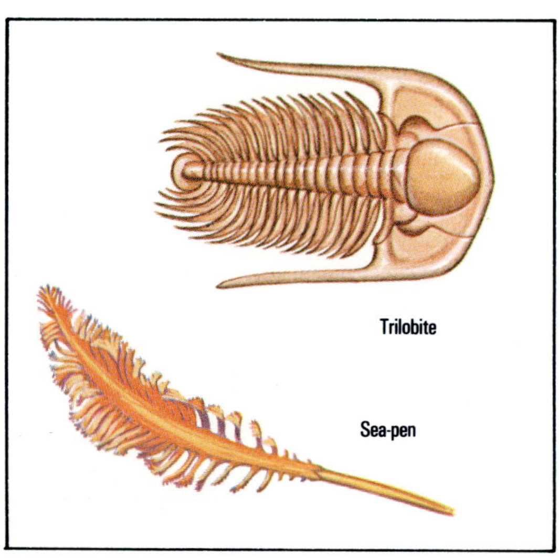

Right: Trilobites first appear in Cambrian rocks. Forms like present-day soft corals or sea-pens have been found in Pre-Cambrian rocks in England, South Africa and Australia.

Far right: Pre-Cambrian fossils from the Ediacara Hills in Australia: an annelid worm (bottom), a jellyfish (left) and an unidentified organism.

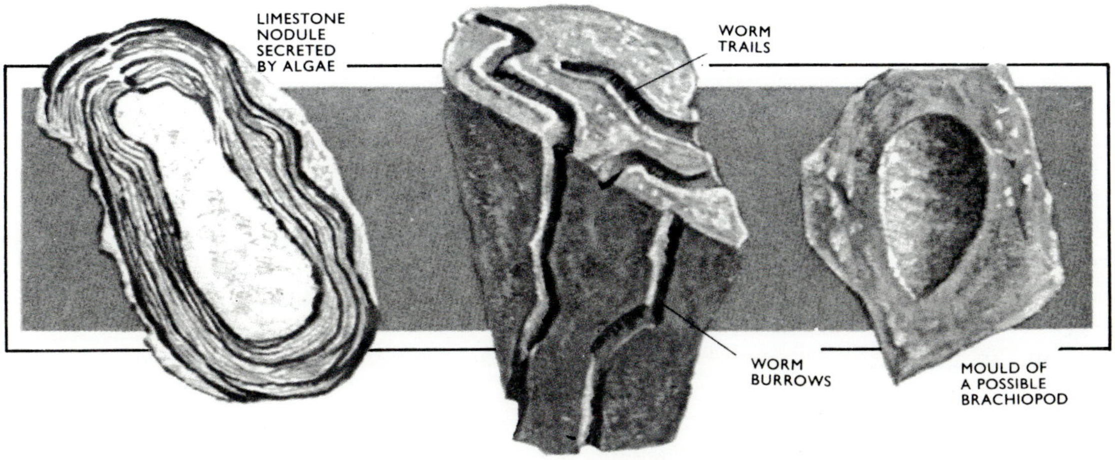

Some of the earliest traces of life: a limestone nodule perhaps secreted by algae; worm tracks and burrows; and a mould of a possible brachiopod.

Some species are found in the oceans today and they are called lamp shells. They look rather like cockle shells and other bivalves, but they belong to a very different group of animals. The shell is much more symmetrical than that of a bivalve mollusc and it conceals two 'arms' which are used to waft food particles into the mouth when the shell is open. Brachiopods live on the sea-bed and are anchored to it by a muscular stalk.

Graptolites

Towards the end of the Cambrian period there appeared a new kind of animal called a graptolite. Graptolites were very small animals and they lived in thread-like colonies. Each thread supported a number of tiny horny cups and each cup contained a single graptolite animal. The early graptolite colonies were fan-like structures, but later ones became simpler and consisted of only one or two branches. We know very little about the soft parts of the graptolite animals because they are quite extinct and the fossils are usually only flattened impressions in shales. They probably floated freely in the sea and they rapidly spread throughout the world. They became abundant in the Ordovician period, but then they dwindled and disappeared completely about 400 million years ago.

Below: Artist's impression of life in the Cambrian seas, showing corals, jellyfishes, trilobites and worms.

The Age of Fishes

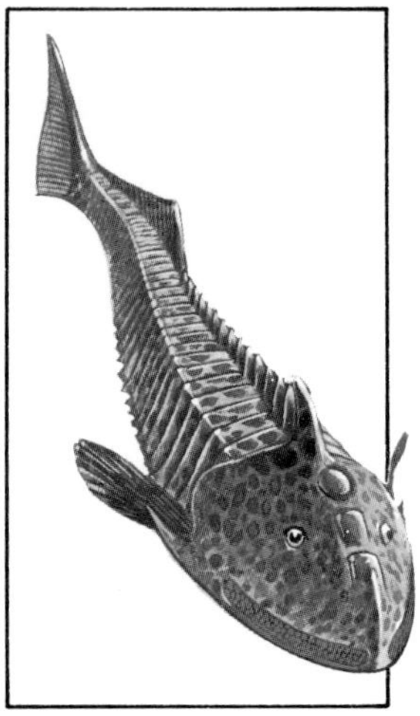

The first fishes were jawless and fed by digging in the mud. They were heavily armoured with bony plates and scales, especially in the the head region.

Although animal life was abundant during Cambrian times, and nearly all groups of animals had appeared by then, there were no backboned animals (vertebrates) so far as is known. The earliest traces of backboned animals have been found in some Ordovician rocks in America. They are about 450 million years old and they consist of various bone fragments and fishes' scales.

How the first fishes arose from earlier types of animal is not clear. Many groups of invertebrate animals have been suggested as ancestors of the vertebrates, but the most likely group is that containing the starfishes. This might seem surprising at first, but some members of the starfish group have larvae like those of the acorn worm, and the acorn worm is known to be related to the vertebrates.

Fishes Without Jaws

The oldest complete fossil fishes that we have are about 400 million years old. These fishes lived in Silurian times and most of them were only a few centimetres long. Most of them were heavily armoured, with bony plates and scales, especially in the head region, but the most striking feature of all was the complete absence of jaws. The fishes probably fed by sucking up mud and other debris and filtering it through their gills to extract food material. Many of them were flattened from top to bottom and they were adapted for life on the bottom of the sea or the rivers. The jawless fishes nearly all became extinct after the arrival of the jawed fishes, but the lampreys and the hagfishes survive to the present day.

The First Jawed Fishes

Remains of the first known jawed fishes date from about 370 million years ago. They almost certainly arose from some sort of jawless fish by the gradual transformation of some of the gill bones into the jaws. The early jawed fishes are known as placoderms and, like the primitive jawless fishes, they were partly covered with bony armour. They had teeth and they probably fed on other animals. As well as jaws, the placoderms had paired fins. These two features were important milestones in the evolution of the backboned

Right: Dinichthys was one of the largest of the first known jawed fishes, the placoderms, reaching a length of 10 metres. Their teeth suggest they fed on other fishes. The early shark-like fish illustrated had a cartilaginous skeleton. This early bony fish had ray-fins.

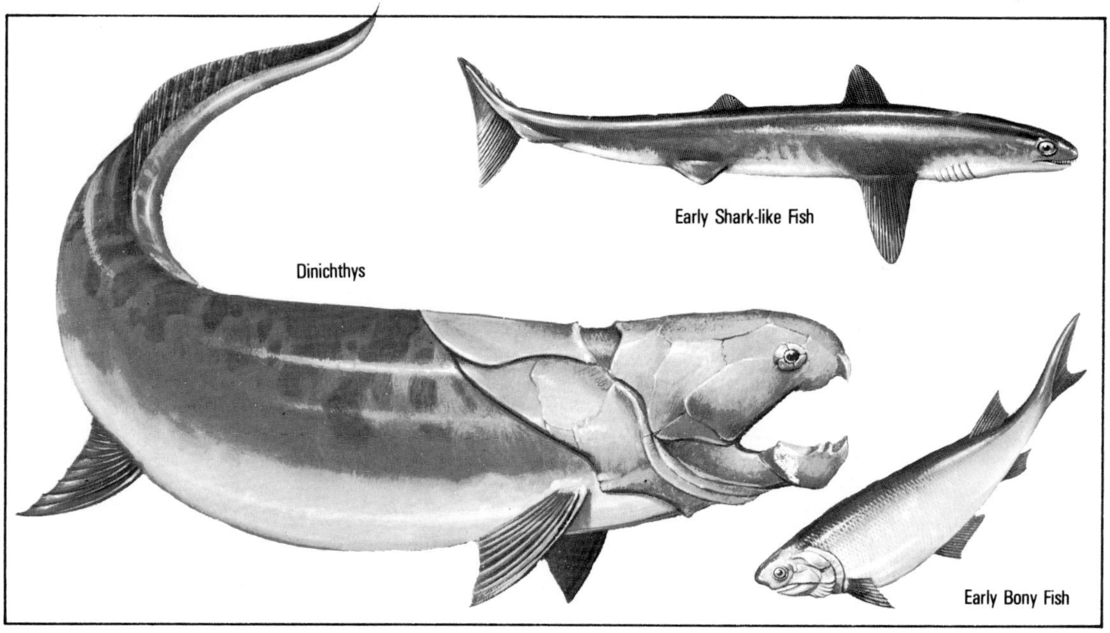

Below: The jaws of vertebrates are believed to have arisen from the bones that supported the third pair of gills in the earlier jawless fishes.

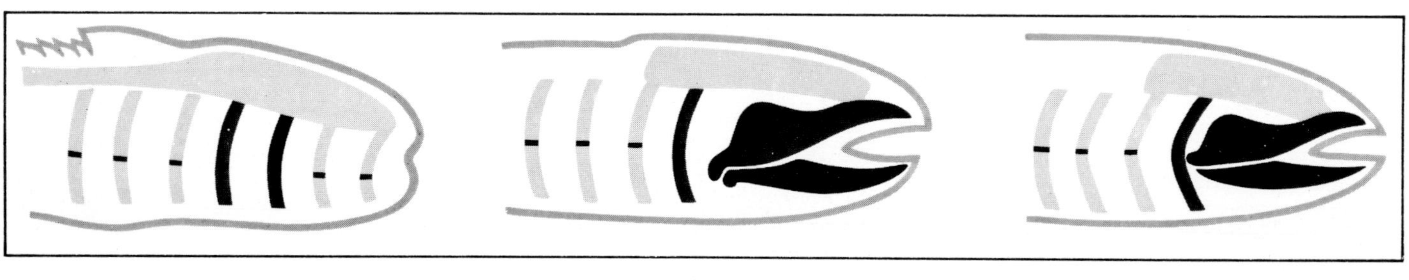

animals. Most of the placoderms were small fishes, less than about 30 centimetres long, but there were a few giant species like Dinichthys.

The Age of Fishes

The Devonian period, which began about 400 million years ago, is often called the Age of Fishes. Many of the jawless fishes were still living, and the placoderms were plentiful, but many new groups of fishes appeared at this time. In fact, all the major groups of fishes had appeared by the end of the Devonian period. Two main lines emerged within the fishes: the shark-like fishes, with their soft cartilaginous skeletons, and the bony fishes. The early sharks were very much like their modern relatives, with powerful jaws and streamlined bodies.

Ray-finned Fishes

The bony fishes had skeletons of true bone. They also possessed air sacs which opened into the back of the throat. Two distinct lines soon emerged among the bony fishes. There were the ray-finned fishes, which include almost all the living fish species, and the lobe-finned fishes. The latter are represented today by just six species of lung fishes and the coelacanth. The fins of the ray-finned fishes are supported on narrow bony spines or rays, whereas those of the lobe-finned fishes are supported by a fleshy lobe in the centre.

In most of the ray-finned fishes the air sacs became modified to form the swim bladder. This is a gas-filled bag situated just above the food canal and its job is to regulate the buoyancy of the fish. A few ray-finned fishes, however, retained the air sac. The bichir, one of the fishes that retained the air sacs, retains several other primitive features, such as heavy scales.

Lobe-finned Fishes

We have very few lobe-finned fishes alive today. Whereas the nostrils of the ray-finned fishes are simply pits on the snout, those of the lobe-finned fishes open into the throat. This means that the fishes can breathe air, just as the modern lung fishes can.

Below: A fossil fish from Devonian rocks. Fossils of marine creatures are more plentiful in these rocks than those of land-dwelling animals since they stood a much better chance of being preserved (see page 214).

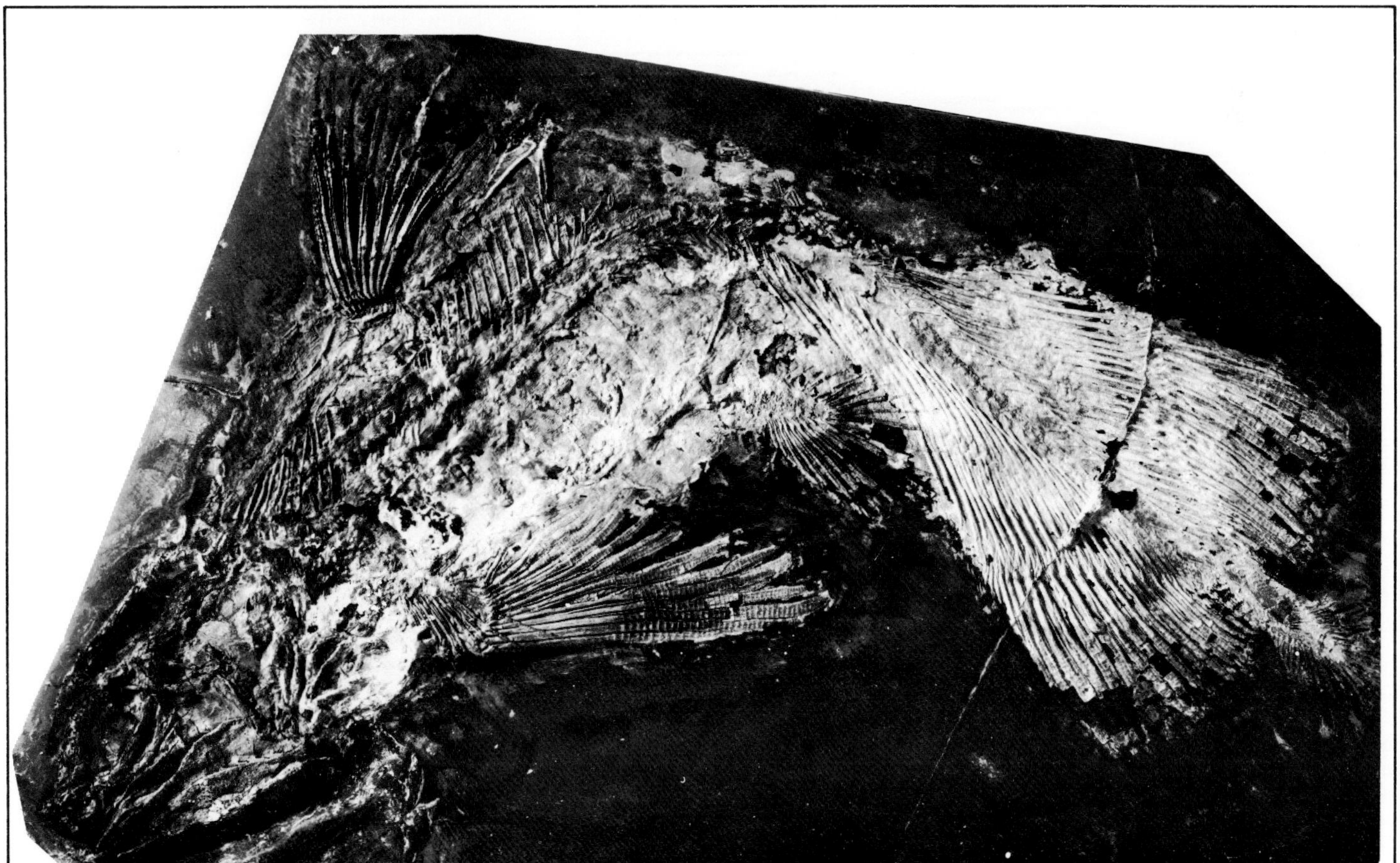

Life Moves to Land

Although backboned animals came into existence something like 450 million years ago, it was a very long time before they managed to conquer the land. At first the only backboned animals were fishes.

At the end of the Silurian period, about 400 million years ago, there were extensive and violent movements of the Earth's crust. They resulted in the lifting up of large areas of the sea-bed, especially in the Northern Hemisphere. The new land was crossed by rivers and streams and it was dotted with lakes. As yet, the land surface was quite bare, with only a few plants here and there. Life was centred in the waters of the rivers and lakes, where numerous fishes swam. This was the Devonian period, or the Age of Fishes.

Below: Fossil and reconstruction of eryops, a prehistoric amphibian about the length of a crocodile.

The lobe-finned fishes were common at this time and we can assume that they were able to drag themselves along on their muscular fins in much the same way that the Australian lung fish does today. We can also assume that they could gulp air into the air sacs leading from their throats. These fishes were thus already prepared for some kind of life on land, but what made them actually leave the water? It used to be thought that periodic droughts dried up their ponds and streams and forced them to wander over the land in search of new homes. This is possible, but it is unlikely that the land provided much food for the larger fishes and there would have been little or nothing to encourage them to stay on the land. In addition, there is no proof that the Devonian period really was as hot and dry as people used to think. A more likely explanation of why the lobe-finned fishes moved on to the land is that it enabled them to escape from competition in the water. It would have been an easy step for the young fishes in the shallows to crawl out onto the mud and they would have found plenty of small insects and other animals there to eat. There was every encouragement for them to stay on the shores and, although they had to go back into the water to breed, their offspring would also have found life on the land rewarding. Their ability to move and to survive on the land gradually improved. Over a period of several million years fins changed

Chased into the shallows, or stranded on the mud of a drying pool, the ray-finned fishes were helpless, but the lobe-fins used their muscular fins to haul themselves about on the mud.

into legs and air sacs turned into lungs. The new animals were the first amphibians.

Fossil Evidence

The story outlined above shows how land vertebrates could have evolved from fishes, but where is the evidence? The Devonian rocks contain numerous fossils showing that the lobe-finned fishes were common, and careful examination of some of these fossils has shown that they really did possess air sacs opening into the throat. In this respect they resemble the modern lung fishes, which gulp air and can also live out of water for a time. It is reasonable to expect that the ancient lobe-finned fishes behaved in a similar way. This sort of evidence strongly supports the idea that the land-living amphibians evolved from fishes.

Much stronger evidence for the evolution of amphibians from fishes is provided by various fossils discovered in Greenland. These fossils, which are believed to be about 350 million years old, show striking resemblances to both lobe-finned fishes and amphibians. The bones of the skull and the spinal column are just like those of the lobe-finned fishes, but the animals definitely had five-fingered limbs. These limbs, and the way in which they were attached to the body, show that the animals definitely walked. Vertebrates had managed to invade the land.

Fossils in the Devonian and Carboniferous rocks indicate that the amphibians remained fish-like for millions of years, although the skeleton gradually became more suited for life on land. Many different types of amphibians appeared during the Carboniferous period, but these animals never really managed to conquer the land. They could never completely escape from the water because they had to return to the water to breed. The real conquest of the land was left to the reptiles.

Some 300 million years ago, a group of amphibians developed a more waterproof covering and they began to lay eggs that could survive on land. Other changes took place gradually inside their bodies, and there came a time when the animals could no longer be called amphibians. They had evolved into reptiles. Freed from the need to return to the water to breed, the early reptiles began to spread out over the Earth. Many plants and insects had now appeared and there was plenty of food for the reptiles. They evolved quite rapidly and produced many different species.

The amphibians, which were rather slow and clumsy creatures, could not compete with their more active descendants and most of the ancient amphibian groups disappeared. Today's frogs and newts are the descendants of a few specialised groups that managed to survive the competition with the reptiles.

The skeleton of a ray-fin (top) compared with the skeleton of a lobe-fin (bottom) from which the typical five-fingered limb developed.

Miobatrachus, an early amphibian.

Ichthyostega, an early amphibian, closely resembled the lobe-finned fishes.

The Age of Reptiles

Reptiles had two very big advantages over the amphibians as far as life on land was concerned: they had scaly, waterproof skins and they were able to lay eggs with tough shells. The reptiles did not, therefore, have to go back to the water to breed.

The early reptiles had many of the characteristics of their amphibian ancestors and they were generally only a few tens of centimetres long. During the Permian period the reptiles improved their ability to live on land and they began to branch out into many different habitats. Some even returned to the sea and eventually became plesiosaurs and fish-like ichthyosaurs. One line evolved into the turtles and another eventually produced the snakes and lizards. Mammals evolved from yet another group of reptiles, but it was a long time before the mammals became important. The Jurassic and Cretaceous periods belonged to the reptiles and these two periods are justly known as the Age of Reptiles.

The early reptiles walked on all four legs, but about 225 million years ago one group started to walk about on its hind legs. The hind legs then gradually became longer than the front ones. These animals were the archosaurs, the ancestors of the great dinosaurs which dominated the world for nearly 100 million years. The dinosaurs have been extinct for more than 70 million years, but the archosaurs live on in the form of the crocodiles and alligators. The crocodiles have changed very little during the millions of years and they tell us a good deal about the structure of the early archosaurs.

Ichthyosaurs

The ichthyosaurs were reptiles that went back to the sea. They evolved a remarkable fish-like body, although they had flippers instead of fins and they still breathed air. In many ways, they were similar to the dolphins of modern seas. The skull was long and narrow and the snout carried numerous conical teeth. The animals must have fed on fishes and perhaps on some of the numerous ammonites in the Jurassic seas. Some fossils have much smaller skeletons associated with them, showing that the ichthyosaurs brought forth living young instead of laying eggs.

Dinosaurs

The name 'dinosaur' is popularly applied to several groups of archosaur reptiles and it is not a particularly scientific name. It conjures up visions of huge, lumbering creatures, but

Archaeopteryx was the first known bird, which had feathers like modern birds. But it also had teeth and a long reptilian tail. Diplodocus was one of the plant-eating dinosaurs which grew to huge proportions.

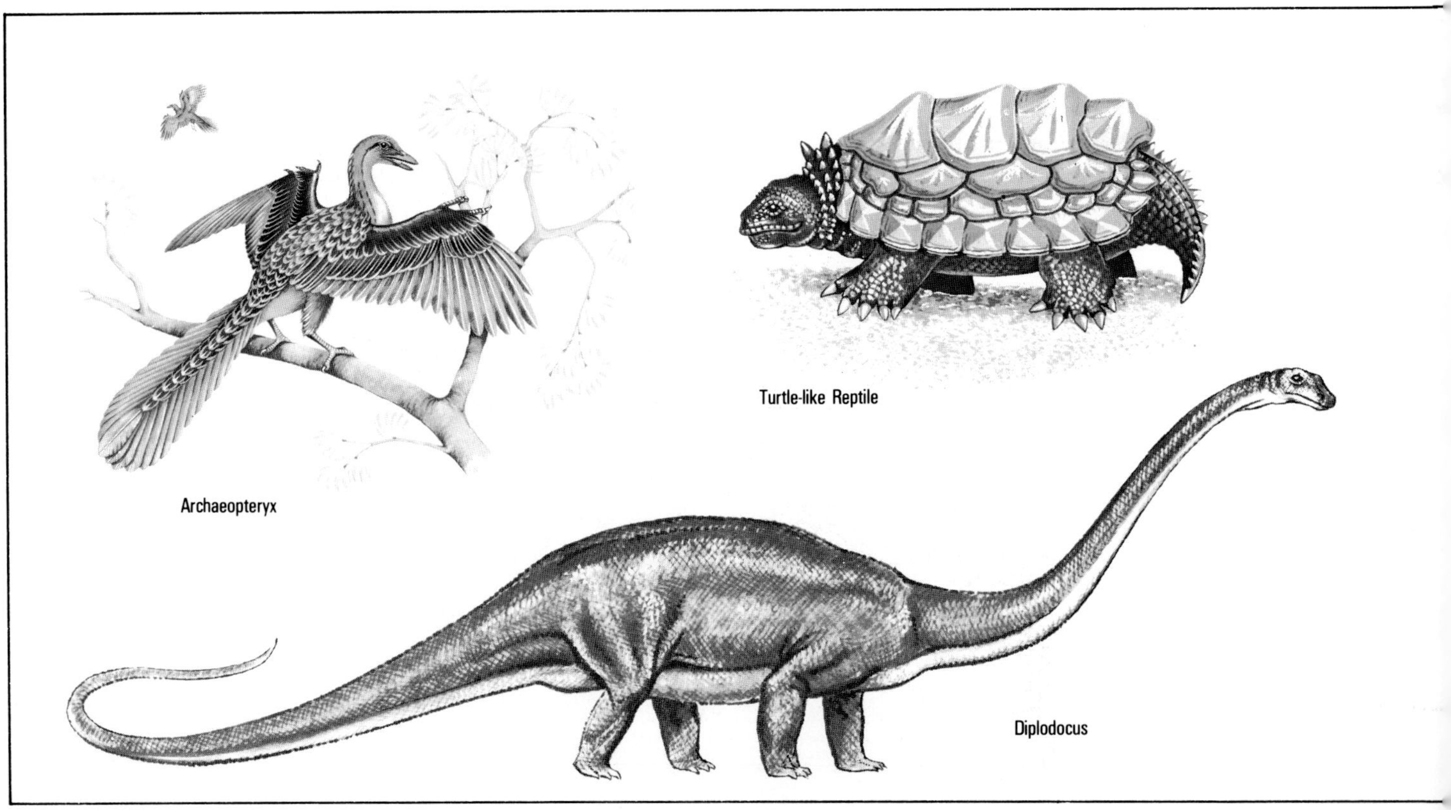

not all the dinosaurs were large. Some were only about a metre long.

The early dinosaurs were all flesh-eaters and they walked on their back legs. Plant-eating types developed later and some of them went back to walking on all four legs, although the back legs still remained much longer than the front ones. Some of these plant-eating dinosaurs reached enormous sizes. Brontosaurus and diplodocus were about 25 metres long and brontosaurus weighed about 30 tonnes. Other plant-eating dinosaurs had bony armour or horns as a defence against the ferocious flesh-eaters such as tyrannosaurus—a 15 metre monster with long dagger-like teeth.

Flying Reptiles

Another group of archosaur reptiles conquered the air. Their fourth finger of the front limb was enormously long. It supported a thin membrane which grew out from the sides of the body and also enveloped the hind legs and tail. This membrane formed a wing, but the animals were not very efficient in the air. They probably did more gliding than flying. There were plenty of insects and the flying reptiles probably caught them in flight. They may also have swooped down to scoop fishes from the surface of seas and lakes. The whole group is known as pterosaurs.

The First Birds

Insects were flying about 300 million years ago and the pterosaurs followed them about 180 million years ago. But birds did not appear until perhaps 150 million years ago. The oldest fossil bird so far discovered is about 140 million years old. It is called archaeopteryx and it had wings, with feathers just like those of modern birds. It also had teeth and a long tail. Archaeopteryx was clearly a bird because of its feathers, but it must have arisen from a group of reptiles.

The Decline of the Reptiles

For about 100 million years the reptiles dominated the land, sea and air. Then, towards the end of the Cretaceous period, they began to decline. By the end of that period, about 70 million years ago, the ruling reptiles had disappeared altogether. We do not know for certain what caused the dinosaurs to disappear. Whatever the reason, the giant reptiles did disappear and the field was clear for the mammals and birds to take over as rulers of the land and air.

Allosaurus was one of the great flesh-eaters. Stegosaurus was protected by bony flaps on its back and large spikes on its tail. Like Styracosaurus, a horned dinosaur, it was a plant-eater.

The Age of Mammals

The early mammals were small shrew-like creatures. Their insignificance helped them to escape the huge flesh-eating reptiles alive at the time.

The mammals are comparative newcomers. One hundred million years ago the world was 'ruled' by the dinosaurs—huge cold-blooded reptiles with tiny brains. The dinosaurs then declined and the last of them disappeared about 70 million years ago. In their place came the warm-blooded and more intelligent mammals. The mammals did not suddenly appear at this time, however: they had been in existence for over 100 million years, but they had been 'overruled'.

The most obvious features of mammals are their hair, their warm blood and their ability to feed their young on milk. These features are of little help to a palaeontologist dealing with fossilised bones, but there are other mammalian features which can be of help. Various bones in the skull and the lower jaw help to distinguish mammals from reptiles.

The Early Mammals

During the Triassic period, some 200 million years ago, there were numerous reptiles that began to pull their sprawling limbs under the body. They also evolved larger brains than the other reptiles. The fossil record shows how these mammal-like reptiles gradually changed into mammals. We do not know when hair and warm-bloodedness appeared, but true mammals were living in the Triassic period about 200 million years ago. The earliest mammals were only the size of mice and rats and they probably ate fruit and insects. The early mammals retained the egg-laying habit, and at this stage one small group of mammals diverged from the rest. They survive today as the monotremes of the Australian region and they still lay eggs. The rest of the mammals, however, soon began to produce living or active young.

Thylacosmilus, a sabre-toothed marsupial, one of the many strange animals which lived in South America while it was cut off from the rest of the world.

We have very few fossils of the early mammals, probably because their small bones did not fossilise well, but it seems that they did not change much during the next 60 million years until the dinosaurs became extinct. About 100 million years ago the mammals had reached the marsupial stage, bringing forth very tiny babies and keeping them in pouches. Shortly after this, a new kind of mammal appeared on the main land mass. It did not have a pouch and the female kept her babies inside her body until they were well developed. She fed her babies through a special organ called a placenta and these mammals were therefore called placental mammals.

The early placental mammals were small insect-eating creatures, not unlike their Triassic ancestors in appearance, but they soon began to evolve into many forms as they filled the niches left by the dinosaurs. Plant-eating and meat-eating forms soon appeared

Right: During the last 60 million years the horse has evolved from a fox-sized creature. The foot bones show how all but the middle toe have diminished and disappeared.

The mammoth was an animal ideally suited for life on the margins of the ice sheets during the Great Ice Age of Pleistocene times.

and some became very large and ungainly creatures. We might say that these strange animals were experimental, for they soon gave way to more modern types of mammals. By about 60 million years ago, early in the Tertiary period, all the main groups of mammals were in existence. From then on they produced a vast range of species which gradually evolved into those we see around us today. We know precisely how some of today's mammals have evolved because they have left fossils of each stage of their evolution. We know that the horse, for instance, has evolved from a little fox-sized creature during the last 60 million years and that the elephant has descended from a pig-sized animal.

Australian Mammals

The placental mammals replaced the marsupials (pouched mammals) in most parts of the world, but Australia had become separated from the rest of the continents before the placental mammals started their advance. A number of bats were able to fly to Australia and various rats and mice reached it by drifting across from Asia on floating logs, but no other placentals arrived in Australia until man started to take them there. The marsupials therefore had the place almost to themselves for 100 million years. They produced a wide variety of pouched mammals to fill all the available habitats. Most of the placental mammals have an equivalent marsupial living in a similar habitat in Australia. The two groups often look alike because they live under similar conditions. There are, for instance, marsupial and placental moles, bear-like koalas, rabbit-like bandicoots and badger-like wombats.

There are also a few marsupials in South America, for this continent was also separated from the rest for a long period. The separation began perhaps 60 million years ago, when marsupials and some of the hoofed mammals had reached the area. Many strange animals evolved during the separation, but most of them died out when the continent was joined to North America about 10 million years ago. Mammals from the north swept down into South America and replaced most of its more primitive inhabitants, but some marsupials survived together with the sloths and armadillos.

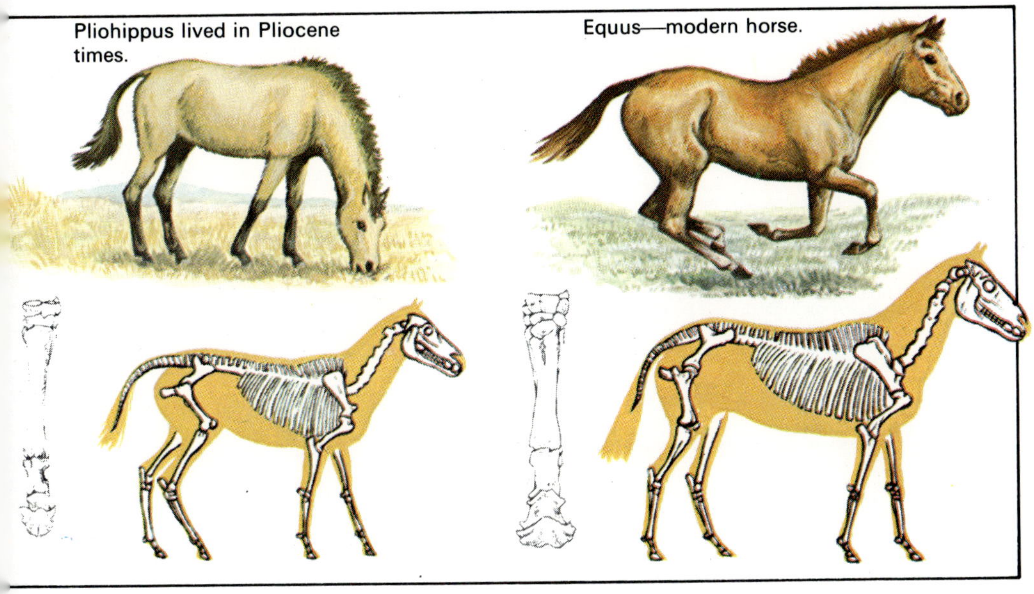

Pliohippus lived in Pliocene times.

Equus—modern horse.

A horse stands on its hoofs which are enlarged nails at the end of a single toe.

The Origins of Man

Man is an animal just as much as cats and dogs are animals. He belongs to a group of mammals called primates and his nearest living relations are the apes. The main difference between man and the other animals is that man has a much better brain. It is this which enables him to talk, to think things out and to make things with his hands.

The first primates appeared on the earth some 70 million years ago. They were small tree-living creatures, rather like the tree shrews that live today. In the next 10 million years the animals evolved to produce a number of creatures rather like today's lemurs and tarsiers. South America had become separated from the rest of the world by this time and the tarsier-like creatures living there gradually gave rise to the New World monkeys. This happened perhaps 40 million years ago. Monkey-like creatures were also developing in the Old World—probably in Africa. By 30 million years ago these Old World primates had diverged into two groups—the monkeys and the apes. The early apes were not very specialized creatures and they lived mainly in the trees. Many kinds of small apes appeared during the next 20 million years and, by about 12 million years ago, the ancestors of today's apes had all branched off from the original group.

An ape called ramapithecus was living in parts of Africa and Asia about 12 million years ago. We have fossils only of its teeth and jaws, but these show definite links with human jaws. Man was therefore beginning to separate from the apes at least 12 million years ago. We have not descended from chimpanzees or gorillas; we merely share a common ancestor with them. *Ramapithecus* probably looked little different from the other apes at first, although he may have been a more upright creature and he may have spent more time on the ground.

Ape Man

At the end of Miocene times, about 12 million years ago, the apes began to dwindle and the fossil record shows that monkeys became more numerous. This is still so today. About two million years ago the climate began to cool down as the Great Ice Age approached. The forests shrank back towards the Equator and the monkeys and tree-living apes went with them. The ground-living descendants of ramapithecus, however, stayed in the open grassy country which replaced the forests. They became more common and many fossils of them have now been found in various parts of Africa. They are called australopithecines—a name which been found in Africa. They are calied australopithecines, meaning 'southern apes'.

A reconstruction of Java Man in his natural surroundings. He was a hunter and lived largely on various antelopes and other animals whose bones are common in the same rock deposits.

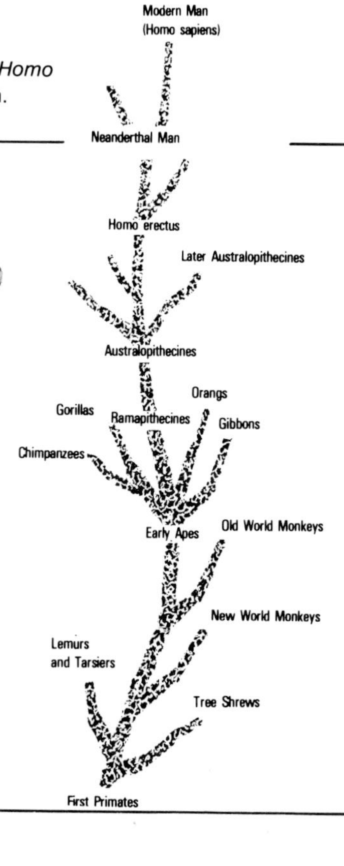

The family tree of *Homo sapiens*, modern man.

The first australopithecine fossils to be discovered were unearthed in South Africa in 1924. They were pieces of a skull and they showed a remarkable combination of human and ape-like features. More fossils have been found since and they show that the australopithecines were very much in between apes and men. They were real 'ape-men'. The skulls had the heavy brow ridges and the projecting jaws of apes and the brain was just about the size of a gorilla brain. The teeth, however, were very like those of modern man and the head was balanced on the top of the neck more or less as it is in modern man. The leg bones and the hip bones indicate that the creatures were about 150 centimetres tall and that they walked in an upright position. They were therefore creatures with the build and posture of men, but with the heads and intelligence of apes. They were undoubtedly hunting animals and they may well have used sticks and stones to kill their prey.

Several different kinds of australopithecines have been discovered, ranging between one million and two million years old. It is likely that there were several distinct lines and that one of them gradually gave rise to true men.

The First Real Man

It is difficult to say just when the ape-like creatures became man because the changes were so gradual. The later australopithecines, however, were not direct ancestors of modern man: they were a sideline which became extinct. By 500,000 years ago real men were living all over Europe, Asia and Africa. They were much more advanced than the australopithecines but they were not very like modern man. One of the best-known is called Java Man, because his remains were first found in Java in 1891. He was about 150 centimetres tall and he walked in an upright position just as we do today. His skull was still ape-like, however, with projecting jaws and heavy brow ridges. The brain had a volume of about 900 cc—much larger than that of the australopithecines, but still much smaller than that of modern man. Java Man was therefore probably not very intelligent, although he made simple stone tools. Java Man used to be called pithecanthropus, which means 'ape man', but he is now called *Homo erectus*. This means 'upright man' and indicates that he was a true man quite closely related to ourselves. Men of this general type were widespread about 300,000 years ago. Modern man, called *Homo sapiens* or 'wise man', has descended directly from them.

Many of the australopithecine fossils have been found in cave deposits. The presence of baboon skulls together with sticks and stones suggests that *Australopithecus* may have hunted the baboons.

Cave Man

One of the best-known of our ancestors was Neanderthal man, who was living in many parts of the Old World until about 50,000 years ago. The Ice Age was still in progress and Neanderthal man in Europe lived mainly in caves. His stone tools are quite common in cave deposits, but the famous cave paintings of southern Europe were not done by him. These are the work of modern man who came on the scene just over 50,000 years ago. All of today's men belong to the one species *Homo sapiens*, but to several different races.

Some activities of Neanderthal man—fashioning stone tools and hardening the points of wooden spears by fire.

Prehistoric Plants

Scattered traces in the rocks show us that plants were living in the world about 3,000 million years ago. These early plants were algae, related to the seaweeds that live today. Algae are soft-bodied plants and they have left few records in the rocks. The fossils that have been found are generally of algae that secreted layers of limestone around themselves. Algae of this sort help to build today's coral reefs.

Below: Fungi preserved in the wood of a Carboniferous tree (top) compared with present-day fungi (bottom). There seems to have been hardly any change in their structures.

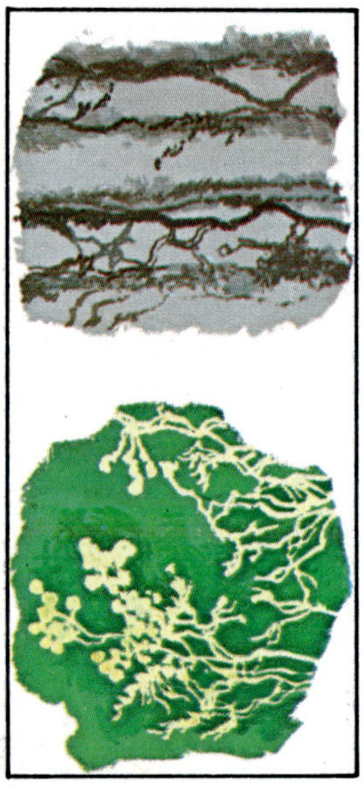

The First Land Plants

Traces of mosses first appear in the Cambrian rocks, but these plants must have been in existence long before the opening of the Cambrian period about 600 million years ago. They presumably arose from the algae. It is likely that the algae started to live on the land and evolved first into liverworts and mosses and then some of these changed gradually into fern-like plants. But again we have no fossils to prove this. The mosses and the ferns could well have descended from separate types of algae. The poor fossil record is due to two main factors: the earliest land plants would have had no hard parts and, being land plants, they would rarely have been in mud or silt.

After the Cambrian period there is a big gap in the fossil record and we have to move forward about 100 million years to find some more plant fossils. These are of strange plants called psilophytes. They had no roots or leaves and the plants merely consisted of branching stems up to a few metres high. Plants of this kind have been found perfectly preserved in some Scottish rocks about 400 million years old. Study of these fossils has shown that the plants had water-conducting tubes and that they carried spore capsules. These ancient plants are thus related to the ferns. During the Devonian period these simple leafless plants gave rise to numerous kinds of small, bushy plants. They were all leafless at first, but leafy plants developed after a while. Many of these were rather like today's club mosses, while others were evolving fern-like appearances and some were developing tough, woody stems.

The Coal Forests

Land plants probably evolved quite rapidly during the Devonian period, when the vertebrate animals were also beginning to conquer the land. Mid-way through the Carboniferous period, about 300 million years ago, there were extensive forests containing a varied assortment of woody plants. We know a great deal about these forests because their remains gradually became converted into coal. Coal is really just a mass of fossilized plants, although the individual plants are not always recognizable. The coal forests grew in vast coastal swamps at a time when there were periodic changes in sea-level. The sea gradually swept in through

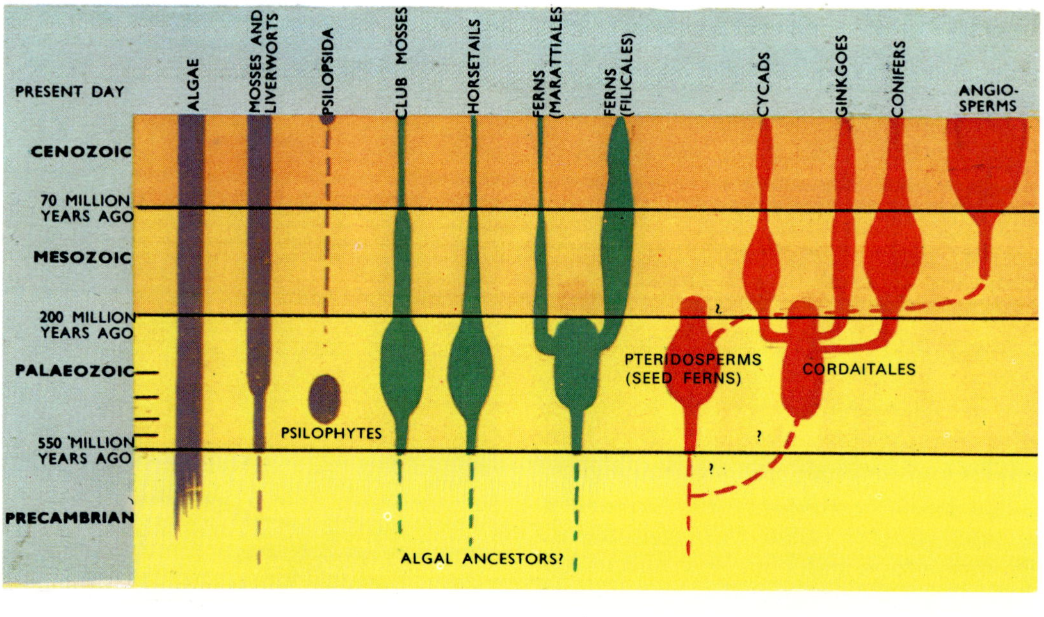

Right: A chart showing the sequence of the main plant groups in geological time. Because of an incomplete fossil record, the evolution from one group to another is uncertain.

the forests and killed the plants. The plants fell and were quickly covered by mud and sand. Later on the sea retreated and the swamp forests spread out again. This happened several times, so that today's coal fields consist of alternating layers (seams) of coal and shale or sandstone. Some of the best plant fossils are found in the shale. They include stems and leaves washed out to sea from the swamps further inland.

Seed Ferns

The coal forests contained many ferns—some of them quite big—and they also contained plants called seed ferns. These were like ferns to look at, but they produced seeds instead of scattering tiny spores. There were some cone-bearing trees called Cordaitales. These were rather like today's monkey puzzle trees, but the main plants were huge horsetails and club mosses. Today's horsetails and club mosses are all small plants (see page 35), but the coal forest ones were woody trees reaching 30 metres in height. There were no flowering plants, although the seed ferns were possibly flowering plants in the making.

The Rise of the Conifers

Towards the end of the Carboniferous period, in which the coal forests were living, the cone-bearing plants began to increase at the expense of the horsetails and club mosses. Conifers not unlike today's pine, larch and cypress arose—probably from the Cordaitales. Cycads (page 37) and ginkgos arose at about the same time as well. The ginkgo or maidenhair tree has survived almost unchanged for millions of years and can certainly qualify for the title of 'living fossil'. It is widely cultivated in gardens.

The First Flowering Plants

The ancient Cordaitales became extinct about 250 million years ago, but the seed ferns lived on until well into the dinosaur era about 125 million years ago. Flowering plants first became common at about this time but, although we have no fossil evidence, they must have been in existence long before that and most probably descended from seed ferns. Whatever their origin, the flowering plants rapidly became the dominant plants in the world as a result of their more efficient reproductive methods (see page 38). The earliest flowers were pollinated by the wind, but many of them later formed associations with insects. Bees, butterflies and other flower-feeding insects began to appear at this time. Their development went on side by side with the development of the flowers. The associations between flowers and insects has become so close that sometimes only one kind of insect can visit a particular kind of flower to collect nectar.

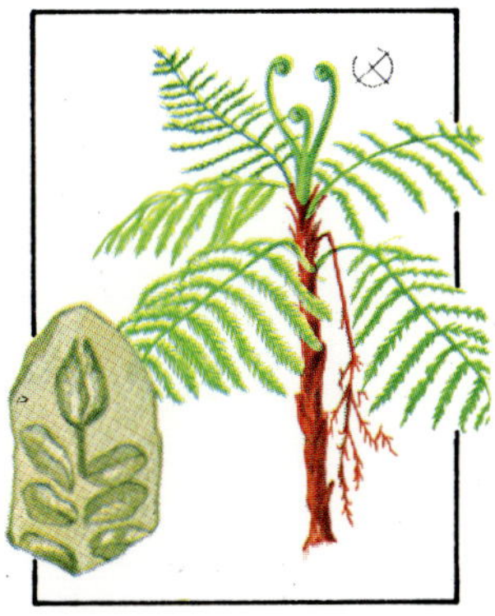

Fossil leaf of a seed fern and a reconstruction of the original plant. Seed ferns were common in Carboniferous times but died out during the Cretaceous period.

Below: A Carboniferous swamp-forest 300 million years ago. There were no flowering plants but the other main branches of the plant kingdom had emerged. The inset pictures show the modern relatives of these prehistoric plants.

The Theory of Evolution

In the previous few pages we have seen how each group of backboned animals gradually arose from an earlier group. In other words, we have traced the evolution of the backboned animals. Evolution means the gradual change of one type of plant or animal into another. The evidence to support this idea of the evolution of living things comes from several directions.

Evidence from Fossils

Fossils provide some of the strongest support for the idea of evolution, as we have already seen in the last few pages. Archaeopteryx was a primitive bird, but it had many reptilian features. This strongly suggests that birds evolved from reptiles, although we can only guess at the earlier stages in the transformation. There is even stronger evidence concerning the development of the horse. There are fossils showing almost every stage between a little fox-like animal and a modern horse. The only logical explanation is that the animals have gradually changed during the last 60 million years. The changes from one generation to the next would have been imperceptible, but over millions of years they added up.

Evidence from Anatomy

A whale's flipper, a bird's wing and a monkey's arm all look different, and they are all used for different jobs, but the arrangement of bones inside them are remarkably similar. This suggests very strongly that all the animals have evolved from the same stock and that they have merely adapted the original skeleton for different functions of swimming, flying and swinging.

Evidence from Embryos

Lizards, birds, rabbits and man all look very different when they are fully grown. In their early stages, however, they all look much alike. All of them pass through a fish-like stage during their development. The only logical explanation for this is that the animals have all descended from some kind of ancestral fish. The fossil record points to the same thing and we can be quite certain that this is the correct explanation.

Young animals also provide evidence for evolution among the invertebrates. Some marine worms and molluscs have very similar young stages. This suggests that the two groups, very different in adult form, have descended from a single ancestral group.

An Old Idea

The idea that living things have evolved is not new. The Greeks suggested it about 2,500 years ago, but they had little evidence to back up the suggestion at the time. The idea cropped up again from time to time during the last thousand years, but most people preferred to believe in special creation. They believed that each kind of plant and animal was created by some supernatural power and that it did not change throughout its existence. The different kinds of animals at each period of the Earth's history were explained by suggesting that worldwide floods periodically wiped out all the animals and that new and slightly better forms were created in their place.

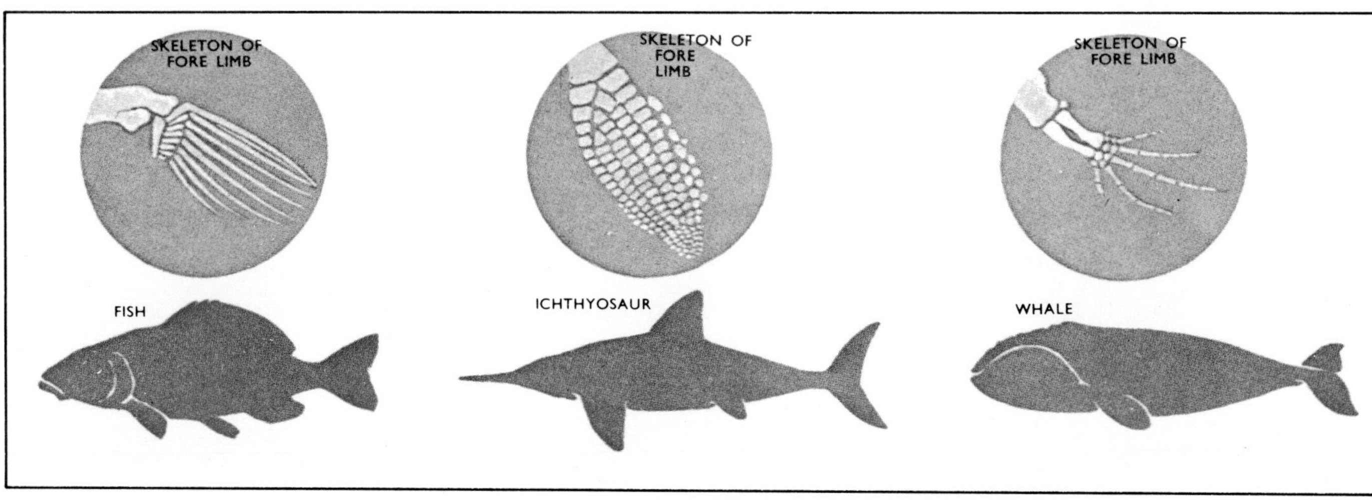

A fish, an ichthyosaur (reptile) and a whale (mammal)—three types of swimming vertebrate. The fore-limbs are homologous (similar in relative position and structure) showing that the three groups have an ancestry, however remote, in common.

One of the main reasons why the idea of evolution was not readily accepted was that no one could explain how or why the evolutionary changes might have taken place. Charles Darwin provided the answers to these questions in the middle of the 19th century and the idea of evolution gradually came to be accepted.

Darwin's Voyage on the 'Beagle'

In 1831, when he was only 22 years old, Charles Darwin began a round-the-world voyage in the survey ship H.M.S. *Beagle*. He saw that animals and plants were beautifully adapted to their surroundings, but he also noticed that the animals and plants in one part of the world were not the same as those in similar habitats elsewhere. Why should so many different types have been created to fill one type of habitat? In the Galapagos Islands of the Pacific he found numerous kinds of finches. They all had a general resemblance to each other and to the finches of the South American mainland, yet they were clearly different species. Why should so many species have been created in this small area and why should they have so many similarities? Darwin came to the conclusion that the various species had not been created individually, but that they had all descended from a common ancestor. In other words, he came to the conclusion that evolution had occurred.

During and after the voyage Darwin collected much more evidence to support the idea—evidence from fossils, evidence from anatomy and embrycology, and evidence from cultivated plants. He knew that crop plants had been developed from wild ones, so why should not similar changes have occurred naturally in the past? Darwin became firmly convinced that evolution had occurred and looked for an explanation.

The Theory of Natural Selection

Darwin's explanation is based on two ideas: the struggle for existence and the survival of the fittest. Plants and animals produce vast numbers of seeds and offspring, but only a few ever survive. Darwin noticed this, and he also noticed that the members of a species vary among themselves. He reasoned that the individuals with the most useful varia-

Darwin discovered a dozen or so species of finch inhabiting the Galapagos islands of the Pacific. The ancestral species of finch is believed to have come from South America 1,000 kilometres to the east. In different parts of the archipelago, new distinct species evolved from this original type, each adapted to a particular form of feeding.

Right: Evidence that molluscs and annelid worms had a common ancestor is provided by the existence of similar larval forms in some species.

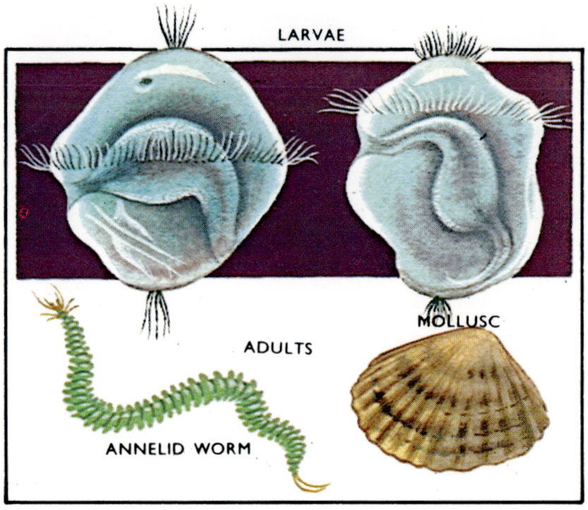

tions would survive best. These would be the ones that would breed and produce the next generation. Offspring tend to resemble their parents and so this next generation would possess the useful variations. There would still be a struggle for existence, and again the fittest would survive. This process would go on generation after generation and the plants or animals would gradually get better and better suited to their surroundings. They would get more and more efficient at catching food and escaping from their enemies. Conditions are not the same everywhere and so a variation that was useful in one place might not be useful in another. A given species might therefore change in two or more directions and give rise to two or more different species, each well suited to its own habitat. Progressive improvement is thus produced entirely by natural means. Darwin called his idea the Theory of Natural Selection and we now believe that all plants and animals have evolved and become adapted to their surroundings by this method.

Convergent Evolution

The process of natural selection ensures that a plant or an animal develops the most efficient shape and structure for its particular way of life. Animals leading similar lives may thus come to resemble each other very closely, although they may be quite unrelated. This is known as convergent evolution. One of the best examples concerns the European mole and the marsupial mole of Australia. Both spend their lives tunnelling in the soil and they are remarkably similar, yet one is a pouched mammal and the other is a placental belonging to a very different group of mammals. The similarities are due solely to their similar modes of life. Convergent evolution also works with plants. Some of the cacti in the American deserts are almost indistinguishable from spurges growing in the deserts of South Africa.

Genetics and Evolution

Every cell in the body of a plant or an animal contains a number of minute thread like structures called chromosomes. Each one carries a number of genes. The genes are the 'instructions' which ensure that the cells (and therefore the whole body) develop in the right way. When plants or animals reproduce they normally combine instructions from both parents. Slightly different combinations of genes are produced in the offspring and these give rise to slight variations in the offspring. They might be variations in size, colour or resistance to disease. Natural selection then gets to work on these variations and favours those which are useful. The species thus become more efficient and better adapted to their surroundings. Sometimes there is a 'mistake' when the instructions are handed on to the offspring. Wrong instructions are usually harmful and the organism usually dies, but sometimes they result in major improvements. Organisms with a useful mistake, or mutation as it is usually called, will survive and breed. The useful feature will thus be

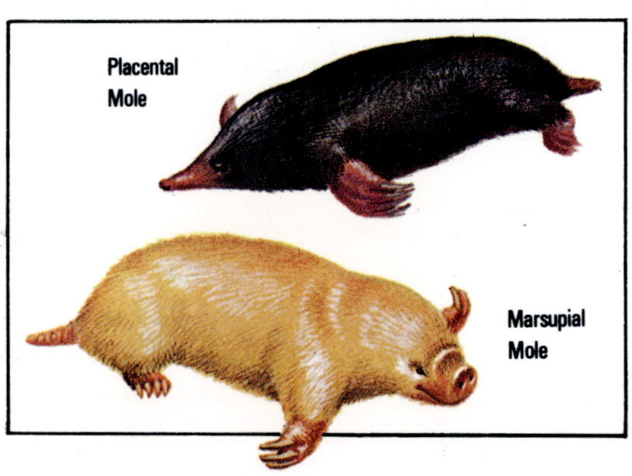

The flightless great auk became extinct in the last century. The placental and marsupial mole provide an example of convergent evolution. Powerful claws give these two burrowing animals a remarkably similar appearance.

handed on. Mistakes or mutations of this kind must have happened many, many times during the course of evolution, resulting in the appearance of new kinds of animals.

Darwin did not know anything about genes and chromosomes when he put forward his theory of natural selection, but he did not need to. He could see that variations were being produced and that was enough for him to explain evolution. The discovery of the genes and chromosomes merely enabled us to explain how the variations were produced.

Evolution Today

It must not be thought that evolution is something that took place in the past and then stopped. It is taking place today. One of the best examples of evolution today concerns the spread of black (melanic) varieties of certain moths. The peppered moth is one of the best known. The normal form is black and white, but completely black individuals sometimes occurred.

The moths rest on tree trunks by day and the normal forms were protected by camouflage among the lichens. The black ones, however, were easily spotted by birds and eaten. After the industrial revolution smoke began to blacken the tree trunks, the black moths survived and began to get more common. They were now better camouflaged on the trees than the normal speckled forms which are now quite rare in industrial regions. The change in the moths came about entirely by natural selection.

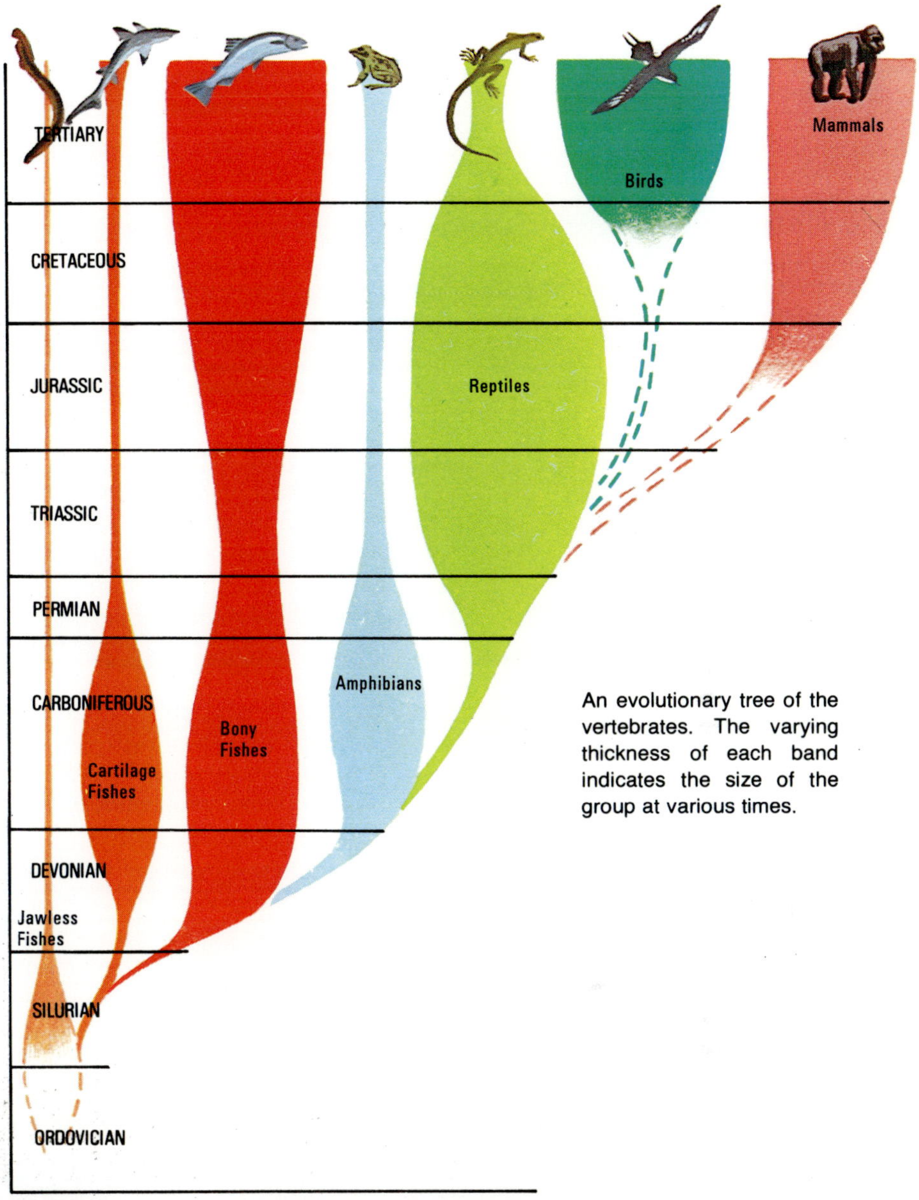

An evolutionary tree of the vertebrates. The varying thickness of each band indicates the size of the group at various times.

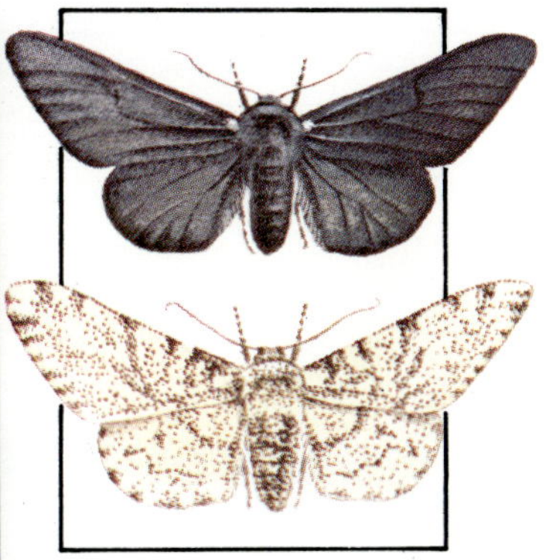

Evolution at work. The black (melanic) form of the peppered moth has increased during the last hundred years or so in industrial areas at the expense of the normal peppered moth.

Living Fossils

In 1938 a strange fish was brought up by a trawler working off the coast of South Africa. The fish was heavily built and nearly five feet long. Its fins were most unusual because, instead of arising directly from the body, they were carried on muscular lobes. They were something of a cross between normal fish fins and the limbs of land animals. None of the fishermen had ever seen a fish like it before and they sent it to a museum. Scientists looked at it and realised that it was a coelacanth.

Scientists knew coelacanths, but only as fossils. They were common 350 million years ago, but they were thought to have become extinct more than 70 million years ago. Yet here they were alive in AD 1938 and very little different from their ancient ancestors. It is not surprising that the coelacanths have been called 'living fossils'.

Remains in the Earth's rocks show us that there has always been a gradual replacement of plants and animals by new types. Why then should the coelacanth have survived? The answer must be that the coelacanth had become very well adapted to the conditions under which it lived and that the later fishes have failed to produce better species for those particular conditions. Conditions in the sea have not changed a great deal during the Earth's history and the features evolved by the ancient animals are still useful today.

There are many other animals that qualify for the title 'living fossils'. Examples include the nautilus which is a distant relative of the octopus, and the king crab, or horseshoe crab, which has remained virtually unchanged for 300 million years. The lung fishes are also living fossils, very similar to creatures that became extinct long ago. The tortoises and crocodiles belong to very ancient groups of reptiles and they have changed very little since they first appeared some 200 million years ago. Some scientists even think that birds are the living descendants of the dinosaurs!

Ancient animal types can survive to become living fossils if they become isolated from the main centres of evolution. New Zealand, for example, is the home of the lizard-like tuatara. This reptile is about 60 centimetres long and it is the only living representative of a group more ancient than the dinosaurs. New Zealand was separated from the rest of the world's land masses before the dinosaurs evolved, but some of these more ancient reptiles had already arrived there. Isolated from competition, they flourished for a long time. The tuatara was common in New Zealand until the middle of the 19th century, but Europeans then started to bring in a variety of mammals which killed off the tuatara. It now lives only on a few offshore islands.

Left: The tuatara is the only living representative of a group of reptiles.
Right: The coelacanth was thought to have become extinct some 70 million years ago. Below: The tortoise has changed very little in 200 million years.

The Balance of Nature

No animal or plant lives alone: each one is intricately bound up with dozens of other organisms in what we can call the web of life.

Plants and animals have been on the Earth for a very long time and, in most places, nature's web has been perfectly developed. The members of each community have become perfectly adapted to each other. There are just the right number of plant-eating animals in each community to keep the plant life in check without any risk of over-grazing. Similarly, there are just enough carnivores to keep the plant-eaters in check. Any increase in the carnivores would push the herbivore population down. Many carnivores would then perish and the populations would return to the normal levels.

Large-scale changes, however, would have a serious effect on the community. Removal of one species would destroy much of nature's web, because all the species in a community are linked up. Removal of a major species could even destroy the habitat itself. Man is doing just this in many places today, often helped by the animals he introduces. He usually throws the community out of balance when he arrives.

Upsetting the Balance

The earliest men were hunters and gatherers. They roamed around in small bands, killing animals and collecting fruits, roots and leaves for food. In some places, though, their effect on the natural environment was out of all proportion to their numbers. By repeated burnings, to drive game, they destroyed huge areas of temperate forest.

When men learned how to grow crops and to domesticate animals they started to settle down in permanent homes. From then on man's effect on the environment has become more widespread. Clearing the land to make way for crops and domestic animals led to the loss of many wild species, both plant and animal. Land clearance is still going on today and it is going on more and more rapidly to accommodate our increasing population. Land is needed for homes, schools, factories and many other buildings as well as for agriculture. Animals are in danger all over the

One species often increases to enormous numbers. In other words, it becomes a pest. The Colorado beetle has ravaged potato crops in North America and Europe.

Removal of the natural vegetation has resulted in soil erosion in many parts of the world. The Tennessee Valley was a particularly badly affected area. Now efforts are being made to repair the damage by replanting the natural grass and tree cover.

world because their habitats are being destroyed. Among these threatened animals are the orang utan, confined to Borneo and neighbouring islands, and the unique lemurs of Madagascar.

Natural communities of plants and animals contain large numbers of different species. They are all kept in check by one another and their numbers remain steady. Artificial communities, however, do not have such stability. There are few species in a field of crops and one species often increases to enormous numbers. In other words, it becomes a pest. One way to keep down pests is to leave as much as possible of the natural community around cultivated land.

Removal of the natural vegetation has resulted in soil erosion in many parts of the world. The land is bare and useless where this has happened.

Strangers from Abroad

When men started to travel from place to place they opened another chapter in the destruction of nature's balance. Plants and animals went with them, sometimes taken deliberately and sometimes accidentally. Many of the species failed to survive in new areas, but some survived only too well. They had no natural enemies in the new lands and they multiplied rapidly, often with disastrous effects on the native plants and animals.

The introduction of the rabbit to Australia has been called the most expensive mistake ever made. Twenty-four rabbits were released by an English settler about 100 years ago. They spread like wildfire and there were millions of them within a few years. They ate the grass and the sheep farmers lost millions of pounds. The disease called myxomatosis has now brought the rabbits under some sort of control, but Australia will never be free of them.

A similar sort of story can be told about the mongoose, which was introduced to the West Indies to control the rats that were destroying the sugar cane fields. The mongoose certainly destroyed the rats, but it also destroyed much of the native wildlife. It then ate the crop that it was supposed to protect.

Many smaller animals have been carried around accidentally. Hundreds of insect species have become spread around the world through being carried unnoticed on plants and other materials. Rats have also been carried all over the world in ships. Both the black rat and the brown rat came from Asia, but they are now found almost everywhere and they do a great deal of damage. The black rat carried the germs of the Black Death, the plague that killed a large proportion of the population in the 1300s.

The introduction of animals to new areas has often proved disastrous. The animals sometimes multiply rapidly and become pests. This has happened with the American mink (right) in Europe.

Food Chains

Lions eat zebras; zebras eat grass. This sequence of events is called a food chain. Every plant and animal is involved in one or more food chains. Each one starts with a plant. This is because the green plants are the only organisms able to incorporate the sun's energy into food. Nature's web is based very largely on these food chains.

Below: A typical food chain beginning with a plant and ending with a flesh-eating mammal.

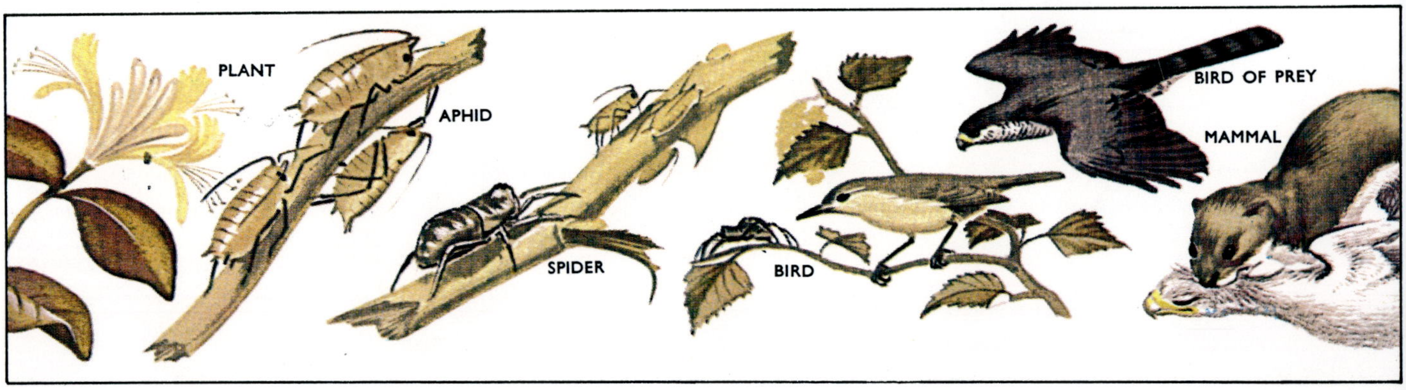

Conservation

Conservation means maintaining the balance of nature that has been built up over millions of years. Man has been destroying this balance over the last few centuries and he now has to make good the damage before it is too late.

Obviously we have to grow crops, but we must try to keep the natural vegetation as much as possible. Some of the lands around the Mediterranean show us the results of over-grazing. The land has been reduced to unproductive desert in many places. Too many trees were removed to make way for crops and animals and too many goats were reared in a small area.

The animals are just as important as the plants. They might provide us with abundant food if they are managed properly. Many of the African antelopes might be herded like cattle and they would give better results than introduced cattle in many places. This is because they are better suited to the conditions and better able to stand up to the various pests and diseases.

The conservation movement has been building up rapidly in recent years and it is showing results. Animals are being re-introduced to places from where they had disappeared. Nature reserves are being set up all over the world in an effort to save wildlife. The African game reserves and parks are famous tourist attractions as well as sanctuaries for the animals. Nature reserves cannot just be left alone. The right conditions must be maintained. Excess animals often have to be killed so that they do not destroy their food resources.

Zoos

Zoos are places where collections of wild animals are kept in captivity. Some zoos exist

Bottom: Wapiti were once common in both eastern and western parts of North America. The only herds that remain are in western reservations.

Below: The American bison was saved from extinction. Now there are thriving herds protected in national parks in North America.

Releasing a rhino in an East African game reserve. Many areas are being restocked with native animals from other places where they are threatened.

simply to provide entertainment for people, but a zoo can do much more than this. Scientists study the animals there and they learn a great deal about them.

Whether we are dealing with zebras or mice, the aim should be to provide the animals with conditions as near as possible to those they find in their native homes. Animals used to be cooped up in small cages, but most zoos are gradually doing away with cages of this kind. They now try to house their animals in paddocks. Some of the enclosures have fences, but many have nothing between the animals and visitors except a deep ditch or a moat. Such an arrangement is much more pleasant for the zoo visitor and it must be more pleasant for the animals than being shut in small cages.

Wildlife parks are becoming very popular today. These go even further than the zoo, for the animals are completely free within the boundaries of the park. It is the visitors who are shut up: they drive around in cars or special 'safari trucks' just as they would in the wilds of Africa.

Zoos and Conservation

A zoo which has interesting exhibits and which attracts a lot of visitors might be considered a successful zoo. But a zoo is not really a success unless it has a good breeding record. There is not much to be proud of in keeping an animal until it dies and then replacing it. It is much better if a zoo can breed its own replacements. It is quite an

Père David's deer. Though extinct in the wild, a herd thrives at Woburn in England.

achievement to breed wild animals because many of them refuse to breed unless they are given just the right conditions.

Zoos which can breed wild animals can play an important part in saving rare species. They can exchange young animals and this means that several zoos can display rare species without actually taking any from the wild. Many animals are threatened with extinction because they have been hunted too much or because their homes have been destroyed. If their numbers get too low they might be too scattered to meet and breed. The only way to save such species is to gather the survivors into a zoo or a wildlife park and breed them. When the numbers have risen, some of the animals can be returned to their homes or released into new homes.

The Hawaiian goose, or ne-ne, is one of several animals that have already been saved by breeding in zoos. In 1950 there were less than 20 of these birds alive in the wild and about the same number in captivity. Today, there are about 800 birds. Many have already returned to their native Hawaii.

Another success story concerns Père David's deer. This fine deer is a native of China and it was unknown in the West until about 100 years ago. It was already extinct in the wild but a few animals survived in parks. Some were brought to Europe and the Duke of Bedford formed a herd at Woburn. The original Chinese herds disappeared, but the deer thrived well at Woburn. Specimens have been sent to many other zoos and they have also been sent back to China.

One of the latest attempts to save a vanishing species concerns the beautiful Arabian oryx. This animal was hunted to extinction in the sandy wastes of Arabia, but a few specimens were captured and taken to Phoenix Zoo in Arizona. The climate there is similar to that in Arabia and the oryx took quite happily to its new home. It began to breed and herds were built up. A few oryxes have now been taken back to Arabia and released in the wild.

Pollution

As the world's population has increased and technical knowledge has advanced so has the amount of waste material. This waste includes polythene bags and containers, detergents and fumes from cars and other machines. The environment can deal with only so much and the waste materials are gradually poisoning or polluting the soil, the atmosphere and the rivers. They are killing wildlife and upsetting the balance of nature. The vast amounts of insecticides and other chemicals used to treat crops contribute to the problem. Many of these substances end up in the sea and become concentrated in animals there. DDT has even been found in Antarctic penguins, thousands of kilometres from where the insecticide was originally used. The control of pollution is one of the most urgent problems facing man today. It is being faced, though, and there is good reason to hope that our awareness of the dangers will lead to a great reduction in pollution.

Elephants thrive in many African countries. Their only enemy is man and poachers still kill large numbers for ivory.

Domestic Animals

So-called 'wild' animals are those creatures which live outside man's control. Most of them are frightened or suspicious of human beings. They cannot be approached, let alone touched. At a certain distance, which varies from animal to animal and even individual to individual, they retreat. This distance is called the flight distance. If cornered, the mildest of them will become frantic and fight.

Domestic animals, in contrast, will allow their owners or regular handlers not only to approach but to stroke them. The flight distance has been completely eliminated.

The process of domestication takes place by a very simple learning process called habituation. Once animals have overcome their initial fear they may soon come to tolerate, even enjoy, human company. The original stimulus to run away disappears.

Domestication is further encouraged by another simple learning process called association. The wild creature perhaps comes to associate human beings with some form of advantage such as food delicacies.

When man first started to domesticate wild creatures long ago in prehistoric times, almost certainly he did so by capturing young animals. Young wild animals are far more easily domesticated than their parents. Having no other experience of man, they very readily accept him without fear. They are also more easily trained, for they have developed no patterns of behaviour of their own. Thus it is far quicker and easier to train a puppy than a full-grown dog.

Breeding Domestic Animals

By crossing carefully chosen animals man could gradually exaggerate certain qualities of appearance or behaviour.

Animals particularly associated with selective breeding before the 18th and 19th centuries were horses, dogs and 'sporting' creatures such as fighting cocks and falcons. Before the age of mechanisation horses were almost indispensable. They were the chief beasts of burden and much in demand for cavalry. Great care was therefore taken in their breeding. King John (King of England, 1199–1216) played his part in improving the stock. He passed laws prohibiting the excessive use of inferior and small horses in breeding.

Dogs were probably the first creatures domesticated and bred by man. Their close relationship with man dates from prehistoric times. Some of our present breeds are very ancient indeed. Bronze Age man had Alsatian dogs 6,000 years ago, while 5,000 years ago the Egyptian Pharaohs used greyhounds for coursing (chasing hares or other small animals).

With the steady growth in human population during the 18th and 19th centuries more and more food was needed. Improved agricultural methods were employed, breeds of farm animals were improved.

Perhaps the most remarkable of all changes have taken place in the pig. Three centuries ago, pigs in England were fierce creatures with most of their weight concentrated in their muscular shoulders. As a result of breeding, today's 'porkers' have their weight more in the middle of their bodies and towards their hindquarters.

Chickens, which are descended from the Red Jungle Fowl of Asia, were probably introduced into Britain about 2,000 years ago. Breeding designed to increase output of eggs is quite a recent development. Formerly they were kept almost exclusively for their meat or cocks were bred for cock-fighting.

All sorts of animals have been domesticated by man in various parts of the world—camels, yaks, elephants, reindeer, llamas, even guinea pigs, antelopes and carp. More are likely to be enlisted for man's benefit.

Livestock breeders are continually improving their techniques. One great advance in modern times has been the use of artificial insemination to improve cattle. This involves introducing semen taken from a bull artificially into cows. A prize bull can now sire many more offspring than it could naturally.

The horse has been one of the most valuable domestic animals. Numerous breeds have been developed to suit different purposes.

Far left: The Indian elephant is a valuable beast of burden in Asia. Left: The domestic sheep looks very different from its wild counterparts.

Index